MUSLIMS IN THE WEST

[CAUGHT BETWEEN RIGHTS & DUTIES]

❧

REDEFINING THE SEPARATION OF

CHURCH & STATE

❧

Sami A. Aldeeb Abu-Sahlieh

Translated by Sheldon Lee Gosline

Foreword by Guy Hennebelle

© 2002

Shangri-La Publications

Warren Center, PA

ISBN 0-9714683-3-8 paperback

ISBN 0-9719496-0-3 hardcover

LCCN 2001099344

© 2002

Sheldon Lee Gosline and

Sami A. Aldeeb Abu-Sahlieh

ISBN 0-9714683-3-8

Paperback $31.00 US / Hardcover $39.50

Published in Warren Center, PA USA

By Shangri-La Publications

Non-Profit Unincorporated Association PA # 2903414

Phone: 570-395-3423 Fax: 570-395-0146 E-mail: shangrila@egypt.net

Library of Congress Cataloging-in-Publication Data

Aldeeb Abu-Sahlieh, Sami Awad.
  [Musulmans en Occident entre droits et devoirs. English]
  Muslims in the West : redefining the separation of church & state /
Sami A. Aldeeb Abu-Sahlieh ; foreword by Guy Hennebelle ; translated by
Sheldon Lee Gosline.
       p. cm.
Includes bibliographical references and index.
  ISBN 0-9719496-0-3 (Cloth Bound : alk. paper) -- ISBN 0-9714683-3-8
(pbk. : alk. paper)
  1. Muslims--Europe, Western--Political activity. 2. Islam and
politics--Europe, Western. 3. Europe, Western--Ethnic relations. 4.
Muslims--Switzerland--Social conditions. 5. Culture
conflict--Switzerland. 6. Switzerland--Ethnic relations. I. Title.
  D1056.2.A7 M87513 2002
  305.891'8204--dc21

                                                          2002003081

2

MUSLIMS IN THE WEST

Redefining the Separation of Church & State

❧❦

Summary Table of Contents
(detailed table at the end of the work)

The Author

Sami A. Aldeeb Abu-Sahlieh, born in 1949, is a Christian Arab of Palestinian origin and Swiss citizenship, holding a doctorate in law from the University of Fribourg. Graduate in political sciences from the Graduate Institute of International Studies of Geneva, Director of Arab and Islamic Law at the Swiss Institute of Comparative Law, Lausanne. He has written many books and articles on Arab and Islamic law besides more general works on the Middle East (see the list in: http://go.to/samipage). Here are some of his books:

- *L'impact de la religion sur l'ordre juridique, cas de l'Égypte, non-musulmans en pays d'islam*, Éditions universitaires, Fribourg, 1979, XVI-405 pages.

- *Discriminations contre les non juifs tant chrétiens que musulmans en Israël*, Pax Christi, Lausanne, 1992, 36 pages.

- *Les musulmans face aux droits de l'homme, religion, droit et politique: étude et documents*, Winkler, Bochum, 1994, 610 pages.

- *Les mouvements islamistes et les droits de l'homme*, Winkler, Bochum, 1998, 128 pages.

- *Mariages entre partenaires suisses et musulmans, connaître et prévenir les conflits, Institut suisse de droit comparé*, Lausanne, 3rd edition, 1998, 44 pages (available also in German).

- *Khitan al-dhukur wal-inath ind al-yahud wal-masihiyyin wal-muslimin: al-jadal al-dini*, Riad El-Rayyes, Beirut, 2000, 562 pages.

- *Khitan al-dhukur wal-inath ind al-yahud wal-masihiyyin wal-muslimin: al-jadal al-tibbi wal-ijtima'i wal-qanuni*, Riad El-Rayyes, Beirut, at press.

- *Circoncision masculine - circoncision féminine: débat religieux, médical, social et juridique*, L'Harmattan, Paris, 2001, 536 pages.

- *Male and Female Circumcision Among Jews, Christians and Muslims: religious, medical, social and legal debate*, Shangri-la Publications, Warren Center (PA 18851, United States), 2001, 400 pages.

- *Les musulmans en Occident entre droits et devoirs*, L'Harmattan, Paris, 2002.

- *Cimetière musulman en Occident: normes juives, chrétiennes, et musulmanes*, L'Harmattan, Paris, 2002, 168 pages.

General Observations

Transliteration

We only present Arabic in transliteration herein. The Arabic alphabet can be transliterated in different ways. We avoid the scholarly form because it is too complicated for a non-specialized reader. The following are equivalents of some Arabic letters:

' (omitted in the beginning and end of a word) = ع + ء ; kh = خ

d = د + ض; dh = ذ + ظ ; sh = ش; s = س + ص; gh = غ

u + w = و ; i + y = ي ; t = ت + ط ; h = ه ـ + ح ; j = ج

We do not distinguish between long and short vowels, or between *shamsi* and *qamari* letters. For example, we write *al-shari'ah* instead of *ash-shari'ah*.

Quotations from the Koran and the Bible

Verse numbering is according to the standard Egyptian system. We primarily use the translation of the Koran by Rashad Khalifa, which can be found at http://www.moslem.org/English.html

Quotations from the Old and New Testament are taken from the *Holy Bible: New Revised Standard Version*, Thomas Nelson Publishers, Nashville, 1992.

Main abbreviations

aCst: Ancient Swiss Constitution of 1874, effective until December 31st, 2000[1].

---

[1] I use the translation published in *Constitutions of the Countries of the world*, Oceana publications, Dobbs Ferry, New York.

CCS: Swiss Civil Code[1].

Covenant on civil rights: International covenant on civil and political rights.

d. (ca): died (circa).

ECHR: European Convention of Human Rights.

LPIL: Federal Law of Private International Law[2].

nCst: New Swiss Constitution of 1998, effective January 1st, 2000[3].

Par.: Paragraph.

UDHR: Universal Declaration of Human Rights.

Footnotes

In footnotes, I mention the author's name and/or first elements of the title. Complete bibliographic data is at the end of book.

Translator's notes

We have decided to use the most basic and standard dictionary definitions for Arabic terms. However, the author and I had considerable discussion concerning one word, *"dar"*. While we have agreed to translate it the usual way, this standard translation, "land" is really incorrect, although most common. The word "land" lends itself to a complete misunderstanding in the West, and particularly in the United States, where "land" tends to mean physical property, a nation, and was most recently in the new phrase "homeland security". The term *"dar"* has a much more far-reaching meaning, encompassing concepts like "ideology", "personal space", "home", "zone", "sphere of influence", "world" or even "universe". This understanding of "dar" is most important to appreciate the Muslim worldview and how it conflicts with the West. Finally, I have added sections to the original text in [brackets] to assist an English speaking audience. Note that the author is not responsible for those sections.

---

[1] We partially use the translation of the *Swiss Civil Code* by Shick, completely revised by Wyler and Wyler.

[2] We use the translation done by Karrer, Arnold and Patochhi.

[3] We use the translation by Susan Emmenegger which can be found in: http://www.uni-wuerzburg.de/law/sz00000_.html

PREFACE TO ENGLISH EDITION BY SHELDON LEE GOSLINE TRANSLATOR AND PUBLISHER

The separation of Church and State is a principle born in the historical, legal, political, and social heritage of the United States. It preserves and protects our religious liberty. Thomas Jefferson, often credited with articulating this concept, was not responsible for its addition to the United States government, although his *Virginia Statute for Religious Freedom* is one of the most important separationist documents of the eighteenth century. Jefferson surely qualifies as one of the most influential men in the early Republic, but he was Ambassador to France during both the Constitutional Convention and Congressional debates over the Bill of Rights, so he had little to do with these founding documents. He did articulate the position in later writings:

> Believing that religion is a matter which lies solely between man and his God, that he owes account to none other for his faith or his worship, that the legislative powers of government reach actions only, and not opinions, I contemplate with sovereign reverence that act of the whole American people which declared that their Legislature should "make no law respecting an establishment of religion, or prohibiting the free exercise thereof," thus building a wall of separation between Church and State (Thomas Jefferson, *Letter to Danbury Baptists, 1802*).

"Congress shall make no law respecting an establishment of religion, or prohibiting the free exercise thereof..." is written into the fiber of the nation's constitution.

James Madison, popularly known as the "Father of that Constitution," was chiefly responsible for the content and form of the First Amendment. His most famous statement on behalf of religious liberty was his *Memorial and Remonstrance Against Religious Assessments*, written to oppose a bill that would have authorized tax support for Christian ministers in the state of Virginia. This text is reproduced at the end of this book.

My historical digression is intended to illustrate how the principle of the separation of Church and State is far from new to the Western democratic system. Furthermore, one can be religious, and even believe that religion is important for public life, without believing that the nation state should have the power to aid or direct religion, preferentially or non-preferentially. What is new, as we enter the 21st century, is the realization that this founding principle of democracy may be its very undoing.

About twenty years ago, the United States started supporting radical religious factions in Afghanistan, to fight against their enemies of the moment, the Soviet Union and Iran. Unwittingly, through their short sighted tunnel vision, our former leaders created a time bomb genii, that has now exploded from its bottle. Only a short time ago, the West in general, and the United States in particular, imagined itself immune to the chaos of war, destruction and religious terrorism they helped engender. Now, the former buffer zone is forgotten and the Russian and Iranian republics are siding with the West to condemn the "terrorists". For decades, we have reveled in contributing to terror and destruction around the globe, claiming the highest moral intent, never imagining it all could wash upon our own shores. Meanwhile, our leaders still think that their own military agendas constitute "justice".

Without bothering to understand Muslims, our leaders continue to welcome inclusion of Islam to the pantheon of faiths, sharing our American theological melting pot. November 1999, a little over two years ago, Representatives Dana Rohrabacher, California, and Thomas M. Davis, Virginia, introduced legislation that a U.S. stamp be issued to recognize the Islamic holy month, Ramadan. Lawmakers noted that Judaism, Christianity, and Islam are the three monotheist religions of the world, and while Jewish and Christian holidays have been recognized on stamps "no Islamic observance is similarly commemorated". The resolution noted more than "five million practicing Muslims in the United States, who represent one of the fastest growing segments of American society". The proposed legislation noted, "those who follow the Islamic faith are a diverse community comprised of all races, colors, and political opinions, who make important and valuable contributions to American society and culture" (http://usinfo.state.gov/usa/islam).

Since September 11th 2001, the Western world has been waiting for a strong united statement from Islamic religious leaders to condemn the atrocities committed by a group of Muslims in the West. It will not come. This book brilliantly outlines why such condemnation has not been forthcoming and why such radical interpretations of Islam and Koran are not only possible in their faith system but also comprise the core nature of their worldview. In the immediate aftermath, Muslim-Americans were subjected to harassment and hostility. Meanwhile, terrorist attacks paved the way for Muslims to establish closer ties to American society.

Coincidentally, for the first time in U.S. history, the post office issued Eid stamps, roughly coinciding with Thanksgiving, Christmas, Hanukkah and Kwanzaa. In Washington, on November 13th, 2001, a beautifully simple stamp done in Arabic calligraphy was issued. This Eid stamp, was designed by Mohamed Zakariya, and features the Arabic phrase *Eid mubarak*, which translates "blessed festival," and can be paraphrased, "May your religious holiday be blessed." The Eid Mubarak stamp commemorates the two most important festivals in the Islamic calendar. *Eid al-Adha* marks the end of the *hajj*, the annual period designated for Muslims to make pilgrimage to Mecca, while *Eid al-Fitr* celebrates end of the Ramadan fast. The appearance of this commemorative now seems to express an ironic twist.

On another government web page, the U.S. showed Muslim troops praying on an aircraft carrier before going on a mission to bomb fellow Muslims, in a misguided effort to express solidarity with Islam. In truth, it just proves that we are infidels! In a similar attempt at religious sensitivity, U.S. President Bush hosted an "Iftaar" (Ramadan break-the-fast dinner) at the White House the evening of November 19th, for representatives of some 53 Muslim nations - reportedly the first such gathering.

This is the same person who started his campaign for President at Bob Jones University, an extremely fundamentalist Christian institution (http://www.nobojo.vom). How can any Muslim take this new religious open-mindedness seriously, from a man who first described planned military actions as a "crusade"? These are sad attempts to placate Muslims in the U.S., in light of military actions in Afghanistan. They also indicate a slow but insidious development, and that we, as a nation, are completely unaware of the forces we are unleashing. Following is the White House text:

THE WHITE HOUSE
Office of the Press Secretary
November 15, 2001

As the new moon signals the holy month of Ramadan, I extend warm greetings to Muslims throughout the United States and around the world.

The Islam that we know is a faith devoted to the worship of one God, as revealed through The Holy Qu'ran. It teaches the value and importance of charity, mercy, and peace. And it is one of the fastest growing religions in America, with millions of American believers today.

The American Muslim community is as varied as the many Muslim communities across the world. Muslims from diverse backgrounds pray together in mosques all across our great land. And American Muslims serve in every walk of life, including our armed forces.

The Holy Qu'ran says: "Piety does not lie in turning your face to the East or West. Piety lies in believing in God." (2:177). Americans now have turned to acts of charity, sending relief to the Afghan people, who have suffered for so many years. America is proud to play a leading role in the humanitarian relief efforts in Afghanistan, through airdrops and truck convoys of food, medicine, and other much-needed supplies. Today we are committed to working for the long-term reconstruction of that troubled land.

We send our sincerest wishes to Muslims in America and around the world for health, prosperity, and happiness during Ramadan and throughout the coming year.

(Distributed by the Office of International Information Programs, U.S. Department of State. Web site: http://usinfo.state.gov)

The sentiments of this letter may be well intended, but are they falling on deaf ears? I fear so. For some reason, this letter fails to mention the bombing of Red Cross warehouses in Kabul. After all, this same Western leader bombed Afghanistan and is now planning to spread this war on terrorism to more global proportions; hunting down a Muslim radical, who many in the Muslim world also consider a chief spokesman for their faith. The witch-hunt continues, for Americans now need someone to hate in order to unify and keep their military - industrial complex healthy. Nearby, Israel and Palestine have intensified their bloodshed, and on the eve of Christmas 2001, Yasser Arafat was denied access to the holy city of Bethlehem for no clear reason. There still is no peace in sight as we go to press in March 2002.

Is Islam free to be critical of its radical groups? How could a group of people so comfortable in the West, hate that society and its peoples so much. For many reasons, the answer is unclear. Dr. Aldeeb guides us easily through the intricate maze of Muslim social norms into a deep understanding of how they think. He logically outlines a rational course to apply principles of the separation of Church and State. Revelations presented herein are just as shocking as they are enlightening.

While the Western powers, led by the U.S., continue a witch hunt for one man, a few leaders, and a radical totalitarian State, the root crisis we are now faced with is implanted in the core structure of Muslim society and embedded in the Koran itself. It is rooted within the matrix of Muslim society, and as that society has greater hold on the West, the situation will only worsen.

The problem is partly that "east" and "west" are not just compass directions. They are worldview ideologies; progressive vs. conservative. The Muslim worldview may be summed up in a thorough understanding of "*Dar al-Islam*" – the world, sphere of influence or zone of Islam. At its heart, this concept is utopian; expressing a wish that all Muslims should live together in unity, peace and harmony. In reality, divisive factions were already developing in the golden age of Muhammad's own lifetime. They certainly erupted shortly after his death, but the myth of unity persisted, to become a chief rallying cry for war and conquest. Islam was born with an overly developed sense of "us" and "them", which led to conquest. Muslims in the West still have this foundational mandate from their faith to hate us (i.e.: any non-Muslim) and to wage war. Thus, Muslims are a growing threat to the Western democratic system, like a cancerous organism, quietly growing until it can destroy its host. The Muslim legal concept undermines national sovereignty. When critical mass is reached in their population, they will attempt to exert Islamic law. Now that we have let the genii out of the bottle will we ever be able to get it back in? Are we in the West ready for this new challenge to the separation of Church and State?

Sheldon Lee Gosline,
Shangri-La Publications
Publisher and Translator
(gosline@egypt.net)

FOREWORD BY
GUY HENNEBELLE, DIRECTOR OF
PANORAMIQUES MAGAZINE

When the author of this book asked me to write a two-page preface for him, I was intrigued by the proposal he addressed to the inspirator of a volume of the magazine *Panoramiques*, whose title is criticized by him: *Is Islam Free to be Critical?* But this obvious contradiction was not displeasing for me to explore, because *Panoramiques*, founded in 1991, is a bimonthly publication that contradicts the warhorses against politically correctness; alas, a present wound in the West in general, and France, my country, in particular. Nevertheless, this volume (distributed, not without paradox, in Algeria, under the title, "Islam opens up to free criticism"- at the request of my Algerian partner) constitutes a first of its kind. It is the first time, to my knowledge, that Muslim believers (united by an Islamic magazine from France) have accepted the principle of academic debate, fair play and fifty-fifty dialogue with atheists, agnostics and critics of Muslim origin! Exchange of views advised against, or otherwise forbidden, by Islam itself, that enjoins its adherents to kill apostates (Dr. Aldeeb recalls this in this book).

It is not altogether surprising that this author initiated such debate, in light of his origins (as a Christian Palestinian). By definition he is not Muslim and therefore open to originate dialogue. In this work he calls a cat "a cat" and refuses the practice, too frequent in Muslim surroundings, to duplicate language or conceptual restriction that in French we call *jésuitisme* and in Islam, especially Shiite, *taqiyyah*[1]. He does not hide, for example, that only demographic mechanics will likely

---

[1] The term *al-taqiyyah* is translated as *dissimulation*. Concerning this concept, see Part I, chap. II.2.

bring about a Muslim majority in Switzerland by the year 2020. This projection led French author Jean-Paul Gourévitch to likewise write his third volume, *African France*, in a trilogy on consequences of immigration to France.

For a long time until now, the responsible press, especially among leftists and extreme-leftists in France, has forbidden the idea that assimilation of first generation immigrants from Arabia and Africa is a potential problem. Now we are beginning to realize that such population influxes intensify problems that only, yesterday were being caused by an influx of immigrants with European origin: Italian, Spanish, Polish, Portuguese, or even Jews of central Europe. Hence, following republican principles that a man is a man, any man is worth any man, it was assumed that these new immigration waves would have no greater affect on society-at-large than previously, and racists alone would dread demographic changes.

In French, the Algeria Jacques Soustelle did not hesitate to replace the term *assimilation* with the term *integration*. He forged this concept in the last quarter hour of May 13th, 1958, to thwart an independence movement, while guaranteeing to the eight million Muslims of Algeria (by now, up to thirty-five million…) equality with the million Europeans, while notably merging the two electoral colleges. In so doing, Soustelle tactfully introduced an entirely new range of family laws to this fully-fledged new French population, irrespective of all incompatible Muslim arrangements, with respect to laws of a secular and democratic republic, such as polygamy, sexual inequality, and inheritance.

Yes, Sami Aldeeb, you are right to analyze all present or future consequences of the presence of millions and millions of Muslim-origin neo-citizens in the West, and in particular your country, Switzerland. I also do not forget that, following Maxim Rodinson, legitimate claims by Palestinians are ignored as a result of unjust infernal Jewish victims of yesterday (victims of victims, as designated by Edward Said). I also do not want to forget that the Christian Souha officially converted to Islam to become Mrs. Yasser Arafat! This same iniquitous Islamic requirement is not required of the non-Muslim wife, but only of a future non-Muslim husband! How to believe in a secular and democratic Palestine in these conditions? How to believe Muslims when they declare that they fully admit the laws of democratic countries, meanwhile they asked and obtained in France from the Ministry of the Interior to suppress passages that recognize the right to change one's religion?

At the time of the French Revolution, an elected (one mentions accordingly Abbé Grégoire or Clermont-Tonnerre), who proclaimed firmly "it is necessary that the Republic recognizes all Jews as individuals and never as a community". Even though it seems preferable to somewhat moderate the harshness of the subject to accord with modern political sensibilities, I would rather not. I hope that France, and more extensively Europe and the West in general will, through their own virtues and freedoms, promote the birth of an *ijtihadi* Islam, which means an updated Islam. One should repeat incessantly that it is far better to be an Arab, or Muslim, in Europe than in any Arab or Muslim country! One should reject without any hesitation the claims of Muslims who would want butter and the money of butter at a time. One should clearly tell the stubborn: *Love it, or leave it*. If we allow you to reconstitute the mental, behavioral and legal norms that led to your decline, you would end up by dragging us into a tragic regression that now makes one billion two hundred million Muslims wallow in misery, from Morocco to Indonesia.

For our part, in the West, this firmness of mind must accompany a resumption of our faltering birth rate and a mixed marriage acceleration. In default, mini-Kosovos will be created with the consequences observed in the Balkans and elsewhere.

Guy Hennebelle
Director of *Panoramiques Magazine*

INTRODUCTION

I will not speak here of Islam, but of Muslim people. Islam, like Christianity or Judaism, is an abstraction that does not exist as an entity. The use of the word Islam, in titles like *Islam in the Republic*[1] and *Is Islam Free to be Critical?*[2], is wholly erroneous. These titles should be *Muslims in the Republic* and *Are Muslims Free to be Critical?* In this work, I only use "Islam" in quotes.

This book, which will also be available in French, is devoted to problems created by Muslims residing in a Western country, such as Switzerland. Even though the data concerning these problems differs somewhat from one country to another, Muslims raise nearly identical problems everywhere they settle in the West; where now between fifteen and twenty million Muslims live. The information is just as applicable to the situation found in the United States, which has more than five million Muslims, and most recently has felt the tragic effects of this cultural clash.

To understand these problems, the first part describes the classic Muslim view of minorities and the current implications. The second section concerns linguistic, ethnic and religious minorities specifically in Switzerland, [although there are similar laws in other countries, especially in the United States, which was the first modern nation to embrace religious freedom.] The third part explores several domains of Muslim values, to see what extend these values can be accommodated in Switzerland. [By extension, these proposals apply to other modern nations in the West.] I list these as follows: recognition, freedom of religion, school, family law, food prohibitions and cemeteries.

The Muslim minority in Switzerland is now the third largest religious community, following Protestants and Catholics. At its

---

[1] *Rapport établi par le Haut Conseil à l'intégration en France*, November 2000.
[2] Title of the periodical *Panoramique*, n° 50, 2001.

present growth rate, in less than twenty years, it will be the largest religious community, and even reach population majority. If the Muslim community is not integrated in time, and its value system does not adapt to larger society, they will represent a real risk to the democratic and legal system in Switzerland, [and indeed every Western country.] The endangering of territorial unity is already felt in ex-Yugoslavia; now ravaged by such religious factions. This risk must be taken seriously in all Western countries (the United States, France, Germany, Britain and Italy) where increasingly high numbers of Muslims live.

I know this work touches on a very sensitive topic, in this period of tension between the Western world and the Muslim world. A reason for this tension is lack of intention transparency on both sides. Nothing is worse than to pretend all is going well and then to awake one morning, as on September 11th, 2001, with a horror that we could have easily avoided with healthier reports and greater global understanding. Therefore, a reciprocal information work, such as this one, is just as beneficial to the Muslim community as for the West (concerning September 11th, see appendices 1 and 2 at the end of this work). To appreciate problems constitutes a predisposition to find their solution.

Muhammad (d. 632) said, "If the judge provides an effort and gives back a suitable judgment, he has gained two merits, but if he is mistaken in his judgment he has just one merit"[1]. I do not pretend to have diagnosed all problems, nor propose infallible solutions, but I hope at least to have achieved some merit for my effort. It is incumbent upon other researchers to pursue this effort and, possibly, to correct findings in it. In this regard, I remain open to all suggestions or constructive remarks from my readers.

Before finishing this introduction, I wish to express my deep gratitude to those that corrected and commented on this text. I thank in particular Sheldon Lee Gosline of Shangri-La Publications for translating this work into English. I remain however uniquely responsible for mistakes and opinions herein, except for the preface, foreword and [bracketed] textual inserts.

Sami A. Aldeeb Abu-Sahlieh, Ochettaz 17, 1025 St-Sulpice, Switzerland, e-mail: Sami.Aldeeb@isdc-dfjp.unil.ch

---

[1] Al-Bukhari, narrative 6805.

PART I.
THE MUSLIM VIEW OF MINORITIES

Arabia in the days of Muhammad was known for its tolerance. In Mecca, no less than 360 idols cohabited. With the creation of the first Muslim nation state by Muhammad in 622, the world was seen anew and divided according to his religious criteria. Regions dominated by Muslims came to be called the Land of Islam (*Dar al-Islam*)[1]. Inhabitants of these regions are either believers (Muslims) or unbelievers (*kafir*). These last are divided according to their degree of disbelief into *People of the Book*, polytheists and apostates, with a particular statute for Arabia. Religious adherence excels all other familial, tribal or racial affiliations. Therefore, classic and modern Muslim jurists only recognize religious minorities. Outside the Land of Islam, there is the Land of Disbelief (*Dar al-kufr*). We will begin by discussing these divisions and their legal implications.

Chapter I.
Division inside the land of Islam

1) Muslims

The Koran states "believers are brothers" (49:10)[2]. All Muslim converts belong to one Islamic nation (*ummah*) that the Koran

---

[1] "*Dar al-Islam*" is translated throughout this work as *Land of Islam*, the terminology adopted by many Muslim and non-Muslim scholars. It is also often translated as Abode of Islam, Domain of Islam, World of Islam, etc. No single English word can express the range of meanings attributed to "*dar*", which can refer to anything from an apartment room to the universe.

[2] The numbers quoted inside the text between brackets without any mention refer to the Koran.

qualifies as "the best community ever raised among the peoples" (3:110). Muslims are convinced that one day all humanity will become Muslim, thus extending the realm of Islam to the entire world. [This totalitarian religious fervor has global implications.]

For the Jewish believer, the Bible imposes itself as a legal code to follow at all times and in all places. One reads:

- You must diligently observe everything that I command you; do not add to it or take anything from it (Deuteronomy 13:1).
- The revealed things belong to us and to our children forever, to observe all the words of this law (Deuteronomy 29:28).
- It is a statute forever throughout your generations in all your settlements (Leviticus 23:14).

Quoting these verses, Maimonides (d. 1204) wrote, "It is clearly stated in Torah that it contains the Law, which stands for ever, may not be changed, and nothing may be taken from it or added to it". Accordingly, if one pretends the opposite, "he shall die by hanging"[1]. This punishment is also predicted for anyone who "uproots any of our verbal traditions or says that God had charged him to interpret the Law in such and such a way, he is a false prophet and is to be hanged even though he give a sign"[2].

One finds this same concept among Muslims for whom the Koran, - literal word of God -, and the Tradition of Muhammad (*Sunnah*) –gathered in different compilations - constitute the first two sources of all law. From these two sources, classic Muslim jurists developed a legal system called *shari'ah* (literally: the way). All Muslims must submit. The Koran says in this respect:

Those who do not rule in accordance with God's revelations are disbelievers ... unjust, ... wicked (5:44, 45, 47).
No believing man or believing woman, if God and His messenger issue any command, has any choice regarding that command. Anyone who disobeys God and His messenger has gone far astray (33:36).

Muhammad Mitwalli Al-Sha'rawi (d. 1998), religious leader and Egyptian politician, explained that revelation is called upon to decide equivocal questions, thus freeing humanity from the anguish of solving a difficult case by discussion, or by exhaustive repetition of experiences. The Muslim does not have to look outside Islam for solutions to any problem, since Islam offers absolute eternal and good solutions[3]. He adds:

---

[1] Maimonides: *The Book of Knowledge*, p. 23-24.
[2] *Ibid.*, p. 25.
[3] Al-Sha'rawi: *Qadaya islamiyyah*, p. 35-39.

> If I were the person responsible of this country or the person charged to apply God's law, I would give a delay of one year to anyone who rejects Islam, granting him the right to say that he is no longer a Muslim. Then I would dispense him of the application of Islamic law, condemning him to death as apostate[1].

This concept of revealed law is reflected in different Islamic declarations on human rights[2]. Thus, one promulgated in 1981, by the *Islamic Council of Europe* (whose seat is in London), affirmed repeatedly that human rights are founded on divine will. The first passage of the preamble states, "Since fourteen centuries, Islam defined, by divine law, human rights, in their entirety as well as in their implications". The preamble adds:

- Strong of our faith in the fact that God is the sovereign master of all things in this immediate life as in the ultimate life...
- Strong of our conviction that human intelligence is incapable to elaborate a better way in view to assure service of life without God's guidance and revelation:

We, Muslims, ... we proclaim this Declaration of human rights made in the name of Islam, as one can understand them of the very noble Koran and the very pure prophetic Tradition (*Sunnah*).

Therefore, these rights present themselves as eternal rights that cannot be suppressed or rectified, abrogated or invalidated. These rights have been defined by the Creator -to him the praise! - and no human creature has the right to either invalidate or attack them.

Jewish and Muslim concepts of law emanating from God, as supreme sovereign legislator, are different from the concept of law in the Christianized Western countries, concept based on the idea of people's sovereignty that decides the laws that govern it, in the public interest (*res publica*). Instead of speaking of Judeo-Christian culture, one should speak of Judeo-Muslim culture, which is similar to a totalitarian and dictatorial concept of law.

This Judeo-Muslim concept could not resist time and modernization. Indeed, nearly all Constitutions of Arab countries affirm that Islam is the religion of the State and that Islamic law is *a* main source, or even *the* main source of the law. Nevertheless, Islamic law now concerns only family law and

---

[1] *Ibid.*, p. 28-29.

[2] The Arab and Islamic Countries issued several Declarations concerning human rights. Some of these declarations conform to Islamic law. Eleven of these declarations are translated into French in: Aldeeb Abu-Sahlieh, *Les musulmans face aux droits de l'homme*, annexes 1-11, p. 462-522.

inheritance, and penal law in some countries such as Saudi Arabia and Iran. Laws imported mainly from the West, to start with the Constitution itself, the judicial system, the civil law, the commercial law and the penal law, govern other legal domains. In this regard, the Muslim world lives today in a situation of schizophrenia, between religious ideals and a desire to acquire an independence from divinity. This situation creates internal violent conflict between three main trends:

- There are those that extol a return to Islamic law as part of their faith, with some adaptation to the present situation through a circumstantial interpretation to save appearances.

- The second trend is constituted by those who, guided by a sense of realities, prefer the *status quo*, and consider Islamic law unable to manage a modern society.

- The third trend would like to evacuate the remaining Islamic norms applied today, which are contrary to a modern perspective of human rights, notably with regard to women's and non-Muslims' rights.

I should specify here that I do not share the Muslim belief that the Koran is God's divine word. The Muslim argument holds that Muhammad was illiterate and, therefore, incapable of producing the Koran without God. Even though Muhammad was illiterate (which is contested), we must recognize that the Koran came from his mouth and was brought about by his Companions, either orally or in writing. For this reason, I mention Muhammad in the bibliography as "author" of the Koran[1]. If I use in this work the expression The Koran says, not Muhammad, my purpose is to distinguish the Koran verses from the narratives assigned to Muhammad - rightly or wrongly.

For understanding the following developments, we should point out here that Muslims are divided into two main groups: Sunnites and Shiites. The Sunnites, who form the majority (about 90%), adhere to four main legal schools: the Hanafite school (founded by Abu-Hanifah, d. 767), the Malikite school (founded by Malik, d. 795), Shafi'ite school (founded by Al-Shafi'i, d. 819) and hanbalite school (founded by Ibn-Hanbal, d. 855).

---

[1] *Tribune de Genève* published in August 8, 1994 a cartoon on the Koran. On its cover was mentioned the title "The Koran" followed by the name of the author "Muhmmad". Fawzia Al-Ashmawi polemized because of this cartoon (see part III, chap. II.3.B).

Muslims classify unbelievers according to their degree of disbelief in Islam: *People of the Book*, apostates and polytheists. [Even other Muslims, following a different form of Islam, can be viewed as falling in a category of disbelief.]

2) People of the Book

According to the Koranic perception, before Muhammad, God sent different prophets to transmit His law to humanity. Muhammad is the last of these prophets and his message constitutes the achievement of the previous messages. All of humanity must therefore rally to his message and must follow it. Muhammad endeavored in his life to achieve this project. He entered into discussions with Jews and Christians so that they recognize him, invoking the fact that their sacred books foresee a savior's arrival. But these two groups refused, saying that their books do not mention the name of Muhammad. He accordingly retorted then that other faiths had falsified their books to make his name disappear[1] and accused them of having been unfaithful to their prophets: the Jews believing in the Gibts and the Taghouts and adoring Moses, their high priests and Ozayr[2], and Christians adoring God, Jesus and Mary[3]. In the end, Muhammad had to accept that his spiritual mission was not shared by the other faith communities, attributing their rejection to divine will:

> Even if you show the followers of the scripture every kind of miracle, they will not follow your Qiblah. Nor shall you follow their Qiblah. They do not even follow each others' Qiblah. If you acquiesce to their wishes, after the knowledge that has come to you, you will belong with the transgressors (2:145).
> Had God willed, He could have made you one congregation. But He thus puts you to the test through the revelations He has given each of you. You shall compete in righteousness. To God is your final destiny - all of you. Then He will inform you of everything you had disputed (5:48; to also see 11:118; 16:93 and 42:8).

He recommends to his Companions to adopt a correct attitude with *People of the Book*, urging this last group to reach a common point of understanding with the Muslims:

> Do not argue with the people of the scripture (Jews, Christians, and Muslims) except in the nicest possible manner - unless they transgress - and say, "We believe in what was revealed to us and in what was

---

[1] Koran 3:78; 4:46; 5:13, 15, 41; 6:91; 7:157, 162.
[2] Koran 4:54; 9:30-31.
[3] Koran 4:172; 5:17, 73, 116; 19:30, 35.

> revealed to you, and our god and your god is one and the same; to Him
> we are submitters" (29:46, also see 16:125).
> Say, "O followers of the scripture, let us come to a logical agreement
> between us and you: that we shall not worship except God; that we
> never set up any idols besides Him, nor set up any human beings as
> lords beside God". If they turn away, say, "Bear witness that we are
> submitters" (3:64).

Muhammad considers himself Abraham's heir, and Abraham as the first *Muslim*; a term meaning *submitted*. Thus, Muhammad thinks himself even nearer to Abraham in faith than Jews or Christians, "Abraham was neither Jewish, nor Christian; he was a monotheist submitter. He never was an idol worshiper" (3:67; also see 2:128-140; 3:96-97). He rejects pretensions of Jews and Christians that believe they alone will be saved, "Some have said, 'No one will enter Paradise except Jews or Christians!' Such is their wishful thinking. Say, 'Show us your proof, if you are right'. Indeed, those who submit themselves absolutely to God alone, while leading a righteous life, will receive their recompense from their Lord; they have nothing to fear, nor will they grieve" (2:111-112; also 2:120, 135; 4:171; 5:77). Muhammad however was not different from them on this level while hurling down both to hell, together with polytheists, "Those who disbelieved among the people of the scripture, and the idol worshipers, have incurred the fire of *Gehenna* forever. They are the worst creatures" (98:6; also 3:85). Accordingly, his reports of contact with Jews are tenser than with Christians:

> You will find that the worst enemies of the believers are the Jews and
> the idol worshipers. And you will find that the closest people in
> friendship to the believers are those who say, "We are Christian". This
> is because they have priests and monks among them, and they are not
> arrogant (5:82).

This theological debate determines non-Muslim legal status, mainly controlled by four verses:

> You shall fight back against those who do not believe in God, nor in
> the Last Day, nor do they prohibit what God and His messenger have
> prohibited, nor do they abide by the religion of truth-among those who
> received the scripture - until they pay the due tax, willingly or
> unwillingly (9:29).
> Surely, those who believe, those who are Jewish, the Christians, and
> the Sabians; anyone who believes in God, and believes in the Last Day,
> and leads a righteous life, will receive their recompense from their
> Lord. They have nothing to fear, nor will they grieve. Covenant with
> Israel (2:62).
> Surely, those who believe, those who are Jewish, the Sabians, and the
> Christians; any of them who believe in God and believe in the Last

> Day, and lead a righteous life, have nothing to fear, nor will they grieve (5:69).
> Those who believe, those who are Jewish, the Sabians, the Christians, the Zoroastrians, and the idol worshipers, God is the One who will judge among them on the Day of Resurrection. God witnesses all things (22:17).

Classic jurists understood from these verses that the *People of the Book* (Jews, Christians, Sabians, and Zoroastrians, to whom one could add Samaritans) have the right to live within the Land of Islam in spite of theological divergences that separate them from Muslims. Certainly, the hope was to one day see them become Muslim, but the Koran rejects recourse to force to convert them, "There shall be no compulsion in religion" (2:256). The cohabitation between Muslims and *People of the Book* is not on equal terms, but of the dominant over the dominated. The *People of the Book* have to pay a tribute, in a state of humiliation (9:29), and to submit to discriminatory norms, notably concerning family law. So for example Muslims may take women from among the *People of the Book*, but their men are not allowed to take Muslim women as wives (2:221; 5:5; 60:10). The *People of the Book* are called *dhimmis*, protected by Muslims, but these people should be closely observe because of their faith, and regarded with constant distrust, even though they may have strong relationship ties:

> O you who believe, do not take Jews and Christians as allies; these are allies of one another. Those among you who ally themselves with these belong with them. God does not guide the transgressors (5:51; to also see 3:28 and 9:8).
> O you who believe, do not ally yourselves even with your parents and your siblings, if they prefer disbelieving over believing. Those among you who ally themselves with them are transgressing (9:23).

One must not exclude reports based on justice, except for a case of hostility:

> God does not enjoin you from befriending those who do not fight you because of religion, and do not evict you from your homes. You may befriend them and be equitable toward them. God loves the equitable. God enjoins you only from befriending those who fight you because of religion, evict you from your homes, and band together with others to banish you. You shall not befriend them. Those who befriend them are the transgressors (60:8-9).

To solve contradictions that exist between the tolerant verses and those less tolerant ones, classic jurists resort to the theory of abrogation: a verse on a particular topic is abrogated by a later verse concerning the same topic[1]. However, classic jurists could not resolve conflicting passages by context or date. Some considered all tolerant verses of Koran concerning the non-Muslims abrogated by the so-called *verse of the sword*:

> Once the Sacred Months are past, you may kill idol worshipers when you encounter them, punish them, and resist every move they make. If they repent and observe the prayers and give the obligatory alms (*zakat*), you shall let them go. God is Forgiver, Most Merciful (9:5)[2].

Whatever the relation between Muslims and other religious communities, numerous persons did convert to Islam over time. Those that remained faithful to their faith could benefit from certain legislative and judicial autonomy, notably concerning family law. The Muslim State was then more a collector of tax than an administrator of society, with Jews and Christians involved in administration far more than the less trained Bedouin, who had come to occupy their countries. This is why historically Muslim authorities retained both Christians and Jews as government officials during the course of their administration. The Koran states in this respect:

> We have sent down the Torah, containing guidance and light. Ruling in accordance with it were the Jewish prophets, as well as rabbis and priests, as dictated to them in God's scripture, and as witnessed by them. Therefore, do not reverence human beings; you shall reverence Me instead. And do not trade away My revelations for a cheap price. Those who do not rule in accordance with God's revelations are the disbelievers ... Subsequent to them, we sent Jesus, the son of Mary, confirming the previous scripture, the Torah. We gave him the Gospel, containing guidance and light, and confirming the previous scriptures, the Torah, and augmenting its guidance and light, and to enlighten the righteous The *People of the Gospel* shall rule in accordance with God's revelations therein. Those who do not rule in accordance with God's revelations are the wicked (5:44 and 46).

This multi-confessional legal system persists up to today in some Arab countries with more or less no change, but on the whole, the approach tends toward unification [and Islamic cultural assimulation.] So in both Jordan and Syria, non-Muslim religious communities apply their religious laws concerning family law, with the exception of inheritance, and have their own religious courts, while Egypt suppressed such courts.

---

[1] This theory is based on the Koran 2:106; 16:101; 22:52.

[2] Ibn-Hazm: *Ma'rifat al-nasikh*, vol. II, p. 146-148; Ibn-Salamah: *Al-nasikh*, p. 19, 27, 29, 42, 45, 49, 54, 57, 61 etc.

3) Apostates

The Koran says, "There shall be no compulsion in religion" (2:256). While all are free to choose, they are encouraged to become Muslim. But a Muslim, either born of a Muslim family or a convert, does not have the right to leave his religion. It is therefore a uni-directional religious freedom, [or really not an expression of religious freedom at all.] The Koran does not foresee a precise punishment against an apostate although it speaks repeatedly by using the term *kufr* (disbelief)[1], or the term *riddah* (abjuration)[2]. Only punishments in the next life are foreseen, if one ignors verse 9:74, that speaks of "painful retribution in this life and in the Hereafter", without making specifications. Narratives of Muhammad are more explicit:

> One that changes his religion, kill him[3].
> It is not permitted to attempt to the life of the Muslim except in the three following cases: disbelief after faith, adultery after marriage and homicide without motive[4].

Mawerdi defines apostates as follows:

> Those that being legally Muslim, either of birth, or following conversion, quit the faith, and the two categories are, to the point of view of apostasy, on the same line[5].

On the basis of Koranic verses and Narratives of Muhammad, classic jurists foresee the death penalty for an apostate, after having granted him a delay of reflection for three days. If apostacy concerns a woman, some jurists recommend putting her in jail until her death, or her return to Islam[6]. It is necessary to add measures of civil order: the marriage of the apostate is dissolved, his children are removed, his inheritance is opened and he is deprived of inheritance rights. Collective apostasy relates to war. The fate reserved for apostates is thus worse than that reserved for an enemy, no truce being permitted for apostates.

---

[1] See verses 2:217 and 47:25-27.

[2] See verses 2:208; 3:86-90, 177; 4:137; 9:66, 74, 16:106-109.

[3] Al-Bukhari, narratives 2794 and 6411; Al-Tirmidhi, narrative 1378; Al-Nisa'i, narratives 3991 and 3992.

[4] Ahmad, narratives 23169 and 24518.

[5] Mawerdi: *Les statuts gouvernementaux*, p. 109.

[6] Aldeeb Abu-Sahlieh, *L'impact de la religion*, p. 60-63.

4) Polytheists

In the beginning of the faith, it seems that Muhammad wanted to make some concessions to polytheists. One passage of the Koran, recorded by Al-Tabari, recognized three of the pre-existing Arab divinities: Al-Lat, Al-Uzzah and Manat. But, facing his Companions that saw in this concession a breach against monotheism, Muhammad denounced this passage as revealed by Satan (i.e.: the source of Salman Rushdie's *Satanic Verses*). Although this passage disappeared from the Koran, traces remain that confirm a provocative polemic (53:19-23). Muhammad admitted the possibility of a pact with polytheists (9:3-4). But it was also denounced (9:7-11) and polytheists were summoned, in conformity with the *verse of the sword* (9:5), either to convert or undergo war until death.

5) Particular status of Arabia

By the end of his life, tolerance toward the *People of the Book* did not apply to those among them that lived in Arabia. Muhammad, on his deathbed, called Umar (d. 644), the future 2nd caliph, and told him, "Two religions must not coexist in the Arabian Peninsula"[1]. It was no longer sufficient to pay tribute as their coreligionists in the other regions dominated by Muslims. Recalling this narrative, Mawerdi writes that non-Muslims were not admitted to stay in the Hijaz more than three days. Their same cadavers would not be buried there and, "if [death] took place, they will be exhumed and transferred elsewhere, because burial equaled staying for ever"[2].

Classic Muslim jurists did not settle the geographical limits in which this norm had to apply. Today Saudi Arabia alone invokes this norm to restrict any freedom of worship for non-Muslims.

---

[1] Malik, narrative 1388.
[2] Mawerdi: *Les statuts gouvernementaux*, p. 357.

Chapter II.
Land of Islam & Land of Disbelief

1) Classic religious border

Classic Muslim jurists consider all regions under Muslim domination as the Land of Islam (*Dar al-Islam*), whether or not all inhabitants are Muslim. On the other side of this border is the Land of War (*Dar al-harb*), often called the Land of Disbelief (*Dar al-kufr*) that should pass to Muslim domination, some day, and its inhabitants convert to Islam.

Before Muhammad's departure from Mecca, the Koran summoned Muslims not to resort to war, even though they were attacked (16:127; 13:22-23). After their departure from Mecca and creation of a Muslim State in Medina, marking the beginning of the Muslim calendar, Muslims were allowed to fight those that fought them (2:190-193 and 216; 8:61; 22:39-40). Finally, they were permitted to undertake holy war (9:3-5)[1]. The goal of this war is to spread the Land of Islam everywhere and to convert all to Islam. According to the traditionalists, Muhammad revealed messages to the different chiefs of his time, demanding that they become Muslim. If they were monotheist and wanted to continue following their own religion, they had to submit themselves to the political authority of Muslims and pay tribute. If they refused both solutions, they had to prepare for war. If they were non-monotheist, they could only choose between conversion and war[2].

The Land of War can benefit from a peace treaty (*ahd*), thus becoming a Land of Treaty (*Dar ahd*). According to Abu-Yousof (d. 798), High Judge of Baghdad, "A representative of the Imam is not allowed to make peace with an enemy, when he has superior forces; but if his purpose was to mildly lead them to Islam or to become tributaries, it is permitted until an arrangement is reached on their side"[3]. Here Abu-Yousof merely paraphrases the Koran, "Never falter and cry for peace when you can gain the upperhand"(47:35).

---

[1] These stages outlined by Mawlawi: *Al-usus al-shar'iyyah*, p. 33-47.
[2] See Hamidullah: *Documents*, vol. II, p. 21, 22, 34 and 41; Hamidullah: *Majmu'at al-watha'iq*, p. 110, 116, 145, 162.
[3] Abou-Yousof: *Le livre de l'impôt foncier*, p. 319.

Three centuries later, Mawerdi (d. 1058) mentions among the duties of the chief of State:

> To fight those who, after having been invited, refuse to convert to Islam, until they convert or become tributaries, for the purpose of establishing the laws of Allah by making them superior to all other religions[1].

He states that if any adversaries convert to Islam, "they get the same rights as us, are submitted to the same charges, and remain masters of their own territory and of their own goods". If they demand grace and ask for an armistice, this armistice is not acceptable unless it is very difficult to defeat them, and on condition that they accept to pay; the armistice must be as short as possible and not exceed ten years; after ten years, the armistice is no longer valid[2].

Ibn-Khaldun (d. 1406), three centuries after Mawerdi, distinguishes between a war conducted by Muslims and a war conducted by the followers of other religions. The offensive war of Muslims is legitimate since they have a universal mission to lead all populations to join the Islamic religion, either by force or voluntarily. This is not the case with followers of other religions; who do not have a universal mission; they are permitted to make war only for self-defense[3].

2) Classic religious border and migration

To escape persecution, Muhammad, accompanied by some of his Companions, left Mecca, his native city, in September of 622, and went to Yathrib, his mother's home city, later named Medina. That event marks the beginning of the Islamic era, the era of *Hegira*, era of migration. Those who left for Medina were called *muhajirin* (the immigrants). Those who gave them good reception were called *ansar* (the supporters).

Some Muslims, however, remained in Mecca and practiced their faith in secret. Constrained to participate in the fight against the troops of Muhammad, some were killed. Referring to this tragic episode, the following verses urged the Muslims in Mecca to join the Community of believers:

---

[1] Mawerdi: *Les statuts gouvernementaux*, p. 31.
[2] *Ibid.*, p. 98-105.
[3] Ibn-Khaldun: *Muqaddimat Ibn-Khaldun*, p. 202.

> Those whose lives are terminated by the angels, while in a state of wronging their souls, the angels will ask them, "What was the matter with you?" They will answer, "We were oppressed on earth". The angels will say, "Was God's earth not spacious enough for you to emigrate therein?" For these, the final abode is Hell, and a miserable destiny. Exempted are the weak men, women, and children who do not possess the strength, nor the means to find a way out (4:97-98).

These two verses urge each Muslim living in an infidel country to leave and join the Muslim community, unless unable. Other verses express the same sense (4:100; 9:20). The purpose of this migration was to protect them from persecution, to weaken the infidel community and to participate in the war effort of the Muslim community. Taken together, the Koran uses two terms to express faith: *those who believe*, and *those who emigrate and strive in the way of Allah* (2:218; 8:72, 74 and 75; 8:20; 16:110).

Verse 8:72 establishes an alliance between the immigrants and those who gave them hospitality. It forbids such an alliance with Muslims who remain in the infidel country "as long as they have not emigrated". But if these Muslims remaining outside the community seek help in a "matter of religion", then it is the duty of the Muslim community to help them, except against a people to which the Muslim community is specifically bound by treaty.

Verse 4:89 urges Muslims not to choose friends from infidels "unless they emigrate to the way of God" (4:89). The Koran displays mistrust toward nomads, these eternal migrants without fixed domicile who, after declaring allegiance to Muhammad, returned to the desert (*ta'rib*) to escape his control in a critical moment when the Muslim community was in need of warriors for defense and expansion interests (see verses 9:97; 9:90, 99, 101, 120 and 49:14).

The Muslim immigrants had abandoned all their goods behind them and they were called to put an end to any link with the infidels, including family bonds (9:23). They had to be taken in charge by other members of the community. The Koran urges those who are rich to help them (24:22). The agreement, established by Muhammad between the immigrants, the *ansar* and the Jews living in Medina confirms that these three groups constituted one community[1]. The Koran gives a part of the war's spoil to the immigrants and it even places them before the actual

---

[1] Hamidullah: *Al-watha'iq al-siyasiyyah*, p. 59.

residents (59:8-10). It establishes a fraternity between all believers (49:10; 3:103; 9:11) implying inheritance rights[1], rights reserved thereafter to next of kin (33:6).

Classic Muslim jurists thought migration toward the Land of Islam would continue as long as there remained a division between the Land of Islam and the Land of Disbelief. They quote a narrative of Muhammad that said, "Migration [to the Muslim community] will never stop as long as the infidels are fought"[2]. Any Muslim in the Land of Disbelief must emigrate toward the Land of Islam. He can remain there only if he lives according to Islamic religious norms or if he is not able to emigrate because of illness, weakness or constraint[3]. Ibn-Qudamah (d. 1223) writes that even though a Muslim can accomplish his religious duties, in the Land of Disbelief, it is preferable that he emigrates toward the Land of Islam to be able to make the *jihad* against unbelievers, and to enlarge the number of the Muslim community[4]. If the Muslim living in the Land of Disbelief must emigrate toward the Land of Islam for a stronger reason, classic Muslim jurists regard with an evil eye any Muslim who migrates from the Land of Islam toward the Land of Disbelief[5]. Al-Jurjani (d. 1413) defined migration as "the act of terminating one's sojourn among the infidels and of joining the Land of Islam"[6]. It is the only correct migration admitted by classic jurists.

Relying on the authority of Malik (d. 795), Ibn-Rushd (d. 1126), imam of the Great Mosque of Cordoba and grandfather of Averroes, states that the obligation of migration is maintained until the day of resurrection. He quotes Koranic verses 4:97-98 and 8:72 and the saying of Muhammad, "I consider myself rid of any Muslim who sojourns among polytheists". Those converted to Islam in the Land of Disbelief must immigrate to the Land of Islam so that the Islamic norms may be applied to them. For a stronger reason, a Muslim cannot travel to the Land of Disbelief for trade or other purposes since the laws of Disbelief will be

---

[1] This situation resembles the first Christian community (*Acts* 4:32-34).
[2] Al-Nisa'i, narratives 4102 and 4103.
[3] Al-Shafi'i: *Kitab al-um*, vol. 4, p. 169-170.
[4] Ibn-Qudamah: *Al-mughni*, vol. 10, p. 514-515.
[5] See Khadduri: *War and peace*, p. 170-174.
[6] Al-Jurjani: *Al-ta'rifat*, p. 257.

applied to him, unless he wants to ransom a Muslim captive. If he goes to the Land of Disbelief willingly, without constraint, he cannot preside over the prayer and his testimony is rejected. Ibn-Rushd urges the Muslim authority to establish controls on roads so no Muslim can travel to the Land of Disbelief, especially if he is transporting forbidden commodities, which could strengthen the enemy against the Muslims. Ibn-Rushd adds, "God fixed to everybody a fate that he will reach and a wealth that he will obtain"[1].

Ibn-al-'Arabi (d. 1148), judge of Seville, is also opposed to the sojourn of Muslims in the Land of Disbelief as well as in the Land of Schism (*Dar al-bid'ah*) (by virtue of verse 6:68). He also directs Muslims to emigrate from a country, which is dominated by the illicit (*haram*), where they are in danger for their health, their persons, their goods and their families. He quotes Abraham (29:26 and 37:99) and Moses (28:21) who escaped for reason of fear[2]. The same position is taken by the great Andalusian Sufi Ibn-Arabi (d. 1240).

> Make sure to emigrate and not to stay among the infidels, because to stay among them constitutes an insult to the religion of Islam, an elevation of the word of the infidelity over the word of Allah. God, indeed, had not ordered the fight but to make the word of God superior, and the word of infidels inferior. Take care not to sojourn nor to enter under protection (*dhimmah*) of an infidel, as long as possible. You must know that he who sojourns among the infidels - although he can leave - has no share in Islam, since the Prophet says: "I consider myself rid of any Muslim who sojourns among the polytheists". He does not recognise in him the qualities of a Muslim. God says about those who died among the infidels: "Those whom the angles take in death while they wrong themselves, the angels will say, 'What was your stand?' They will say, 'We were abased in the land'. The angels will say, 'Was not God's earth wide, so that you might have emigrated in it?' Such as those, their abode shall be Gehenna; how wretched a destination!"(4:97).

> For this reason, we have forbidden to the people in this époque to visit Jerusalem (*bayt al-maqdis*) or to sojourn in it because it is in the hands of the infidels. The authority belongs to them, as well as domination over the Muslims. The Muslims with them stay in the worst situations - may God safeguard us from the domination of passions. Those Muslims who visit today Jerusalem or sojourn

---

[1] Ibn-Rushd: *Kitab al-muqaddimat*, p. 611-613.
[2] Ibn-al-Arabi: *Ahkam al-Qur'an*, vol. 1, p. 484-486.

> there are those about whom Allah says: "Their works are vain, and on the day of resurrection we assign no weight to them" (18:104). Because of that, emigrate from any human creature condemned by the religious law, and by the Truth in his Book or by the Prophet of Allah[1] [2].

In application of this migration doctrine, Muslims left countries reconquored by Christians. Thus, in 1091, the Christian reconquest of Sicily was achieved after an Islamic occupation of more than 270 years. A large number of Muslims left the island and found refuge on the other side of the Mediterranean. Imam Al-Mazari, from Mazara (in Sicily; d. 1141, in North Africa) called to Muslims living in Sicily not to remain in the Land of Disbelief. This rule, however, has exceptions:

- Sojourn in an enemy country for an imperative reason.
- Voluntary sojourn in ignorance of the fact that the sojourn is forbidden.
- Sojourn in an enemy territory hoping to snatch it from the occupying force and return it to Muslims, or hoping to lead the infidels on the straight way, or, at least, to divert them from any heresy[2].

With the capitulation of Toledo in 1085, the great majority of Muslims left the city. Those who remained could safeguard their mode of life and their propriety, their habitual residencies, as well as fiscal regime and religious freedom by paying tribute[3]. Such Muslims that stayed were despised by both those who emigrated, and those who had not been conquered. They were called *ahl al-dajn*, or *mudajjan*, words used when referring to tamed or domestic animals as opposed to free or wild animals. They became known in Spanish as *mudéjar*. However, the tolerance of the Christian kings of Spain toward their subjects, Jews as well as Muslims, did not last. Many Muslims converted to Christianity, but continued to live out their faith secretly, exposing themselves to the fury of the Inquisition. They were called *Moriscos*. This situation ended when it was decided to expel them all, like the Jews before them, in 1492. Expulsion was concluded by 1610[4].

---

[1] Ibn-Arabi: *Al-wassaya*, p. 43.
[2] Arab text and French translation of the *fatwa* of Al-Mazari, in: *Turki: Consultation juridique d'Al-Imam Al-Mazari*, p. 697-704.
[3] Quesada: *La population mudéjare*, p. 134.
[4] *Chrétiens, musulmans et juifs dans l'Espagne médiévale*, p. 313, 333.

The *Moriscos* under Christian authority hid their religion by resorting to the dissimulation (*al-taqiyyah*) as permitted by the Koran:

> The believers never ally themselves with the disbelievers, instead of the believers. Whoever does this is exiled from GOD. Exempted are those who are forced to do this to avoid persecution (3:28).
> Those who disbelieve in God, after having acquired faith, and become fully content with disbelief, have incurred wrath from God. The only ones to be excused are those who are forced to profess disbelief, while their hearts are full of faith (16:106).

This dissimulation (*al-taqiyyah*) consists in saying or showing the opposite of what one truly believes to save oneself, or others, from eminent danger. Both Sunnite and Shiite jurists allowed this approach[1].

Legitimating such an attitude, one religious decision or decree (*fatwa*) by Mufti Ahmad Ibn-Jumaira, dated December 1504, provides precise regulations to fit their hostile *milieu*. Thus if Christians obliged occupied Muslims to insult the Prophet Muhammad: they should pronounce his name as "Hamed", as Christians do, and not think of the Messenger of God, but of Satan or of some Jew called Hamed. If they are forced to go to Church at the time of Islamic prayer: they will be dispensed from doing the later, and their worship in Church will be considered as the Koranic prescription of prayer toward Mecca. If they are prevented from doing their prayers during the day: they should do them at night. The ritual ablution could also be replaced according to the circumstances: they can plunge in the sea, or rub the body with a clean substance, soil or wood. If they are obliged to drink wine or to eat pork: they may, but knowing it is an impure act and observe a mental reserve. If they are forced to renounce their faith: they should try to be evasive; if they are pressed: they should inwardly deny what they are obliged to say[2].

---

[1] See in the Internet http://www.islamic-paths.org/Home/English/Sects/ Shiite/Chapter_6b_Part01.htm#al-Taqiyya/Dissimulation%20(Part %201%20of%203), http://www.emamreza.net/eng/lib/ency/chapter6 %20b/part2_1.htm, http://www.ummah.net/moa-on-line/khutoot2.htm l#TAQIYYAH; See also Taqiyyah, in: *Al-Mawsu'ah al-fiqhiyyah*, vol. 13, p. 185-200.

[2] Cardaillac: *Morisques et chrétiens*, p. 88-90; Sabbagh, p. 49-53.

The preceding *fatwa* concerns Muslims who could not emigrate from their country[1]. Concerning those who were able to leave, Al-Wansharisi (d. 1508) stated, in two *fatwas*, that they should not remain; an opinion contrasting with that of Al-Mazari, whom he quotes without commentary[2]. He says that emigration from the Land of Disbelief to the Land of Islam remains obligatory until the day of resurrection. The same obligation exists to leave a Land of Revolt (*fitnah*). He reports that Malik forbids a person to sojourn in a locality where he had to behave with injustice. If he does not find a just country, he should choose a country with less injustice. Al-Wansharisi quotes here verse 4:97.

Exception is made for those who cannot move because they are paralyzed, in captivity or very sick or feeble. They must, however, keep in mind that they will emigrate whenever possible. Al-Wansharisi adds that it is forbidden to sojourn among infidels as it is forbidden to eat pork or to kill a person without reason. He who refuses to emigrate abandons the community[3] and denies Islam. He cannot fulfill the prayer without having the infidels laugh at him, a fact condemned by the Koran (5:58), neither can he fulfill the obligatory alms (*zakat*) due to the imam, an important element of Islam, nor the fast of Ramadan, nor pilgrimage to Mecca, nor *jihad*. A sojourn in the Land of Disbelief is contrary to the words of Muhammad, "The Muslim should not degrade"; and "The superior hand is better than the inferior one". Such a sojourn exposes the Muslim to perversion in matters of religion. Supposing that adults can avoid perversion, what about children, unable persons and feeble women? In addition, by staying among infidels, the descendants and women of Muslims risk being diverted from their religion by non-Muslims through marriage and by adopting their clothes, bad customs and language. If a Muslim loses the Arabic language, he also loses rituals linked to it. Lastly, Muslims cannot trust infidels who can find pretexts to overwhelm them with taxes, and fail in their engagements[4].

---

[1] Sabbagh, p. 53.

[2] *Al-Wansharisi*, vol. 2, p. 133-134 and vol. 10, p. 107-109.

[3] *Ibid.*, vol. 2, p. 119-133.

[4] *Ibid.*, vol. 2, p. 137-141.

3) Present religious border

Today, national criteria overstep religious criteria. After having undergone colonization, the Muslim world, notably after the end of the Ottoman empire and suppression of the Caliphate in 1924, was divided into separate modern nations, often at war with each other, with minimal religious links as through the *Organization of Islamic Conference* which acts as intermediary, without much effect. These modern Muslim nations are members of the United Nations. We are currently facing a new geopolitical structure, as modern Muslim authors try to adapt old divisions of Land of Islam and Land of War to this new political reality.

Abu-Zahrah (d. 1974) affirms that the present world is united in one organization (the United Nations) whose members are committed to respecting its laws. Islam requires in this case the respect of all agreements by virtue of the Koran [17:34]. Because of that, countries, which are members of this world organization, can no longer be considered as the Land of War, but must be treated as being a Land of Treaty (*Dar ahd*)[1].

Mawlawi says that if the Land of Islam is the country where Islamic norms are integrally applied, one may conclude that most Muslim countries no longer can be considered as a Land of Islam. Is it sufficient that a country applies family law to be considered Muslim? What about Turkey, which does not apply these laws: is it still a Muslim country? If the criteria is the practice of religious rituals, then what about some non-Muslim countries where Muslims practice their rituals more freely than in the so-called Muslim countries? Surely these are not Muslim countries, but there are few differences between them and Muslim countries, which do not apply Islamic laws and allow only Islamic rituals. Mawlawi is of the opinion that non-Muslim countries which are not in war or which have treaties with Muslim countries must be considered as a Land of Treaty (*Dar ahd*) or Land of Mission (*Dar da'wah*)[2]. Conscious of the negative connotation of the term "Land of Mission", Tariq Ramadan, a Swiss Muslim activist,

---

[1] Abu-Zahrah: *Al-ilaqat al-duwaliyyah fil-islam*, p. 57. See also Al-Zuhayli: *Athar al-harb*, p. 108-109 and 195-196.

[2] Mawlawi: *Al-usus al-shar'iyyah*, p. 98-104.

prefers the term "Land of Testimony" (*Dar al-shahadah*)[1], without departing from the classic notion:

> Muslims are asked to spread the knowledge of Islam among Muslims as well as non-Muslims. The *mu'min* [believer] is the one who has known and eventually accepts, whereas the *kafir* [unbeliever] is the one who has known and then refuses, then denies[2].

Present law books in Arabic use neutral terms, without religious connotation, but religious books generally replace the term Land of War (*Dar al-harb*) with Land of Disbelief (*Dar al-kufr*), and inhabitants of these countries are most often designated not as enemy (*harbi*), but as unbelieving (*kafir*), a qualifier given to all non-Muslims, including Christians and Jews, even among Muslim country nationals who sometimes occupy ministerial stations in these countries.

The fundamentalist movements within Arab and Islamic countries would like to reintroduce the old division between the Land of Islam and Land of War[3]. Accordingly, the 2nd article of 1984 Constitutional model of Jarishah stipulates:

> The Islamic Community constitutes one community. The best entity among those that compose it is the most pious; all barriers: frontiers, nationalities (*qawmiyyat*), and links of blood (*asabiyyat*), are void[4].

The *Islamic Council of Europe*[5] 1983 Constitutional Model holds any state adopting this model is "part of the Muslim world, and its Muslim people are integral with the Muslim nation" (article 2), adding, "It is the duty of a state to strive by any means to seek unity and solidarity with the Muslim nation" (article 72).

Muhammad sent some of his Companions to Abyssinia to protect them from persecutions by the inhabitants of Mecca. He gave them a message for the king of Abyssinia, asking him to welcome them and to become a Muslim. To call the unbeliever to

---

[1] Ramadan: *To be a European Muslim*, p. 145-147.

[2] *Ibid.*, p. 134.

[3] We refer here to different constitutional models issued by Muslim fundamentalists who consider themselves in conformity with Islamic law. These models should replace the Constitutions of Arab and Islamic countries inspired by the West. Six of these constitutional models are translated into French in: Aldeeb Abu-Sahlieh: *Les musulmans face aux droits de l'homme*, annexes 12-17, p. 522-569.

[4] Text in: Aldeeb Abu-Sahlieh: *Les musulmans face aux droits de l'homme*, p. 566-569.

[5] *Ibid.*, p. 557-565.

Islam remains a constant concern of all Muslims. The 1983 Constitutional model of the *Islamic Council of Europe* says, "The state and society are based on the following principles: [...] obligation to engage in the Islamic mission (*da'wah islamiyyah*)" (article 3). The 1952 Constitutional model of the Liberation Party states, "the appeal to Islam is the principal duty of the nation" (article 10)[1]. The freedom to change one's religion is, however, uni-directional: conversion of Muslims to another religion is expressly forbidden. In addition, *jihad* is not excluded as a means of extending the authority of Islam. The Constitutional model of the Liberation Party says, "*Jihad* is a duty for all Muslims" (Art. 90). The commentary specifies that one should begin by calling the infidels to the Islamic faith. If they refuse to convert, then they can be fought. This Constitutional model forbids treaties of absolute neutrality because they reduce the authority of Muslims, as well as treaties of permanent delimitation of frontiers, because such delimitation means the non-transmission of the Islamic faith and the end of *jihad*[2].

Some countries give their citizenship only to Muslims (for example Saudi Arabia and other Golf countries); in other countries, adhesion to Islam makes citizenship acquision easier (for example in Egypt)[3]. Meanwhile, Arab countries still continue to apply Islamic family law to any Muslim, whatever his or her country of origin. For example, a French man who converts to Islam is submitted to Islamic law in Egypt. He may contract a polygamous marriage and repudiate his wife; upon death, a daughter receives half of what a son receives as inheritance [4].

The classic Islamic concept played an important role in the creation of new Islamic nation states, following Soviet downfall, as well as the sporadic emergence of independence or autonomy, demonstrated by Muslim minorities in the Balkans. This is the result of classic Islamic norms, which forbid Muslims from submitting to any non-Muslim judicial, legislative and/or executive power. Whenever Muslims reach a significant

---

[1] *Ibid.*, p. 528-540.

[2] *Ibid.*, p. 452-453.

[3] *Ibid.*, p. 93-94.

[4] On Egypt, see Aldeeb Abu-Sahlieh: *L'impact de la religion*, p. 189; on Morocco, see Manaf: *Problèmes du couple mixte*, p. 156.

percentage of the population in countries such as England, Germany, France, Italy, Switzerland, Holland or the United States, they put themselves into a similar problem as the Balkans. Note here that Muslims in England formed their own parliament in 1992[1]. Already in 1982, they founded an *Islamic Shari'ah Council* in London, proclaiming that their Islamic court could make decisions concerning Muslim family law. Such a court dissolves Islamic marriages, but with regard to civil aspects of the contract the couple must still address British courts. Anyone who gets a divorce by this Council can get remarried[2]. Still in London, Imam Omar Al-Bakri preaches holy war against Britain, and calls for election and citizen involvement boycotts. He no longer sees the use of a driver's license, as according to him, it constitutes a divine permission[3]. Likewise, in the U.S., black Muslims founded the *Nation of Islam*, in 1930. Its goal is still to create an independent Muslim country[4].

4) Religious border and present migration

Colonization of Islamic countries by European nations raised the same problems as the reconquest of the Iberian Peninsula. Should Muslim countries occupied by foreign forces be considered as being part of the Land of Disbelief? If such is the case, should Muslims emigrate from these, their native countries, and proceed to some Muslim country? Al-Wazani (d. 1923), Mufti of Fes (Morocco), mentions a *fatwa* issued by Judge Mawlay Abd-al-Hadi forbidding a Muslim from staying under the protection of infidels whenever he has a chance to go to a Muslim country.

According to this *fatwa*, a Muslim who frequents the infidels' homes loses both his faith and life in this world, and disobeys his master, Muhammad, because the Malikite school unanimously forbids conclusion of any peace with infidels, except under duress. Such a Muslim cannot preside over prayer and his testimony is rejected, because Islam is superior and nothing should be superior to Islam. More serious is when someone trades with infidels. Even more condemned is someone who not only

---

[1] See http://www.islamicthought.org/mp-intro.html
[2] The Islamic Shari'a Council, London.
[3] Lathion, p. 6.
[4] See http://www.noi.org/

trades with them, but also gives information against fellow Muslims: he must be considered a spy and sentenced to death. Most culpable is a person who goes to the enemy and indicates a way to occupy Muslim territory, "To love an infidel, and wish his domination over fellow Muslims is a sign of infidelity; it constitutes apostasy"[1].

Al-Wazani mentions also the *fatwa* of Abu-al-Abbas Ibn-Zaki concerning Muslims

> - who stay in their country occupied by the Christians and fight against them;
> - who remain in the country after the conclusion of peace, believing that their presence is temporary and that they are not required to pay a tribute. If this is required of them, they escape to the country of Islam;
> - who have the intention to live in their country and to pay tribute to the Christians.

This *fatwa* claims that the first group serves his religion; the dust of his feet is a benediction. The second group commits an odious act (*makruh*). However, if he executes his intention to flee whenever compelled to pay tribute, he will be saved, if God wishes. The third group is the worst; such a person has lost his faith and his life in this world. He deserves the extremest punishment: if he spies against Muslims, he deserves the death penalty; if he fights on the side of Christians, he must be treated the same as Christians: he can be killed and his goods can be taken. The students and muezzins who remain under the authority of Christians are students and muezzins of misfortune: they cannot preside over prayer and their testimony is rejected. They must repent upon leaving these countries, dominated by infidels[2].

Al-Wazani affirms that the duty to emigrate from the Land of Disbelief to the Land of Islam is maintained until the day of resurrection, as reported by classic Muslim jurists. This is also the case for a country dominated by evil and wrong. If a Muslim does not find a just country, he must choose a less evil country. Nobody can be dispensed from his obligation to emigrate from his country if occupied by infidels, unless there is no possibility

---

[1] Al-Wazani: *Al-nawazil al-sughra*, vol. I, p. 418.
[2] *Ibid.*, vol. I, p. 419.

to do so, due to sickness or extreme weakness. In such cases, he must be mindful of leaving his country whenever possible[1].

In the early years of colonialism, Muslim jurists and leaders tried to apply the rule of emigration. A considerable number of Muslims emigrated from North Africa to Turkey. In 1920, when India was declared a Land of Disbelief, a great wave of emigrants went to Afghanistan. That migration was catastrophic for them; they eventually returned to India, impoverished and frustrated. Hundreds died on the way[2].

The majority of Muslims, however, were obliged to stay together with their leaders and religious teachers, to fit the new reality, particularly because colonial regimes were, generally and in their own interest, tolerant concerning religious questions. They permitted Muslims not only to practice their religion freely in the Western conception of religion, but also to maintain their own laws with their own courts and judges for many social, civil and economic questions[3].

After the creation of Pakistan, Muslim Indians had to choose between staying in India or emigration to Pakistan. Mawlana Abul-Kalam Azad declared in 1942 to the Indian National Congress, "I am proud to be Indian. I am an integral part of this united and indivisible nation... I most never renounce this right". After independence, he became Minister of National Education of the Indian government. Addressing Muslim university students, he said that if they dreamt of living in "Medina", it would be better to join Pakistan, but if they chose to live in India they should accept the situation of Mecca, which meant to be a minority community[4].

Today, with the end of colonization, we have the opposite problem, the emigration of Muslims toward non-Muslim countries that previously had colonized them. Some of these

---

[1] *Ibid.*, vol. I, p. 446. French occupation of Algeria, see *fatwas* sollicited by Emir Abd-al-Qadir and his opinion in: *Abd-al-Qadir: Tuhfat al-za'ir*, p. 316-329, 384-393, 411-422 and 471-480. On India and Algeria, see Peters: *Dar al-harb*, p. 579-587.

[2] Masud: *The obligation to migrate*, p. 40-41. See the *fatwas* on India in Hunter: *The Indian Muslims*, p. 185-187.

[3] Lewis: *La situation des populations musulmanes*, p. 29-30.

[4] Levrat: *Une expérience de dialogue*, p. 136-137.

Muslims even acquired the citizenship of these Western countries. There is also the problem of non-Muslim country citizens that converted to Islam and the one of autochthonous Muslim minorities that live in countries with a non-Muslim majority as in the Balkans, Israel and the United States. Is it necessary to ask all Muslims to leave non-Muslim countries (the Land of Disbelief) and to immigrate to Muslim countries (the Land of Islam)? To what extend must classic Islamic norms be maintained in a world where religious borders are no longer national borders?

We saw already that Muslim minorities in countries having a non-Muslim majority obtained political independence, and others hope to obtain such independence in the near future. While waiting for this day, one notes tendencies among different Muslim authors to refer to classic Islamic teachings.

Muslim extremist groups even consider their own "Muslim" countries as being in the Land of Disbelief, as long as these countries do not apply fully Islamic law. They ask their followers to emigrate and to go in the mountains to prepare for the conquest of their countries, as Muhammad did with Mecca. [The United States is still fighting such groups in the mountains of Afghanistan.] In Egypt, the police call these groups: *Al-takfir wal-hijrah* (anathema and migration). Their real name is however *Al-jama'ah al-islamiyyah* (Muslim brotherhood or community), which implies that they consider themselves the only Muslims. Currently, this group is responsible for many attacks in Egypt. Its ideologist was Sayyid Qutb; hung by President Jamal Abdel-Nasser, in 1966. He specified in his commentary of verse 8:72 that emigration was required of Muslims until the day Mecca was conquered. If all Arabia would submit to Islam, a Muslim no longer would be obliged to immigrate, as he found himself henceforth in the country of Islam. Today, however, the world has reversed to the *jahiliyyah* (period of ignorance before Islam) and the authority is no longer that of God, but of the *Taghout* (the tyrant, the devil). It is a new situation for Muslims, which implies a reassertion of the division Land of Islam / Land of Migration (*Dar al-islam / Dar al-hijrah*). This situation will continue until Islam expands anew, and then there is no need for migration[1].

---

[1] Qutb: *Fi dhilal al-Qur'an*, vol. III, p. 1560.

Muslim movements ask all Muslim countries to open borders for migration by any Muslims living in non-Muslim countries. The 1984 Constitutional model of Jarishah stipulates that a nation's leader "opens the door of immigration into the Land of Islam to believers" (article 19). The 1983 Constitutional model of the *Islamic Council of Europe*[1] grants, to any Muslim, the right to achieve citizenship in a Muslim nation state (article 14). The 1981, Second Islamic Declaration of Human Rights published by the *Islamic Council of Europe*[2] states in article 23(c):

> The Land of Islam (*Dar al-islam*) is one. It is a homeland for every Muslim, whose movement within (its domain) cannot be restricted by any geographical impediments nor any political boundaries. Every Muslim country must receive any Muslim who emigrates there, or who enters; as a brother welcomes his brother, "Those who entered the city and the faith before them love those who flee unto them for refuge, and find in their breasts no need for that which had been given them, but prefer the fugitives above themselves though poverty become their lot. Whoever is saved from his own avarice is successful" (59:9).

One modern author and professor at the Universities of Jordan, Tripoli (Libya) and, now in Riyadh, considers the question of the occupation of Muslim countries by colonial infidels who apply their laws. Those who are occupied are in a particular situation, which obliges them, under constraint, to ally with the infidel to avoid his evil by virtue of the principle of dissimulation (*al-taqiyyah*) instituted by the Koran (3:28). Dissimulation must however remain exterior, and the Muslim must never trust the enemy. It is however not obligatory: a Muslim can always abandon it and say the truth, even when he risks his life[3]. On the other hand, dissimulation is not permitted when confronted with an unjust authority[4]. Evoking verses 4:97-98, this author adds that if the Muslim fears that his faith will weaken, he must leave this land, even if it is his native country and his home. He must leave the Land of Disbelief and go to the Land of Islam, where he can follow the norms of Islam. The obligation of immigration is maintained until the day of resurrection and it is an obligation for each Muslim who fears for his faith, regardless of where he stays.

---

[1] Text in: Aldeeb Abu-Sahlieh: *Les musulmans face aux droits de l'homme*, p. 557-565.

[2] *Ibid.*, p. 486-496.

[3] Al-Hasan: *Al-ilaqat al-duwaliyyah fil-Qur'an wal-sunnah*, p. 245-252.

[4] *Ibid.*, p. 252-253.

Nothing should prevent him from accomplishing this end: his goods, his interests, his parents, his friends, the suffering he risks encountering by immigrating, as long as there exists a land where his religion can be safe.

This professor, however, forbids an immigrant whose goal is to escape holy war (*jihad*). Islam requires *jihad* to transform a country governed by infidelity into a country governed by Islam. If a Muslim can rely on the help of his fellow believers, living in his country or on Islamic forces living in proximity to his country, he is obliged to stay because the Koran requires him to fight the neighboring enemy (9:123). In this case, he who remains has merit over one who immigrates. Muhammad said, "O Fadik: Do prayer, give the obligatory alms (*zakat*), emigrate from evil and live in your country wherever you like... and you will be considered as an immigrant"[1]. The author refers to two distinct situations: the non-application of Islamic law by Muslim countries and the occupation of Palestine by Israel. In the face of these two situations, one should make recourse sometimes to dissimulation (*al-taqiyyah*), sometimes to emigration and sometimes to holy war (*jihad*)[2].

Concerning the problem created by the occupation of Palestine by Jews, the Great Mufti of Jordan, Abd-Allah Al-Qalqili, issued a *fatwa* forbidding Muslims to leave their country, because this will be a defeat worse than occupation itself. These Muslims must stay even if they must suffer. He quotes the Koran, "O you who believe, you shall be steadfast, you shall persevere, you shall be united, you shall observe God, that you may succeed" (3:200).

Speaking about the Koranic obligation to immigrate, Al-Qalqili says that this duty was prescribed for two reasons:
- Muslims could not maintain their faith in Mecca before its conquest.
- Muslims needed men who could participate in the war effort against enemies.

Immigration to a Muslim community remains an obligation for a Muslim when these two conditions are realized. Thus:
- It is an obligation for a Muslim who goes to America or another country where laws opposed to his religion are applied and where he cannot practice his religion, and is exposed to perversion, risks having children ignorant of their religion and, after his death, does

---

[1] *Ibid.*, p. 259.
[2] *Ibid.*, p. 258-260.

not find somebody to pray over his remains. Such a Muslim
engenders children who abandon their religion and sometimes fight
against their nation and against the religion of their fathers.
- It is an obligation for a Muslim whose country needs him to
participate in battle.

In these two cases, a Muslim has no right to leave his country,
and if he is already outside his country, he must emigrate from
there to a Muslim country. Al-Qalqili adds that if somebody is
constrained from leaving his country, he should seek out where a
Muslim community exists, and whose members help each other
to maintain Islamic identity. Those who emigrate from their
country and go to countries where they lose their faith and
engender infidel children commit a great sin; they prefer the life
in this world to the next[1].

The Guide for the Muslim in Foreign Countries, edited by a
Shiite Lebanese publisher in 1990, recalls the prohibition against
going to the Land of Disbelief. It quotes Koranic verses relating
to this subject and a saying of Imam Al-Sadiq, "There are seven
deadly sins: voluntary homicide, false accusation of adultery,
desertion in battle, return to nomadism after emigration, eating
unjustly an orphan's goods, acceptation of usury and all that is
punished with hell by Allah"[2]. The *return to nomadism* refers to
Bedouins converted to Islam in the time of Muhammad who went
back to the desert, dissolving their links with the Islamic
community; refusing to participate in its wars.

This guide claims that the Muslim must always feel a barrier
between himself and the impure Land of Disbelief. It quotes the
Koranic verse, "The polytheists only are unclean" (9:28). This
barrier must prevent the Muslim from integrating himself into
this society. He must have the feeling that he is in an unjust
society and that his presence in this Land of Disbelief is an
exceptional presence, dictated by the necessity that he must flee
as much as possible, "Indeed, what is for a Muslim worse than to
loose his eternal life for a temporary pleasure or a brief interest?"[3].

This guide accuses parents who send their children to foreign
countries, especially their girls without relatives to supervise
them. It explains that foreign countries attract these Muslim

---

[1] Al-Qalqili: *Al-fatawi al-urduniyyah*, p. 7-12.
[2] *Dalil al-muslim*, p. 15-20.
[3] *Ibid.*, p. 29.

children with scholarships or by granting them political asylum or even citizenship through marriage with one of their citizens. This is intended to separate them from their Muslim *milieu* according to the missionaries' plan, which failed to convert them to Christianity, and which now tries to distort their personality. After the failure of military and economic colonialism against Muslim countries, foreign countries cannot find any other means than to impose their domination over Muslim brains[1].

However, *The Guide for the Muslim in Foreign Countries* denies that it is in favor of cutting Muslims off from the Western world; its purpose is only to vaccinate them against the defects of that Land of Disbelief. The Muslim has to choose either to leave the Land of Disbelief or to immune himself spiritually against it. The purpose of the book is then to help a Muslim to safeguard his or her identity and his or her purity in the Land of Disbelief[2]. For this purpose, it establishes the following principles:

- It is forbidden for a Muslim to go to a Land of Disbelief if the way of life in this Land can undermine faith, regardless of the reason for travel: tourism, studies, trade or permanent sojourn. Undermining faith means committing any sin, small or great, such as shaving his beard, shaking hands with a foreign woman, abandoning prayer and fasting, eating impure foods, drinking alcohol, etc.
- If the risk to undermine faith concerns solely a woman and children, the Muslim must leave them in his Muslim country. Because of that, the Guide speaks only about duties of Muslim men, and not about those of Muslim women.
- If a Muslim needs to travel to a Land of Disbelief for medical treatment or for other important reasons, and he simultaneously risks undermining faith, this travel is permitted within the limits of necessity.
- In all cases, it is preferable not to live in the company of sinners or of those who are in error, unless there is a valid reason. He who lives among the sinners receives part of their maledictions, which hit them. He who lives in the Land of Islam benefits from the benedictions which it receives[3].

Concerning those who must travel to the Land of Disbelief, they must respect Islamic norms, developed in this guide. We mention here:

- To accomplish daily prayers. Not to eat impure foods, not to drink alcohol; nor to sit at a table where alcohol is consumed. Not to direct

---

[1] *Ibid.*, p. 30-31.
[2] *Ibid.*, p. 32-33.
[3] *Ibid.*, p. 63-66.

the face or back toward Mecca while on the toilet, because Western toilets are not oriented according to Islamic norms.
- Not to touch a foreign woman. Marriage with a pagan (non-monotheist) or apostate is forbidden. Marriage with a Jewish or Christian woman should only be temporary. If a virgin, the Muslim must ask her father's consent. In divorce, it is forbidden to leave children with the woman. Unless unavoidable, a woman must be treated by a female physician or nurse, and a man by a male physician or nurse if treatment involves touching or seeing "disgraceful parts" (*awrah*).
- Not to bury a Muslim in the cemetery of infidels unless unavoidable due to the impossibility of sending the body to a Muslim country.
- It is permitted to work in a supermarket if one is not obliged to sell pork or alcohol. It is forbidden to sell or purchase lottery tickets or musical instruments[1].
- Medical students must avoid staying among women, and if impossible, they must take care not to be influenced. They must not touch a woman's body or look on her "disgraceful parts" unless required for treatment. They must not look upon an image of a human body with desire. They must not practice on a Muslim corpse unless life depends on it and a non-Muslim corpse is not available[2].
- To seek to convert infidels to Islam. This has to be considered by the Muslim as a payment for having left the Land of Islam[3].

The magazine of the *Saudi Commission of Fatwa* publishes the following *fatwa* of Sheik Ibn-Baz (d. 1999):

Question: Is it licit for a student to live with a family in a foreign country in order to learn the language better?

Answer: It is illicit for a student to live with such a family because he risks contamination by the morals of the infidels and of their women. The question remains whether such travel is licit in itself. It is in fact forbidden to travel in the Land of Disbelief for study except in case of extreme necessity and on condition that the student is lucid and prudent... Muhammad says, "God does not admit the acts of a Muslim if he frequents the polytheists"... He says also, "I consider myself rid of any Muslim who sojourns among the polytheists". Many other sayings of Muhammad have the same sense. Thus, the Muslim must avoid travel in the Land of Disbelief, except in extreme necessity. Unless the traveler is lucid and prudent and intents to convert others to Islam ... in this case, his travel is meritorious[4].

The journal of this religious authority twice published the same editorial to warn against the sending of students for language courses organized in the West, including programs of

---

[1] *Ibid.*, p. 69-79 and 83-89.

[2] *Ibid.*, p. 80-83.

[3] *Ibid.*, p. 44.

[4] *Majallat al-buhuth al-islamiyyah* (Riyad), n° 27, 1990, p. 83-84.

entertainment and sojourn in infidel families. The headline is expressive, "Warnings against travel in the infidel country and the dangers of such a travel for religion and morals"[1].

One Saudi woman demanded that the government forbid Saudi girls from registering in mixed foreign schools, faculties or universities. She also wants girls to be obliged to wear Islamic clothes[2].

Abdallah Ibn Abd-al-Muhsin Al-Turki, of the University of Imam Muhammad Ibn-Sa'ud, wrote the preface to a book on the reasons for and economic consequences of scientist emigration from the Muslim world. He says that such emigration is due to the fault of both: Muslim societies and Muslim scientists. If Muslim societies had not ceased to follow the teachings of Islam, they would not have suffered from this problem. Concerning Muslim scientists, if they had steadfast zeal and a feeling for their Islamic national duty, they would have remained in their places, to fulfill the needs of their societies even if they had to suffer some difficulties and to sacrifice some of their interests.

Al-Turki adds that besides the arguments presented in the book, there is a necessity "to recall to our Muslim scientist brothers who emigrated and refused to return to the Land of Islam that it is not allowed for a Muslim, according to the Islamic law, to live in a Land of Disbelief and take it as his homeland and domicile". He points out that, besides the underdevelopment in Muslim countries, the emigration of the brains has consequences on the children of these scientists who risk abandoning Islam. These scientists should think, "the seduction of the life, including scientific position, notoriety or economic security, has no value if their sons and daughters leave the Islamic religion"[3].

The author of this book points out that educated children who go to Western countries provide these countries an annual help estimated at millions of dollars. Some of them work in sensitive fields such as the creation of atomic bombs and whose secrets go to Israeli atomic installations, which in turn threaten Muslims[4].

---

[1] *Majallat al-buhuth al-islamiyyah* (Riyad), n° 10, 1984, p. 7-10 and n° 16, 1986, p. 7-10.

[2] Hammad: *Masirat al-mar'ah al-su'udiyyah*, p. 105.

[3] Mursi: *Hijrat al-ulama*, p. III-V.

[4] *Ibid.*, p. 4-5.

Another debate concerns Muslims who take citizenship of a non-Muslim country. One author strongly considers such a Muslim an apostate, because he submits to Western laws instead of Islamic laws. He even asks Muslim citizens in a non-Muslim country, including converts, to give up their citizenship and return to live among their Muslim brothers[1]. This problem was submitted by the *Islamic Center of Washington* to the *Academy of Islamic Law*, and concerns the *Organization of Islamic Conference*. Members of this Academy were divided, so that they could not make a clear response[2]. We will reconsider this point in detail in the following discussion of Muslim naturalization.

Facing the impossibility of forbidding any Muslim from emigrating to the Land of Disbelief and their naturalization, Al-Jaza'iri, preacher of the Prophet's Mosque in Medina, recommended the creation of a commission of all Muslim countries, with the goal of protecting immigrant rights by providing a budget to which all Muslim countries must contribute according to their ability, and whose goal is:

- To construct mosques to pray there and to learn their religion.
- To provide imams and books.
- To unite Muslims and create only one group that will be connected exclusively to the same commission.
- To organize a religious teaching for immigrants.
- To create a cooperation between immigrants for their own butcher shop and cemetery.
- To create a commission of three religious scientists in every country of immigration whose goal is to solve conflicts between immigrants in order to avoid addressing themselves to the non-Muslim courts; to conclude and dissolve their marriages; to share their inheritance according to a will established in accordance with Islamic law; to create a cash-box to help in every mosque; to establish economic law between them and a bank to receive deposits according to Islamic norms.

Al-Jaza'iri believes these measures will prevent Muslims from dissolving into the unbelieving and atheistic Western society[3].

We must here take note of the fact that some Muslims living in Muslim countries claim for their coreligionists living in non-Muslim countries the application of the Islamic family law, in the

---

[1] Al-Jaza'iri: *Tabdil al-jinsiyyah*; Al-Jaza'iri: *I'lam al-anam*, p. 723.
[2] *Majallat majma al-fiqh al-islami*, n° 3, part 2, 1987, p. 1104, see also p. 1103, 1113, 1119, 1129, 1149-1158 1327-1338, 1399.
[3] Al-Jaza'iri: *I'lam al-anam*, p. 726-729.

same way Muslim countries apply to their non-Muslim communities their own religious family laws. An Egyptian professor writes:

> The non-Muslim nations, who pretend to be the most civilized, do not reserve for Muslim citizens any particular treatment in matters of family law considered by them as public order applied equally for all. This is not the case of Islam that applies to non-Muslims their own family laws. What a beautiful equity is Islam![1].

Another Egyptian professor wishes the creation of a Muslim family code applicable to Muslims living in the non-Muslim countries who opt for such a code. This code should be inspired entirely by Islamic law in a contemporary interpretation, which would be the most compatible with universal values. The purpose is "to allow the coexistence between the members of the Muslim community and other communities respecting the culture and the legitimate interests of this growing Muslim community"[2].

The application of such a code, according to this professor, could be limited to Muslims established in Europe and whose links with their country of origin are interrupted. But it will not be applicable either to European Muslims or to Muslims not established in Europe, whose links with their country of origin remain strong. This unified code could avoid, theoretically, the principal discriminations attributed to the Islamic law, i.e. discrimination on the basis of sex or religion. It should:
- exclude the impediment to inheritance for disparity of religion;
- limit polygamy to exceptional cases according to the spirit of the Islamic law;
- limit or subordinate divorce by unilateral repudiation to conditions which are similar to those of divorce in order not to deny the rights of the defending party.

In this way, adds this professor, "it is possible to elaborate on the basis of Islamic norms an Islamic family law which allows Muslims living in the West to realize their principal objective which is to establish their identity without being in disharmony with the society in which they are trying to integrate"[3].

The proposition of the two Egyptian professors is not new. Already in 1980, the Seminar of Kuwait on Human Rights in Islam organized by the *International Commission of Jurists*,

---

[1] Salamah: *Mabadi al-qanun al-duwali*, p. 172.
[2] Riad: *Pour un code européen de droit musulman*, p. 380.
[3] *Ibid.*, p. 381-382.

Kuwait University and the *Union of Arab Lawyers* mentioned a similar idea:

> The Seminar calls all nations to respect minority rights in exercise of their cultural traditions and religious rituals, and the right to refer in their personal statute to their religious convictions, and it recommends providing the necessary support to all initiatives that encourage this spirit and strengthen this orientation and outlook[1].

It is important here to mention the point of view of a Muslim author of ex-Yugoslavia in a doctoral thesis, presented in Saudi Arabia. After noting that acquiring citizenship in a non-Muslim country by a Muslim constitutes apostasy[2], this author indicates that it is not possible to apply Islamic norms that impose migration toward the Land of Islam and forbid naturalization to Muslim minorities. Indeed Muslim minorities do not live voluntarily under non-Muslim domination, but are forced there and acquire citizenship in spite of them according to the *right of blood* or the *right of soil*. Therefore, they are not sinful, nor guilty of wrongdoing. Further, these Muslims can be considered obliged, according to Islamic law, to accept citizenship of a non-Muslim country, since this citizenship confers benefit and rights from the nation state. But this author adds that such Muslims must keep in mind the idea that they are forced to acquire this citizenship, without which they would not be able to have a worthwhile life. Meanwhile, they must use all means at their disposal to spread Islam, and be ready when a Muslim nation will come about, to answer the call and immigrate[3].

This author allows a Muslim to emigrate from a Muslim country to a non-Muslim country and to acquire its citizenship in the following conditions:

- His country of origin does not need him.
- This Muslim cannot have a life in his country very equal to the one procured in the non-Muslim country.
- He must not be harmful to a Muslim in his work.
- He must not commit what is illicit according to Islam.
- He and his family are secure and he can without danger practice his religion.
- He does not ask for the citizenship of the non-Muslim country unless this country does not grant any work for unnaturalized people.

---

[1] Aldeeb Abu-Sahlieh: *Les musulmans face aux droits de l'homme*, p. 500.
[2] Tupuliak: *Al-ahkam*, p. 79-82.
[3] *Ibid.*, p. 82-86.

- He intends to return to his country of origin at the first opportunity.
- He disapproves of evil he commits while acquiring this citizenship, at least in his heart.

The author in question mentions the verse, "Those who disbelieve in God, after having acquired faith, and become fully content with disbelief, have incurred wrath from God. The only ones to be excused are those who are forced to profess disbelief, while their hearts are full of faith" (16:106). He concludes that if the Muslim must disavow faith out of necessity, for stronger reason he may acquire foreign citizenship to protect his faith, his life, his possessions and his family. He also mentions a narrative of Muhammad that affirms, "All countries are God's countries, and all believers are God's servants. Remain anywhere you feel well"[1]. He then answers objections over the naturalization of a Muslim:

- The marriage of a naturalized Muslim takes place according to civil law. The author answers that such a civil marriage is however done by a Muslim for show. After the civil marriage he concludes a religious marriage before an imam or a religious person according to Islamic norms.
- The inheritance of a Muslim is shared according to Western law, contrary to Islamic law. The author answers that a Muslim has always the right to dictate his will according to Islamic law, denying inheritance to those who do not have the right thereby.
- A Muslim can be forced to serve in the non-Muslim army, sometimes against fellow Muslims. The author answers that the military service in most Western countries is voluntary and can be exchanged against an amount of money. On the other hand, Muslim minorities in ex-Yugoslavia adhered to the army to learn to handle weapons. Most who took part in the Yugoslav army ran away, not to participate in the war against fellow Muslims.
- A Muslim can be submitted to Western laws, contrary to Islamic law. The author answers that this is also the case in many so-called Muslim countries that apply Western law. A naturalized Muslim who submits to Western law has the benefit of excuse for constraint.
- Muslim children are educated according to programs based on disbelief, without links to Islam. The author answers that non-Muslim countries allow Muslims to educate their children in Islamic schools and centers[2].

It is important here to say a word concerning the politics of migration adopted by Maghreb countries. These countries conceived of emigration as having three purposes: to have fewer

---

[1] *Ibid.*, p. 86-88.
[2] *Ibid.*, p. 88-91.

unemployed persons, to obtain more currency to finance development, and to enable the emigrants to acquire a professional training in Europe which would help their respective country's development after their return. This was considered advantageous for the receiving countries as well as for the exporting countries [1]. They conceived of this migration as provisional. The national Algerian Charter promulgated in 1976 (Title VI, V, 5) indicates the return of immigrants as one of "the major objectives of the socialist revolution". It adds, "From their side, the emigrants will make their return to the country... one of their fundamental aspirations". The return is encouraged by administrative simplifications and tax facilities, priority for housing or acquisition of land for building[2].

These countries did not envisage losing their children for the benefit of the receiving countries. Because of that, they were hostile to the idea of dual-nationality. Even when they support it, it remains for them a stopgap measure. Thus, according to article 30 of the Tunisian decree 63-6 of February 28th 1963, the voluntary acquisition of foreign citizenship has as a consequence the automatic and irrevocable loss of Tunisian citizenship. The law 75-79 of 14 November 1975 has modified this article: the loss of Tunisian citizenship is henceforth facultative and occurs by decree of the Tunisian government. This reform was aimed principally, according to the Tunisian press, at satisfying the complaints of Tunisians working in foreign countries. They wanted to "obtain for a time" the citizenship of the receiving country in order to "lay claims to the social advantages reserved for nationals of these countries" and "to avoid all forms of discrimination"[3].

This desire of the country of origin to keep their children is evident in the agreements signed by Algeria and Tunisia with France on military service. The Franco-Algerian agreement of 1983, as well as the Franco-Tunisian convention of 1982, replaced the expression "Dual-nationals", with "young people". The agreement with Algeria, contrary to usual agreements that

---

[1] Belguendouz: *Les jeunes maghrébins en Europe*, p. 69.

[2] Khelil: *L'intégration des Maghrébins en France*, p. 19.

[3] *Al-Amal*, Tunis, 12.11.1975, quoted by *Immigration et nationalité*, p. 27.

link the service of Dual-nationals with the criteria of residence, leaves the choice open. Often, concerning Algerians at least, young people choose, usually under pressure from their parents, or sometimes their parents themselves choose for them, to perform Algerian military service. Once the choice is made, it is irrevocable according to the above agreement[1].

Concerning Algeria, the *French Commission on Citizenship* indicates that this country has for long time been reluctant to permit the acquisition of French citizenship by its citizens established in France. It accepted unwillingly that children born in France after January 1st 1963, to an Algerian father be considered French by virtue of the double *jus soli* (child born in France to a father born before independence in Algeria); such children are Algerians according to Algerian law. It seems, however, that the attitude of the Algerian authorities is changing and that they envisage limiting their influence to the maintenance of cultural links[2].

This new conciliatory attitude by Algeria can be explained by its economic difficulties. In the first years after independence, the official policy was to permanently claim the country's descendents, to remind them that their sojourn in France was only provisional, that their destiny was with their homeland. To stay in France was considered a desertion, to acquire French citizenship a betrayal, to marry a French a shame. When the Algerian government, confronted by its very high demographic rate, understood the importance of emigration for the stability of the country, it stopped its blackmail of Algerians living in France, "If you take French citizenship, you loose forever your Algerian citizenship". The Algerian authorities accepted with realism the departure of hundreds of thousands of persons that it could no longer nourish and to whom it could no longer offer a job[3].

Concerning Morocco, the *French Commission on Citizenship* indicates that it also exercises a strong influence on its nationals established in France, but by different means than that of Algeria. However, its attitude has not yet provoked difficulties analogous to those existing with Algeria. Explanations are various: the

---

[1] Khelil: *L'intégration des Maghrébins en France*, p. 96-97.
[2] *Être français aujourd'hui et demain*, tome 2, p. 46-47.
[3] Kacet: *Le droit à la France*, p. 71-72.

relations between Morocco and France are traditionally good; Moroccan children born in France become French only at eighteen years old; and as familial reunification was introduced later for the Moroccan immigration, the question of military service has not been raised, therefore there is no Franco-Moroccan convention on this matter[1].

Mr. Ennaceur, ambassadorial representative of Tunisia in Geneva, explains that immigration began in the sixties in an organized framework and it had been regulated by bilateral conventions between the sending and the receiving countries by fixing the modalities of co-operation and providing for mixed structures for follow-up and for consultation between the concerned authorities. But since stopping immigration in the beginning of the seventies, the receiving country acted alone and thus confronted the sending countries with a series of *faits accomplis*. This attitude is reflected in many decisions taken unilaterally and without consultation, such as the norms inciting to return, the revision of conditions of sojourn and of familial reunification, or the adoption of a policy of integration that seems to become a collective option for the European countries[2].

Ennaceur expresses satisfaction that attempts of European countries to integrate migrants, chiefly those of second generation, has failed, taking into consideration the small number of persons who have renounced their citizenship of origin. For Ennaceur, "integration does not at all mean the alienation of identity or the renunciation of its fundamental attributes. Integration should not be translated, necessarily, by naturalization and rejection of one's citizenship of origin". He indicates that Dual-nationals among the second generation represent 18.8%, while 75.2% of young second generation North Africans insist on keeping their citizenship of origin[3].

Belguendouz, professor in the Faculty of Law of Rabat, contests the economic contribution of Moroccan emigrants to their country of origin and strongly criticizes those who plead in favor of integration in their country of reception. He quotes Ahmed Alaoui, Minister of State, who declared in 1986, before

---

[1] *Être français aujourd'hui et demain*, tome 2, p. 47-48.
[2] Ennaceur: *L'immigration maghrébine en Europe*, p. 117-118.
[3] *Ibid.*, p. 123.

the *Amicales of Moroccan Workers and Tradesmen in France,* "our young people in foreign countries are and remain Moroccans: if they acquire foreign citizenship they do not loose Moroccan citizenship through a principle of perpetual allegiance, and fundamentally, the youths should have double allegiance without forgetting their country"[1]. He denounces this manner of accepting and excusing naturalization[2], and efforts of the receiving country to integrate his compatriots, "These incitements to assimilation, despite some nuances or contradictory aspects, do not care about the existence of originating countries and cultures. Everything takes place as if the countries of origin do not have their own civilization, their own cultural and national identity"[3].

Belguendouz asks the North African countries to prepare the ground to permit the return of their children because "there will not be a possible voluntary return if there is no minimum of security and of stability for the emigrants: nations have the obligation to offer them such guarantees"[4]. He adds:

> The more application of this plan is delayed, the more costly will be the reinsertion not only in the economic field, but also on familial, cultural, social, and psychological levels especially for those concerned, their families and their society, and under conditions which will be more constraining, more difficult, and perhaps also more dramatic due to, among other things, a hardening by European countries as a consequence of exacerbation of the crisis, intensification of racism, and political repercussions that these could provoke[5].

These words recall the position of Al-Wansharisi although the religious arguments are missing here.

Another Moroccan author, although he excludes "any hope of return for the immigrants", says that the two parties, European and North African, must manage the question of integrating immigrants by respecting their economic and social rights without any discrimination, but they must also "favor the blooming of their cultural and religious identity, and permit them to safeguard solid links with their country of origin, on the political level as well as on the economic and cultural level". "In this way, emigration can play a determining role in the extension

---

[1] Belguendouz: *Les jeunes maghrébins en Europe*, p. 93.
[2] *Ibid.*, p. 94-95.
[3] *Ibid.*, p. 97.
[4] *Ibid.*, p. 99.
[5] *Ibid.*, p. 99-100.

of democracy and of respect for human rights to the south of the Mediterranean and in the promotion of a real co-operation between the two entities, the North African and the European"[1].

5) Naturalization of the Muslim

In spite of opposition from Muslim doctrine, emigration is an ineluctable phenomenon that Muslim countries cannot prevent, except by assuring their nationals material security and satisfactory intellectual freedom. This is far and wide the case today. The problem today is not to prevent Muslims from emigrating, but rather not to lose them completely, notably through naturalization.

One book on naturalization was published in Arabic, in Paris, in 1988, and reprinted in 1993. The title of this book simply claims, "Change of citizenship is apostasy and treason". Its author, very probably an Algerian, believes that a Muslim who opts for the citizenship of a non-Muslim country is an apostate, because he commits a forbidden act according to the Koran and the Tradition of Muhammad. This Muslim must thus give up this citizenship, so God may forgive this sin. Accordingly, anyone who remains in his new citizenship, and dies, will go to hell[2].

Among reasons that encourage Western countries to bestow their citizenship on Muslims are the following according to this author:
- The small increase in the number of Westerners. In this case, naturalization reduces the number of Muslims.
- The exploitation of Muslims to improve the economic situation of non-Muslims. However a Muslim should never agree to be exploited by a non-Muslim.
- The progressive attraction of Muslims to disbelief and atheism. In this case, naturalization is a loss for the Muslim and a gain for unbelievers and atheists[3].

He explains that a Muslim who takes the citizenship of another Muslim country, does not change his statute, since all Muslims are brothers. But the Muslim that takes the citizenship of a non-Muslim country such as the U.S., France, England, Germany or any other unbelieving and atheistic country, this Muslim becomes

---

[1] Oualalou: *L'immigration maghrébine en Europe*, p. 46.
[2] Al-Jaza'iri: *Tabdil*, p. 20-21.
[3] *Ibid.*, p. 21-24.

an apostate, to which one proposes repentance for three days and three nights. If he refuses to returns to his Islamic citizenship, he is liable of the death penalty. The author mentions the narrative of Muhammad in this respect, "One that changes his religion, kill him"; "Letting anyone's blood is only permitted in three cases: the married man who commits adultery, the death sentence in application of the law of retaliation, and for one who abandons religion quitting the community". Therefore, the Muslim that acquires non-Muslim citizenship must be considered as having abandoned his religion and treated as an apostate: his wife will be repudiated, his possessions will be confiscated to benefit the public treasury, and after his death no one will pray for him nor will any one bury him in the Muslim cemetery, according to the verse, "You shall not observe the funeral prayer for any of them when he dies, nor shall you stand at his grave. They have disbelieved in God and His messenger, and died in a state of wickedness" (9:84)[1]. The author goes on to present proofs how a naturalized Muslim becomes an apostate.

- The Muslim who naturalizes himself to obtain benefits from a foreign country accepts the validity of the unbelieving laws instead of Islamic laws. However, according to many Koranic verses, the Muslim that rejects Islamic law becomes an apostate[2].
- The Muslim that naturalizes himself becomes an ally of unbelievers and atheists. Many Koranic verses forbid such an alliance, of which these, "The believers never ally themselves with the disbelievers, instead of the believers. Whoever does this is exiled from God. Exempted are those who are forced to do this to avoid persecution" (3:28); "O you who believe, you shall not befriend My enemies and your enemies, extending love and friendship to them, even though they have disbelieved in the truth that has come to you" (60:1). According to these verses, Muslims are not allowed to ally with unbelievers... except if one fears them, resorting to dissimulation (*al-taqiyyah*) to avoid danger[3].
- The Koran forbids Muslims from remaining among non-Muslims. The author mentions the Koranic verses that incite emigration from the Land of Disbelief to the Land of Islam. For stronger reason, the Muslim is forbidden to acquire citizenship of a non-Muslim country[4].
- A Muslim that naturalizes himself and stays in an unbelieving country exposes his children and his family to the disbelief. This

---

[1] *Ibid.*, p. 25-27.
[2] *Ibid.*, p. 31-44.
[3] *Ibid.*, p. 45-76.
[4] *Ibid.*, p. 77-93.

Muslim no longer has any religion and looks like a feather that wind displaces at will. His purpose is only to fill his stomach and to satisfy his sex. This Muslim becomes member of the army of the hostile camp and fights his own Muslim brothers to satisfy people from whom he took citizenship. So the Muslim breaks all links with Islam. Muhammad says in this respect, "One who carries weapons against us is no more ours"[1].

- The naturalized is a traitor to his people and his homeland. The Koran forbids treason. This Muslim left his country, exchanged it for an unbelieving country and submitted himself to its laws instead of Islamic laws[2].

The author reports *fatwas* of Muslim religious authorities that affirm that acquirement by a Muslim of the citizenship of a non-Muslim country constitutes apostasy. These *fatwas* were given out at the time of the French colonial domination over Algeria and Tunisia. The French authorities had opened the way for naturalization of Muslims. Those who accepted French citizenship submitted to French laws. According to this author, these *fatwas* have a general reach that passes the colonial period as naturalization implies submission of a Muslim to foreign national law and, therefore, constitutes an apostasy for a Muslim[3].

This author goes on to ask the citizens of non-Muslim countries that convert to Islam to give up their citizenship and to leave their country to join a Muslim country. If these countries refuse to welcome them, these new Muslims can oppose them with the verse, "If they repent and observe the prayers and give the obligatory alms (*zakat*), then they are your brethren in religion" (9:11). Elsewhere, God eternally guaranteed immigrants to find a room for security, "Anyone who emigrates in the cause of God will find on earth great bounties and richness. Anyone who gives up his home, emigrating toward God and His messenger, when death catches up with him, his recompense is reserved with God. God is Forgiver, Most Merciful" (4:100). Any Muslim is thus required to leave the Land of Disbelief, not to remain in the company of unbelievers and atheists, and not to submit to their laws. One who does not obey God and Muhammad is no longer a Muslim[4]. This author even refuses the idea of Dual-nationality

---

[1] *Ibid.*, p. 105-113.

[2] *Ibid.*, p. 151-157.

[3] See these *fatwas* in: *Al-Jaza'iri: Tabdil*, p. 175-233.

[4] *Ibid.*, p. 95-103.

and criticizes Muslim countries that permit it. He advances the following arguments against Dual-nationality:
- Dual-nationals submit to unbeliever laws and reject Islamic law. Dual-nationality thus constitutes an apostasy.
- Dual-nationality is hypocrisy, forbidden by the Koran, "When they meet those who believe, they say, 'We believe'; but when they are alone with their evil ones, they say, 'We are really with you: We were only jesting'" (2:14). It is also a matter of ruse and deception, forbidden in Islamic law.
- Dual-nationals look like unbelievers. Muhammad says, "One who looks like a group is part of it"[1].

Al-Jaza'iri, preacher of the Prophet's Mosque in Medina, also considered the question of naturalization. He notes three *fatwas* to this topic:
- A *fatwa* of sheik Hamani, President of the Supreme Islamic Council in Algeria, considers acquirement of citizenship of an unbelieving country is an apostasy. The naturalized cannot marry a Muslim, he is deprived of succession, and he will not be washed nor buried in the Muslim cemetery.
- Saudi *fatwa* no 4801, of 1982, concerned one Algerian imam in France who wanted to know if he could acquire French citizenship. This *fatwa* affirms, "It is not permitted to voluntarily acquire the citizenship of an unbelieving country because it implies acceptance of its norms, submission to its laws, subjection and alliance to this country. Furthermore, it is clear that France is an unbelieving country as government and as people, while you are a Muslim. It is therefore not permitted for you to acquire French citizenship".
- Saudi *fatwa* no 2393, issued one year later, concerns a naturalized Egyptian in Canada. It states:
"Muslims are not allowed to acquire citizenship of a country whose government is unbelieving because it means alliance with unbelievers and acceptance of mistakes that they follow. As for residing without taking citizenship, it is forbidden in principle for these reasons:
- God says, "Those whose lives are terminated by the angels, while in a state of wronging their souls, the angels will ask them, "What was the matter with you?" They will answer, "We were oppressed on earth". The angels will say, "Was God's earth not spacious enough for you to emigrate therein?" For these, the final abode is Hell, and a miserable destiny. Exempted are the weak men, women, and children who do not possess the strength, nor the means to find a way out" (4:97-98).
- Muhammad says, "I will abandon any Muslim that lives among polytheists", and other narratives that follow this sense.
- Muslims are unanimous that it is necessary to emigrate from polytheist countries toward the Land of Islam when possible. But a

---

[1] *Ibid.*, p. 137-148.

religious scientist may remain among unbelievers to teach them
Islam and call them to convert, provided he does not follow
perversion, and that there is hope of influencing and guiding them"[1].

Affirming these *fatwas*, Al-Jaza'iri writes that, contrary to the
Algerian *fatwa*, the two Saudi *fatwas*, while forbidding
naturalization, do not consider the naturalized as unbeliever[2]. He
notes that with the expansion of secularism, adherence to a
religion becomes a free affair. Thus, one can become British or
French without becoming Christian, and one can become
Pakistani without becoming Muslim. Therefore, one who
acquires the citizenship of a non-Muslim country while keeping
faith and avoiding what is forbidden by religion does not become
an unbeliever. Al-Jaza'iri adds that to treat as apostates millions
of Muslims living in countries of disbelief does not solve their
problems but complicates them, as long as it is not possible to
bring back all such Muslims to Muslim countries. Realizing this
impossibility, he recommends creating a commission of all
Muslim countries to protect immigrant rights and to prevent their
assimulation into unbelieving and atheistic societies[3].

As mentioned above, the problem of acquiring citizenship of a
non-Muslim country has been proposed by the *Islamic Center of
Washington* to the *Academy of Islamic law* that depends on the
Organization of Islamic conference. The academy could offer no
answer to this question, due to divergences between its members[4].

Let us note here that Morocco acknowledges the principle of
perpetual allegiance concerning citizenship. A Moroccan cannot
renounce his citizenship on his own free will; he needs further
"authorization by decree to renounce Moroccan citizenship"
(article 19 of the Law on Citizenship). A Moroccan author states
that the loss of citizenship is a purely theoretical question since
by virtue of the principle of the perpetual allegiance the
Moroccan is born and dies Moroccan. The Office of Citizenship
in the Ministry of Justice does not even have a particular form for
giving up Moroccan citizenship[5]. By virtue of this norm, even

---

[1] Al-Jaza'iri: *I'lam al-anam*, p. 723-725.
[2] *Ibid.*, p. 725.
[3] *Ibid.*, p. 726-729.
[4] *Majallat majma al-fiqh al-islami*, n° 3, part 2, 1987, p. 1104; see also
   p. 1103, 1113, 1119, 1129, 1149-1158 1327-1338, 1399.
[5] Zukaghi: Ahkam al-qanun al-duwali al-khas, vol. I, p. 75.

Jews who have left Morocco for Israel retain always, in the eyes of Morocco, their Moroccan citizenship; they can come back at any time.

6) Migration: integration or disintegration

We have just seen that classic and modern Muslim authors are opposed to migration of the Muslims toward the Land of Disbelief. Yet, due to present geopolitical reality, some end up tolerating migration, even accepting naturalization of Muslims living in these countries.

An additional element is introduced by the perception that Muslims have a right to live in non-Muslim countries because they have participated in their defense and economic construction or were born there. "Could France be ungrateful toward these veterans or their descendants?", wonders one French Muslim author[1]. The Charter of the Islamic Faith in France[2] says in its preamble, "Yesterday, with their blood shed in Verdun or Mount Cassino, today by their labor, intelligence, creativity, Muslims of France contribute to the defense and to the glory of the nation as well as to its prosperity and to its radiance in the world". Article 33 adds:

> Full members, on the spiritual level, of the vast cultural and religious community of the Islamic Ummah, Muslims of France are not less conscious of the privileged links which tie them to France, which is for many of them a country of birth or of election. Beyond the diversity of their ethnic, linguistic, and cultural origins, Muslims of France intend to work for the emergence of an Islam of France, open toward the Muslim world and anchored in the reality of French society as well. Claiming not to have any particular foreign religious authority, Muslims of France work toward the expression of an Islam that permits to live profoundly the Koranic message in peaceful harmony with the French culture.

Dalil Boubakeur, Leader of the Great Mosque of Paris, explains the question of citizenship of a Muslim in a non-Muslim land:

> - In time of peace, the national and civic adhesion to a non-Muslim nation is legitimate for a Muslim because it constitutes for him a

---

[1] Khelil: L'intégration des Maghrébins en France, p. 13.

[2] Text in: Azeroual: *Foi et République*, p. 181-186, and in: *Praxis juridique et religion*, vol. 11, fascicule 2, 1994, p. 167-181. This text has been initiated by the Great Mosque of Paris and presented on December 10th, 1994 to the Government by the Consultative council of Muslims in France (CCMF, created in September of 1993).

fulfillment of his rights and of his participative socio-economic and cultural life to the nation he adheres to. However, each modern Muslim author nuances this position somewhat, the essential being to avoid a "dilution" of the Muslim identity by the process of acculturation.

- This citizenship must always assume completely and fairly, with conscience and responsibility, its options, even in case of conflict. The Western notion of nation, adopted by almost all the Arab and Islamic world, is compatible with Islam, as religion and community.

- "The love of nation (*watan*) is a form of faith", states a genuine *narrative* of the Prophet. Generally, an accepted jurisprudence in the political tradition of Islam maintains, "Obedience is imperative toward he who is master of a territory"[1].

This is a new and problematic challenge to the separation of Church and State. The current and increasing presence of Muslims in non-Muslim countries does not satisfy Muslims themselves, who live constantly in a conflict between their religious norms and national norms. Nor does it please host countries that do not know how to integrate them, without endangering secularism and faith diversity. The separation of Church and State as a principle is opposed to the ultimate aim of the Muslim. Some, besides, do not hesitate to view the present Muslim migratory influx as an invasion. The term "invasion" is explicitly used by the program of the *National Front* of 1985; it was repeated by Giscard d'Estaing in *Figaro Magazine*, in September of 1991. Many arguments are evoked: their high birth rate; the rise of unemployment in France; the progress of Islamic fundamentalism; the attacks attributed to Middle-Eastern groups; the differences between their values and those of Europeans, in particular their family behavior and status of women[2]. Some French did not hesitate, during the Gulf war, to see in Muslim immigrants a fifth column[3].

The solution should be, according to Jean-Marie Le Pen, to encourage by financial assistance those who are born in a country, which is not a member of the European Community to return home[4]. Le Pen would like also to limit the number of those who become French citizens with the suppression of the *lex soli*, a

---

[1] Azeroual: *Foi et République*, p. 34.
[2] Barreau: *De l'immigration*, p. 64.
[3] Jelen: *Ils feront de bons français*, p. 231.
[4] Le Pen: *Pour la France*, p. 123.

provision that automatically grants French citizenship to any individual born in France[1].

The alternative solution is to integrate them, a solution whose feasibility is doubted by some. According to Barreau, it is difficult for Muslims to live in a society where they are a minority; Islamic law only recognizes one kind of situation: that in which the Muslim is naturally the master of the city and where he applies his Islamic law. The submission to an infidel authority is not envisaged[2].

Those who are more optimistic reply that integration is an ineluctable fact. Most young second generation Arabs are culturally French, and speak Arabic or Berber poorly. They are no longer able to appropriate this "heritage", which was never really transmitted to them. Once the first generation of immigrant North Africans (illiterate, and whose language is Arabic or Berber) disappears, the second will loose its anchorage in the Arab-Islamic civilization. For these reasons, integration and assimilation of the *Beurs* (Arabs born in France) are "as sure as the movement of life and death"[3]. According to this opinion, no culture from the Third World can resist more than one generation against the lamination of the European post-industrial culture. The women of Muslim origin gradually adjust their fecundity to conform to that of the French. The *Beurettes* (Arab girls born in France) begin emancipating themselves from the familial system. The number of mixed marriages increases and the children of these marriages will no longer have any unique or separate ethnic origin. These long-term factors reveal that the resistance to integration is largely a myth[4].

However, one cannot be very optimistic when considering Christian and Muslim communities in the Balkans who, after having cohabited for centuries, remain separate. As noted above, this situation could repeat itself in other Western countries if the number of Muslims reaches a critical mass, large enough to permit self-affirmation and assertion of its values on the wider Western society. All Western country policy makers must

---

[1] *Ibid.*, p. 118.
[2] Barreau: *De l'immigration*, p. 68-69.
[3] Jelen: *Ils feront de bons français*, p. 225.
[4] *Ibid.*, p. 224.

manage the situation better by integrating their Muslim populations. Western leaders must re-examine and fully understand the Islamic system and worldview. But are Muslims themselves ready to address these issues? Will non-Muslims lead them in this direction? Nothing is less certain right now. Claims by Muslims to have exclusive cemeteries or burial plots, and acceptance of this claim by certain Swiss cantons, is proof among many other such examples that Muslim integration is really not viable.

PART II.
MINORITIES IN SWITZERLAND

Chapter I.
Minorities in general

When one speaks of minorities, one generally refers to national minorities. There is no accepted international definition of this notion. Switzerland made a declaration during the ratification of the *Framework Convention for the Protection of National Minorities* of the Council of Europe, specifying the meaning of national minority:

> Switzerland declares that in Switzerland national minorities in the sense of the Framework Convention are groups of individuals numerically inferior to the rest of the population of the country or of a canton, whose members are Swiss nationals, have long-standing, firm and lasting ties with Switzerland and are guided by the will to safeguard together what constitutes their common identity, in particular their culture, their traditions, their religion or their language[1].

It is clear from this definition that Switzerland unites the notion of national minority to citizenship. Therefore, a non-national cannot invoke special protection granted to a person belonging to a national minority. He is nevertheless protected by article 27 of the *Covenant on civil rights*. As our book considers religious minorities, it will further elaborate the Swiss definition. A Muslim community, consisting of Swiss citizens or foreigners, considers itself as having a unique identity that, although living in Switzerland, is connected to Islamic nation that unites all Muslim believers independent of their national adherence.

In the Constitution of 1998, there is no specific disposition protecting minorities as such. They are protected nevertheless,

---

[1] *Feuille fédérale* 1998 1033, 1047, ch. 22; This declaration is contained in the ratification instrument deposited October 21th, 1998 in: http://conventions.coe.int/Treaty/EN/CadreListeTraites.htm

indirectly, by the guarantee against discrimination by constitutional rights, notably by the two following articles:

Article 7 - Human dignity ought to be respected and protected.

Article 8 - 1) Everyone is equal before the law.

2) Nobody may be discriminated against, namely for his or her origin, race, sex, age, language, social position, way of life, religious, philosophical, or political convictions, or because of a corporal or mental disability.

3) Men and women have equal rights. The law provides for legal and factual equality, particularly in the family, during education, and at the workplace. Men and women have the right to equal pay for work of equal value.

4) The law provides for measures to eliminate disadvantages of disabled people.

Other constitutional norms provide particular importance for national minority protection. It is the case of freedom of speech or freedom of conscience and worship. Some cantonal Constitutions refer to the notion of minority. So article 4 of the Constitution of the canton of Bern stipulates, for example, that it considers linguistic, cultural and regional minority needs and, to this effect, some particular prerogatives can be assigned to these minorities.

Besides the constitutional norms, article 261bis of the Penal Code, in effect since January 1st, 1995, punishes by confinement up to three years or fine up to 40,000.- Sfr:

- Whoever publicly incites hatred or discrimination against a person or a group of persons on the basis of their race, ethnicity or religion.
- Whoever publicly promotes an ideology that systematically disparages or slanders members of a race, ethnic group or religion.
- Whoever organizes, supports or participates in a propaganda action with this same goal.
- Whoever publicly through word, writing, illustration, gesture, act of violence, or in any other way disparages or discriminates against a person or a group of persons on the basis of their race, ethnicity or religion, in a way that offends their human dignity or, for any one of these reasons, denies, flagrantly whitewashes or seeks to justify, genocide or other crimes against humanity.
- Whoever withholds, on the basis of race, ethnicity or religion, a service or product from a person or a group of persons that is offered to the public at large.

Article 171c of the Military Penal Code has the same content, except that it adds the possibility of a merely disciplinary sanction in cases of little gravity. These Swiss norms go beyond requirements ensuing from the *Convention on the Elimination of all Forms of Racial Discrimination*, as they expressly include among punished acts the discrimination founded on religious motives and refusal of a service or product offered to the public at large. The penal disposition does not protect groups solely, as in the Convention, but also individuals[1].

August 23rd, 1995, the Swiss Federal Council, created the *Federal Commission Against Racism* that began working September 1st, 1995. In December of 1998, a motion emanating from some bourgeois parties asked for its dissolution[2], for reasons the Commission was superfluous, that its mandate was too large and contained impossible formulas to put into practice. The Swiss Federal Council rejected this proposal, finding that the Commission's activity created favorable echoes within administration and close to medias and politicians[3]. We blamed this Commission's too critical position toward Switzerland and not enough toward Muslims whose rights are unreasonably defended. We will come back to this point later[4].

In addition to internal norms, Switzerland adhered to numerous international conventions relating directly or indirectly to minority protection. We mention here some of them:

- *Convention for the Protection of Human Rights and Fundamental Freedoms* as amended by Protocol No. 11, 4 November 1950, in force in Switzerland since 28 November 1974.
- *European Charter for Regional or Minority Languages*, 2 October 1992, in force for Switzerland since 1st April 1998.
- *European Code of Social Security*, 16 April 1964, in force for Switzerland since 17 September 1978.
- *European Outline Convention on Transfrontier Co-operation between Territorial Communities or Authorities*, 21 May 1980, in force for Switzerland since 4 June 1982.
- *International Covenant on Economic, Social and Cultural Rights*, 16 December 1966, in force for Switzerland since 18 September 1992.
- *International Covenant on Civil and Political Rights*, 16 December 1966, in force for Switzerland since 18 September 1992.

---

[1] Deuxième et troisième rapports périodiques présentés par la Suisse, par. 102.

[2] Postulate Mörgeli dated 22.12.1999 "Dissolution de la Commission fédérale contre le racisme" (CN 99.3645).

[3] See the position of the Federal Council on the postulate Mörgeli dated 22.12.1999.

[4] See part III, chap. I.1, chap. II.3.B and chap. IV.3.B.

- *International Convention on Elimination of all Forms of Racial Discrimination*, 21 December 1965, in force for Switzerland since 29 December 1994.
- *Framework Convention for the Protection of National Minorities*, adopted by the Committee of Ministers of the European Council 10 November 1994, in force for Switzerland since 1st February 1998.

Having seen the general norms, we will say some words concerning the linguistic and ethnic minority before treating the religious minorities, notably the Muslim one.

Chapter II.
Linguistic and ethnic minorities

Switzerland is a Federal State formed of twenty-six sovereign cantons and half-cantons (articles 1 and 3 nCst) with large legislative, judicial and executive prerogatives; they may conclude treaties with foreign countries within the scope of their powers (article 56 nCst). The cantons are then divided into municipalities whose autonomy "is guaranteed in the limits fixed by the cantonal law" (article 50 nCst).

Switzerland also has linguistic borders. Four languages are considered national: German, French, Italian and Romansh (article 4 nCst). The first three are official languages, and Romansh is an official language for communicating with persons of Romansh language. The cantons "designate their official languages. In order to preserve harmony between linguistic communities, they shall respect the traditional territorial distribution of languages, and take into account the indigenous linguistic minorities" (article 70 nCst). According to the 1990 census, German is spoken by 63.6% of the population, French by 19.2%, Italian by 7.6% and Romansh by 0.6%. Of the 26 cantons and half-cantons, 17 are German speaking, 4 are French speaking, 1 is Italian speaking (Tessin, with a small German speaking minority), 3 are bilingual (Bern, with a German speaking majority; Fribourg and Valais with a French-speaking majority), and 1 is trilingual (Grison, with a German speaking majority). About 8.9% of the population has another mother tongue than the four national languages. Current laws do not recognize autochthonous linguistic minority status for any non-native linguistic minorities, such as Turks, Albanians, or Arabs, regardless of their number, whether they are Swiss or not.

Ethnic minorities, in the strict sense, do not exist in Switzerland. The only group bearing this title are nomads or "people of the road", numbering about 25,000 people of which 4,000 to 5,000 are unsettled. Most nomads in Switzerland are members of the Jenisch group, although some are part of Roma or Sinti[1].

Chapter III.
Religious minorities

Traditionally Christian, Switzerland is today a multi-confessional country with numerous sects. It passed through periods of Catholic and Protestant conflicts that threatened its territorial unity. The Constitution of 1874 endeavored to cut wings to the religious communities by confiscating their power concerning civil status (article 53 par. 1), marriage (article 54), jurisdiction (article 58 par. 2) and cemetery (article 53 par. 2), by guaranteeing freedom of religion and worship (article 49), by assuring maintenance of public order and confessional peace between various religious communities and uninvolvement of ecclesiastical authorities in citizens' and state's rights (article 50 par. 2). Since Switzerland, like the United States, is a secular nation, religious communities have no legislative function there. Certainly, the Catholic Church, in both Switzerland and the United States, has religious courts, but their decisions are not enforceable. [This is basic to the separation of Church and State in both nations.]

The new Swiss Constitution of 1998 is based on the idea that Switzerland has surpassed the religious conflicts that the old Constitution tried to remedy. Commenting the article on freedom of conscience and worship, the Message of the Swiss Federal Council optimistically states that the new Constitution "puts emphasis henceforth on individual religious freedom rather than on guaranteeing religious peace, that is no longer a menace as in

---

[1] Présentation du rapport initial de la Suisse devant le Comité de l'ONU pour l'élimination de la discrimination raciale, March 1998, p. 11, par. 28.

the past"[1]. For this reason, it guarantees various rights without lingering on obstacles in realizing these rights, nor in evoking the jurisdiction of the Church or the question of the cemeteries. But article 72, par. 1, specifies that the regulation of the relationship between Church and State is a cantonal matter. Par. 2 adds, "The Confederation and the cantons may, within the framework of their powers, take measures to maintain public peace between the members of the various religious communities". It omits, wrongly, the question of the "encroachments by religious authorities on the rights of citizens and the state", of which speaks article 50, par. 2 of the 1874 Constitution.

If the relations between Catholics, Protestants and the State became more cordial, Switzerland must face now newcomers on the religious scene, such as sects, whose danger was clear after the massacres perpetrated in October 1994, in December 1995 and in March 1997 in three countries: Switzerland, Canada and France, by the *Order of the Solar Temple*, founded in Geneva in 1984. These three massacres caused the death of 74 people, 19 of them being Swiss. Sects make the object of distrust on behalf of the traditional Churches that see in them a competition, but also on behalf of the nation that is held to protect individual freedoms while remedying abuses. In its *Report on sects* of July 1st, 1999, the *Commission of the National Council* offered the following recommendations:

1) Federal Council elaborates a policy concerning sects.
2) Federal Council coordinates the execution of this policy.
3) Federal Council institutes a service of information and consultation and informs the public regularly.
4) Federal Council encourages interdisciplinary research on doctrinating movements and coordinates collaboration that must bring activities of research and consultation closer.
5) Federal Council must verify the enforcement of the laws, in particular concerning the protection of children, consumers and health, and favors the harmonious practices among the cantons[2].

On June 29th, 2000, the Swiss Federal Council rejected these propositions, finding that present laws are sufficient, that the term *sect* is often used in a discriminatory manner, that it is not incumbent upon the Confederation to determine what

---

[1] *Message relatif à une nouvelle Constitution fédérale*, p. 157.
[2] *Sectes ou mouvements endoctrinants en Suisse*, p. 9232.

associations belong to dangerous doctrinal movements nor to give a valid definition for the notion of *sect*[1].

Muslims constitute the most recent and numerous religious community in Switzerland. As the result of the 2000 census is not yet known, we examine here the census of 1970, 1980 and 1990.

In 1970, Switzerland counted 16,353 Muslims. In 1980, this number passed to 56,625, of which 2,941 have the Swiss citizenship, on 6,365,960 inhabitants. In 1990, they were 152,217, of which 7,735 have the Swiss citizenship, on 6,873,87 inhabitants. The following picture gives the population distribution for Switzerland according to the main religious communities in 1990:

	Men	Women	Total
Swiss Muslims	3,223	4,512	7,735
Foreign Muslims	93,560	50,922	144,482
Muslims' total	**96,783**	**55,434**	**152,217**
Foreigners	724,868	520,564	1,245,432
Catholics			3,314,271
Protestants			2,747,821
Jews			17,577
Total Inhabitants of Switzerland			6,873,687

These numbers show that the Muslim community constitutes today the third religious community in Switzerland. One will also notice that the number of the Muslim men surpasses by 41,349 the number of the Muslim women. This means that Muslim men will get married with non-Muslim women, to compensate this deficit. It is necessary to keep in mind that Muslim women are not allowed to marry non-Muslims, according to Islamic law, unless potential husbands convert to Islam. An undetermined percentage of Swiss men and women convert to Islam due to marriage with a Muslim. Children of the mixed marriages will be Muslim, such being the norm in Islamic law, a norm which is

---

[1] wysiwyg://16/http://www.cesnur.org/testi/ch2K_june2.htm

respected by Muslim husbands, and rarely challenged by their wives.

Note that the Muslim community in Switzerland nearly tripled every ten years in the last three decades, from 16,353 in 1970, to 56,625 in 1980, and to 152,217 in 1990. This last number does not include seasonal workers, nor people authorized for short stays, nor claimants of asylum, nor those without papers. These last would comprise, according to certain speculation, between 150,000 and 300,000, many being Muslim. It is important to wait for the census of 2000 to see if this trend continues. If so, we can predict the Muslim community in Switzerland currently numbers 450,000 people, and in ten years about a million and a half, and in twenty years four millions and half. It means that Muslims will form the majority of Swiss inhabitants by 2020 and would constitute the main religious community in Switzerland, if one accounts for elevated birthrate among Muslims compared to non-Muslims, mixed marriages and migratory fluxes. Even reducing this forecast for the year 2020 by half, such a growth of the Muslim community necessarily implies a change in the Swiss legal and political system according to the principle, "Quantity makes quality".

A small part of these Muslims are Swiss citizens, but their number will increase with the present tendency to facilitate naturalization and permanent residence of Muslims in Switzerland. Muslims come from different countries, notably ex-Yugoslavia, Albania, Turkey and North Africa. They are regular workers or illegal immigrants, students or claimants of political asylum. They follow different religious sects, but most notably Sunnite. One finds among them very divergent currents, from fundamentalists to liberals. There is no representative Muslim organization in Switzerland nor is there any Swiss Muslim union, but some Muslim associations are trying to organize in certain cantons to be able to negotiate solutions with the cantonal authorities over concrete issues. Some of these associations receive financial support from Saudi Arabia, Turkey, Algeria and other countries and individuals. They do not receive direct financial Swiss authority support, but some may receive donations and present themselves as charitable institutions to obtain tax advantages.

Chapter IV.
Minorities, the individual and the State

On internal or international level, two entities exist whose rights should be preserved and reconciled: the individual and the minority group. The rights of these two entities are complementary, in the sense that an individual can come to full bloom within his or her group. At the same time, these two rights are against each other: the minority can become oppressive to the point of depriving the individual of his fundamental rights. A minority that executes its dissidents, discriminates against women or deprives physical integrity according to its religious norms cannot invoke religious freedom or cultural difference. The *Commission of the National Council* said in its *Report on sects*:

The Commission thinks that, even in the name of a belief, it is not permitted to violate human rights, recognized fundamental values, fundamental freedoms (freedom of self-determination for example), nor basic principles of democracy. At the same time, the Commission is conscious that a guaranteed right by the Constitution can be limited only in determined and precise conditions: this limitation must be for public interest, lean on a legal basis and respect the principle of proportionality[1].

If sects awaken distrust, the nation state generally displays certain kindliness toward the main religious communities: Jewish, Christian and Muslim. This may be because one thinks that these communities made their proof by centuries of existence and the large number of their followers, or because one does not dare attack them, or on the contrary because the nation state imposed its political supremacy facing the religious power. This is the relatively fragile balance between Church and State that allows for personal faith convictions for all citizens.

Certainly, Switzerland is beginning to worry about its security. The 1998 *Report on State protection* points out that the main participants in violent conflict are Turkish-Kurdish groups, Albanian groups of Kosovo, fundamentalist Algerians, Middle East groups and Tamil groups. Four of these groups are Muslim[2]. The report also notes "without being the direct target of international terrorism, Switzerland [like the United States] has been affected by the increase of extremism and terrorism. It

---

[1] *Sectes ou mouvements endoctrinants en Suisse*, p. 9201-9202.
[2] *Rapport sur la protection de l'État*, p. 20.

continues to play an important role as logistic basis and shelter for many such groups"[1]. In this perspective, a federal law, adopted March 21st, 1997, instituted measures aiming "to assure the respect of democratic and constitutional foundations in Switzerland as well as to protect the freedoms of its population" (article 1). To achieve these aims, "the Confederation takes preventive measures ... to detect potential dangers linked to terrorism, prohibited secret services and violent extremism. The gathered information should allow the concerned federal and cantonal authorities to intervene in time according to the applicable laws" (article 2 par. 1).

Secularism is a factor-key in coordinating individual rights. This is a crucial element in preserving the balanced separation between Church and State. With religious groups the problem goes beyond a matter of security and relates to the legal system. In Switzerland, the nation state took measures to keep Catholic and Protestant communities in check, to assure a pacific cohabitation. However, with the arrival of the Muslim community whose religious norms are fundamentally hostile to secularism, there is a high risk that Switzerland passes again in a zone of turbulence. It is not certain that the nation grants the same importance to this problem as to the problem of security. Especially due to a euphoria inspired by the inter-religious dialogue instituted by Catholic and Protestant authorities that, ingenuously, are too beneficial to the claims of the Muslim community, as in matter of separate cemeteries exclusively reserved for Muslims, without understanding the results of such claims. We will see this question later.

To know what the future holds, it is necessary to see to what extend the claims of Muslims living in Switzerland coincide with the Swiss legal system. This is what we will investigate in the following part.

We have to mention here that the questions treated in the following part are rarely treated by the conventions on minorities, although they are part of the claims of the religious minorities in the countries where they live.

---

[1] *Ibid.*, p. 21.

PART III.
MUSLIMS IN SWITZERLAND

Chapter I.
Recognition of Islam

One may recognize a community on two levels: the public level, and the official level. One must also see to what extend a minority recognizes a nation state with which it deals.

1) Recognition by the public

Muslims complain that they are poorly accepted in Switzerland. The *Federal Commission Against Racism*, whose opinion often reflects the Muslim point of view, states in a press release:

> When the Muslim minority living in Switzerland asks for freedom of worship, it is often confronted with insecurity, institutional difficulties and sometimes, pure and simple dismissal.
>
> Needs of Muslims provoke debates within the population and authorities, concerning construction of a cemetery or mosque, veil, teaching religion in school, naturalization demands or official recognition. The *Federal Commission Against Racism* is preoccupied by discriminations to which Muslims, and people thought to be Muslim, are exposed...
>
> No one must be discriminated against because he is considered Muslim, when looking for work, in the workplace or at the time of applying for naturalization, etc.
>
> No one must be considered as belonging to a religion, whatever his actual religion, nor convicted, due to his country of origin or his name....
>
> Every human being must have the right to practice his religion without restriction, as long as he does not infringe upon the rights of another person or the Constitution.
>
> On the political level, the debate over Muslims should not serve as an instrument, but be considered objectively[1].

---

[1] Les musulmanes et les musulmans en Suisse, communiqué de presse, in: *Tangram*, n° 8, March 2000, p. 100-101.

In the issue n° 7 of October 1999, dedicated to Muslims in Switzerland, the *Tangram Magazine* of this Commission includes numerous articles that follow this sense written by Christians and Muslims[1]. The editorial, written by two Muslim members of the Commission, affirm:

> In Switzerland, needs expressed by Muslims are taken up quickly by medias, often with negative connotation, and provoke debates within the population when it is for example question of constructing an Islamic cemetery or when the demand for naturalization of a girl born in Switzerland is rejected because she wears a veil.... Even in Switzerland, the picture of Islam rests largely on prejudices, generalizations, improper clichés and information distributed by the sensationalist press. This picture continues to be filled today by the Crusades (11th to 13th centuries), by the threat of the Turks at the gates of Vienna (1529), by the tales of *One thousand and One Nights*, or by the pictures and the writings of 19th century orientalists.
>
> This is why there is fear of Islam, whose partisans attack tourists in Egypt, make revolution in Iran and require women be veiled from head to foot in Afghanistan. In this context, the campaigns waged against Islam reach their target easily. Are there no other possibilities? Is it not time to correct this picture that makes Islam our enemy[2]?

This editorial is followed by numerous litanies that go in the same sense. Pastor Jean-Claude Basset does not escape the rule. He thinks that there is "nothing surprising in reactions caused by the irruption of a new socio-cultural community in Switzerland; in any case nothing that goes beyond natural resistance by any social body confronted with the presence of a new entity: resistance to changes that oblige self-examination, ensue novelty and require sharing because of the cohabitation in a democratic nation state". He also proposes that the situation of Muslims in Switzerland is unique:

> The presence of Muslims provokes a certain number of negative reactions in the picture that give medias about Islam in general and about Muslims in particular. This reaction is so obvious and no similar reaction is fomented toward Buddhism and Buddhists whose presence and influence continue to increase, in Switzerland as in Europe. If there is a possible comparison with the negative treatment of Islam by medias, it is on a level usually reserved for these religious and spiritual minorities that one commonly calls sects.

---

[1] *Tangram*, n° 7, October 1999, editorial, p. 3, by Taner Hatipoglu and Samia Osman.
[2] Loc. cit.

In this sense, one can speak of latent anti-Islamism, not as a deliberate project of discrimination against Muslims, but specific resistance to Islam and Muslim community.

Pastor Basset thinks that this anti-Islamism is nourished by two very distinct sources in the Swiss society:

The devote Christians and the partisans of a pure and hard secularism. For the first, representing 5% of the population, mostly but not solely Protestant, Islam appears in direct contradiction to the Gospel of Jesus Christ and a threat for the Christian faith. Islam is considered as a deed of the devil. For the second, Islam is discerned as a regression in relation to the progress of the century of light and as a threat for the separation, dearly acquired, between politics and religion[1].

He also thinks that it requires mutual effort to pass this mindset:

One should not hide that, if Muslims' integration in the Swiss society implies for them a real effort of adaptation and re-interpretation of their sources, the welcoming community has also to review some of its presupposition and redefine the basis of a society which became more culturally and religiously diverse[2].

We will see whether this distrust is not uni-directional, and if Muslims also transport a negative attitude concerning Switzerland.

2) Recognition by authorities

The *Islamic Cultural Foundation of Geneva* states that one of its objectives is "to make a pressing effort so that the Swiss government recognizes the Islamic religion as an official religion, like other religions in Switzerland and to dedicate cemeteries reserved for Muslims in all Swiss cities"[3].

In 1997, Fawzia Al-Ashmawi, Professor in the Arabic section of the university of Geneva, declared in a conference held in Casablanca, on *Islam and Muslims in Europe*:

In spite of the myth of the Swiss neutrality and in spite of the presence of the *Human Rights Commission* in Switzerland, Muslims in Switzerland do not benefit from freedoms or rights received by other religious followers, such as Jews for example. Indeed, although the number of Jews is less than half the Muslim community in Switzerland, Judaism is recognized in Switzerland as a religion while Islam is not.

---

[1] Basset: *Aux sources de l'anti-islamisme en Suisse*, p. 20.
[2] *Ibid.*, p. 20.
[3] *Bulletin of the Islamic Cultural Foundation of Geneva Concerning the Prayers* 2000/2001.

Switzerland is a secular nation state, like other European nations, which means the separation between the religion and the state. But it recognizes only some religions as official religion for its citizens. So the Swiss nation recognizes Catholics', Protestants' and Jews' religions, but not the Muslims' religion[1].

During the 150th anniversary of the Swiss Federal State, in *Forum 98* held in Brig September 18th and 19th, 1998, Fawzia Al-Ashmawi asked Flavio Cotti, then president of the Confederation, the following question:

As Muslim population in Switzerland is the third largest religious community... is Switzerland considering an official recognition of Islam as a religion of the Swiss population?

Flavio Cotti answered her:

The Muslim community of Switzerland has the right to be recognized and integrated into our society, but the Swiss government does not recognize any religion. We are a neutral country and we adopt secularism. We are a democratic and federal government that grants to every canton and each municipality the freedom to determine its involvement with different religious communities. So this recognition is not the task of the federal government, but of the cantons and municipalities[2].

In spite of the clarity of this answer, Fawzia Al-Ashmawi insists in her book *La condition des musulmans en Suisse* on the question of recognition. She thinks that the "non-recognition of Islam as one of the religions of the population of Switzerland is the basis of almost all the social discriminations against Muslims living in this country"[3]. In an interview she had with Ismail Amin, president of the *Union of Muslim organizations* in Zurich, he affirms that the objective of his organization is to obtain an "official recognition of Islam, as a religion of the population living in Switzerland". He adds:

Once the official status is achieved, we will be able to ask for:
- The establishment of a real mosque that will be an institution with a place of prayer, a library, a school to teach Arabic and Koranic sciences, a social service, a meeting room.
- The creation of a chair for Islamic Sciences in the Faculty of Theology in a German-speaking canton and another chair in a French-speaking canton. These chairs must be financed by Swiss authorities, as are the chairs for Hebrew and Christian studies.
- The perception of a tax that will be part of obligatory alms (*zakat*), similar to the ecclesiastical tax allocated for churches of the country.

---

[1] Al-Ashmawi: *Kalimah*, p. 311-312.
[2] Al-Ashmawi: *La condition des musulmans en Suisse*, p. 114.
[3] *Ibid.*, p. 50.

- The establishment of a cemetery where Muslims may be buried according to Islamic tradition.

Ismail Amin thinks the best means to encourage the integration of Muslims in Switzerland is "recognition of their Muslim identity, and this through official recognition of Islam". According to him, Muslims are discriminated "because Islam is not recognized as an official religion of a segment of the population in Switzerland"[1].

One can read many similar declarations by other Muslims in Switzerland. Neither Fawzia Al-Ashmawi, nor Ismail Amin specify what they mean by recognition of Islam. Both are of Egyptian origin. They probably think of the Egyptian model where "Islam is the state religion... and the principal source of legislation is Islamic jurisprudence" (article 2 of the Constitution), the two elements being united between them. Do they ignore that Switzerland is different from Egypt in spite of their long sojourn in Switzerland? ...probably, because they have little real understanding of the separation of Church and State.

Insistence by Muslims for Swiss recognition of *Islam*, and not of the *Muslim community*, can be explained by the fact that they do not structure themselves on the cantonal or federal levels. Therefore, they present themselves as a large number of persons instead of a structured group. By addressing themselves to the Confederation, they would probably want bypass the different cantons with their very varied systems, and ask, once that Islam is recognized, that the Confederation adopts laws and measures imposed to all the cantons. It is not excluded that they would like to apply the Islamic family law instead of the federal one: since you recognize Islam, you have also to recognize Islamic law, which is part of Islam! One implies the other! It is not therefore a simple *ignorance* of the Swiss legal system on behalf of Muslims, but a *stratagem* aimed at getting round the Swiss legal system. As pointed out to me by a person responsible for an Islamic Center in Zurich, thinking that I was Muslim, "We ask today one thing, and progressively we will ask something more".

The recognition of Islam is not possible in Switzerland on the federal level for the simple reason that the federal state is neutral on religious matters. Contrary to what Fawzia Al-Ashmawi

---

[1] *Ibid.*, p. 115-117.

imagines, Switzerland does not recognize Catholicism, or Protestantism, or Judaism, or any other faith system!

It is exact that both the 1874 and 1998 Swiss Constitutions start with the formula "In the name of God Almighty". The federal Message says that this formula

> perpetuates a tradition, observed since the first pacts that bound the Confederates. Its mention in the preamble... establishes an important link with the tradition. In summary, it recalls that there is, above the nation state and the human being, a transcendent power, relativizing terrestrial value. As there are different religions and philosophical views, this power is not necessarily marked by a Christian seal; the nation state cannot offer any obligatory belief and each person can lend his own understanding to the term God Almighty.

The Message adds,

> The guarantee of freedom of conscience and worship forbids the Confederation and the cantons to behave toward any religion in a hostile manner (including those that choose a private philosophical concept as religious reference)[1].

One can say therefore, as did Flavio Cotti, that the Confederation does not recognize any particular religion, contrary to Egypt. Furthermore, the Confederation does not recognize any religious community. On the contrary, it stripped away the prerogatives of the two main religious communities of the country, Protestant and Catholic, concerning civil status, marriage, cemeteries and jurisdiction. Article 72 par. 1 nCst precises, "the regulation of the relationship between Church and State is a cantonal matter". The Confederation merely imposes respect of religious freedom to the cantons and intervenes with these last to "take measures to maintain public peace between the members of the various religious communities" (article 72 par. 2).

It is for the cantons to consider the manner of regulating the different religious communities, taking into consideration historic tradition, while respecting the fundamental rights, in particular freedom of religion and worship (article 15) and the principle of equality (article 8). But, according to the Message of the Swiss Federal Council concerning the *Popular initiative for complete separation between Church and State*, of September 6th, 1978[2], the Constitution does not force the cantons to observe total religious neutrality. They may decide to bestow a public statute to

---

[1] *Message of the Federal Council*, 20.11.1996, p. 124-125.
[2] *Feuille fédérale* 1978 II 676ss.

certain religious communities and not to others. One notes that there are as many systems as cantons. The cantons of Neuchâtel and Geneva do not bestow any public statute to religious communities. In most other cantons, the two main traditional Churches benefit from a public statute. It is also the case for the Catholic Church and the Jewish community in some cantons. Thirteen of the 26 cantonal Constitutions foresee the possibility of bestowing the public statute to other religious communities. Thus in four cantons, the Jewish community received the public statute.

In any case, Swiss cantons do not recognize a *religion*, but rather a *religious community*, implying a democratic organization with by-laws that define modes of adherence and representatives. Such communities must present a request to obtain a public statute. It is thus never a question of abstractly recognizing Islam, Catholicism, Protestantism or Judaism. Nothing forbids the Muslim community from applying for the public statute where the canton permits it, but it must organize itself first and have representatives. It is only in case of dismissal of such a demand, that this community can complain about discrimination. Thus, the critiques of Fawzia Al-Ashmawi and other Muslims toward Switzerland show ignorance of the law or dishonesty.

In addition to the possibility of obtaining a public statute, the Muslim community has the right to organize itself, on local, cantonal or federal levels, as a foundation or an association according to article 52 CCS that stipulates:

1) Associations of persons organized into corporations, and institutions devoted to a special purpose and independent, receive the right of personality, by entry in the commercial register.
2) Public corporations and institutions, societies not for profit, religious foundations and family foundations require no such entry.
3) Associations or institutions for immoral or unlawful purposes cannot acquire legal personality.

The right of association is guaranteed (article 23 nCst) not only for citizens, but also for foreigners. Switzerland differs from most Muslim countries where the creation of a foundation or an association is submitted to previous authorization on behalf of the nation state that exercises control over its activities[1]. This situation could probably explain why Muslims ask for

---

[1] See Aldeeb Abu-Sahlieh: *Les ONG de défense des droits de l'homme.*

recognition on behalf of "Switzerland", being ignorant of the difference between Muslim countries and Switzerland. Swiss law *ipso facto* recognizes any foundation or association created in accordance with the law. There is no need for any formal recognition on behalf of public authorities. It applies to Muslims as well as all other religious community. So too, the Swiss Jewish community is organized mainly as a private association.

Evidently there is a difference between a private association and a public statute as regards to the financial advantages. As indicated by Ismail Amin, president of the *Union of Muslim organizations* in Zurich, Muslims would like Switzerland to recognize Islam to obtain financial benefits.

The system for financing religious communities differs from canton to canton; there are no two identical systems[1]. On the federal level it is noted in article 49 par. 6 aCst, "No one shall be bound to pay taxes the proceeds of which are specifically appropriated to cover the cost of worship within a religious community to which he does not belong". Even though this article is not taken in the new Constitution, the principle remains valid on the basis of the decisions of the Federal Court in this matter. In 24 cantons, officially recognized Churches - or their parishes - possess power concerning fiscal sovereignty; perception of tax can be obligatory or optional, and it takes place on the cantonal or the local level. Unrecognized communities must manage alone, as is the case for the Muslim community. Juridical entities pay ecclesiastical tax in certain cantons; this situation creates problems, for in addition to these entities, there are individuals whose freedom of religion is violated by this tax. The canton of Vaud does not have an ecclesiastical tax and draws in the general cash-box to finance Catholic and Reformed Churches. In this canton, as in some cantons where municipalities (or parishes) do not make use of this imposition right, and where Churches are financed in whole or in part by means of general fiscal assets, non-believers and people having declared to come out of the Church can deduct from local tax slip a certain percentage, correspondent to the share that represents expenses of the Church in the budget of the municipality of their domicile.

---

[1] See *L'impôt d'Église*.

According to the Federal Court, such a deduction is not however possible on the cantonal level.

A popular initiative aiming to introduce in the Constitution an article imposing "complete separation of Church and State" for all Swiss territory was presented in 1976. In its Message of September 1978, the Swiss Federal Council recommended its rejection in order to not undermine the federal structure of the country by encroaching on canton sovereignty in ecclesiastical matters, and imposing on them a centralizing approach, without consideration for cultural and confessional diversity. According to the Swiss Federal Council, the citizens of every canton should remain free to determine relations between Church and State. Submitted to the popular vote in March of 1980, the initiative was refused massively by 1,052,575 No, against 281,475 Yes, and by all cantons.

We favor separation of Church and State as practiced in Neuchâtel and Geneva. For us, any religious community, including the Muslim community, must finance its activities and religious personnel by contributions of its members. Such was proposed in Switzerland the initiative of 1976, had it been adopted. [In this respect, nothing prevents the nation state from financing social activities in these communities, without discrimination, but the nation should not provide salaries for clergy. The United States is ahead in this matter. This position was first stated in Thomas Jefferson's *Bill for Religious Freedom* and reiterated in Madison's *Memorial and Remonstrance*. Refer to the end of this work for these documents.] When adopted, these religious associations can find subsidies for actions whose purpose is a better reciprocal knowledge between immigrants and Switzerland. For example, the office in charge of foreigners in Neuchâtel repeatedly financed feasts at the end of Ramadan fast[1].

It is necessary to add that if one bestows any public statute to the Muslim community, one risks to open the door to claims without end on its behalf, notably the change of laws concerning the family (as authorization of polygamy and repudiation), the establishment of religious court, etc. This community will then constitute a religious state within the nation state, as one will see it in the following point.

---

[1] Mahnig: *L'intégration*, p. 107.

3) Recognition of Switzerland by Muslims

Let us recall first of all that the Arab-Muslim world recognizes to the Muslim, Christian, Jewish, Samaritan and Zoroastrian religious communities, legislative or even judicial autonomy more or less extended in the field of family law, which is considered a part of the religious freedom. A Muslim is held to submit to his religious law and jurisdiction; otherwise he is taxed of apostasy. Muslims in non-Muslim countries would like to have similar privileges as those recognized by non-Muslims in Muslim countries, in virtue of the principle of reciprocity and religious freedom. As we have seen, the reticence of Muslims facing emigration has mostly been the fact that they will not be able to abide to Islamic law and jurisdiction in non-Muslim countries.

The Muslim legal concept undermines a main attribute of national sovereignty. Switzerland dispossessed Churches of civil status, marriage and jurisdiction as we saw above. When the Pope of Rome declared in 1870 the dogma of infallibility, Switzerland became alarmed, fearing a breach to its sovereignty. For Switzerland, the law and courts emanate from the people, and not an outside power, such as the Pope, representative of Christ, or Allah in person. A Muslim community that would want to apply in Switzerland the Islamic law - whose formulation has not been made by the Swiss people -, and create its own courts would propose to return Switzerland again to the situation that prevailed before the Constitution of 1874.

Fawzia Al-Ashmawi considers that Switzerland discriminates Muslims living in Switzerland by applying to them its law especially concerning marriage, divorce and inheritance[1]. To the question of "what new legislations are necessary to integrate Muslims in Switzerland?", Sheik Yahya Basalamah, Imam of the *Islamic Cultural Foundation of Geneva* answers:

> First the official recognition of Islam by the Swiss authorities that will integrate the 2nd generation Muslims into the country. I also think that the mechanism of secularization must be more moderated and flexible so that Muslim identity can be adapted to this mechanism[2].

Hani Ramadan, Imam and Director of the *Islamic Center of Geneva*, wrote in a book titled *Articles on Islam and Barbarism*:

---

[1] Al-Ashmawi: *La condition des musulmans en Suisse*, p. 46.
[2] *Ibid.*, p. 121.

Man lives in a universe whose deep essence is unknown. He asks questions on the interior aspect of things. Therefore prophecy is necessary in order to have some lucid answers on a certain questions that would perpetually return man anguished in front of his ignorance. This is also valid as regards faith and law… If the human does not obey divine law, he ends up managing his natural habitat, the universe, in an abominable way. It is just what happens today. Let us thus be conscious that the world could not be managed appropriately without recourse to divine law. Islam means submission to God: to obey unconditionally the law [of God]. "No believing man or believing woman, if God and His messenger issue any command, has any choice regarding that command. Anyone who disobeys God and His messenger has gone far astray" (Koran 33:36)[1].

Fawzia Al-Ashmawi reports of Hani Ramadan the following:

The biggest problem that will face Muslims will be official recognition of Islam by Swiss authorities. The Muslim must get ready for this recognition and must have a federation that represents them. This federation or "Islamic" parliament should be established according to the Swiss model with a Muslim representative from every canton. This Islamic parliament will be a forum where the Muslim will be able to make decisions and advance complaints concerning the Muslim questions before communicating them to Swiss authorities… This Islamic parliament should get official recognition of Islam by Swiss authorities. In my opinion, it is the most important question for social integration of Muslims in this country[2].

In an article titled "Islam proposes to the West a dialogue without compromise", Hani Ramadan thinks that the system constructed on democracy and human rights creates emptiness, and this emptiness must be filled by religion. However, he pursues, "the return (of the West) to Christianity would be a solution. But the Christian faith, by giving back to Caesar what belongs to Caesar, disengaged itself completely from history. The State has put aside the Church, marginalized it and compromised its authority. As for Judaism, it remains attached to an obsolete idea of an elect race, that considerably reduces the extent of its message". Islam alone remains able to propose faith, morals and "a system of laws… a government that does not reject the democratic principle of elections, but which considers divine law

---

[1] Ramadan: *Articles sur l'islam et la barbarie*, p. 17.
[2] Al-Ashmawi: *La condition des musulmans*, p. 124.

alone as sovereign. It is effectively a comprehensive system which questions the principles of secularism"[1].

The opinion of Hafid Ouardiri, spokesman of the *Islamic Cultural Foundation of Geneva*, is hardly different from that of Hani Ramadan. He explains:

> The foreign Muslim must be content to live a temporary Islam, that is an Islam without claims. An Islam that adjusts willy-nilly to laws in force, even though these often reduce him. This foreigner, whether a worker, an intellectual or a scientific, has no choice. In clear language, if he is not happy, he can return home. If we know what waits him at home (the worse) we understand, without condemning him, why should he resign.

The situation differs for a Muslim who becomes a citizen. Hafid Ouardiri explains:

> The European Muslim is something else. He is a citizen, therefore equal to others.... He must respect laws and must serve his homeland in accordance with requirements of citizenship... But here is the problem. For the faithful Muslim citizen, above citizenship there is his faith, with its laws, its practice, its principles and its values... He is therefore confronted with a dilemma. The law that governs citizenship is sometimes in contradiction with the one of his faith. Is Islam incompatible with the European citizenship or the reverse? For the Muslim, the obstacle comes from the narrowness of secular laws and not the opposite. Facing this situation, a Muslim citizen must either expose himself to a refusal on behalf of the authority and, in the name of secularism, to live a reduced and incomplete Islam in relation to divine prescriptions; or to claim the right to greater openness and understanding on behalf of the political authority. He will claim from this authority a larger political, legal and cultural field in order to express legally and live indispensable Islamic values[2].

Tariq Ramadan, Muslim activist and brother of Hani Ramadan, wrote:

> When individuals or Muslim associations challenge the public authorities to find solutions to various problems, they do not translate a will to be treated differently; well rather – since they are going to live here – they ask that one takes in consideration their presence and their identity in the setting of laws elaborated in their absence[3].

Certainly, Swiss laws have been elaborated in the absence of Muslims. But now Muslims are there; what can they do? Must

---

[1] Ramadan: *Articles sur l'islam et la barbarie*, p. 43 (L'islam propose à l'Occident un dialogue sans compromission, article published in: *Tribune de Genève*, 9.9.1994).

[2] Hafid Ouardiri: Musulman et citoyen européen: quel avenir? in: *Le Courrier*, 19.11.1993.

[3] Ramadan: *Les musulmans dans la laïcité*, p. 97-98.

they simply accept these laws, or impose their own laws? In his dialogue with Tariq Ramadan, Jacques Neirynck expresses a fear:

> If a Muslim community is a minority in a country which is a State based on law, a tolerant State - not a State that persecutes the faith – as in the case of most Western Europe countries, the Muslim must accept the law honestly as it exists. He can and he must use margins that exist inside this law, to come as close as possible to Islamic concepts.

Tariq Ramadan answers, "Precisely"; Jacques Neirynck adds:

> But without violating local law! This position is very important. It is a message that Western discerns in a wrong way. Hostility toward Muslims comes from the idea that once they will be sufficiently numerous, they are not going to obey the common law any more and one is going to find again two communities, living next to each other, with their own laws, with their own courts. The situation is going to become first inextricable, and then contradictory, as in Israel or Lebanon[1].

Elsewhere, Tariq Ramadan wrote that the Muslim must not only accomplish the worship practices (prayer, fasting, obligatory alms and pilgrimage), but also respect other Islamic norms regarding social affaires: marriage, divorces, contracts, trade, and so forth. "In this respect, every issue must be studied in light of both the Islamic and the legal environment so as to find a way to remain faithful to the Islamic teachings and to respect the enforced laws. This by no means signifies that Muslims, or any other being should be forced to act against their conscience"[2].

While noting that there is no contradiction to be *Muslim* and *European citizen*, he recognizes that one must "clarify the nature of the articulation which exists between the prescriptions of the Islamic references and the concrete reality of citizenship in a European country". He affirms:

> Millions of Muslims – when coming into these [European] countries as workers, students, refugees or after a family reunion – have tacitly or explicitly recognized the binding character of the constitution or the laws of the country they enter into and then live in. By signing a work contract or asking for a visa, they acknowledge the validity and authority of the constitution, the laws and the State all at once. This is clear for residents and passing workings and it is even more obvious in the case of citizens who take a solemn oath to respect their country's fundamental laws. As for young Muslims of second and subsequent generations, they are either citizens, and as such naturally bound by the legislation, or residents, who are bound by the agreement previously made by their parents[3].

---

[1] Neirynck and Ramadan, p. 208.
[2] Ramadan: *To be a European Muslim*, p. 132-133.
[3] *Ibid.*, p. 163-164.

That is reassuring, but what if Swiss law enters into conflict with Islamic law? Which has prevalence? Tariq Ramadan answers:

> In social, political and even financial fields, human affairs are based on agreements and contracts and ... their respect is binding and must have priority in Muslims' eyes. Faysal Mawlawi aptly notes that, according to the great majority of *ulama*, Muslims are also bound by the decisions and acts of a perverted ruler or dictator "as long as he does not commit a sin or something against the Islamic teaching". In such a situation they are no longer bound by his acts since, by doing so, *he has betrayed the tacit agreement they had that both, himself and his people, were to respect the authority of Islamic sources. Therefore, they have the right, and the duty, to take over from him, by all legal means*[1].

Tariq Ramadan adds:

> Concerning Western legislation, the scope of permission is wider than that of compulsion. Nevertheless, it could happen that citizenship would lead someone to face or to feel a great tension between their faith, their conscience, and the duties related to their nationality. In such situation, they would have to refer to the legal notion of the clause of conscience, which allows them to make it clear that some actions or types of behavior are in contradiction with their faith[2].

He mentions here the case of war, to which we will return. There are also transactions, which are forbidden by their faith and Islamic law. "Some of them are compulsory (banks, insurance, ritual slaughter, burial) and need specific considerations. Muslims in these cases should find a way to protect their identity. A close assessment of the situation has to be undertaken by both the average Muslim and the *ulama*, so as to determine the degree of compulsion (and thus the degree of necessity)... It is only after this that an adapted *fatwa* should be formulated"[3].

Does not one risk undermining political sovereignty in legislative matters? Tariq Ramadan answers:

> This by no means signifies that Muslims are seeking to throw away the foundations of the nation or to appeal to "particular laws for Muslims" as we have heard here and there. Clearly, and more specifically, Muslims as citizens have the right – within the framework of the national legislation – to be recognized as Muslims and it could be that some laws no longer match the current landscape of Western societies. Such laws – very few of them in fact – should be reconsidered or, at least, their foundations discussed. Henceforth, as part of their European societies, Muslims have the duty, according to Islamic teachings, to protect their identity, to

---

[1] *Ibid.*, p. 170-171.
[2] *Ibid.*, p. 175.
[3] *Ibid.*, p. 176-177.

> respect their commitment toward the laws and, within the wide space of freedom provided, to strive and to act across all the different fields (social, legal, economical and political) to bring about a Muslim personality as well as a Western landscape which, to the largest extend could match[1].

Can a person invoke the clause of conscience everywhere? Tariq Ramadan claims there are some issues "which partake of the essence of the Islamic faith … and as such, they take priority and must be taken into account wherever the Muslim lives. Freedom of worship, respect of the principle of justice, and the prohibition of killing for power or money are of this nature: non-respect for these rulings shakes the foundation of the Muslim identity". Other issues such as school, education, marriage, and burial do not fall into the same level of consideration in light of the Islamic teachings. "They are certainly of great importance but still it is possible to find solutions within the framework of the legislation, namely in accordance with the terms of the tacit or explicit covenant that exists with the country. Therefore, they have nothing to do with a possible clause of conscience but rather require the true involvement of Muslims so that they can find appropriate solutions"[2].

Without doubt, the Muslim citizen, like any other Swiss citizen, has the right to modify the laws through the legal means so that these acquire conformity with his conscience and his convictions. But how far can one satisfy the Muslim conscience? In Muslim countries, fundamentalist Muslims make limitless demands, resembling the onion-like Russian doll. Tariq Ramadan recognizes that Muslims in the West formulate some extreme requirements. He writes in this respect:

> Some radical Islamic groups claim that a Muslim cannot be bound by a constitution, which allows interest, alcohol and other behavior, which contradicts Islamic teachings. Yet, if European constitutions effectively allow such transactions or behavior, they do not oblige Muslims to resort to them or to act in such a way. Therefore they must, on the one hand, respect the running legislation – since their presence is based on a tacit or explicit pact – and, on the other, avoid all kinds of activities or involvements that oppose their belief[3].

---

[1] *Ibid.*, p. 177-178.
[2] *Ibid.*, p. 178.
[3] *Ibid.*, p. 171.

Unless a poll among Muslims, it is not easy to know to what extend Muslims follow the ideas of Hani Ramadan, Tariq Ramadan and Hafid Ouardiri. But it often happened to us to hear Muslims saying that they refuse to submit to the unbelieving laws and to be judged by the unbelieving courts. As we will see it, some even get married and divorced before the imam of a mosque, in Swiss norms violation[1].

One of problems in ex-Yugoslavia was that of the allegiance of Muslims. The Yugoslavian army divided according to the national and religious adherences. Soldiers who were supposed to defend the country killed each other. In his discussion with Tariq Ramadan, Jacques Neirynck evokes what he calls "extreme situations":

> A French citizen of Muslim faith can be, in case of war, employed as a soldier and sent to the Middle East without asking his opinion. It already occurred in Iraq, for example. And he is placed there in a paradoxical situation, because he becomes the mercenary forced by the Christians to face his Muslim brothers. It recalls the situation of *Harkis* in Algeria during the war of independence of this country. What should this Muslim make in that case?

Tariq Ramadan answers:

> The principle first is the one of the justice. So, if a conflict begins indeed, and the Muslim, who is in the inimical party, defends an unjust motive, then the involvement to this war can be legitimized. The Koran speaks of such a case where two Muslim parties oppose one another: it is then necessary to take the part of justice and equity. The Prophet said, "Help your brother (Muslim), be he just or unjust". His Companions wondered, "okay to help him if he is just, but how to help him if he is unjust?" The Prophet answered, "Stop his injustice!" The answer is explicit.
>
> If, on the contrary, the war is for colonial purpose for example, or to expropriate lands or for any other motive, it is then impossible for a Muslim to be engaged in such a war. He should invoke the objection of conscience. Note that things must be clear: it is not about advancing objection of conscience solely when the war that opposes Muslims is unjust. Objection of conscience must concern any engagement in unjust war, with any adversary.

Tariq Ramadan mentions the case of Cassius Clay who refused to fight in Vietnam, "The enterprise was unjust and illegitimate; a Muslim was not able in any way to warrant it. A lot of Christians

---

[1] See part III, chap. IV.2.B.

also refused to fight"[1]. Elsewhere he mentions Joseph who preferred jail to injustice, "My Lord, prison is better to me than what they invite me to do" (12:33).

The answer is acceptable. But what about a Muslim community becomes important enough in a Western country? Can it then refuse to submit to non-Islamic law and jurisdiction? What if it asks for secession or legislative autonomy? What then should be the attitude of the Muslim soldier in that country? [This last question may potentially arise in the United States right now, where Muslim military personel are required to fight against fellow Muslims in the War Against Terrorism.] Does the answer lie is in the Balkans?

Chapter II.
Freedom of religion and worship

Religious minorities in all domains of life invoke the argument of freedom of religion. We will limit discussion here to the following questions: freedom to adhere, religious brands, freedom of opinion, holidays, prayers, Ramadan fasting, mosques and religious personnel. Questions of school, family law, prohibited food and cemeteries will be been considered separately.

1) Freedom to adhere

A) Islamic norms

We already looked at religious freedom while considering the *People of the Book* and apostasy. In brief, any individual is free, or even encouraged, to become Muslim. To become Muslim, it is sufficient to pronounce the following formula, "I testify that there is no other divinity than Allah and that Muhammad is Allah's messenger". If it is a man, he normally must be circumcised. Muhammad says, "One who becomes Muslim must circumcise himself even though he is aged"[2]. He can be required to take a Muslim name or at least neutral sounding one. It is the case of the

---

[1] Neirynck and Ramadan, p. 208-209. See also Ramadan: *To be a European Muslim*, p. 175-176.
[2] Narrative quoted by Al-Sukkari, p. 50.

Swiss journalist Albert Huber (who became Ahmed Huber), of the French philosopher Roger Garaudy (who became Raja Garaudy), of British pop star Cat Stevens (who became Yusuf Islam) and of American boxer Cassius Clay (who became Muhammad Ali)[1]. To convert can present a certain advantage for a man: he can repudiate his wife for example and marry up to four women at one time, get the double-share in succession, and obtain the guardianship of his children. If convert is a woman, she can free herself of her non-Muslim husband, obtain the guardianship of her children and have a share in the inheritance of her Muslim husband.

This freedom to become Muslim and its advantages contrast with the prohibition to leave Islam and its disadvantages that carries the threat of death of the apostate. Only two Arab nations foresee expressly such a sanction, Mauritania and Sudan, but elsewhere the apostate is not more in security; his family may kill him. The apostate cannot get married. If he apostatized after marriage, his marriage is dissolved, his children are removed and his succession is opened. He cannot hold public office. It is prohibited to convert someone who is Muslim. A convert will rarely find a priest who will accept to baptize him, and if done, baptism will always be kept secret. Groups of Christian converts currently exist in North Africa and other Muslim countries, but they live in fear of being discovered and the Church cannot openly involve with them. A Western Christian organization takes care of these converts secretly[2].

These Islamic norms are the basis of controversies that took place at the time of discussions of the UDHR, whose article 18 stipulates:

> Everyone has the right to freedom of thought, conscience and religion; this right includes freedom to change his religion or belief, and freedom, either alone or in community with others and in public or private, to manifest his religion or belief in teaching, practice, worship and observance.

---

[1] The Official Saudi Gazette (*Um al-Qura*) publishes regularly the names of the converts to Islam and the names they adopted. Internet has narratives of converts to Islam who changed their names.

[2] The name of this organization is: *Middle East Concern*. It has a secret address in the Middle East, and another in the United States.

The mention of the *freedom to change his religion or belief* provoked a very quick Muslim reaction, notably from Saudi Arabia, sustained by Iraq, Syria[1] and Egypt[2]. The same problem was raised during the discussion of the *Declaration on the Elimination of All Forms of Intolerance and of Discrimination Based on Religion or Belief* of 1981[3].

B) Swiss norms

The Islamic norms, that recognize a uni-directional freedom favoring Muslims, are contrary to international and Swiss norms. Religious freedom is affirmed in article 49 aCst, which states:

1) Freedom of creed and belief is inviolable.
2) No one may be forced to participate in a religious association, to attend religious teaching or to perform a religious act nor be subjected to penalties of any sort because of his religious beliefs.

The new Constitution of 1998 is more broadly stated. Article 15 stipulates:

1) The freedom of religion and conscience is guaranteed.
2) Every person has the right to freely choose his or her religion or non-denominational belief and to profess them alone or in community with others.
3) Every person has the right to join or belong to a religious community and to receive religious education.
4) No person may be forced to join a religious community, to conduct a religious act or participate in religious education.

In Switzerland, anyone can become Muslim, and Muslims are known to extensively proselytize, even in jails. One Catholic chaplain noted, "A recent survey done in a jail at Fleury-Mérogis (France) indicated clearly that during Ramadan, 25% of Muslims observing the fast were originally non-Muslim convicts, who were converted to Islam by co-convicts during their incarceration.

---

[1] *GA*, 3rd Commission, vol. 2, 127th session, p. 402-403.

[2] *GA*, 3rd session, plenary session 180, 1980, p. 913.

[3] The representative of Iran said that Muslims are not allowed to change their religion. Those who change their religion are killed (*GA*, 3rd Commission, 26.10.1981, A/C.3/36/SR.29, p. 5). In the name of the *Organization of Islamic conference*, the representative of Iraq said that the members of this organization do not accept the norms, which contradict the Islamic norms (*GA*, 3rd Commission, 9.10.1981, A/C 36/SR. 43, p. 10). The representatives of Syria (*GA*, 3rd Commission, 9.10.1981, A/C 36/SR. 43, p. 12) and Egypt confirmed the Iraqi declaration (*GA*, 3rd Commission, 9.11.1981, A/C.3/36/SR.43, p. 9).

Similarly, one observes an analogous phenomenon in French-speaking cantons of Switzerland". The chaplain added:

> It is a fact that for young marginalized Europeans, missing reference marks and meaning for existence, Islam, a religion with simple principles, strict rules, and claims, can play an unexpected structural role in front of a Christianity which is diluted in a wave of humanism, impoverished of most religious expression, constantly shown in derision by media, whereas Islam is put forward as fresh and vital[1].

Imams do not permit to celebrate a religious ceremony at the time of the marriage with a Muslim woman unless the man converts to Islam, and some also exercise a pressure so that a Christian woman who wants to marry a Muslim man becomes Muslim. We will come back on this question. Even though some converts to Islam may have difficulties with their parents, they do not complain of discrimination. The few Muslims converted to Christianity in Switzerland keep secret their origin, fearing reprisals on behalf of Muslims. Whereas converts to Islam overtly participate in broadcasts of radio and television to praise the merits of Islam, a Christian of Muslim origin would never dare to do the same. No Muslim leader in Switzerland denounced the Islamic norm of apostasy. Challenged by Jacques Neirynck, Tariq Ramadan tries to explain this norm in a diplomatic way:

> One often says that Islam forbids apostasy and one refers to certain scholarly opinion that has a literal and strict analysis of tradition of the Prophet affirming, "One who changes religion, kill him". This type of reading exists and no one can deny that certain authorities were held or hold themselves again to this first and literal sense. Other Islamic scholars over the centuries interpreted this *hadith* [narrative] differently through a contextualization, which is necessary to understand it... They have shown that one who would leave the faith for personal conviction without trying to betray Islam and Muslims thereafter, in any way, this individual does not enter into the category of the aforesaid *hadith*. They rely on the Koranic verse, which indicates that God alone judges such act. The necessary attitude is therefore a minimal respect for the faith that one leaves and a sensitivity by those that continue to practice it[2].

Tariq Ramadan does not specify about what this minimal respect consists. Would a Muslim who becomes Christian have to hide his new faith or at least not overtly profess it, for fear of hurting a Muslim? Elsewhere, Tariq Ramadan writes:

---

[1] Arbez: *Détenus musulmans dans les prisons suisses*, p. 9-10.
[2] Neirynck and Ramadan, p. 145.

> The duty of a Muslim is to spread the Message and to make it known, no more no less. Whether someone accepts Islam or not is not the Muslim's concern, for the inclination of every individual heart depends on God's Will. … Muslims are asked to spread the knowledge of Islam among Muslims as well as non-Muslims. The *mu'min* [believer] is the one who has known and eventually accepts, whereas the *kafir* [unbeliever] is one who has known and then refuses, denies[1].

Everyone thus falls into these awful *believer / unbeliever* categories. The term *kafir*, the biggest insult in the Arabic language, applies equally to Christians or Jews that do not want to become Muslim. His brother, Hani Ramadan, Director of the *Islamic Center of Geneva*, writes:

> As for apostasy, it may truly lead to condemnation to death according to Islamic law, but this punishment cannot be enforced unless a person overtly manifests hostile or disrespectful behavior to [Islamic] law[2].

One would be curious to know what is meant by "hostile and disrespectful behavior of the law". Elsewhere, Hani Ramadan writes:

> It is incorrect to say that Islam legitimizes the "murder of apostates".… If an individual overtly denies the foundation of Islamic State, that is belief in an unique God, he should exclude himself of the Muslim community which forms the majority – and that is not forbidden – or he could associate with that community while avoiding to express conspicuously his opinions which would be a troubling factor and harm the public order. In this context, an apostate former Muslim, who has declared his hostility overtly against the Islamic State and Muslim community, is liable of the death penalty. The fact that the same person collaborates with a foreign nation state to destabilize power, to foment unrest, or to maintain the hate of other persons, constitutes an aggravating circumstance[3].

These explanations are far from clear. Hani Ramadan maintains confusion between treason (punished whatever its author's religion) and the change of religion (freedom of conscience) to lead astray the reader. He should rather tell us whether someone has the right to change his religion and to express his belief in

---

[1] Ramadan: *To be a European Muslim*, p. 134.

[2] Ramadan: *Articles sur l'islam et la barbarie*, p. 43 (Pas de contrainte en religion, affirme le Koran, article published in: *Tribune de Genève*, 29.6.1993).

[3] Ramadan: *Articles sur l'islam et la barbarie*, p. 48-49 (La tolérance de l'islam en cinq points, article published in: *Le Courrier*, 22.3.1997). See also p. 70-72 (Point fort, article published in: *Tribune de Genève*, 13-14.4.1995).

public as Muslim or Christian, freely, without undergoing consequences on the penal or civil level. The answer is definitely no in Islamic law and in Muslim countries. Useless to deny what happens or attempt extreme convolutions of logic.

2) Religious brands

A) Islamic norms

In Islamic law, a child, whose parents are Muslim, is inevitably Muslim, even though the parents are of a contrary opinion. Once adult, the child has no right to change religion. We will come back to a child's religion in the chapter on family law. What interest us here are religious brands. Christians consider baptism the bath to faith. Although they believe that baptism marks the baptized in an indelible way, it does not leave a physical trace, such as male circumcision among Jews, Muslims and some Christian groups (100% in Egypt and 60% to the United States). Muslims also practice female circumcision (about 97% of Egyptian women are circumcised[1]), along with Jewish Fallachas and some Christian groups (as in Egypt). These groups insist on maintaining these customs in the name of religious freedom and cultural rights.

B) Swiss norms

Article 10 nCst stipulates:
> 1) Every person has the right to life …
> 2) Every person has the right to personal liberty, particularly to corporal and mental integrity and freedom of movement.
> 3) Torture and any other form of cruel, inhuman, or degrading treatment or punishment are prohibited.

On the other hand, article 122, numeral 1, par. 2 of the Penal Code says:
> Anyone who has mutilated a person's body, one of the limbs or one of the important organs, or rendered the limb or the organ unfit to function [...], will be sentenced to a maximum of 10 years reclusion or to between 6 months and 5 years of imprisonment.

In appearance, these Swiss norms, which can be found in all national legislations, should be sufficient to forbid male and female circumcision in Switzerland and elsewhere. Unfortunately, no legislator, either Swiss or international, deduces such consequences of these principles. They only condemn female

---

[1] *Egyptian Demographic and Health Survey*, p. 171-183.

circumcision in all degrees, but keep silent about male circumcision in any degree, mainly for a political reason: the fear of being labeled anti-Semitic. Female circumcision is condemned in a declaration of the *Central commission of medical ethics* of the *Swiss academy of medical sciences* published in the Bulletin of the Swiss Physicians, August 24th, 1983. It invokes the aforementioned article 122 of the Penal Code [1]. This condemnation was reiterated by the Swiss Federal Council March 1st, 1993. We have to notice here that neither the UDHR, nor the ECHR expressly mention the right to physical integrity. This omission may not be a coincidence.

During a Symposium of the *Swiss Academy of Human and Social Sciences* (Gerzensee, 29 September-3 October 1997), I questioned Heinrich Koller, the main redactor of the new Constitution, whether article 10 par. 2, might apply to male circumcision. He answered, "Do you think therefore that we should forbid religious circumcision to Jews and Muslims!?" He added that Swiss public opinion is opposed to female circumcision, but not yet to male circumcision.

In current Swiss law, male circumcision is allowed for medical or religious reasons. In this last case, it should be paid by the party in question not by insurance. One however finds abuses on behalf of physicians who present religious circumcision as medical circumcision, so that insurances will agree to pay for it[2].

We will not linger on this question, to which we already dedicated a book. Four degrees of female circumcision and four degrees of male circumcision exist. We consider any religious brand as a violation of the child's physical integrity and a threat to his religious freedom. This applies to both male and female circumcision since these two practices consist in amputating a healthy part of the human body without serious medical reason and without the patient's consent, expose the child to the sexual, psychological and physical harm, and sometimes cause death. Some authors even consider these practices a torture. The attitude of legislators is discriminating against boys and makes them

---

[1] Declaration published by *Bulletin des médecins suisses*, vol. 64, 1983, cahier 34, 24.8.1983, p. 1275.

[2] Aldeeb Abu-Sahlieh: *Male & Female Circumcision*, and *Circoncision masculine*. Concerning Switzerland, see p. 304 and 406-408.

accomplices in this crime. Consent of parents cannot be taken into consideration since male circumcision is for physicians' financial gain not in the child's interest. Certainly, parents would not allow the amputation of even the small finger of their healthy child, yet they are convinced that there is no pain or physical loss in amputating sensitive sexual organs. Parents should no longer be able to justify this breach of physical integrity by their right to raise their child in the religion of their choice: to raise a child does not mean to mistreat him. In this respect, the Swiss Federal Court says that when obedience to principles of a belief concretely and significantly injures a child's well being, his interest is more important than his parents' interest. This is especially true when a child's health is threatened[1].

Male and female circumcisions lead to misunderstandings among couples, notably mixed ones involving Muslim or Jewish partners. This sometimes leads to divorce. Our booklet on marriage between Swiss and Muslim partners recommends that mixed couples agree in writing, to respect the physical integrity of their sons and daughters until their majority. Sons and daughters may then freely decide if they want to submit to these practices. If the spouses live in Switzerland, such an agreement has a chance to be respected. It is a completely different situation if they were residing in the country of origin of the Muslim partner. Often, the Muslim family imposes its customs and insists on the circumcision of the children in spite of parental resistance. To avoid the family's seizure of these children, the booklet says it is better to let them remain in Switzerland until majority[2].

3) Freedom of opinion

A) Islamic norms

As noted, Islamic law never permits apostasy. This concept of apostasy not only consists of abandoning Islam, but also expressing any opinion that could in any way be thought of as against "Islamic norms". The best known case is that of Salman Rushdie against whom Imam Khumeini issued on February 14th, 1989 a *fatwa* calling for his death, following the publication of

---

[1] Federal Court decision 119 Ia 178.
[2] Aldeeb: *Mariages entre partenaires suisses et musulmans*, p. 28-29 and 36.

his *Satanic Verses*. But by far this is not the only case. Lately, Nawal Al-Saadawi has been dragged before Egyptian courts accused of apostasy because she asked for equality between men and women in inheritance and criticized the pilgrimage to Mecca[1]. Likewise, a fundamentalist group successfully instituted a suit for apostasy against professor Abu-Zayd from Cairo University, for his liberal interpretation of the Koran. This matter went before the Egyptian Court of Cassation, which confirmed his condemnation August 5th, 1996[2], and required the separation of Abu-Zayd from his wife. The couple left Egypt and asked for asylum in the Netherlands, for fear to being killed. Muhammad Mahmud Taha, founder of the Republican Brothers in Sudan, presented a theory reducing the normative reach of the Koran. He was condemned by a Sudanese Court and hung January 18th, 1985[3]. The Egyptian philosopher Faraj Fodah was murdered on June 7th, 1992 by a fundamentalist Muslim, because of his opinions. Al-Mahdawi, an old Libyan judge, was dragged before courts numerous years because his book entitled *Proof by the Koran* questioned the tradition of Muhammad and some Islamic norms. The Court of Appeals in Benghazi acquitted him on June 27th, 1999, but prohibited distribution or reprint of his book[4].

Prohibition to criticize any Islamic norm concerns both Muslims and non-Muslims. Certainly, Muslims know that non-Muslims do not accept the Koran as God's word or that Muhammad is His prophet, but non-Muslims living in Muslim countries must not overtly state this. By comparison, Muslims never miss an opportunity to put down Christian norms and faith. Works criticizing non-Muslims are handed out as pamphlets on Cairo sidewalks, but no Christian in Egypt would dare publish a book to answer these tracts, or do the same concerning Muslims.

---

[1] See on the trial against Nawal Al-Saadawi: www.geocities.com/nawalsaadawi

[2] Decision published by Al-Mujtama al-madani (Cairo), September 1996.

[3] On this Sudanese philosopher, see Aldeeb Abu-Sahlieh: *Droit familial des pays arabes*, p. 39-41. Text and commentary of the judgement in: Kabbashi, p. 80-96 (the author was the judge who condemned Taha).

[4] Al-Mahdawi: *Al-bayan bil-Qur'an*.

Muslims often brag about being the most open to other religions. Christians are trapped by this argument. So Jacques Neirynck, in a debate with Tariq Ramadan, noted that the *Catholic Catechism*, published in 1992, mentions Judaism, atheism, and materialism, but not Islam, which is simply ignored. There is not even one quote from the Koran or any mention of Muhammad. He even adds, "Useless to recall that the reciprocal is not true and that Islam holds in high reverence Jesus' person, abundantly quoted in the Koran"[1].

It is necessary to remember however that the Jesus of the Koran is not the one of the *New Testament* and Christians. On the other hand, Muslims never mention *Gospels* recognized by Christians, and repeatedly cite the apocryphal *Gospel of Barnabas*, that probably dates of the 14th century, because this pseudo-Gospel speaks of Muhammad and presents a Christ somewhat according to the picture in the Koran. In 1996, the *Ministry of the Awqaf and Islamic Affairs* of Qatar republished the English translation[2], mentioning on the title page this claim by Paul,

> About Barnabas, the commandment is, "If he comes unto you, receive him" (Colossians 4:10).

Also, book exhibitions held in the West offer versions of the Koran in Arabic and different translations. On the other hand it is not possible to find Christian or Jewish holy books in any book exhibitions in Arabic countries of the Gulf, such as the United Arab Emirates, Kuwait, not to mention Saudi Arabia. In Qatar, a Muslim asked me if I could provide him the Gospel in Arabic. I contacted Christian religious leaders in that country, but all indicated that it would be more prudent to send him the Gospel from Switzerland.

B) Swiss norms

This uni-directional Islamic perspective poses a problem in Switzerland where expressing a religious opinion is part of the freedom of opinion. This freedom did not exist in the 1874 Constitution, but since 1965 the Federal Court considered it a constitutional right[3]. It was integrated in article 16 of the New

---

[1] Neirynck and Ramadan, p. 13.
[2] *The Gospel of Barnabas*.
[3] Federal Court decision 96 I 219; 96 I 586.

Constitution under the title "freedom of opinion and information" This article stipulates:

    1) The freedom of opinion and information is guaranteed.

    2) All persons have the right to form, express, and disseminate opinions freely.

    3) All persons have the right to receive information freely, to gather it from generally accessible sources, and to disseminate it.

It is over-simplistic to believe that the freedom of opinion is absolute in Switzerland. Article 261 of the Penal Code says:

> Whoever publicly and maliciously insults or ridicules the religious creed of others, especially faith in God, or desecrates the religious sanctity, whoever maliciously prevents, disturbs or publicly ridicules a worship guaranteed by the Constitution, whoever maliciously profanes any place or any object serving a faith guaranteed by the Constitution or such a worship, shall be sentenced to the prison for not over six months or fined.

Other limits are foreseen by the abovementioned article 261bis concerning racial discrimination, adopted June 18th, 1993 and enforced since January 1st 1995. This article is extensively used by Jews to defend their positions, even against Swiss Federal Counselor in the issue of the Jewish property in the Swiss banks. They used it to confiscate anti-Semitic works (for example the book by Roger Garaudy, *Founding Myths of Israeli Politics*) and to condemn their authors and distributors as well as the booksellers who sold them, some of whom were Muslim. On the other hand, Swiss Government and Public supported Salman Rushdie - certainly because he was condemned to death, which cannot be tolerated by Switzerland - without forbidding the sale of his book that was found offensive by many Muslims[1]. This left a bitter taste for Swiss Muslims, who think of themselves as victims of a double standard policy.

Switzerland followed other matters concerning freedom of opinion in relation with Muslims.

There is the Voltaire matter that began July of 1993, on the occasion of the tercentenary of his birth, in 1694. A French producer, Hervé Loichemol, wanted to use public funds in the city of Geneva for a theatrical presentation of Voltaire's work *Muhammad or Fanaticism*. Geneva cultural affairs authorities refused to finance this presentation arguing, "We do not want to

---

[1] See Aldeeb Abu-Sahlieh: *Les musulmans face aux droits de l'homme*, p. 396-399.

offend the Muslim community of Geneva". The vexed producer organized a public debate in order to discuss this affair with local media representatives, authorities and the Muslim community. Representatives of the *Islamic Cultural Foundation of Geneva* and the *Islamic Center of Geneva* joined with Geneva authorities against the French producer, and the presentation was banned[1].

Also, beginning August 1994, Fawzia Al-Ashmawi, Muslim Professor in the University of Geneva, wrote a letter to the local press[2] with the title *Do not touch my Koran*. We give here the entire letter she sent us:

Dr Fawzia Al-Ashmawi–University of Geneva

Professor – Section of Arab and Islamic Civilization

Do not touch my Koran

The Newspaper *Tribune de Genève* published August 8, 1994 a humorous drawing of the Koran; in its cover was represented the title of the work "The Koran" preceded of the name of its author "Muhammad". Obviously, the redaction of this Newspaper knows that Muhammad is not the author of the Koran. It is absurd, in 1994, in a Western country calling itself "civilized and neutral", to insist displaying such ignorance. So much that the West will keep this attitude of indifference and lack of interest *vis-à-vis* Muslims, it must not wonder about violent reactions on behalf of fundamentalists, when one touches upon what is most holy, the Koran.

How many times is it necessary to repeat that Muhammad is not the author of the Koran: The Koran is the word revealed of God, transmitted to Muhammad through the intermediary of the angel Gabriel, after the 22nd year of Muhammad's life. The Koran is not a writing but a reading, a compiled oral revelation, united in a volume, 5 years after the death of Muhammad. He being illiterate, his associates wrote down these revelations, on parchment. One of Muhammad's widows, Hafza, - an intelligent and shrewd Muslim woman from the seventh century -, carefully kept the complete text of these revelations. It is this text that constitutes the official Koran that we have now. This text is immutable and incorruptible.

On the other hand, Koranic interpretation can be modified. It must be now readapted to the evolution of the customs in modern Arab-Islamic societies, and nothing prevents Muslim women from participating in this task. It is not by provocation, nor blasphemous writings that Muslim women would make any modification of their personal or social status, but by the perseverance to claim their right to be recognized by men as being equal in religious matters, in conformity with this Koranic verse that says, "The believing men and women are allies of one another. They advocate righteousness and

---

[1] Al-Ashmawi: *La condition des musulmans*, p. 61-62.
[2] *Le Courrier*, 19.8.1994.

forbid evil, they observe the prayers and give the obligatory alms (*zakat*), and they obey God and His messenger" (9: 71).

So, if Taslima Nasrine indeed attacked the Koran, she is no longer one of us, she blasphemed and deserves the fate that waits all who attack God and his revealed word: they are excluded from the Muslim community. Why does the West matter about this fact and becomes the advocate of the devil? The West does not have the right to sustain the excluded persons of the Muslim nation. The cases of Salman Rushdie and Taslima Nasrine are not related to freedom of opinion, as pretends the Pen Club, it is a case of lese-majesty and defamation against God and Muhammad. We are a billion Muslims, throughout the world, watching over our holy and immutable book, the Koran, so that no satanic verses may infiltrate. A billion Muslims tell the West: do not touch my Koran!

Le Courrier, which published this letter, added a commentary by Patrice Mugny, "With her prose, this professor who exercises her talents in the University of Geneva incontestably represents the intellectual face of bloodthirsty fanaticism that effects many regions"[1]. Following this letter, about twenty articles appeared in the French speaking Swiss press accusing Fawzia Al-Ashmawi of propagating religious fanaticism. The Dean of Arts Faculty presented the University's position to the press. He explained that as a professor, using her title publicly, she should know, more than any other person, the seriousness of her position. Her intentions are not sufficient excuse, as her position constitutes an official declaration. The Dean notes that in the present context of the death penalty issued against Salman Rushdie and Taslima Nasrine, which revolts all free men, the declaration of Fawzia Al-Ashmawi can have only one sense, even though not in her intention, and it contributes to intolerance and fanaticism. He added that the Arts Faculty cannot tolerate such attacks against Salman Rushdie and Taslima Nasrine, and is morally obliged to say so, with the hope that adequate legislation will in future limit the impunity of such declaration. The Faculty therefore addressed an official reprimand to Fawzia Al-Ashmawi for irresponsibility in her public declaration. The Dean added, "This declaration is much more regrettable as it nourishes racism and hostility in the press toward the Arab world, which is totally unacceptable". He indicated that the University sanction stops there since, in an interview, September 5th, 1994, Fawzia Al-Ashmawi presented her apology and clearly specified she was opposed to any

---

[1] *Ibid.*, 19.8.1994.

violence and condemnation to death as regards the two writers, and had only called for dismissal from the community of believers, comparable to excommunication [1]. Addressing this affair, Fawzia Al-Ashmawi writes:

> The polemic caused by the case of Al-Ashmawi illustrate that Muslims who respect their religion and observe Islamic values and rituals, are accused of fanaticism as much by the media as by the native population. This reveals a limited and erroneous understanding of Muslims' sensitivities. This polemic also underlines the fragile nature of freedom of opinion, granted to Muslims in Switzerland [2].

In this matter, only the paragraph concerning Salman Rushdie and Taslima Nasrine drew critical attention. But the first paragraph is no less problematic. In a defensive letter published in *Le Courrier* August 22nd, 1994, Fawzia Al-Ashmawi wrote, "My letter was intended to ask the local press not to touch the Koran, the holy book of all Muslims. One does not jest with what is holy; local newspapers must respect all religious convictions: Jewish, Muslim or Hindu". But Fawzia Al-Ashmawi forgets an important element: while she has the right to believe the Koran is revealed by God to Muhammad, can she impose her convictions on five billion non-Muslims, who do not agree with her?

I myself have been attacked three times by Muslims. The first was a petition of December 13th, 1996 on behalf of Muslims addressed to the *Federal Commission Against Racism* aiming to forbid the distribution of my booklet on *Mixed marriages between Swiss and Muslims* (2nd edition of June 1996, published by the Swiss Institute of Comparative Law). The Commission organized a meeting of reconciliation between the director of the institute and myself on the one hand, and two representatives of the Muslim community. The declared goal of the Commission was to suppress this booklet, but the direction refused, only accepting the introduction of some formal modifications, precisions and bibliographic references. The new version was submitted for approval of the same Commission, which declared its incompetence. Nevertheless, this Commission continued attacking the booklet [3].

---

[1] *Ibid.*, 9.9.1994.

[2] Al-Ashmawi: *La condition des musulmans*, p. 61.

[3] This Commission solicited and published an article against my booklet in its periodical *Tangram*, n° 7, October 1999, p. 43-45.

In another instance, a Moroccan Muslim reacted to my letter to the editor entitled, "Commission against or for racism?"[1]. Here is my letter:

> January 18th, 2000 I participated in a symposium organized by the *Federal Commission Against Racism* on "Muslims in Switzerland".
>
> During this symposium, Switzerland has been accused on several counts. One heard of grievances from both Muslims and the Commission that Switzerland discriminates against Muslims. But no word was said about Islamic discriminatory norms concerning family law that reverberate in Switzerland, norms explained in the booklet *Marriages between Swiss and Muslim partners*, published by the Swiss Institute of Comparative Law in Lausanne. Why these two weighty measures? Most surprising was to see the Commission sustaining the claim of Muslims to have their own cemeteries in Switzerland, without considering problems that such a claim could provoke in Switzerland and without wondering for what reason Muslims refuse to be buried with non-Muslims. The symposium had no debate on this. Listeners had to listen without questioning.
>
> Muslim officials invoke two reasons for their refusal to be buried with others:
>
> 1) They want to have tombs face Mecca: However the Earth is round and so any direction is the tomb one still faces (and backs) Mecca.
> 2) They want permanent tombs: However the small size of Switzerland cannot accommodate the Muslim minority with more space than received by the non-Muslim majority.
>
> The third reason, which is never cited by Muslims in Switzerland, but it is mentioned by Islamic law, is the following: Muslims must not be buried next to unbelievers. This xenophobia should be fought, not sustained, by the *Federal Commission Against Racism*.
>
> A Muslim representative in the *Federal Commission Against Racism* asked Switzerland "not only tolerance, but also acceptance of Muslims". Is it not also necessary that Muslims accept "non-Muslims" in Switzerland? Why should the acceptance stop at the doorstep of the tomb?

In reaction against this letter, Ahmed Bennani, a Swiss of Moroccan origin who considers himself as atheist, addressed a letter to the *Federal Commission Against Racism*, to Ruth Metzler, Federal Councilwoman responsible for the Justice and Police Department, and to the press. In his letter, he wonders if "the incitement to religious hatred does not fall under the law". He adds, "for about ten years, Dr. Aldeeb nourishes hate and contempt of Islam in all its diversity, so it is necessary to stop his acts. I suggest setting up an academic and scientific commission to analyze his slanderous writings and declarations against an

---

[1] See this article in: *Le Temps*, 20.1.2000.

important group in Switzerland". Making reference to my function, Bennani writes, "most heartrending in this affair, is that the Swiss Institute of Comparative Law confided in him responsibility as a specialist of Islamic law. It is totally surrealistic and certainly the Institute in question loses all credibility". I addressed to Bennani and those who received his letter a list of my publications, inviting them to face my ideas with other ideas, not with inquisition[1]. My letter to Bennani remained unanswered.

Finally, a Swiss Muslim of Algerian origin sent a penal complaint to the Court of Lausanne April 19th, 2000 aimed at forbidding my booklet *Marriages between Swiss and Muslim partners* (published by the Swiss Institute of Comparative Law). The court did not reply to this complaint.

4) Holidays, prayers and fasting of Ramadan

A) Islamic norms

The Bible prescribes Saturday as the day of sacred rest. One who violates it is liable of the death penalty, according to the Bible (Exodus 31:14). Practicing Jews forbid any activity during this day and would like to impose their attitude on the whole of Israeli society with more or less success. In addition to this weekly rest day, Jews have other religious holy days. In Christian countries, with the exception of some groups, Sunday replaced Saturday as the day of prayer and rest. But as one passed of one to two weekly rest days, Saturday was added. On these two days, public offices and enterprises stop activities, although some people work the weekdays and nights. There are also religious feasts and national holidays that vary from country to country.

The Koran established Friday as the day of obligatory weekly gathering for prayer:

> O you who believe, when the prayer is announced on Friday, you shall hasten to the commemoration of God, and drop all business. This is better for you, if you only knew. Once the prayer is completed, you may spread through the land to seek God's bounties, and continue to remember God frequently, that you may succeed (62:9-10).

On the basis of Muhammad's narratives, classic jurists held that Muslims, except for children, patients, travelers, slaves and

---

[1] See *La Liberté*: Des musulmans veulent la tête d'un chercheur suisse, 22.1.2000.

women, must assemble around noontime, without fixing an exact hour. The quorum varies according to opinion: four, twelve or forty persons. During this gathering, begun by a call, an imam makes a homily and directs prayer[1]. In addition to Friday, Muslims have two days of holy feasts, during which they also assemble for prayer, visit each other and visit family tombs:

- Yom al-fitr, day of the end of fasting of Ramadan, on the 1st day of the month of Shawwal (10th month of the lunar calendar).
- Yom al-adha on the 10th day of the month of Dhou al-hijjah (12th month of the lunar calendar)[2].

There are also five daily prayers that constitute one of the five pillars of the Islamic faith[3]. These prayers, preceded by ablutions, require facing Mecca, unless it is impossible. They take place at the following hours[4]:

- Morning prayer: fixed by apparition of true dawn until before sunrise.
- Noon prayer: after midday until before the time of afternoon.
- Afternoon prayer: fixed between noon and the time of sunset.
- Twilight prayer: fixed between sunset and the disappearance of red twilight.
- Evening prayer: set between disappearance of twilight and the first third of the night.

One may perform two prayers together if hindered due to travel, rain, cold weather or fear, or even for less important reasons according to some classic jurists[5]. Prayers can take place anywhere, including on a road, but best in a mosque. They can be individual, but they must be in a group if there are two people, men separated of women. Note here that participants or an official, when in a house of worship, may nominate the imam who directs prayer. Prayers are obligatory for each Muslim pubescent (older than 7 or 10). Anyone who abandons prayers, deeming them as not obligatory, is considered an apostate, liable of the death penalty. As for one who abandons them for laziness,

---

[1] See *Al-mawsu'ah al-fiqhiyyah*: Salat al-jum'ah, vol. 31, p. 114-118.

[2] See *Al-mawsu'ah al-fiqhiyyah*: Id, vol. 27, p. 192-211.

[3] The five pillars of Islam are the attestation (that there is no other divinity than God and that Muhammad is the messenger of God), the prayer, the obligatory alms, the pilgrimage, and the fasting of Ramadan.

[4] Prayers are fixed by the verses 2:238-239; 4:103; 11:114; 17:78 and the Narratives of Muhammad.

[5] See *Al-mawsu'ah al-fiqhiyyah*: Jam al-salawat, vol. 15, p. 284-292.

some classic jurists say to kill him, and others demand castigation and jail until death or repentance[1].

From the aforesaid, religious norms do not impose holidays, but simply moments dedicated to daily prayers and communal gathering for Friday, and for two holy feasts. Outside of these moments of prayer and gathering, the Muslim can work, as affirmed in the Koran (62:10). Muhammad probably decided in favor of this lack of formalism because he saw that Jews had problems respecting the *Sabbath* rest[2]. Muslim countries did not adjust to a uniform weekly holiday. Some countries now follow a Western system, closing Saturday and Sunday due to international trade. In such countries, foreign embassies fix holiday days freely. The same phenomenon exists for schools and universities. In Saudi Arabia, markets, offices, schools and libraries stop for the hour of daily prayers. In other countries, as Egypt, work continues without interruption, since Muslims can make the prayer another moment. In these countries, civil servants may stop working for prayers.

Concerning the Ramadan fast, one of the five pillars of Islam, it is required and preserved on family, state and society levels. A family's father can require his wife and children of a certain age to fast. On the other hand, the religious state forbids any public violation of fasting. Certainly non-Muslims are not obliged to fast, but they cannot consume food in public. Laws punish such infringement. Some modern states are less demanding, or even hostile to observing the fast of Ramadan for health reasons and economy. Former President Bourguiba (d. 2000) of Tunisia incited his people to not observe the fast and frequently appeared on television eating and drinking during prescribed hours of fasting. But if the Muslim state sometimes is favorable to ending the fast, society is stern toward any who contravene. Some religious groups tour restaurants and bars to castigate those who consume food publicly during Ramadan[3]. This month creates problems for work and school. Some countries grant reduced or

---

[1] See *Al-mawsu'ah al-fiqhiyyah*: Salat, vol. 31, p. 51-132 and Salat al-jama'ah, p 165-191.

[2] See verses 2:65; 4:154; 7:163; 16:124.

[3] Aldeeb Abu-Sahlieh: *Les mouvements islamistes et les droits de l'homme*, p. 97.

special timetables. As a rule, business becomes slow during this month.

B) Swiss norms

The aforesaid religious norms create problems for work and studies in Switzerland, where weekly rest days are Saturday and Sunday, which correspond to Jewish and Christian practice. With regard to other holidays, there are national and religious feasts, according to the cantons, where Catholic majority exists Catholic religious feasts, and where Protestant majority exists Protestant religious feasts. The federal institutions in the cantons conform themselves to the majority's norms. A federal Catholic servant from Fribourg (canton with catholic majority) who works in Vaud (canton with Protestant majority) observes the holidays of the Protestant workplace. March 20th, 1998, Parliament adopted a modification of the federal law concerning work in industry, handicraft and trade. Article 18 foresees that, when employer is informed, workers can suspend work for confessional holidays not recognized by the cantons. So other religious people than Catholics or Protestants can observe their holidays. In this way, Muslims can take a holiday for the two aforesaid religious feasts.

To our knowledge, there was no demand on behalf of Muslims for Friday as a holiday, or to interrupt work for daily prayers. But the Federal Court admitted the right of Muslim convicts to assemble on Friday to make their common prayers, even obliging authorities to have an imam from outside to preside over the prayer – whereas an imam could be chosen among participants.

This matter was brought up in Regensdorf Prison. April 8th, 1987, the director of the jail rejected the request of Nehal Ahmed Syed, a practicing Muslim prisoner, from meeting 19 fellow Muslim prisoners for common prayer on Friday. Having acted without success with the cantonal Ministry of Justice, the plaintiff formed recourse to the Federal Court, which welcomed it favorably.

The Swiss Federal Court concluded that article 50 par. 1 aCst guaranteed the freedom of worship within the limits set by public order and morality. Freedom of worship is not absolute, but restrictions can be brought only if they are resting on a legal basis, justified by a public interest and respecting the principle of proportionality. It notes that in the jail in question, Protestant and

Catholic chaplains have charge over convicts and, when necessary, chaplains from other confessions should be called (article 42 of the Regulation of the penitentiary). Besides, Protestant and Catholic prayers are organized regularly in the establishment. But then, the attacked decision refuses to allow common Muslim prayer on Friday. The Director of Justice of the canton of Zurich held it was not possible, for good order of the establishment, to allow every religious community organizing worship; an exception is only admitted for national Churches. The Federal Court rejected this argument, concluding that organization difficulties do not clear authorities of their obligation to assure fundamental religious rights.

The Federal Court notes that freedom of conscience and of worship imposes upon the nation state a neutral religious attitude. But, according to tradition, it does not exclude certain advantage granted to recognized churches as communities of public law, notably concerning tax. However this advantage cannot affect religious life. So if only recognized communities, such as national churches, could meet for worship, one could no longer speak of religious freedom. This norm does not address penitentiary establishments differently. To refuse meeting of Muslims on Friday for prayer violates freedom of worship and equality of treatment, "because between national churches and other religious communities no difference exists regarding worship, nor any essential difference in facts that can justify treatment disparity".

The Federal Court took into consideration the difficulty to satisfy everybody. It judged "admissible to organize interdenominational celebrations for adherents of connected confessions. Thus, Christian sects cannot require the possibility to hold their own worship with their own pastor when their adherents can participate in an interdenominational Christian celebration. But then, Muslims cannot take part at Christian celebrations". The Federal Court indicated, "It is true that the Ministry of Justice observes that the Muslim convicts of Regensdorf belong to different sects and would require organization of several separate meetings for Friday prayer. But this manner of seeing things is not acceptable. As one can ask different Christians from different sects to have a common celebration, in the same way one can ask Muslims from different sects to have a common celebration without violating freedom of worship"[1].

This problem also relates to public schools, whose legislation is adapted to prescriptions of the Christian majority since it is impossible, except to reduce the study time, to satisfy all believers. There is not therefore class on Sunday, or during federal or cantonal Christian feasts. For other religions, the situation has long been precarious. It depends on the Authorities who sometimes granted holidays for their religious feasts. In the forties, the Federal Court set a narrow interpretation of the Constitutional norm that states, "Religious beliefs do not exempt anyone from carrying out civic duties" (article 49 par. 5 aCst). School obligation being precisely a "civic duty", Jews did not have the right to miss school on Saturday[2]. Things changed. In a motion of 1988, the Federal Court blamed the canton of Zurich for having applied the cantonal legislation in a petty way and it granted a holiday of five days to participate in a big religious feast[3]. In another case of 1991, the Federal Court specified that school legislation limits religious freedom, but inversely, religious freedom limits school legislation. Stating otherwise: it does not only depend on the legislator to be liberal; the Constitution obliges him to take into consideration, in laws, the religious freedom of pupils. He must not restrict it more than what is required for public interest, that is reasonable execution of educational mandate, and he should respect, in regimentation of holidays; the proportionality principle[4].

Jewish and Christian sects that celebrate Saturday have the advantage that this day precedes Sunday. The proximity of the two days together resulted, for social reasons, in a longer weekend and the regression of the school on Saturday. Several cantons abandoned the school that day; others reduced it to one half-day, dedicated to various light activities. Muslims have less luck. Professor Jean-François Aubert, although a liberal, believes it very unlikely that they ever get a dispensation for Friday, which is a day entirely dedicated for study. It weighs too heavily

---

[1] Federal Court decision 113 Ia 304, JdT 1989 I 268.
[2] Federal Court decision 66 I 157, du 20.9.1940.
[3] Federal Court decision 114 Ia 129, du 19.2.1988.
[4] Federal Court decision 117 II 311 and 315.

to be ousted in the name of religious freedom. On the other hand, he thinks Muslims can ask, in virtue of the Constitution and international conventions, for compensation, for example free time on Friday, for prayers as the prisoners in the previous case[1]. One should notice here, as we saw before, Islamic norms do not prescribe a one-day holiday for Friday, but only a gathering for prayer reserved for males of a certain age. Yet, little should oppose conceding two feast days to Muslims. The *Federal Commission Against Racism* indicates:

> It is necessary to look for pragmatic solutions, not vague ones, which apply to all religious minorities and not only a particular group, for instance Muslims. Rules that allow parents to excuse their children for school absences some days per year without particular explanation can be used by members of all religious communities without indicating the religious adherence[2].

Can one allow Muslim pupils to interrupt courses to accomplish prayers? Neither Jean-François Aubert nor the Commission addresses this question that may arise in Switzerland, like in Italy in 2000. There, a Pakistani father asked the head of a village school near Bologna to allow his nine-year-old girl to pray alone. Ten of the fourteen teachers were opposed. This affair provoked strong controversy in Bologna between the Catholic Church, Muslim community and Evangelical Church; this last supported the Muslim community[3]. We think that such a demand on behalf of the Muslim community in the name of religious freedom cannot be accepted since their religion permits accomplishing unfulfilled prayers at a later hour. Fundamentalist Muslims wanted the University of Cairo courses interrupted, but the Egyptian State, whose official religion is Islam, did not accept this demand. Why ask Western countries to be more agreeable to Muslims' demands than Muslim countries?

The Ramadan fast also creates problems. Certainly, workers can take their yearly holidays during this month, but they cannot ask to reduce the work-time, as do some Muslim countries. The situation is even more difficult for school since the schoolchild cannot take a holiday during this month or have special programs.

---

[1] Aubert: *L'islam et l'école publique*, p. 489-491.

[2] Les musulmanes et les musulmans en Suisse, communiqué, in: *Tangram*, n° 8, March 2000, p. 101.

[3] Corriere della Sera, 16.4.2000.

In neighboring France, the *High Council for Integration* definitely rejected such an arrangement. It thinks that respect for fasting has severe effect: lack of attention and tiredness of pupils, increase of absenteeism and school results decrease. Another difficulty emerges at the end of fasting each day, some pupils ask to leave studies then. The *High Council* notes that the Polyvalent Romain Rolland School in Goussainville had a "committee of pupils" that, after discussing with teachers, made the following compromise: pupils broke the Ramadan fast symbolically by eating a date or sweet without leaving class[1].

5) Mosques and religious personnel

A) Islamic norms

In Muslim countries, there is confusion between Church and State. This confusion is practically required by the Islamic religion. One function of the State is to assure the propagation of Islamic religion, and that religion be respected by its Muslim citizens; even paying for buildings and personnel of Islamic faith.

Islamic law guarantees freedom of worship to recognized religious minorities. The situation differs from one country to another. Thus, in Egypt, it is still not easy to get a permit to construct or repair a Church. Oman bestows lands freely for Church construction.

Saudi Arabia represents the most extreme case, since it forbids any freedom of worship to non-Muslims. Thousands of Christians that work there do not have right to attend Church and cannot meet even in private places to pray in community. Those found out are arrested and sent back in their countries[2]. Answering a letter from pastor Georges Tartar to the Embassy of Saudi Arabia in France[3], a sheik teaching at the University of Medina answered that the whole Saudi Arabia "is considered by Islam a mosque, where two religions could not possibly coexist. Also as it is inconceivable to construct a mosque inside a Church, it is unacceptable to erect a Church in a country that constitutes a

---

[1] *Haut Conseil de l'intégration*, par. 4.4.2.
[2] *Amnesty International Report* 1993, p. 252. See also State Department: Country reports on human rights practices for 1996, February 1997, p. 1371.
[3] *Le Monde*, 28.7.1987.

mosque"[1]. Actually, this attitude of Saudi Arabia comes from the prohibition against non-Muslims residing in Saudi Arabia, according to Muhammad's narrative, "Two religions must not coexist in the Arabian Peninsula"[2], as mentioned before[3].

B) Swiss norms

Article 50 par. 1 aCst stipulated, "The free exercise of acts of worship is guaranteed within the limits set by public order and morality". The 1998 Constitution does not expressly foresee the freedom of acts of worship. The Message of the Swiss Federal Council explains that this freedom is included in article 15 par. 2 that stipulates, "Every person has the right to freely choose his or her religion or philosophical convictions and to profess them alone or in community with others"[4].

As noted above, relations between Church and State are regulated by the cantons. These relations are very complex and differ from a canton to another. Some cantons recognize the statute of public entity to some religious communities and finance their worship buildings and religious personnel. One objective of Muslims that ask for Swiss recognition of Islam is to obtain financial help and the creation of a chair for Islamic Sciences in the Faculty of Theology in a German-speaking canton and another chair in a French-speaking canton financed by Swiss authorities, as are the chairs for Hebrew and Christian studies[5].

Today, Muslims in Switzerland have some mosques and many places of worship. Muslim countries that try to exercise a certain control on their nationals often finance the personnel and places of worship. Thus, with regard to the Turkish community, it is the Cultural Attaché of the Turkish Consulate, through the religious attaché office, that names imams to direct and control the Muslim centers[6]. Conflicts between different political parties in Turkey affect Switzerland, every group trying to place its imam. Some Turks directly bring an imam, at their expense, from Turkey. Saudi Arabia likewise has a big influence, notably through the

---

[1] *Ibid.*, 20.8.1987.
[2] Malik, narrative 1388.
[3] See part I, chap. I.5.
[4] *Message*, p. 158.
[5] Al-Ashmawi: *La condition des musulmans en Suisse*, p. 115-117.
[6] *Le Nouveau Quotidien*, 6.5.1993.

Islamic Cultural Foundation of Geneva and the *Islamic Center of Basel* that it finances. The *Islamic Cultural Foundation of Geneva* is in competition with the *Islamic Center of Geneva*, founded by Saïd Ramadan, which belongs to the movement of *Muslim Brothers*. A place of worship was constructed in 1996 in the city of Bienne, with an important financial contribution of the Swiss authorities proceeding from the parochial tax surplus[1].

Here arises the question of reciprocity. Muslims in Switzerland invoke this principle concerning cemetery and family law. They think that since Muslim countries allow the non-Muslims to have their own cemeteries and the application of their own family law, non-Muslim countries should permit the same thing for Muslims living there. Can one link construction of mosques in Switzerland to construction of Churches in Saudi Arabia or elsewhere according to the principle of reciprocity? The *Federal Commission Against Racism* rejects such an argument, noting, "our democracy is too precious to depend on absolute theocratic behavior"[2]. Such a declaration pleases Muslim members of this Commission who thereby do not have to criticize Saudi Arabia.

The principle of reciprocity, applied generally in commercial reports, cannot be considered for domains of fundamental rights, for lack of which society would sink into barbarism. Thus, Switzerland cannot take the freedom to cut a Saudi thief's hands since Swiss thieves risk having their hands removed in Saudi Arabia. In the same way, one cannot forbid Muslims living in Switzerland, even Saudis, from practicing their faith under the pretext that the freedom of worship of non-Muslims in that country is not respected. It does not mean that Switzerland must close its eyes to violations of religious freedom in Muslim countries. We must require these countries to respect this freedom, notably when it is about constructing mosques financed by Saudi Arabia. Otherwise, one risks opposition of Swiss people when voting on construction projects of Islamic religious places, as was twice the case in Basel and Bern[3].

---

[1] Al-Ashmawi: *La condition des musulmans*, p. 38.

[2] Les musulmanes et les musulmans en Suisse, communiqué, in: *Tangram*, n° 8, March 2000, p. 100.

[3] Mahnig: *L'intégration*, p. 103-104.

Questioned by Jacques Neirynck about construction of worship places for Christians in Saudi Arabia according to reciprocity, Tariq Ramadan, Swiss Muslim activist, notes that Muhammad's narrative, concerning two religions not coexisting in Arabia, is true, but raises questions in its application, adding:

> The only statement of this text should not let us forget superior principles of Islam, which are the respect of other's faiths, the freedom of conscience and worship and the refusal of any constraint concerning religion. If it is clear that one does not imagine a Church actually in Mecca or Medina because these are Muslim spaces carrying a holy dimension, it is not the same case for the other cities and regions of the country.
>
> Moreover, if one accounts for the fact that the same government allows Christians to work on its soil, one is obliged to say that, invoking this specific text, the Saudi government betrays the superior principles of Islam in the field of law[1].

Was this position the beginning of openness toward religious tolerance or, on the contrary, a camouflaged incitement to forbid Christians to work in Saudi Arabia? His brother, Hani Ramadan, Director of the *Islamic Center of Geneva*, justified the absence of Churches and Christian symbols in Saudi Arabia as follows:

> You cannot decently blame the monotheist Islam for wanting to preserve the purity of its faith in its holy places. The "religious symbols" of which you speak, and are supposed to represent God, oppose the universal precepts that one finds in the same Bible, "You shall have no other gods before me. You shall not make for yourself an idol, whether in the form of anything that is in the heaven above, or that is on the earth beneath or that is in the water under the earth". Hence, who more than Muslims respect this divine order[2]?

October 30th, 1993, during the Islamic-Christian dialogue in Yverdon organized by Protestant leaders, Professor Fawzia Al-Ashmawi of the University of Geneva justified the attitude of Saudi Arabia by the fact, "this country is a big mosque and one cannot build a Church inside a mosque". Yet a soccer stadium exists in Saudi Arabia. Would anyone put a stadium in a mosque? Why does one tolerate a soccer stadium in this "big mosque" while not the presence of a Church, or even a Synagogue?

We have already noted that imams in Switzerland received their education in the Muslim countries that send them. This situation

---

[1] Neirynck and Ramadan, p. 26-27.

[2] Ramadan: *Articles sur l'islam et la barbarie*, p. 43 (Pas de contrainte en religion, affirme le Coran, article published in: *Tribune de Genève*, 29.6.1993).

intensifies the problem of integration. The *Federal Commission Against Racism* indicates:

> Spiritual directors have an important role in supporting immigrants and can contribute to cultural integration. The *Federal Commission Against Racism* is struggling so that spiritual directors benefit liberal regulation concerning their admission and work permits. This regulation must take account of the special character of every community concerned. One must ask spiritual directors to encourage integration[1].

This last wish is seldom realized. How can one ask spiritual directors to encourage the integration when they do not understand Swiss society? If Muslim countries delegate spiritual directors, they are part of a foreign institutional setting that exercises control and sanctions them. They will not have independence, and would rather apply the Islamic norms of their own countries. For this reason, we think it is preferable for religious personnel of the different communities be educated in Switzerland, and that this education conform with the Swiss Constitution and laws, notably with regard to sexual and religious non-discrimination and religious freedom. [A similar solution could be found in other Western countries, such as the United States, where immigration concerns are strongly felt now.]

The same problem exists for public chaplainries. These aim to allow people prevented from worshiping where they want to benefit from religious freedom.

Muslims ask for Muslim chaplainry available in various public institutions. Since 1997, official negotiations relating to this question have been held in Geneva, between local government and Muslim associations, including a number of 2nd generation young physicians. These last obtained permission from the chief of the *Department of Health and Social Affairs* to provide a Muslim chaplainry and became closely active with Muslim patients in hospitals and jails of the canton[2]. We already mentioned the decision of the Federal Court concerning the right of Muslims to meet Friday for communal prayer with an external imam.

---

[1] Les musulmanes et les musulmans en Suisse, communiqué, in: *Tangram*, n° 8, March 2000, p. 101.

[2] Al-Ashmawi: *La condition des musulmans en Suisse*, p. 33.

One Catholic chaplain in the Geneva prison notes, "as a rule, Muslim convicts have only Friday prayer for spiritual aid, presided by an imam. With regard to private interviews, where it is possible to confidentially express his situation and to find follow-up support every week, Muslim convicts who want may call upon Catholic or Protestant chaplains, knowing that these are kindly open to all faith convictions, without proselytism"[1]. The chaplain in question also confided that imams are not interest in this kind of activity and do not have contacts with the Catholic or Protestant chaplains.

In the Swiss army, paragraph 2 of the December 20th, 1996 regulation concerning the chaplainry service reports, "Any soldier has the right to spiritual direction. It is the commanders' duty to respect this right in the setting of military service". Paragraph 3 adds, "Spiritual aid is assured by chaplains of the Evangelical-Reformed and Roman Catholic confession". Paragraph 5 stipulates "The chaplain facilitates the spiritual aid of all soldiers, even though they do not belong to their Church". One notes in these norms that the army has chaplains for the main Catholic and Protestant communities, and such chaplains must provide their services for all. Nothing is provided for the Jewish and Muslim communities. Although the latter is more numerous, it is mainly foreign and not as involved in the army. The problem will develop when a greater number of Muslims enter military service. To have a Muslim chaplain, it would be necessary to determine what Muslim religious authority the Army would consult since there is little unity within the Muslim community.

Hospitals arrange a service of religious chaplainry. Some religious personnel come to visit patients regularly, without being called. It is done among both Christians and Jews. At present Muslims do not make use of this service. This practice can only develop if religious personnel are informed by hospital administration of patients belonging to a particular religious group. But now the administration is confronted with the problem of data protection, to avoid patient rights abuse[2].

---

[1] Arbez: *Détenus musulmans dans les prisons suisses*, p. 6.
[2] Pahud de Mortanges: *Fragen zur Integration*, p. 98-99.

Chapter III.
School and religion

School is the place to learn "living together" *par excellence*. It is also where confrontations and resistances can emerge in social conflicts. To determine the limits of Muslim minority' rights, we will explore five questions concerning religion and the school: religious education, distinct religious signs, co-education, course content and Muslim schools. The reader will find in the other chapters the questions concerning holidays (part III, chap. II.4), relations between parents and children over religious education (part III, chap. IV.8) and prohibited food (part III, chap. V).

1) Religious education

A) Islamic norms

To compare between the secular Swiss education system and the education as conceived by Muslims, we will present the situation in Egypt. In that country, religious education is provided for in the Constitution of 1971 as follows:

> Article 12 – Society shall be committed to safeguarding and protecting morals, promoting genuine Egyptian traditions and abiding by the high standards of religious education, moral and national values, the historical heritage of the people, scientific facts, socialist conduct and public manners within the limits of the law. The nation state is committed to abiding by these principles and promoting them.
>
> Article 19 – Religious education shall be a principal subject in the courses of general education.

In Egypt, there is a general education that leads to academic studies and professional teaching. It is divided mainly into two categories:

> - Azharite education: Al-Azhar is the most important Islamic center in the Sunnite Islamic world. In order to fulfill its religious mission, it was endowed by a modern university with numerous faculties and branches, including scientists, in Cairo and other Egyptian cities, but also by college-prep schools. Only Muslims, Egyptians or foreigners, can be registered in Al-Azhar schools and University. Programs of study, approved by Al-Azhar and the government, insist on religious matters and Arabic language. Any academic student, whatever is his branch, must pass religious teaching.
>
> - Civil education: It is provided by governmental or private schools. Private schools are either national, founded by Egyptian Christians, or foreigner, founded by foreign nations such as France, England, etc.; they submit to the Egyptian State except those for diplomatic corps children and those established in agreement with a foreign nation.

> Egyptian private schools, as with any public school, follow programs, either established or approved by the government. They are opened to all, without distinction of religion.

In civil schools, religion occupies weekly just three hours for the primary cycle on a total of 27 to 34 hours of study, and two hours in preparatory and secondary cycles for a total of 34 to 39 hours. In comparison, in Al-Azhar schools, religion occupies weekly 24 hours for the 6th primary year on a total of 42 hours, and 13 hours for the 3rd preparatory year on a total of 39 hours.

Egyptian civil schools teach both Muslim and Christian religion, according to official governmental programs. Parents cannot exclude their children from religious education, nor choose the religion of their children. If one parent is Muslim, the children are inevitably considered Muslim and educated accordingly, even in case of parental apostasy (abandonment of Islam). A commission named by the Ministry of education, composed mainly by orthodox Coptic elements with one Catholic and one Protestant representative, establishes the official course on religion for Christians. This commission tries to establish a manual that covers norms accepted by all Christian communities. For Catholic schools, a *Catechism Center* in Cairo prepares manuals distributed in addition of those imposed by the government. Different communities teach religion to their adherents through the so-called Sunday schools (which meet Friday evening, the official holiday).

Religious education is indicated on the top of the certificate. To be able to pass from one year to the next, it is necessary to pass exams in this subject, but failure is rare. Religion grades are not posted with other grades. University acceptance is based on average grades, with religion grades excluded.

Often students in the same class are not interested in the faith of their colleagues. There are no ecumenical meetings. Government school libraries contain no Christian religious books. This official block against other religions contrasts sharply with the fact that Christians are obliged to learn Islamic notions through the Arabic language. This attitude follows Islamic norms that forbid the Muslim to learn the religion of others, as one will see in point 4 dedicated to the content of courses. Arabic manuals are made and taught exclusively by Muslims, even in Christian schools. Christians must learn Koranic verses and other Islamic elements.

So Christian pupils are obliged to learn the Muslim religion in the Arabic course, whereas Muslim colleagues remain completely ignorant of the Christian faith. Their will to convert Christians is strong[1].

B) Swiss norms

As Switzerland includes many school systems in the different cantons, we will limit discussion here to the general setting established by the Federal Constitution and to the situation in one canton where we live, the canton of Vaud.

On the federal level, par. 2 and 3 of article 49 aCst stipulated:

2) No one may be forced to participate in a religious association, to attend religious teaching or to perform a religious act nor be subjected to penalties of any sort because of his religious beliefs.

3) The holder of the paternal or tutorial authority shall determine the religious education of children in conformity with the foregoing principles until they have completed their sixteenth year.

This article must be completed by article 27 par. 3 aCst, which says, "It shall be possible for the adherents of all religious beliefs to attend public schools without being affected in any way in their freedom of creed or conscience". Article 303 CCS precises:

1) The father and mother provide for religious training of the child.

2) A contract that restricts this power is void.

3) A Child who has completed his sixteen years has the right to choose his own religious faith.

The new Constitution alleviated arrangements of old Constitution over religious teaching without changing its sense. Par. 3 and 4 of article 15 indicate:

3) Every person has the right to join or belong to a religious community and to receive religious education.

4) No person may be forced to join a religious community, to conduct a religious act or participate in religious education.

This article no longer addresses the right of parents since this right is provided for by article 303 CCS, still in force.

Article 62 par. 2 nCst includes an alleviated disposition by comparison with par. 3 of article 27 aCst, "The cantons shall ensure a sufficient primary education open to all children". The findings of the Swiss Federal Council concerning the Constitution states:

---

[1] For more details, see Aldeeb Abu-Sahlieh: *L'enseignement religieux en Égypte*.

> Freedom of conscience and belief implies the principle of the confessional neutrality of the nation state, that is an opening to all religious and philosophical convictions. But this principle does not require of the nation an attitude deprived of any religious or philosophical aspects. The State can privilege, in certain limits (for example, by recognizing national Churches), some religious communities without carrying reach to the religious freedom[1].

The neutral confessional character of the public schools does not limit itself to religious teaching, which must not be characterized as proselytizing. It concerns also the organization of the schools and the attitudes of the teachers, as we will see when we will speak about the distinct religious signs. One can observe in the aforesaid Swiss federal norms the following three fundamental principles:

1) The Constitution guarantees religious freedom to either adhere or not to adhere to a religious community, to either follow or not to follow religious teachings.
2) The father and mother provide for the religious training of the child until 16 years old. At this age, the child is free to choose his own faith.
3) The Constitution forbids obligatory religious education in public schools, which must be organized in the respect of confessional neutrality.

In the canton of Vaud, article 17 par. 3 of its Constitution stipulates, "Teaching must comply to principles of democracy". Article 18 par. 3 adds, "Public schools shall be frequented by adherents of all religious beliefs without being affected in any way in their freedom of creed or conscience". Par. 4 indicates however, "In public schools, religious teaching must comply with principles of Christianity and be distinct from other teachings". The law of June 12th, 1984, concerning the school addressed this religious teaching:

> Article 4 - The school respects the religious, moral and political convictions of the children and their parents. Notably, all type of propaganda is forbidden.
> Article 53 - Teaching biblical history, in conformity with the principles of Christianity, is given to pupils as optional. The department dispenses of this teaching one who demands it out of conscience.

Article 89 of the Regulation of application of October 23, 1985 adds, "The parents who want to dispense children of the biblical history must, in principle, in the beginning of the school year,

---

[1] Message, p. 158.

address a written demand to the director. The master is immediately informed of this demand".

The public school in the Vaud Canton counts fourteen years of schooling of which eleven are obligatory:
- Two years for small children.
- Six years in common.
- Three years optional: on the basis of grades attained, one divides pupils after six years into three groups for last three years: pre-gymnasium option, general option and training option.
- Three years of specialization according to the options: gymnasium leading to the maturity certificate and then to the university, training with special gymnasium for a profession, and basic training.

During none of these years, does the school give religious education. The religious communities are in charge of the religious education of their adherents. However, the school teaches biblical history for one hour per week during the six first years. During the following three optional years, there are courses on Christian culture. During the 1st and 2nd years of gymnasium, there is no religious course. Only in the 3rd year of gymnasium are optional courses on religion offered. None of these courses concerning biblical history and religion is obligatory. Parents can ask that the school excuse their child. If he is older than 16 years, the child himself can choose not to attend. These courses do not have exams and, therefore, there are no grades.

Public schools follow manuals established by the French-speaking *Association of biblical teaching* (so-called ENBIRO), approved by both Protestants and Catholics and by the Public Instruction. These manuals are distributed to pupils freely with other school manuals. Public school teachers, independent of religious adherence, give biblical history teaching on the basis of these manuals. So, an atheist may teach this subject. But a teacher can ask to be dispensed of teaching it for reasons of conscience.

The ENBIRO's manuals have important gabs. To teach the Bible, notably the *Old Testament*, is not comfortable task and risks offending some political sensitivities. As a Christian Palestinian, I have been antagonized by the biblical expressions *Elect People* and *Promised Land*. Pastor Claude Schwab, president of ENBIRO, told me that Swiss Jews also complain because these manuals use the term *Palestine* to designate the territory where events of the Bible occurred. They also wanted to suppress the history of Stephen martyrdom, stoned by Jews. ENBIRO tempts to remedy these problems as much as possible. Thus, it intends to use the term *Palestine/Israel*, but how does one reconcile the irreconcilable? It seems an impossible mission.

These manuals gave me the opportunity to clash with Jews. A Communiqué of the *Geneva union against intolerance*, dated May 27th, 1991, attacked a Missal of the Fundamentalist Monastery of Barroux, approved by the Vatican, containing "serious incitements to anti-Semitism". This Missal asks all to "pray for the treacherous Jews". It adds, "God, grant the prayer that we address you for this blind people. Make them come out of their darkness". Following this communiqué, I sent the following reader's letter to the Swiss press:

> According to the ATS (Swiss Telegraphic Agency) of May 27th, 1991, The *Geneva union against intolerance* protested against the auxiliary bishop of Geneva Mgr. Amédée Grab, for the publication in France of an anti-Semitic Missal, which demanded to "pray for the treacherous Jews".
>
> This Union is right to protest against racist formulas in religious books.
>
> Unfortunately, this is not a unique instance of racism. There are many books of religious education and catechism in the French-speaking cantons of Switzerland, books taught to our children in both schools and Churches.
>
> I had in fact opportunity to read them all, and I have been alarmed by the repeated use (about hundred times) of *People of God*, *Elect people*, etc. Such expressions, taught to our children make them believe that there is a people above other peoples of this world, that the God of love is a racist God. These racist expressions often reappear in our Churches, in prayers, in preaching and in the parochial bulletins.
>
> I wish all books of religious education and catechism circulating in Switzerland, from Christians, Jews and Muslims, be reviewed to eliminate all suspicion of racism, so tomorrow our children will not be emulators of Hitler, or other racists that clutter our already polluted world.

My reader's letter was not pleasing to Zionists in Switzerland, who answered July 9th, 1991 in *Tribune de Genève* under the signature of a certain Maurice Cohen, as follows:

> We are taken aback and burst out laughing to read the smirking letter of Mr. Aldeeb (*La Tribune* of June 12th), which all while reproving the infamous "anti-Semitic French missal", recommends that this holy book be censored, in order to comply, no doubt, with the charter of the PLO which, as one knows, desires the destruction of Israel.
>
> It is no more necessary to say that Israel is the elect people, because otherwise Mr. Aldeeb, the death in the soul, would be obliged to say the God of Israel is a racist God. The Eternal, according to Mr. Aldeeb,

assumed a heavy responsibility in choosing Israel to give him the Book. Mr. Aldeeb wants good to the Lord, and it is why he reproaches Him in a friendly way this gap of language that, fortunately, he believes, can be corrected easily.

But God, decidedly, will not make otherwise. In every paragraph of the Torah, the Eternal says, "I am the God of Israel" and of nobody else. He even designated to His People the land that He destines to it. Should we then make an autodafé of this inexhaustible bestseller, the Torah?

Alas! Christians, for reasons that concern themselves, cluttered the Holy Book of Jews, they call *Old Testament,* and it is little likely that they will agree today to leave it.

Twice alas! Muhammad, in his Koran, covers the *Kitab* (The Book) with praise, and Mr. Aldeeb knows that it did not mean any other book than the Torah.

Thrice alas! There is no UN agency that may be influenced by oil-producing countries capable of censoring the Lord.

Aldeeb means wolf in Arabic. But how does one say pavement?

But all the same, what inconsistency on behalf of the Eternal!

I replied to the letter of Maurice Cohen in the following unpublished letter:

Mr. Maurice Cohen (*Tribune* of July 9th) should be reassured. My letter of June 12th does not recommend censorship of the Bible "in order to comply with the Charter of the PLO" (Mr. Cohen's words). My goal is simpler: to eliminate from our Christian, Jewish and Muslim books of religious education and catechism concepts such as *Elect People, People of God,* etc.

Certainly, the Bible contains such racist concepts, and many others (to read for example chapters 9 and 10 of the Esdras Book). But, it is not the only religion that uses such racist concepts. No one demands to censor these books that belong to the inheritance of humanity and prove the progress of the spirit in history.

All that I ask, is that one does not teach outdated racist concepts to our children as if they were unchangeable dogmas, even though these concepts come from religious books.

Anyone who believes that human beings are equal must care that religion does not convey racism and intolerance. It is time that organizations, Swiss and international, fighting against these two curses, open their eyes to this very serious and very dangerous problem. Their present silence is inadmissible and reprehensible. If this is your opinion, contact me.

Fawzia Al-Ashmawi reproached Swiss school manuals for "containing only some rudimentary information on Islam and Muslims... with a strong emphasis on the tendency for fundamentalism that ravages the Muslim world... As most Muslim children in Switzerland attend public schools, they feel frustrated and have difficulties in adjusting to the secular educational system"[1].

Every society has its own debate over religious education in schools to avoid religious confrontations and to assure social peace. In Switzerland, this debate is augmented because of the increased cosmopolitan character of society and diversity of faiths. I discussed this with the president of ENBIRO, Pastor Claude Schwab, himself a biblical history teacher in the *Normal School* of Lausanne.

According to Pastor Schwab, confessional religious teaching must remain outside school. However, it is necessary to introduce religious sciences, openly discussing all religions, without distinction and without proselytism. For this pastor, Swiss pupils, who are in their majority Christian, must be aware of Christian civilization roots, but at the same time, they must be open to other religions. On the other hand, non-Christian pupils have the right to know the roots of the society that welcomes them.

Professor Roland Campiche already wrote in 1991, "There is no reason why school children know less about God than on the geography of Maghreb". This professor proposes that the *God question* should be addressed to the school in three ways:
- Cultural angle: Christian tradition deeply marks the history and relations of this country. To be unaware of this inheritance, in particular its biblical component, is to be unaware of its roots.
- Comparative angle: How can we expect tolerant attitudes toward Muslim Turks if our knowledge of their religious tradition summarizes in stereotypes and *a prioris*? Teaching religious history is needed if one wants to avoid ethnocentricism that locks many in theoretical ghettos. This type of teaching should include new religious movements. The young generation, often targeted with propaganda, has the right to a minimum of preliminary information.
- Ethical angle: to acquire tools permitting the elaboration of ethical judgment should be considered as a part of citizen's rights[2].

2) Distinctive religious signs in the school

Every society, or even each ethnic or religious group, elaborates its own signs that distinguish it from others and that

---

[1] Al-Ashmawi: *La condition des musulmans*, p. 55.
[2] Roland J. Campiche: Il n'y a pas de raison que les écoliers en sachent moins sur Dieu que sur la géographie du Maghreb, in: *Le Nouveau Quotidien*, 29.11.1991, p. 10.

obey religious or social injunctions, but these signs are not always tolerated. What is obligatory in certain places for modesty is forbidden elsewhere and is considered subversive. Some signs take part in the social or even political cog and can lead to penal condemnations.

A) Islamic norms

The Muslim sartorial norms obey two religious considerations: the prohibition to look like unbelievers and the restrictions concerning modesty.

Prohibition to look like unbelievers is based on a narrative of Muhammad, "One who looks like a group is part of it"[1]. We have also to mention the two following Koranic verses:

> This is my path - a straight one. You shall follow it, and do not follow any other paths, lest they divert you from His path. These are His commandments to you, that you may be saved (6:153).
> Do not be like those who forgot God, so He made them forget themselves. These are the wicked (59:19).

Some classic jurists extrapolate from this the death penalty for those that look like unbelievers and refuse to amend[2]. The prohibition to look like unbelievers covers many domains. So according to the Islamic norms, the Muslim should abstain from shaving the beard and mustaches, while limiting to care for them, norms affirmed recently in some *fatwas* and applied by the Talibans in Afghanistan[3]. But in certain Muslim countries, the beard is considered subversive. Under Sadate, the government raged against beards. Egyptian schools are enjoined to send home, under pretext of cleanliness, students who grow a beard until they shave it. Concerning male clothing, there is the question of wearing the turban and traditional dress or hat and suit in Western style. Today one notices in a city such as Cairo that male Western fashion triumphed, but youths are returning to long white robes, believing that religious perfection consists in being dressed like Muhammad in the 7th century. The triumph of Western fashion is also found in female clothing, but one often reads advertisements along the streets of Cairo praising Muslim fashion, clothing that consists of a long dress, a veil covering the hair and neck, with

---

[1] Ahmad, narrative 5114.
[2] See Al-Luwayhiq, p. 126-127.
[3] *24 Heures*, 25.3.1997.

gloves, all in dark cloth, seems somewhat inappropriate to a hot climate.

In addition to the prohibition to look like unbelievers, men's and women's dress obeys to religious norms on modesty. Indeed, from the Koran and narratives of Muhammad, classic jurists conclude that some parts of the human body are *awrah*[1] (lit.: one-eyed, deficient, repugnant) or *saw'ah*[2] (lit.: bad, ugly). It is prohibited to either expose them or to look at them. The goal of this prohibition is to resist temptation to dissolute living. Women being thought of as the supreme temptation, Islamic law has stricter norms for them. According to some sources, Muhammad said, "There is no more harmful temptation for men than women"[3]. The application of this norm differs from one country to the other. In extreme cases, women cover themselves in public from head to foot, and one does not see their hands, hair, or eyes. They never present themselves to male guests, and men take meals in the absence of women. When they travel in public, they are put in the back of the bus, in a compartment where windows are drawn with black curtains; they are separated from men by another black curtain. It is the case notably in Saudi Arabia and countries of the Gulf. Men in these countries refuse to touch a woman's hand, and vice-versa. In Saudi Arabia, a woman cannot drive a car "because it leads her to unveil her face or part of her face... and because promiscuity with men provokes subversion and incites vice", according to one *fatwa*[4].

In Egypt, the State imposed, in two decrees of 1994, a school uniform and a *certain* standard for Muslim pupils, to avoid a complete veil (*niqab*) covering the entire face and hands. Christian schools must also require uniforms for their pupils, but do not dare oppose the veil. A Muslim father attacked Egyptian norms for unconstitutionality, but the constitutional court confirmed them by concluding that the State could prescribe the sartorial norms, the Koran not foreseeing any categorical and

---

[1] This term is in the verses 24:32 and 58, and 33:13.
[2] This term is in the verses 5:31, 7:20, 22 and 26-27, 20:121.
[3] This narrative of Muhammad is quoted in an Egyptian school textbook: Al-Sanhouri: *Al-usrah fil-tashri al-islami*, p. 203.
[4] *Majallat al-buhuth al-islamiyyah*, n° 24, 1989, p. 75, and n° 30, 1990-1991, p. 297-298.

clear norms in this domain. The court specified that a woman does not have freedom to choose her dress, this not being a private matter. It is not necessary that a woman's dress pass limits of moderation[1].

Some national and Muslim intellectuals consider Muslim dress, notably female dress, as an oppression of women, or even a hindrance to social progress, because it shuts in women and limits their movement. For religious movements, Muslim dress is a sign of virtue and modesty, not hesitating to carry extreme value judgment against those that follow Western fashion and are not veiled, sometimes calling them prostitutes.

B) Swiss norms

Switzerland is a multi-cultural and multi-confessional country. Each has the right to exhibit his religious signs to mark his difference, and to clothe himself as he chooses while not offending public modesty. This does not prevent authorities from addressing some litigations concerning this matter

One case concerned a motorcyclist Sikh required to pay a fine for not respecting a red light and not wearing a protective helmet. The Sikh argued against the second charge before the Federal Court, since his religion forbids allowing his head to be uncovered in public, and so it was not possible for him to carry the helmet with the turban. Any coercive act obliging him to remove his turban would constitute discrimination. The Federal Court answered that according to article 49 par. 1 aCst, "Freedom of creed and conscience is inviolable". Freedom of religion guarantees the right to have religious or ideological convictions and, in certain limits, to express them, to propagate them and to practice them. Religious dress is protected, but freedom of conscience and belief can be limited provided there is legal basis, major public interest and respect of the proportionality principle. So article 49 par. 5 aCst says, "Religious beliefs do not exempt anyone from carrying out civic duties". The Federal Court recalled the judgment of July 12th, 1978 of the *European Commission of Human Rights*, in which a motor-cyclist was obliged to carry a helmet in the interest of public security which, according to article 9 par. 2 ECHR, justifies a reach to freedom of religion. Therefore, the freedom of conscience and belief of Sikhs,

---

[1] *Official Gazette* n° 21, 30.5.1996, p. 1026-1041.

most notably evident in the wearing of a turban, is not injured by the obligation to wear a protective helmet imposed to drivers of mopeds. And as his religious norms do not forbid the helmet nor impose exclusively the turban, the Sikh in question could exchange his turban for a helmet when driving a moped[1].

In another case concerning Muslims, the Foreigners' Police in Bienne refused the renewal of the residence permit of Turkish women since they did not want to provide photos without the veil. In the proceedings of this case, the Foreigners' Federal office decreed November 15, 1993 a guideline inviting the local and cantonal authorities to suppleness by allowing Muslims to wear veils in their identity photographs[2].

In Neuchâtel Canton, the school commission decided, in 1998, to expel an eleven year old Muslim student from public school in Chaux-de-Fonds because she wore an "Islamic veil that denotes sexual discrimination in relation to men, discrimination much more important since the minor girl cannot oppose to her father's will"[3]. The *Department of Education and Culture* admitted the father's recourse, based on the position adopted in 1996 by the *Intercantonal Conference for Public Instruction in French-speaking cantons and Tessin*. Accordingly, it allowed pupils to carry traditional religious symbols (as cross, kippa or veil). The cantonal administrative court then confirmed this decision in June of 1999[4].

In June of 1999, Geneva University Hospitals refused a practicum for three Muslim medical students who wished to wear Islamic veils during their work. The *Federal Commission Against Racism* did not consider this refusal as discriminatory[5]. These three students yielded before the administrative decision and accepted the solution to follow their practicum in a private hospital in Geneva. Annotating this case, Fawzia Al-Ashmawi (who does not even wear a veil!) writes, "the Muslim population was shocked by the politicization over the question of wearing

---

[1] Federal Court decision 119 IV 260, JdT 1994 I 707.

[2] Al-Ashmawi: *La condition des musulmans en Suisse*, p. 49.

[3] Journal de Genève et Gazette de Lausanne, 4.2.1998.

[4] Deuxième et troisième rapports périodiques présentés par la Suisse, par. 183.

[5] *Ibid.*, par. 184.

the Islamic veil, a religious obligation for all practicing Muslims, which should not be a justifying pretext for discrimination against Muslim women"[1].

Switzerland has not yet witnessed debate concerning the veil like France, where it has provoked several litigations and court decisions. Swiss constitutionalist Jean-François Aubert wonders "if Muslim girls can wear veils in school, during courses, or if the school authorities can oblige them to remove them". He answers, "For us, the answer is clear, the wearing of the veil is permitted and one cannot even understand that there are so many stories concerning this point". For him, authorities can forbid extravagant dresses, those that embarrass work or disturb communication making it difficult to identify pupils. None of these reasons is opposable to the veil. The veil of which Jean-François Aubert speaks is "a material that hides hair and neck, but allows the face to be seen". He does not consider veils that "cover the face and hide with grating as one encounters in some oriental countries"[2].

Answering objections based on sexual equality, Professor Jean-François Aubert explains that the veil does suggest inequality only by association of ideas: because it is prescribed in the Koran, because this same book contains, in other places, verses without ambiguity on the subordination of women, because it is notorious that more literal Muslims adhere to the superiority of the male sex. The association of ideas is incontestably strong, but it is not decisive. The inequality is not indeed the only religious message the veil communicates. There is another message that is quite distinct, female modesty, which can appear excessive, but which is hard to condemn. After all, the time is not so long ago when our mothers or grandmothers also observed a reserved attitude in public. He adds:

> One could say: this is not chosen by them, it is their fathers who impose it... Non-Muslim parents also impose things that do not suit their children. Then children become adult, they will make, of all these precepts, what is pleasing to them. But, as minor, it is necessary to shelter them somewhere, normally in their family, where they are most beloved and best treated. It seems to us that this is not the role of the State, except in exceptional cases, to force the children to disobedience. And then, to conclude, it is necessary to see where the intransigence of

---

[1] Al-Ashmawi: *La condition des musulmans en Suisse*, p. 48.
[2] Aubert: *L'islam et l'école publique*, p. 482.

> the State leads: the most practicing family will simply withdraw their children from public school and educate them in an imam school or at home. What a beautiful result for the integration and advancement of female cause[1]!

If one admits individual freedom to bear some religious signs within certain limits, the nation state still has a problem, as it must display confessional neutrality. Can the State exhibit distinctive religious signs in public places? The question was expressed through crucifixes in classrooms, and secondly through the veil of a Muslim schoolmistress, in a Geneva public school.

In the first case, on September 26th, 1990, Swiss Federal Court accepted a claim presented by a teacher and parents of pupils in the Catholic canton of Tessin, that a crucifix in the classroom be removed[2]. To avoid conflict, the Court specified that its decision concerns only "the presence of the crucifix in a room used for teaching pupils of various faiths, who have not yet completed their religious majority age". It excludes from its decision "the presence of a crucifix in other public places, as courts or where executive or legislative authorities meet". It adds that its decision may have been different "if it concerned the presence of a crucifix in a place of common use in the school, such as the entrance hall, passageway, dining hall or room intended for worship or optional religious education". It held that the freedom of conscience and belief does not require absolute neutrality of the State in a religious matter. To sustain the opposite would question the present relations between Church and State in the cantons and other religious aspects such as dominical or federal fasting. According to the Court, "secularism of the State means an obligation of neutrality that imposes abstaining, in public acts, of any confessional consideration susceptible to compromise citizen freedom in a pluralistic society".

Hani Ramadan, Imam of the *Islamic Center of Geneva*, approved this decision. He wrote, "It is obvious that the school space must remain imperatively neutral: a cross on the wall, or Koranic verses displayed in the corner of a class are not compatible with secularism"[3]. On the other hand, he strongly

---

[1] *Ibid.*, p. 485-486.

[2] Federal Court decision 116 Ia 252, JdT 1992 I 5.

[3] Ramadan: *Articles sur l'islam et la barbarie*, p. 91 (Nous n'avons rien à cacher, article published in: *Le Courrier*, 11.2.1997).

criticized the decision of the Federal Court forbidding a Muslim schoolmistress from wearing a veil in a Geneva public school.

This affair concerns a Swiss citizen, born in 1965, hired as schoolmistress on September 1st, 1990. She became Muslim in March of 1991 and married, October 19th, 1991, an Algerian. She wore the Islamic veil for the first time in class at the end of the school year 1990-1991 by respect of the Koranic prescription enjoining to women to veil before adults and pubescent males. In May 1995, the inspector of the school in Vernier informed the General administration of primary schools of the canton of Geneva that the schoolmistress wore an Islamic veil regularly in school, adding to never have heard parents' remark on this subject. August 23rd, 1996, the General administration forbad the teacher from wearing the veil in the exercise of her professional activities and responsibilities, for such contradicted the law of public instruction that stipulates:

> Article 6 - Public teaching guarantees respect of political and confessional convictions of pupils and parents.
> Article 120 par. 2 - Civil servants must be secular. Exception to this norm can be accepted only for the academic body teaching.

Article 27 par. 3 aCst proclaims, "It shall be possible for the adherents of all religious beliefs to attend public schools without being affected in any way in their freedom of creed or conscience". The General administration of education concluded that wearing the veil constitutes "a conspicuous model of identification imposed by the teacher to the pupils, moreover in a public and secular school system". The schoolmistress fought against this decision in the State Council of Geneva, August 26, 1996, which rejected her claim on October 16th, 1996, for the following reasons:

> The teacher must (...) adopt the objectives assigned to the public school as well as the liabilities imposed to the school authorities, including strictly neutral confessional obligation (...).
> The litigious dress (...) represents (...), independently of the intention of the teacher, a vector of a religious message sufficiently strong (...) which does not limit to the personal realm of the plaintiff but rebound in the institution that she represents, i.e., the public school[1].

The plaintiff appealed to the Federal Court on November 25th, 1996, invoking that the prohibition of the veil is a violation of the

---

[1] Council of the State of Geneva, decision 16.10.1996 (unpublished).

"intangible core of religious freedom" according to article 9 ECHR. The Federal Court rejected her claim and confirmed the decision of the State Council of Geneva, on November 12th, 1997. It notified its decision November 18th, 1997[1].

In a preliminary analysis, the Federal Court said that, contrary to what the schoolmistress claimed, "there is no doubt that wearing the veil and ample clothes is not for aesthetic reasons, but in order to obey religious requirements (...). It constitutes a strong religious symbol which shows immediately visible sign to a third party, clearly indicating adherence to a particular religion".

Swiss Federal Court noted, "according to article 9 par. 2 ECHR, the freedom to express religion or conviction can be restricted, contrary to the interior freedom which has an absolute character as it cannot, by nature, reach public order, and therefore escapes all restriction. Even though it is especially important for the plaintiff, and even though it may not be only an expression of religious conviction, but obeys an imperative religious requirement, wearing the veil and ample clothes remains an external demonstration which does not belong to the intangible core of religious freedom".

The Federal Court indicates, "civil servants are submitted to special public rules, to which they adhered freely and to which they hold interest. This fact justifies that they benefit public liberties in a limited measure". It recalled articles 6 and 120 par. 2 of the cantonal law of November 6th, 1940 on public instruction and articles 164ss of the canton's Constitution according to which this canton has full separation of Church and State. "In this case, concludes the Federal Court, the prohibition made to use a veil clearly indicating adherence to a determined confession concretizes the will of Geneva legislature, expressed in the aforementioned arrangements, to respect in school matters religious neutrality and separation of Church and State. Therefore, even though the undertaken decree included a serious breach of religious freedom, it had sufficient legal basis".

Answering the objection that Geneva decision does not address public interest, the Federal Court stated:

> By showing strong religious signs inside the walls of the school, or
> even in class, the plaintiff can infringe the religious feelings of her

---

[1] Federal Court decision 123 Ia 296.

pupils, of other pupils in the school and their parents. Certainly, neither the pupils nor their parents complained. But it does not mean that none were upset. Possibly some gave up intervening directly to not make situations worse, while hoping for a spontaneous official school reaction. Besides, the public opinion expressed concern about this problem. The plaintiff had numerous interviews and the High Council adopted a resolution following the decision taken by the State Council. Likewise, if school authorities did not immediately intervene with a decision after the inspector informed them of the practice, this must not be seen as implicit assent. It is reasonable that school authorities first attempted to address matters quietly.

The decision is in conformity with the principle of confessional neutrality at school, whose goal is not only to protect religious convictions of pupils and parents, but also to assure religious peace that, in some aspects, remains fragile. In this consideration, schools would risk becoming a place of religious confrontation if teachers were allowed by their behavior, notably their dress, to show strongly their convictions in this domain.

Thus, there is an important public interest to forbid the wearing of the Muslim veil.

In respect to the proportionality principle, the Federal Court adds:

Freedom of conscience and belief obliges the State to observe confessional and religious neutrality; the citizen can prevail himself in this respect of individual rights. (...). Neutrality aims to take into consideration, without partisanship, all existing concepts in a pluralistic society. The principle that the State must not favor or penalize a person for religious motives has general application and it ensues directly from articles 49 and 50 aCst. Finally, secularism of the State summarizes itself in an obligation of neutrality that imposes abstention, in the public acts, from any confessional or religious consideration susceptible to compromising citizens' freedom in a pluralistic society. In this sense, it aims to preserve the freedom of religion and to maintain in a spirit of tolerance, the confessional peace.

This neutrality has particular importance in public schools, because education is obligatory for all, with no difference between faiths. In this matter, article 27 par. 3 aCst, according to which "It shall be possible for the adherents of all religious beliefs to attend public schools without being affected in any way in their freedom of creed or conscience", is the corollary of the freedom of conscience and belief. (...)

Thus, the attitude of teachers has important role. Even by their lone behavior, they have a strong influence on their pupils; they represent a model for pupils who are especially receptive by reason of their young age - to which they are not able in principle to resist - and by reason of the hierarchical nature of this relation. In fact, the teacher is holder of school authority and represents the State, to which his behavior is imputed. It is therefore especially important that he exercises functions that transmit knowledge and develop faculties, while remaining confessionally neutral.

After extensive analysis of this neutrality requirement, the court concluded:

> To forbid wearing the veil puts the plaintiff in front of a difficult alternative: not to respect a precept of her religion she considers important, or to affront the risk not to teach in public schools.
>
> On the other hand, the veil is an obvious religious sign. Besides, the plaintiff teaches in primary school young suggestible children. Certainly, she is not blamed for proselytism or for trying to convince pupils of a particular faith. But she cannot avoid the questions of the pupils. It appears rather delicate to invoke aesthetic elements or sensitivity in respect to cold weather ... as the children realize that this argument is a loophole. She is therefore unable to answer them without exposing her convictions. However, the plaintiff detains part of school authority and personifies the school even though other teachers there hold other religious opinions. Such a representation appears with difficulty conceivable with the principle of non-identification, as the behavior of a civil servant should be imputed to the State. Finally, it is necessary to recall that the canton of Geneva opted for full separation of Church and State that results notably in a secular public education.
>
> Furthermore, one should notice that wearing the veil is with difficulty reconcilable with the principle of sexual equality (cf. Sami Aldeeb, *Musulmans en terre européenne*, *PJA* 1/96 p. 42ss. spec. letter d p. 49). However, it is a fundamental value of our society, dedicated by explicit constitutional disposition (article 4 par. 2 aCst), which must be taken in consideration by the school.
>
> Besides, confessional peace finally remains in spite of all, fragile, and the attitude of the plaintiff is susceptible to provoke negative reaction, or even confrontation, that one should avoid. It is necessary to take in consideration, while weighing the interests, that wearing the veil would lead to accept strong sartorial symbols of other religions, for example the cassock or the kippa (the State Council admits that teachers carry in the school a discreet religious signs, as a jewel ...). Such consequences could jeopardize the principle of confessional neutrality in school. One can finally note that it would be difficult to conceive forbidding the crucifix in public school and in the same time to admit that teachers carry strong religious symbols, of any faith.

Note here that in the present case the Federal Court forbids wearing the Islamic veil in public schools only for teachers, and not for pupils. The *Federal Commission Against Racism*, still extremely favorable for Muslims, was pleased with this decision because it advises the cantonal and local authorities to resolve with pragmatism the problems bound to minority reports. It says not to be favorable to the general prohibition of the veil, but believes that people holding symbolic function of authority (such as an educational staff) should renounce its use[1]. Muslims, on the other hand, criticized this decision. Thus, Hani Ramadan, Imam of the *Islamic Center of Geneva*, denounced the decision of Geneva[2] as well as that of the Federal Court. In an article titled "For a plural secularism", he wrote:

> It is necessary to first consider that the five judges who compose the Federal Court are not infallible. Anti-religious intellectuals who shout victory should have the decency to consider that human decisions are susceptible to mistakes, and are not Gospel. Because, in short, they have just legitimized in a bewildering way a wrongful action that simply consists in forbidding a religious practice, in opposition to article 9 ECHR, … article 49 of our Constitution… and article 18 of the International Covenant… The entire Muslim community of this country, all institutions and mosques, are deeply shocked by this religious discrimination, of which they are victims. Neither the Geneva Department of Public Instruction, nor the State Council, nor the Federal Court consulted imams or any Swiss Muslim representatives before reaching this decision… [Muslims] will never be able to admit that this State establishes itself as defender of ideology, aiming to exclude the signs of religious adherence from public space in general and school space in particular. Instead of protecting individual freedoms, this is a type of "secularism" that attacks conscience, and tries to impose its unique and singular view. The public domain is not the sole property of atheists and free thinkers that claim the right to furnish it, as they like… Some atheists and free thinkers want to construct the outside world to their own image: without God, without religious sign, emptied of all living and visible spirituality form… These masters of modern thought, seated on the shaky throne of republican secularism to which they avow real devotion, promulgate decrees that aim to expel of the secular domain everything that closely recalls God's existence[3].

Elsewhere, Hani Ramadan qualifies those that are opposed to wearing the Islamic veil at school as "secular torturers"[4].

Feeling supported by fundamentalist Muslims of Geneva, the schoolmistress appealed May 16th, 1998 to the European Court of Human Rights, but this one, in its decision of February 15th, 2001,

---

[1] Les musulmanes et les musulmans en Suisse, communiqué de presse, in: *Tangram*, n° 8, March 2000, p. 100-101.

[2] See Ramadan: *Articles sur l'islam et la barbarie*, p. 80-97.

[3] *Ibid.*, p. 98-101 (Pour une laïcité plurielle, article published in: *Journal de Genève*, 5.12.1997, and *Le Courrier*, 24.1.1998).

[4] Ramadan: *La femme en islam*, p. 53.

considered her demand as inadmissible[1]. The schoolmistress presented two main grievances:

> 1) The plaintiff thinks that the prohibition to wear the veil while teaching violates her rights, guaranteed in article 9 ECHR, to freely express religion, that this prohibition did not pursue a legitimate goal and that wearing the veil did not create any manifest trouble in the school.

The Court answers that "in a democratic society, where several religions coexist in one population, it may be necessary restricting the religious freedom to reconcile various groups and to assure respect of all convictions". It adds, "Considering the circumstances known by the court and the terms of three decisions, the court holds that the measure pursued legitimate goals according to article 9 par. 2: the protection of the rights and freedoms of others, public safety and public order". The restriction of the plaintiff's right to express her religion freely is justified "by the necessity to protect, in a democratic society, the right of pupils in public schools to receive a formation dispensed in context of religious neutrality. Religious convictions have been fully taken into account in front of the imperatives to protect the rights and freedoms of others and to preserve the public safety and public order. It is also clear that the litigious decisions are based on these imperatives and not on objections to the plaintiff's religious convictions".

The Court "admits that it is very difficult to appreciate the impact that a strong visible sign such as wearing the veil can have on the freedom of conscience and belief of young children. Indeed, the plaintiff taught in a class of children between four and eight years and therefore of pupils being in an age where they ask a lot of questions and can be more influenced than pupils of more advanced age. How would one be able thus to deny a proselytizing effect from wearing the veil, imposed on women by Koranic prescription which is, as noted by the Federal Court, with difficulty reconcilable with the principle of sex equality? Also, it seems difficult to reconcile the Islamic veil with the message of tolerance, of respect of others and especially of equality and non-discrimination that in a democracy any teacher must transmit to his pupils".

---

[1] Decision of 15.2.2001 recorded as n° 42393/98 in case Lucia Dahlab vs. Switzerland. In: http://hudoc.echr.coe.int/hudoc/ViewRoot.asp.

The Court adds, "While balancing the right of the schoolmistress to express her religion and the right of the pupils to protection through the safeguard of religious peace, the Court thinks that in view of the circumstances and, notably, the low age of the pupils who are under the care of the plaintiff as representative of the State, Geneva authorities did not go beyond their margin of appreciation and therefore the measure they took was not unreasonable". It concludes, "the prohibition of the veil in the education setting constituted a necessary measure in a democratic society".

> 2) The plaintiff considers the prohibition expressed by the Swiss authorities as sexual discrimination, according to article 14 ECHR, as a Muslim man could teach in public school without incurring prohibition of any nature.

The Court answered, "The prohibition not to wear the Islamic veil during the professional activities does not aim her adherence to the female sex, but follows the legitimate goal of respecting neutrality of public primary school education. Such measure may also apply to conspicuous male clothing in similar circumstances".

3) Co-education

A) Islamic norms

Islamic law established norms forbidding promiscuity between men and women and imposed strict sartorial measures. It is sufficient here to mention two passages from the Koran:

> Tell the believing women to subdue their eyes, and maintain their chastity. They shall not reveal any parts of their bodies, except that which is necessary. They shall cover their chests, and shall not relax this code in the presence of other than their husbands, their fathers, the fathers of their husbands, their sons, the sons of their husbands, their brothers, the sons of their brothers, the sons of their sisters, other women, the male servants or employees whose sexual drive has been nullified, or the children who have not reached puberty. They shall not strike their feet when they walk in order to shake and reveal certain details of their bodies (24:31).
>
> Tell the believing men that they shall subdue their eyes, and to maintain their chastity. This is purer for them (24:30).

The Koran (7:27-28) and many narratives of Muhammad also forbid public nudity. From these two sources, classic Muslim jurists determine which body parts cannot be exposed, parts qualified as *awrah* [1] (lit.: one-eyed, deficient, repugnant) or *saw'ah* [2] (lit.: bad, ugly):

- In male-to-male relations: are considered as repugnant the parts from navel to knee. So it is forbidden for a man to look at the thigh of another man.
- In female-to-female relations: repugnant parts also extend from navel to knee. Some forbid the non-Muslim woman from looking at the body of a Muslim woman to avoid that she describes the Muslim woman to her non-Muslim husband.
- In female-to-male relations: the woman can look at any part of her husband's body. With regard to her father's body, brother and paternal or maternal uncle, she does not have the right to look at his body between navel and knee. For other people, it is forbidden for woman to look at their body, but some classic jurists prohibit her from only looking at the part between navel and knee.
- In male-to-female relations: some classic jurists say that all the woman's body is repugnant, including her nails. Some jurists exclude the face and hands. All invoke the Koranic verses and narratives of Muhammad in support of their opinion.

As a result of these norms, co-education between boys and girls should be forbidden. This prohibition also extends to universities in countries such as Saudi Arabia. If the Egyptian State University, contrary to the University of Al-Azhar, permits the co-education, this situation is criticized by Muslim surroundings and it leads fundamentalists to impose separation between students within classrooms.

Prohibition of co-education extends to sports, notably swimming, because men and women expose body parts forbidden to be seen by the opposite sex. In this respect, Iran organizes sport competitions solely reserved for women. Such rules are not respected everywhere, especially on beaches, causing anger amongst fundamentalist Muslims[3].

B) Swiss norms

Swiss public schools are mixed, from primary grades to university. They are opened to all without discrimination for sex or religion. I am not aware of problems with Muslims who send their children to public schools, although their attitude constitutes a violation of Islamic norms. However, parents refuse that their

---

[1] This term is in the verses 24:32 and 58, and 33:13.
[2] This term is in the verses 5:31, 7:20, 22 and 26-27, 20:121.
[3] For more details, see Aldeeb Abu-Sahlieh: *Limites du sport en droit musulman et arabe.*

daughters participate in the mixed events, only permitting obligatory school activities. For the moment, only the swimming courses created some problems.

In Lausanne, parents of two pupils, an Afghan and a Turk, asked not to require from their daughters lessons of swimming pool. Authorization was granted, "because it was necessary to avoid by any means to harden conflict", which would have led to more extreme marginalization for the girls, explained the school's dean, adding, "No one is going to force them to wear a swimsuit, it is necessary to be patient!"[1]

Another case of swimming pool emerged in the canton of Zurich. The cantonal authorities refused dispensation of swimming courses asked by a Turkish father for his 11-year-old daughter. Requisite dispensation was found on religious motives, the father claiming that Islam forbade men and women to swim together. The father appealed then to the Federal Court in his own name and as legal representative for his daughter, presenting his case as a violation of religious freedom, guaranteed by article 49 aCst and article 9 ECHR.

In its decision of June 18th, 1993, the Federal Court admitted his recourse. It concluded that it was up to the parents to choose religious education of children younger than sixteen, as a component of their own religious freedom. The father can invoke his right to represent his daughter as well as his own right. When parents are married, one can presume that each parent acts in agreement with the other, unless they show otherwise.

The Swiss Federal Court indicates that according to articles 49 par. 1st and 5 aCst and article 9 ECHR, the cantons cannot restrict religious freedom beyond what is required for public interest and the principle of proportionality. It specifies, "the constitutional guarantee of religious freedom does not only protect Western Churches or communities; the protective field extends to all religions, independent of the number of followers in Switzerland. Islamic religion is thereby protected". It adds that individuals can deduce from the religious freedom the right to behave according to the precepts of their religion and personal convictions. Religious freedom also extends to all expressions of religious life, as long as generally recognized moral requirements in our

---

[1] Le Nouveau Quotidien, 19.11.1993.

civilization are respected. Thus, faith dictates suitable behavior in given situations. The religious prescriptions concerning the clothing can be included in the protective field of the religious freedom. The Federal Court notes some religions, such as Islam, have requirements in all domains of human activity, but one should distinguish behaviors expressing belief from other behaviors; otherwise the reach of religious freedom would be limitless.

The Federal Court understood that Islamic norms do not allow children of different sexes to swim together, as commonly done in primary school. It refers to prescriptions of the Koran, particularly verses 24:31 and 33:59. It concluded that some Islamic adherents forbid women or girls to bathe with men unless their parents were nearby. It does not matter if a majority or a minority of Muslims observes this norm. Demonstration of a belief is even protected when it ensues from a minority religious view. There is no reason to examine whether, in country of origin (Turkey), the rule in question is extensively observed or not. Obligation to participate in mixed swimming courses represents therefore, in this regard, a breach of religious freedom.

The Federal Court saw that according to article 49 par. 5 aCst, "Religious beliefs do not exempt anyone from carrying out civic duties". But when the legislator defines citizen's duties, he must also consider public interest and the principle of proportionality. School constitutes a civic duty and can be required against the will of parents, because the general interest is most important. School must provide for the greatest common denominator. One cannot admit a general school activity dispensation when requirements of a religion are especially strict, because a very neat and efficient education would not be assured anymore.

The Federal Court noted that it is necessary to balance private interests with public interests when fervent followers prevail themselves of an essential rule of their religion. Indeed, they are facing the following alternative: not to respect a religious prescription or to violate State's norms. It not only results in conflict of conscience, but also a conflict between family life and school activities, conflict in which children may suffer. When interests of parents and child oppose, there is no justification to privilege the child's good unless observance of religious prescription causes concrete and tangible difficulties. It would be thus in cases risking a child's health, or if formation was compromised concerning equality (including the equality between men and women) and would no longer be guaranteed, or if the child was deprived of indispensable education. However, says the Federal Court, requisite dispensation does not concern an indispensable discipline that would compromise acquirement of schooling of value, and the girl will not be underprivileged in this case. It notes besides that the father promised he would instruct his daughter in swimming, adding, "It is obvious that he will meet some practical problems, but there is no reason to doubt his sincerity on this point".

The Federal Court added, "One no longer sees what problems of school organization the concession of requisite dispensation could cause; one no longer sees what very neat and efficient teaching it would compromise. Such a dispensation can be compared to those that foresees the cantonal school legislation for Jewish or Adventist children who can give up school activities on Saturday". It rejects the idea that the dispensation could compromise the integration of foreigners, "Other country nationals who stay in Switzerland are submitted to the same legal order than the Swiss citizens. They have no legal obligation however, when they come from other cultures, to adapt their way of life to the one of Switzerland. The principle of integration is not a rule of law that could justify some disproportionate reaches to the religious freedom"[1].

The Federal Court has been criticized for not having required the mother to sign the recourse. According to the criticism, the Federal Court should have insisted on this fact, notably vis-à-vis of patriarchal culture nationals. On the other hand, one criticized the argument of the Federal Court according to which the concession of the dispensation does not disturb education within the primary school in question. Indeed, prescriptions of clothing, and rules concerning public swimming have no relation with the question to know if education is possibly disrupted. These prescriptions would be only the woman's humiliation. The goal put forward of the protection of female sex means imposing the tutelage of the woman, in violation of the equality of treatment between men and women. Some have also criticized the Federal

---

[1] Federal Court decision 119 I 178.

Court for disregarding the political consequences of this affair. The attitude of the foreigners who refuse to integrate could provoke reactions of defense among the local population and so lead to racist feelings[1].

Tariq Ramadan asks in this respect that Muslim girls be regrouped with an instructor for swimming courses in the respect of principles of the Islamic modesty[2]. Annotating the decision of the Federal Court, professor Jean-François Aubert has the same proposition and believes that it would not be very difficult, nor very expensive, to organize separate courses in private swimming pools or on the calm sides of a lake, but then obligatory, for girls – and maybe also for boys – that do not wish to mix sexes[3].

Let us be liberal as suggested by professor Jean-François Aubert. What would be the position of the Swiss authorities if Muslim parents require that the State organize separate classes for girls in the name of the religious freedom? This question will no longer linger.

In this respect, the *Cultural Association of Muslim Women* rent a swimming pool a few hours some days for them alone in order to be able to conform themselves to Islamic norms. One advertising circular, made by this Muslim association, announced a "Swimming pool exclusively for women in the Hauterive Sports Center (Neuchâtel Canton), from 12.30 to 14.30". It indicates, "The dress should be composed of a long short (bicyclist) and a one-piece swimsuit (or tee-shirt), with a bathing cap". It adds, "Boys are admitted until the age of 6 years". Certainly, Swiss law cannot oblige a Muslim to frequent a mixed swimming pool, but a Muslim husband can not force his wife to only frequent some swimming pools reserved for women. Such a constraint could be considered a reason for divorce.

4) Content of courses

A) Islamic norms

If the Muslims contributed extensively to the progress of sciences and philosophy, one always observed, as in the West, a

---

[1] See Blaise Knapp: *Annuaire international de justice constitutionnelle*, 1993, p. 672-674.
[2] Ramadan: *Les musulmans dans la laïcité*, Tawhid, p. 122.
[3] Aubert: *L'islam à l'école publique*, p. 494.

conflict between the religious surroundings and scientists. It is sufficient to recall the case of Galileo (d. 1642) who has been forbidden, in 1633, by the Church to teach his theory concerning the rotation of the Earth around the Sun. Although the Church admitted his theory in the 19th century, it recognized its error only in 1992 in the Pope's speech to the Pontifical academy of sciences. The Pope qualified this case as a "sad misunderstanding"[1]. The same problem was raised in our time by Ibn-Baz (d. 1999), the highest Saudi religious authority, who repeated that the theory of the rotation of the Earth around the Sun contradicts the Koran. One who professes it should be put to death for apostasy[2].

Other topics meet reticence so much at the Christians as at Muslims. It is notably the case of Darwin whose evolutionist theory is rejected by fundamentalist Christians and Muslims. Fundamentalist Muslims also ask to throw out the philosophical writings of Averroes.

Egypt knew several resounding cases in report with education, most famous being the one of Taha Husayn (d. 1976) who, in a book of 1926 taught at Cairo University, qualified the story of Abraham and Ishmael as legend, although it is mentioned in the Koran. The Public attorney, thanks to a particular political conjuncture, classified the claim of the religious authorities, but the author suppressed incriminated passages in subsequent editions. Fundamentalist Muslims frequently profane his memorial at the entrance of the Arts Faculty of Cairo University.

One will recall here a certain reticence on behalf of Muslims to read the texts of other religions. After riots of January 18th to 19th, 1977, Sadate gathered the Muslim and Christian religious leaders. Pope Shenouda, head of the Orthodox Coptic Church, proposed making common books on religion and social ethics. Sadate answered, "I agree that it is necessary to write books with a new style for our children. We want to speak to them with the language of the century. There should be common books. It is an excellent idea"[3]. Some days after, *Al-I'tisam*, Islamic magazine, warned the Minister of the education against this proposition,

---

[1] *The Galileo Case*. See also Allègre, p. 11-52.
[2] Majallat al-kifah al-arabi, 27.11.1995.
[3] *Al-Ahram*, 9.2.1977.

"Take guard to disdain your religion. Take guard to anger God and his Prophet. Take guard to commit a sin that history will record in a black page and of which you will carry the burden until the day of the resurrection. Know, oh Minister, that the shaking of the religion of our sons is the supreme goal of the enemies of Islam and the enemies of the homeland: the missionaries, the communists and the colonizers". It reminded him that Muhammad had forbidden Muslims to read the religious books of others. It noted that Umar, the 2nd caliph, read a Jewish text. Angered, Muhammad said, "People, I received all the words and their seals. They were summarized to me and I delivered them to you white and pure. Do not deceive yourself and do not let deceivers abuse you". The magazine in question reported other Narratives of Muhammad reproving the reading of the religious texts of others. Following these attacks, the proposition of the Pope Shenouda collapsed[1].

Jews seem to have the same attitude. *Jerusalem Post* reported December 25th 2001, that a teacher, in Beit Shemesh, decided to burn in the school courtyard a copy of the New Testament in Hebrew he found with one of his sixth-grade students. The teacher said, "God sent it and He gave us the privilege, and we'll be able to burn the *New Testament*". He consulted with the principal, Rabbi Yair. After receiving approval, the teacher took his class outside and burnt the *New Testament*. Rabbi David Spector, the rabbinic decision-maker for the school, ruled that missionary material should be burned, but it is the sole responsibility of the owner to do it and the burning should take place in private. He cited traditional and modern rabbis, including Rabbi Moshe Feinstein, who wrote that he had burned missionary texts, which he called "books of incitement and brainwashing". Such burning is permissible even if the texts include the name of God, Spector said[2].

B) Swiss norms

The problem of the contents of the courses has not yet emerged in Switzerland. Note here a polemic around Tariq Ramadan who wrote in a book:

---

[1] See Aldeeb Abu-Sahlieh: *Les musulmans face aux droits de l'homme*, p. 112-113.

[2] http://www.jpost.com/Editions/2001/12/25/News/News.40531.html

> Biology courses may contain teachings that are not in conformity with principles of Islam. It is sometimes the same for courses of history or philosophy. It is not about dispensation of those courses. Rather, one should offer youngsters, in parallel, courses that permit them to know what are the answers given by Islam to these problems in the various courses. This would be a concrete factor of enrichment[1].

We do not have anything against such a concept, provided that the Muslims do not pretend *a priori* the infallible character of "the principles of Islam" and that they accept to put them in question without seeing a reach to their faith. Without it, one will lead to a new Galileo case in biology. The aforesaid proposition of Tariq Ramadan provoked a quick reaction on behalf of professors of the College of Saussure in Geneva where Tariq Ramadan teaches. They wrote a manifesto in which they require, "That no religious group should in any case interfere on the content of our courses"[2].

In neighboring France, the *High Council for integration* considers the content of courses among the intangible principles and that it "would not be tolerable that pupils or parents challenge, in the name of religion, this or that part of the program of biology, literature, philosophy, drawing or physical training"[3].

In a dialogue with Tariq Ramadan, Jacques Neirynck thinks that one would live better the religious pluralism "if this pluralism was respected in schools. On the one hand, there should be hours of religious teaching where children separate to follow education of their religion. On the other hand, in certain moments, they should meet to learn about the faith of others". Tariq Ramadan answers to this proposition:

> It is necessary to have a profound debate on the content of this formation. Opinions are divergent and very sensitive on these questions. It is necessary to remain prudent and to respect stages with a clear debate on objectives[4].

Tariq Ramadan expresses here the refusal of Muslims to learn about the religious norms of others, by fear of proselytism whereas courses imposed to Christians in the Muslim countries are full of Muslim religious elements, as we have seen before.

---

[1] Ramadan: *Les musulmans dans la laïcité*, p. 122, note 55.

[2] Florence Duarte: *Les profs de biologie ont peur de l'islam*, in: Hebdo, 7.3.1996.

[3] Haut Conseil de l'intégration, par. 3.3.5.

[4] Neirynck and Ramadan, p. 225-226.

5) Schools for the Muslims

A) Islamic norms

In the Muslim countries, Christian religious communities have their own schools, frequented by Christians and Muslims; they are very appreciated by both. Contrary to the governmental public schools, they are not free of charge, but do not get a subsidy on behalf of the State. They often function thanks to Western Christian grants. Their programs are fixed and approved by the government. Besides the Christian private schools, there are Muslim religious schools, which are reserved for Muslims alone. It is notably the case of schools of Al-Azhar that assures a parallel pre-academic and academic education to the one offered by the public establishments.

B) Swiss norms

In addition to public schools, there are private schools in Switzerland, some of which are run by Christian or Jewish communities. Whereas Jewish schools are reserved for Jewish pupils, Christian schools are often open to all, without distinction of religious convictions.

In his dialogue with Tariq Ramadan, Jacques Neirynck wonders whether it would not be better that Muslims in the Western countries manage their own schools to avoid the problems with Muslim pupils and teachers. He thinks that a Muslim school can contribute to reduce delinquency in the disinherited suburbs of Lyon, Strasbourg or Marseille. He says that in Saudi Arabia "there is no delinquency, because sanctions are immediately applied. If one removes this system of sanctions, some Muslim youngsters feel themselves completely disoriented. What the Muslim kid can find in the secular school is a course of abstract and philosophical morals, and that will not help him".

Tariq Ramadan notes that some Muslims think effectively, "the only solution is the creation of Islamic schools that protect the children while transmitting them their values". But he has an opposite opinion, "It is necessary to make very attention because these schools, according to the way they are conceived, can become ghettos and can create rather than to solve problems". He adds, "It depends on the motivation behind the constitution of these Islamic schools: if it is to have Muslims together and to isolate them from the world, then one risks to provoke troublesome ruptures tomorrow, when youngsters will be again in contact with the society. But if these schools are open projects in interaction with the environment, in a harmonious coordinated development with the *milieu*, they can be interesting"[1].

Fawzia Al-Ashmawi blames Switzerland not to have regular Islamic schools whereas the other religious communities have their own schools next to the public schools[2]. She forgets that it is not the fault of Switzerland. It is up to the Muslim community to open these schools, as do the other communities. She indicates that during the last two years some projects to create Islamic schools have been formulated: these schools intend to promote education in Arabic language, which is liturgical language of the Koran, prayers and the teachings of Islam. The Swiss authorities encouraged these efforts in conformity with the Swiss Constitution[3]. She mentions that in Geneva a small number of private schools, frequented by children of diplomats and the Arab community, give courses of Arabic and Islamic instruction. However, this education is given in irregular manner and outside the class hours. Some Arab countries such as Libya, for example, opened a private school for children of their nationals in Switzerland. The Libyan school is managed by the embassy of that country in Bern. Libya pays for this school, establishes the program and provides school materials[4].

One can fault Arab countries that do not provide language classes for their nationals, as do Spain and Italy, so that their children, independently of their religion, can learn Arabic without being exposed to Islamic religious propaganda.

We should mention here a general problem of children's access to school independent of their religion. The Swiss public schools are open to all children whose parents are sojourning legally in the country. It is otherwise for children whose parents stay illegally. This situation mainly concerns Muslim children of clandestine refugees from Albania and Kosovo. These children can frequent the public schools only in Geneva Canton. Fawzia Al-Ashmawi believes that this situation constitutes a breach of

---

[1] *Ibid.*, p. 213-214.
[2] Al-Ashmawi: *La condition des musulmans*, p. 55-56.
[3] *Ibid.*, p. 56.
[4] *Ibid.*, p. 56.

the *Convention on the Rights of the Child*, which stipulates that every child has the right to receive an education and go to the school whatever the status of his parents[1].

However, with a massive presence of refugees coming from Albania and Kosovo, pupil integration in public schools creates problems because they do not speak the languages used in these schools. In certain schools, the number of foreign pupils is greater than that of Swiss pupils, negatively impacting the quality of education. As a result, some Swiss parents withdrew their children from these public schools and placed them in private schools. Fawzia Al-Ashmawi faults these parents and believes it is the duty of the canton to remedy the situation[2]. But such a correction cannot be done rapidly with such large numbers of foreigners. Some cantons thought to make separate classes for these new foreigners who cannot master the language used at school. This has also led to reproaches by the *Federal Commission Against Racism*, which thought this solution hides a political problem and considers it logical to dismiss foreigners.

According to this Commission, "permanently separate classes for foreign children constitute a discrimination, because child's national or ethnic origin is the only criteria of classifying him as less gifted than others. If it was instituted systematically and following a system of long range planning, such an institutional and structural exclusion would lead eventually to apartheid, whose objective is to prevent equal involvement in the society". "The idea of a separate educational development threatens long-term democratic foundations of cohabitation in a legal State"[3].

It requires great shrewdness and sensitivity to find the magic solution to the problem created by the Muslim refugee influx, [presenting Western nations not only with a large population that cannot speak the national languages, but also a strong cultural resistance to learning anything other than Arabic, the language of the Koran.] Western nations are bound to laws that provide children with the right to schooling, but what can be done if these students will not integrate. The problem presented by Muslim refugees in Switzerland may best be solved by only allowing

---

[1] *Ibid.*, p. 47.
[2] *Ibid.*, p. 55.
[3] Des classes séparées? in: *Tangram*, n° 7, October 1999, p. 86-88.

them to remain for a short period and requiring them to return to their countries of origin once the war finishes, even if they prefer to remain in Switzerland.

Chapter IV.
Family law

Family law, which covers marriage, relations between the spouses and their relations with the children, divorce and inheritance, is the domain most marked by religious norms. This domain passed progressively, with a lot of resistance, from the religious authority to the civil authority. Muslims continue to consider it as part of their faith. Islamic family law is where we find discriminations based on religion and sex, which provoke the greatest conflicts with the Swiss norms, and by extension the greatest conflict in all Western nations.

We will quickly outline the main problems below[1]. The reader can find in the 4th appendix of this book a *Model Contract for Mixed Marriage between Muslims and non-Muslims*. This document provides a proposal for solving the cultural conflict between Muslims and non-Muslims concerning marriage. [As such, it is an important consideration concerning the Muslim challenge to the separation of Church and State.]

1) Passage from religious to civil norms

A) Islamic norms

As noted already, recognized religious communities in Muslim countries often keep a legislative, or even judicial autonomy more or less extended concerning family law. These communities think that the application of their religious norms is part of the religious freedom or the dogmas of the faith. A Muslim who refuses the application of Islamic norms or asks change in these norms is considered as apostate with all the consequences we know. Recently, Nawal Al-Saadawi was taken before the Egyptian courts accused of apostasy because she asked for

---

[1] For more details, see Aldeeb: *Mariages entre partenaires suisses et musulmans*; Aldeeb and Bonomi (ed.): *Le droit musulman de la famille et des successions*.

inheritance equality between men and women[1]. A Muslim who accepts submission to a non-Muslim judge is treated the same.

The multi-legislative and multi-juridictional system that exists in Arab and Muslim countries can appear more tolerant than the unified Western system, but it has the disadvantage of endangering the unity of the country by forming nations within the official nation, putting outlaw those who do not belong to any recognized religious community, and favoring a community in case of law conflicts, as we will see it farther. For these reasons, Egypt suppressed the religious jurisdictions in 1955 and attempted, without success, to promulgate unified family law for the whole population. Thus, the Egyptian Civil Code, yet extensively inspired by the Western codes, does not include a chapter on the family law. Today, Egypt has one Islamic, two Jewish, and several Christian family laws[2].

The Islamic system characteristically emphasizes religious adherence above national adherence. Thus, a Swiss Christian tourist who visits Egypt cannot marry a Muslim woman, nor repudiate his wife, nor contract a polygamous marriage, nor grant to his son the double of what his daughter receives in inheritance. If he converts to Islam, then he will immediately be submitted to the Islamic law and realize all that he could not do by being a Christian. [The law in an Islamic nation is not for all. It is specific and faith based. The modern Western concept of all persons being equal under the law is unknown.] More comically, a Muslim cannot marry several women in Turkey or in Tunisia, these two countries having suppressed polygamy. But if he moves to Egypt, he will be able to do so, since the modification intervened in Turkey and Tunisia is considered contrary to the Koran by Egypt.

B) Swiss norms

The Western countries unified with more or less success their norms concerning family law at the expense of the Churches' power. Thus, in 1874, Switzerland abolished ecclesiastical jurisdiction (article 58 par. 2 aCst) and assigned to civil authorities everything that concerns civil status, the holding of

---

[1] See on the trial against Nawal Al-Saadawi: www.geocities.com/nawalsaadawi.

[2] See Aldeeb Abu-Sahlieh: *L'impact de la religion.*

the registers and marriage, as well as cemeteries (articles 53 and 54 aCst). Henceforth, all Swiss citizens, whatever their religion, are submitted concerning the family to only one Civil Code, and in case of litigation they will address themselves to the same court managed by judges chosen without religious criteria.

Certainly, in Switzerland [as in the United States] the Catholic Church always has its own courts that function besides those of the State to for example annul marriages, but without effect on the State level. It will refuse to bless the marriage of a Catholic who divorced civilly, but it cannot prevent his marriage in the civil status office. However, the Swiss authorities apply to the foreign Muslims their religious laws when the Swiss law refers back to their national law. It is for example the case of Iranians, since Switzerland signed a convention with Iran, April 25th, 1934, that foresees the application of the national law[1]. Nevertheless, Switzerland will elude the application of this law in the domains contrary to the Swiss public order. Therefore, an Iranian will not be able to marry in Switzerland two women, even though they are Iranian citizens. [If the Iranian in question becomes Swiss, it is Swiss law that will be applied to him, not that of Iran.]

As noted before, Muslims in Western countries, including those that have the citizenship of these countries, would like to retain legislative and judicial autonomy in matters of family law, as part of their religious freedom. They invoke the fact that Christian and Jewish communities in Muslim countries have their autonomy in this matter. Fawzia Al-Ashmawi considers discriminatory the application to Muslims living in Switzerland the Swiss Civil Code concerning marriage, divorce and inheritance[2].

However, if such autonomy were granted to Muslims, it would establish a pluri-legislative and pluri-juridictional system in the West; a system discussed in the Koran, and one that Muslim countries would like to abolish to guarantee national unity. [This plurality of religious faith in the West, made possible by freedom of religion, is the current motivation behind their holy war. The Muslim solution is then simple. All law should follow Islam.]

We will review the main questions related to family law to identify points of friction between Islamic and Swiss norms.

---

[1] RS 0.142.114.362.
[2] Al-Ashmawi: *La condition des musulmans en Suisse*, p. 46.

2) Celebration of the marriage

A) Islamic norms

In most Muslim countries, a religious authority or a civil authority with religious connotation generally celebrates the marriage. If these countries insist more and more on the necessity to write down the marriage in a State register, they admit even today the so-called customary marriage which is established in the presence of two witnesses, as long as it is not contested on behalf of the two spouses. This situation is the result of the classic Islamic law, which does not prescribe an official form for the celebration of marriage. The customary marriage is becoming a social curse in a country such as Egypt where students resort to it secretly because of economic difficulties that prevent them from contracting a normal marriage. These marriages are formed and dissolved without any control on behalf of state or family; they imply social insecurity for the women. Some Swiss women already fell into this trap during their travels in Egypt as tourists.

B) Swiss norms

In Switzerland, marriage is a legal and binding institution. The celebration of marriage is the exclusive prerogative of the civil status officers, whatever is the religion or citizenship of partners.

It is forbidden to any foreign diplomatic and consular representatives in Switzerland to celebrate marriage, even for their citizens[1]. Furthermore, "a religious solemnization of the marriage can only take place after the solemnization before the civil status officer" (article 97 par. 3 CCS). This religious solemnization is an optional formality with no legal consequence.

If the spouses get married in Switzerland before an imam, without having concluded civil marriage beforehand, Swiss law does not recognize such a marriage, which can have some unpleasant consequences, notably for the woman abandoned by her husband[2]. On the other hand, the imam exposes himself to penal sanctions[3] and his residence permit may be withdrawn. This

---

[1] Note dated 8.2.1995 from the Swiss Federal Department of Foreign Affairs sent to diplomatic and consular representations in Switzerland.

[2] In France, some Imams have married a second wife through a religious ceremony (Gozlan: *L'islam et la République*, p. 111-117).

[3] Articles 271, 287 and 292 of the Penal Code.

situation brought the *Federal Office of Civil Status* to address a circular letter July 9th, 1999 to more than 120 Muslim communities in Switzerland and to the cantonal authorities of surveillance concerning civil status, in which it is said, "During these last months, our Office has been informed repeatedly of violations of the Swiss law, by the fact that religious personnel including imams proceeded to the celebration of marriages". The circular adds:

> According to law currently in force since 1874 only the marriage celebrated in Switzerland by the civil status officers is valid. A religious blessing can take place only after the celebration of the civil marriage. These norms are also valid for foreign nationals submitted to a religious marriage according to their national law. ...
>
> The respect of these norms by religious personnel responsible of the communities is imperative. In case of violation, they can be punished .... The spouses must also count with annoyances. Even though such a marriage accomplished in this manner had to be recognized in the State of origin, in Switzerland they will always be considered as not married. If the woman gave birth to a child, the filiation would only be established between the child and the mother and not her partner. The newborn will receive the family name of the mother. The father must recognize the child expressly in order to create a link of filiation. In addition of the financial inconveniences (no right to allowance for family and children, etc.) there can be problems related to foreigners' police (residence permit).

If the Swiss law admits the marriage celebrated abroad, it is not yet the case of the Muslim countries. Thus, Morocco does not recognize the marriage implying one or two Moroccan partners celebrated in Switzerland before the civil status officer. Therefore, the embassy of this country proceeds to a new celebration in its local, in spite of the fact that Switzerland does not recognize such prerogative for this Embassy.

3) Religious obstacle to the marriage

A) Islamic norms

Islamic law recognizes obstacle to marriage because of religion. The norms concerning this matter can be summarized as follows:

- Contrary to the Shiites, Sunnites admit marriage of a Muslim with a non-Muslim monotheist (Jewish or Christian). A Buddhist that wants to marry a Muslim must previously convert to Islam or another monotheist religion (Judaism or Christianity). The non-Muslim monotheist woman can keep her faith while marrying a Muslim Sunnite, but this one does not hide his wish that such a marriage will lead her to convert to Islam[1]. Even in the absence of pressure, the woman will feel practically constrained to become Muslim if she does not want to be penalized in inheritance and care of children. The marriage of a Sunnite with a non-Muslim woman, although permitted, remains blameful, notably if the woman is foreign. A book, used for education in the Egyptian public schools, expressly warns Muslim youngsters against this kind of marriage. There is fear that a non-Muslim woman becomes a spy for her country[2]. Sheik Al-Ghazali (d. 1996), notorious Egyptian author, says that one cannot qualify Christians and Jews of Europe and America as *People of the Book* since the Bible and the Gospel have lost any power on them. According to him, the religion at these Christians and Jews is limited to a dominical holiday, a Christmas feast, an anger against Islam and insults against Muhammad. In the past, he says, the Muslim was allowed to marry a woman of the *People of the Book* because she could care for his house and educate his children according to God's teachings. Today this is not possible in a society where wine flows as a stream and sex is without limit[3].

- The Shiites admit the marriage of a Muslim man only with a Muslim woman. If a Muslim marries a Christian woman, she must convert to Islam first, otherwise the marriage is not recognized.
- A Muslim woman can only marry a Muslim man. The non-Muslim man, whatever is his religion, that wants to marry a Muslim woman, must previously convert to Islam. It was for example the case of the French philosopher Roger Garaudy converted to Islam who married a Muslim woman from the family Al-Husayni of Jerusalem. As no one can abandon Islam, the Muslim woman cannot convert to her husband's religion.
- If a non-Muslim woman married with a non-Muslim man becomes Muslim, her marriage is dissolved, except if her husband accepts to follow her in her new religion.
- A person who abandons Islam cannot contract a marriage, being either punished of death or confinement to life, or considered at least as dead. If the apostasy intervenes after the marriage, this one is dissolved. If a Christian converts to Islam to marry a Muslim woman, and comes back to his religion of origin thereafter, he is considered as apostate. Therefore, his marriage is dissolved immediately. The same happens to a Muslim husband who adopts positions judged contrary to Islamic religion.

These restrictions, which are in all family laws of the Arab countries, are based on two Koranic verses (2:221 and 60:10) as

---

[1] See Abu-Zahrah: Al-ahwal al-shakhsiyyah, p. 113-114; Badran: Al-ilaqat al-ijtima'iyyah, p. 66-77.

[2] Al-Sanhouri: *Al-usrah fil-tashri al-islami*, p. 29-34 (textbook taught in the eleventh year).

[3] Al-Ghazali: *Qadaya al-mar'ah*, p. 203-204. See also Al-Jaza'iri: *Zawag al-muslim bi-ghayr al-muslimah*, p. 31 -32.

well as on a truncated passage of the Koran, "God will never permit the disbelievers to prevail over the believers" (4:141). Muhammad said in the same sense, "Islam dominates and will never be dominated". These passages are also to be understood physically: a non-Muslim man cannot go over a Muslim woman.

Badran, law professor in the University of Alexandria and the Arab University of Beirut, recommends the death penalty against the non-Muslim man who marries a Muslim woman. This would be, according to him, the most efficient means to impede non-Muslims from attempting to the honor of Islam and Muslims[1].

Let us finish here by the position of King Hassan II of Morocco. In the French emission *À l'heure de vérité* (Antenne 2, 17 December 1989), he said:

> What I think about mixed marriages is very clear; it is really the calculation of the most improbable probabilities. For one succeeding, there are a hundred, which fail. I think that it is preferable to leave things go as they are, without being neither for, nor against; but at least the environment should be considered, it should be... We speak at the present time of environment, but the environment is much more important: there is the historical environment, there is the environment of authenticity, there is the environment in general and the continental, linguistic, religious environment[2].

B) Swiss norms

The aforesaid uni-directional Islamic norms are contrary to the principles of non-discrimination, of the freedom of marriage and of the equality between man and woman. Therefore, they violate the international norms such as article 16 of the UDHR that stipulates:

> Men and women of full age, without any limitation due to race, nationality or religion, have the right to marry and to found a family. They are entitled to equal rights as to marriage, during marriage and at its dissolution[3].

At the time of the voting on the UDHR, the representative of Egypt rejected this article because it was against Islamic law, which forbids marriage of a Muslim woman with a non-Muslim man[4]. Other Arab and Muslim countries reacted in the same sense. To satisfy them, the passage "without any limitation due to race,

---

[1] Badran: *Al-ilaqat al-ijtima'iyyah*, p. 88.
[2] Quoted by Immigration et nationalité, p. 91-22.
[3] *GA*, 3rd session, plenary session 180, p. 912.
[4] Loc. cit.

nationality or religion" was suppressed from article 23 of the *Covenant on civil rights*.

Article 54 par. 2 aCst stipulated, "The right to marry may not be limited for religious or economic reasons …", while Article 14 nCst states, "The rights to marriage and family are guaranteed", expressiong the same idea. Therefore, the religious obstacle to marriage foreseen by the Islamic law is not admissible in Switzerland. A Muslim woman can marry a non-Muslim man in Switzerland. However, in some traditional communities, she may risk kidnapping, or even being killed by her parents and her coreligionists. She can never return to her country, and if she does in company of her husband, she is immediately separated from him and both may risk their life. In November of 1996, a Christian Swiss man married a Muslim Tunisian woman in Switzerland. Her two brothers kidnapped her and threatened her husband with a weapon. The police who freed the woman stopped them. But the husband and his wife are afraid as she has three other brothers[1]. Once the kidnappers were let out of prison, the spouses began to be anguished. They changed domicile repeatedly, refused to communicate their telephone number and were followed by a psychiatrist.

As noted, Sunnite Islamic law allows a non-Muslim woman to marry a Muslim man without necessarily changing her religion if she confesses a monotheist religion (Jewish or Christian). In spite of that, when the spouses contact after the civil marriage a religious one before a Muslim religious authority or a consulate of a Muslim country, the wife is invited to convert to Islam, with more or less insistence. According to testimonies, an Islamic center operating in Switzerland delays the religious ceremony continually until the non-Muslim woman accepts conversion to Islam. In one specific case, a Christian girl, whose father is a Muslim convert to Christianity, contacted the *Islamic Center of Lausanne* to arrange a possible religious celebration of her marriage with a Muslim man. The woman who welcomed her, a Swiss convert to Islam, explained to her that as a daughter of an apostate, she cannot marry a Muslim man unless she convert to Islam. Having known that his daughter was planning a marriage with a Muslim, the father began to have nightmares, fearing for

---

[1] *24 Heures*, 13.11.1996.

his life in Switzerland. He insisted that his daughter never give her family address, since fundamentalist Muslims could kill him.

To avoid these problems, many Swiss men convert to Islam for show, often without realizing the legal consequences of their act. Indeed, they cannot return to their original religion. If they do, they risk undergoing the aforementioned consequences. The Muslim society does not admit the right of mistake in this matter.

Some wonder what is the sense of a conversion to Islam that the Muslim authorities know formal. In fact, if a non-Muslim converts to Islam, even though it is only for show, his children will be inevitably Muslim according to the Islamic law and will forget incentives for which their father had converted; they do not have the right to change religion at any time of their life.

In France, sheik Soheib Bencheikh, Mufti of Marseille, tries to find a solution to this problem by advancing arguments used before him by the Egyptian philosopher Muhammad Ahmad Khalaf-Allah (d. 1997), that he does not quote[1]. For him, neither the Koran, nor the Narratives of Muhammad forbid marriage of a Muslim woman with a Christian or a Jewish man. In Islamic law, everything that is not expressly forbidden is permitted. He notes that because of this taboo, a lot of girls leave Islam to marry Christians[2].

This enlightened liberal position is not shared by the Muslim community in Switzerland or by persons responsible for this community. In a symposium organized in Bern November 26th, 1998, I asked Hafid Ouardiri, spokesman of the *Islamic Cultural Foundation of Geneva*, if the Mosque of Geneva was ready to declare that a Muslim woman has the right to marry a non-Muslim man[3]. He reacted violently and said that such a declaration will never be made. I put the same question to Tariq Ramadan during a conference that took place in Lausanne June

---

[1] On this philosopher, see Aldeeb Abu-Sahlieh: *Les musulmans face aux droits de l'homme*, p. 134-136.
[2] Gozlan: *L'islam et la République*, p. 125-129.
[3] The symposium was organised par the *Swiss association of catholic journalists*. Its title was: "Muslims and Christians in Switzerland what kind of relations?"

9th, 1999[1]. He answered likewise, saying that Swiss law does not oblige a Muslim girl to marry a non-Muslim man. In fact, the problem is not to oblige a Muslim girl to marry a non-Muslim, but not to stop her from making it by threats on behalf of her family or her religious community. Far from condemning the prohibition of the marriage of a Muslim woman with a non-Muslim man, Tariq Ramadan tries to justify it. He writes:

> The question of mixed marriage for the Muslim is to consider under the realm of family philosophy as translated in the teaching of Islam. The principle, in marriage, is equality of beings and complementary roles and functions.
>
> The man has the duty to provide the family's needs and, in this sense, he has the responsibility to maintain the home. The woman has the right not to provide material needs: it is a right, this is not a duty (as some Muslims present it sometimes), and nothing prevents a woman to work. In the family space, there is in Islam the idea of the woman's right that can put her, on the financial level, in a more or less relative dependence situation.
>
> This situation explains, at the level of the general philosophy, why, in Islam, a Muslim man can marry a woman of the *People of the Book*, Christian or Jewish, since it is a duty for him to respect his wife's faith and to provide needs. The inverse is not possible; a Muslim woman cannot marry a man of another religion because she could be in a situation where the person responsible of the home does not recognize her faith, its practices and its general or particular requirements. The latitude of the possible dependence is more important in this sense with, moreover, the fact that the Muslim recognizes Jewish and Christian faith but a Christian or a Jew does not consider the revelation of Islam as authentic[2].

Hani Ramadan, brother of Tariq Ramadan and Director of the *Islamic Center of Geneva*, presents similar arguments:

> A non-Muslim does not believe in the prophecy of Muhammad. He will have difficulty therefore sharing his wife's religious feelings. The education of children will create him a problem. On the contrary, the Muslim, if he takes for woman a Jew or a Christian, fully recognizes the prophecy of Moses or Jesus. He should not only respect his wife's belief, but also give her means to live in conformity with her convictions. Some Muslim jurists even say that he has the obligation to

---

[1] The conference was organised by the *Association mosaïque* of the University of Lausanne. Its title was: "Is it possible to live according to Islam in Switzerland?"

[2] Neirynck and Ramadan, p. 121.

take his wife to her place of worship (church or synagogue) if she wants it. What better proof of tolerance[1]?

Hani Ramadan forgets that the Swiss Constitution guarantees to a Muslim woman who marries a Christian respect of her religion. With regard to education of children, it must be decided in Switzerland by the two parents, whereas in Islamic law, only the Muslim partner decides.

We can understand the reticence of Swiss Muslim religious authorities to denounce Islamic religious discrimination in this domain. If they made it, they would be disavowed by their community, or at least lose the financial Muslim country support. On the contrary, one does not understand why the *Federal Commission Against Racism* does not denounce this norm.

4) Temporary or enjoyment marriage

A) Islamic norms

Shiite Islamic law has a form of marriage called *zawag al-mut'ah* (literally. enjoyment marriage) translated often as temporary marriage. This kind of marriage is defined expressly in the Iranian Civil Code[2]. According to this code, the husband would be able, in addition to the four regular wives he is permitted in Islam, to take other women in temporary marriage, a union that can last for only one hour or as long as several years, depending on the circumstances in which he finds himself. Some do not hesitate to call this marriage prostitution.

Temporary marriage is forbidden in Sunnite Islamic law. But Sunnite religious authorities allow their co-religionists who are in the West for studies or a mission, to marry monotheist non-Muslim women with the explicit intention of separating them once they finish their stay abroad. Such a marriage permits these students the loophole of engaging in sexual intercourse without technically breaking Islamic law, which of course forbids sexual intercourse outside of marriage[3].

---

[1] Ramadan: *Articles sur l'islam et la barbarie*, p. 50 (La tolérance de l'islam en cinq points, article published in: *Le Courrier*, 22.3.1997).

[2] Articles 1075 and 1077 of the Iranian Civil Code. On this marriage, see Haeri: *Law of desire*.

[3] *Fatwa* of Ibn-Baz, president of the Saudi Commission of *Fatwa* in: *Majallat al-buhuth al-islamiyyah*, n° 25, 1989, p. 89.

This problem raised a big debate in the Muslim community of the United States, following a *fatwa* in favor of marriage with the intention to repudiate after the end of the stay abroad. The *Islamic Center of Washington* submitted the question to the *Academy of Islamic law,* which depends on the *Organization of Islamic conference.* But the Academy refused to decide the case due to divergent opinion among its members, some being in favor of this marriage, and others considering it fraudulent[1]. [This type of marriage of convenience remains a major matter of debate in the United States, where the issue is complicated by the fact that individual states determine specifics regarding marriage laws.]

The customary marriage of the Sunnites as aforementioned is becoming the equivalent of Shiite temporary marriage.

B) Swiss norms

Switzerland, as in other Western countries, knows the *white marriage* problem aimed to facilitate foreigners in obtaining residence permits and citizenships. To our knowledge neither the courts nor the Swiss doctrine discuss the matter of temporary marriage. Certainly, the longevity of marriage is not anymore what it was, a perpetual alliance as still upheld by the Catholic Church. No one can legally oblige two spouses to remain united until the death of one or the other. But Swiss lay does not allow marriage that is of a limited time, in advance of the agreement. [U.S. immigration laws were recently revised to deal with this situation. In the United States, the citizen of an international marriage applying for a residence permit for his or her spouse must not only show financial means of support for the dependent, but also must sign a binding contract with the governement to support this spouse for a time, even if this marriage is dissolved.]

On the other hand, Swiss law does not permit dissolution of a marriage without judicial procedure, so the distinctions between being married and not being married are much clearer. Unacknowledged polygamy due to the nature of Islamic law is the other problem. In Western nations, someone who is already married in any way cannot conclude another marriage. Since polygamous marriage is forbidden in Switzerland, any subsequent attempt to marry another person is seen as illegal.

---

[1] The debate is reported in: *Majallat majma al-fiqh al-islami,* n° 3, part 2, 1987, p. 1107, 1141, 1170, 1232-1233 and 1374-1376.

[This is a longstanding "Church and State" issue in the United States, where Utah was not admitted as a state in the union, until they agreed to officially bann the practice of polygamy.]

5) Polygamy

A) Islamic norms

Polygamy is a practice known in the Bible, which puts no limit to a man's sexual appetite in this domain. Abraham, Jacob, Moses, David and Salomon, to only name a few, were polygamous.

The Koran allows Muhammad to marry as many women as he wants (33:50), but for other Muslims, it limits the number of women at one time to four. However, it recommends to only take one woman if one fears not being equitable with them (4:3) while adding, "You can never be equitable in dealing with more than one wife, no matter how hard you try" (4:129). In addition to these four women, a man could marry an unlimited number of slaves[1]. Among Shiites, a man can even now marry an unlimited number of free women in temporary marriage. The woman, on the other hand, can marry only one man at one time. A woman who marries two men is considered an adulteress, liable of lapidating in certain countries such as Saudi Arabia or Iran.

Polygamy is forbidden in Tunisia and Turkey. In this latter country, however, polygamy is still practiced and the State promulgates from time to time decrees aiming to legitimize the children born out of such marriages. Measures have been taken by certain Arab legislators aiming to limit the polygamy invoking the aforesaid Koranic verses (4:3 and 129). These measures vary from one nation to another, and can be summarized as follows:

- The woman can include in the contract a clause of non-remarriage giving her the right to ask for the divorce if the husband takes another one.
- The woman can ask for the divorce in case of remarriage even in the absence of a contractual clause.
- The husband who wants to marry a new woman must fulfill some conditions submitted to the judge's appreciation.

B) Swiss norms

To our knowledge, no international document speaks in a direct manner about the polygamy in respect to human rights. One can

---

[1] See the verses 4:3 and 25, 23:5-7 and 24:33.

note however here the general norm, which prescribes the equality between man and woman in marriage, whereas Islamic law allows the husband to have several women simultaneously and imposes to the woman to only have at one time only one husband. Also, the norm concerning consent, whereas one does not ask the woman if she wants to marry a man who is already married or to share the husband with other women later. Thus, the UDHR (article 16 par. 2) and the Covenant on civil rights (article 23 par. 3) specify, "Marriage shall be entered into only with the free and full consent of the intending spouses". The *Convention on the Elimination of all Forms of Discrimination against Women* says, "National parties shall take all appropriate measures to eliminate discrimination against women in all matters relating to marriage and family relations and in particular shall ensure, on a basis of equality of men and women .... the same right freely to choose a spouse and to enter into marriage only with their free and full consent" (article 16 par. 1.b).

In Switzerland, polygamy is contrary to the principle of the equality affirmed by article 8 nCst. Besides, it constitutes a penal offence according to article 215 of the Penal Code that stipulates:

> Whoever, being already married, marries another person shall be confined in the penitentiary for not over five years or in the prison for not less than three months.
>
> The unmarried person who knowingly contracts a marriage with a married person shall be confined in the penitentiary for not over three years or in the prison.

Article 96 CCS foresees, "Whoever wants to get remarried must establish that his previous marriage has been dissolved or annulated". Article 105 par. 1 adds that the marriage must be annulated "when at the time of contracting the marriage, one of the parties thereto was already married or that the previous marriage was not dissolved by the divorce or by the death of the other spouse". The proper authority of domicile or any one who has an interest may bring suit for annulment of marriage (article 106 par. 1). The prohibition of polygamy also applies to foreigners that would like to contract a polygamous marriage in Switzerland, substantive prerequisites for marriage being determined by Swiss law (article 44 par. 1 LPIL).

In some cases, foreigners, already married in their country of origin, marry a Swiss woman while hiding their first marriage to get a residence permit. Once having a permit, they divorce and take their first wife in Switzerland. A Swiss national may also contract a marriage abroad and then, without declaring the first marriage, contract another marriage in Switzerland, the first marriage being discovered by intervention of the first spouse[1]. The second marriage in this case is of course void. Indeed, bigamy is punishable even though the first marriage had been contracted abroad, so long as the Swiss law has recognized it[2].

In June of 2001, the press reported the case of a Moroccan sojourning in Lausanne since 1987, who had married a Swiss woman and obtained Swiss citizenship in 1995. He had hidden to everybody that he had another wife and two daughters in Morocco. One year after the divorce from his Swiss wife, he asked for official family regrouping in order to bring his first wife and two daughters from Morocco. The administration thus discovered his polygamy. The reaction of the Federal office of foreigners was immediate. Four months later, it annulled his naturalization because he "had concealed the essential facts that would have led to naturalization refusal". Two months and half later, the Service of the population of Vaud Canton refused him a residence permit. The Administrative court confirmed this decision in November of 2000 because "the concerned person lived in state of bigamy, contravening to a prohibition which is part of the Swiss public order". It concluded, "We are in presence of a foreigner who behaved in a disloyal manner toward his wife and toward the authorities". The Federal Court rejected the recourse of the Moroccan and he had to leave Switzerland before August 31st, 2001[3].

Far from condemning polygamy, Hani Ramadan, Director of the *Islamic Center of Geneva*, a Swiss citizen, made an advocacy in its favor:

> Islam does not impose to men to live according to norms that they would be incapable to respect. Islam does not recognize to the human nature more virtue than it possesses. Rather than to impose a theoretical monogamy, that very often conceals the adultery, Islamic law allowed the polygamy while limiting and codifying it.
>
> One would have the mind very badly turned to criticize the polygamy negatively because it legalizes a situation of fact, and in the

---

[1] Siegenthaler: *Fascination des mers du sud*, p. 295-298.
[2] Message concernant la modification du Code pénal et du Code militaire du 26.6.1985, *Feuille fédérale* 1985 II 1068.
[3] *Le Matin*, 16.6.2001.

same time allows that men live in the shade and illegally some extra-conjugal adventures.

What situation is preferable for the woman? To be taken and rejected to will and at random of meetings, or to be cared of – according to the legal norms – by an officially recognized and responsible husband[1]?

The interested reader can refer, for other arguments, to the booklet of Hani Ramadan[2] that constitutes a real incitement to the violation of the Swiss law. It is sufficient to say here that the polygamy was never a guarantee for the man's fidelity in the Muslim countries. If this were the case, Hani Ramadan should also plead for the polyandry in order to prevent the disloyalty of women. If he does not adventure in this way, it is because the Islamic law does not allow polyandry.

In order to get the establishment of the seat of the *World Trade Organization* in Geneva, Switzerland accepted to give up concerning polygamous couple stay. A clause of this agreement stipulates:

Members of the permanent missions from countries admitting the polygamy will be allowed, from case to case, to take with them two wives simultaneously; alone one of the two can exercise a lucrative activity. The financial situation of the permanent mission as well as the one of the concerned person will be taken, among others, in consideration[3].

6) Dissolution of the marriage

A) Islamic norms

The Koran says:

Repudiation may be retracted twice. The repudiated woman shall be allowed to live in the same home amicably, or leave it amicably. It is not lawful for the husband to take back anything he had given her. However, the couple may fear that they may transgress God's law. If there is fear that they may transgress God's law, then it shall be no sin for either of them in what she gives as ransom to get her freedom. These are God's laws; do not transgress them. Those who transgress God's laws are the unjust (2:229).

On the basis of this verse and Muhammad's narratives, Islamic law foresees three main ways to dissolve marriage: repudiation, ransom and divorce.

---

[1] Ramadan: *La femme en islam*, p. 32-33.
[2] *Ibid.*, p. 35-38.
[3] WT/GC/1, 17.5.1995.

Repudiation is the recognized right of a Muslim man, and to him alone, to end marriage with a one-sided declaration, without justification and without appearing before a court. It can be very well either definitive, or revocable in a certain lapse of time (of about three months) again by a one-sided decision by the husband. It can be exercised by the husband or by a delegate. Having a Koranic basis (2:229), it is admitted by all Arabic countries except Tunisia and Turkey. Muhammad affirmed, "Repudiation is a permitted act which is most detested by God". To counter abuses, some Arab legislators grant woman an indemnity of consolation (*mut'ah*) calculated on the basis of a maintenance of less than two years, taking account of the husband's financial situation, circumstances of the repudiation and the length of marriage. In this respect, some Muslim countries' legislations allow the woman to include in the act of marriage the right to repudiate her husband. This possibility remains however theoretical, since women never dare include such a humiliating clause for the husband in a marriage contract.

The woman can negotiate with her husband repudiation against remittance of a sum of money. Some qualify this procedure as "divorce by mutual consent". The term "ransom" would be more appropriated. Indeed, the Koran uses the term *iftadat* (2:229), evoking the ransom paid for a prisoner's liberation[1]. Even though the woman expresses her will to end the marriage, the husband remains master of the situation: without his agreement, the marriage cannot be dissolved. The ransom can even be sterner than repudiation as it allows the husband to use psychological and financial pressure on his wife.

Divorce, contrary to the two previous procedures, is a dissolution of marriage pronounced by a judge on the basis of motives foreseen by law. The woman, who wants to part from her husband, if she does not manage to get her freedom by ransom, must necessarily address a court to expose reasons for which she wishes to dissolve the marriage. A Husband who does not want to assume liabilities that are incumbent to him in case of repudiation may also use divorce.

---

[1] See this term in the verses 2:85; 2:184; 2:196; 3:91; 5:39; 10:54; 13:18; 37:107; 39:47; 47:4; 57:15; 70:11.

B) Swiss norms

The repudiation and the ransom constitute a violation of the principle of the equality between man and woman, principle dedicated by the UDHR (article 16 par. 1) and the Covenant on civil rights (article 23 par. 4) that speak of "equal rights as to marriage, during marriage and at its dissolution". Article 16.1.c of the *Convention on the Elimination of all Forms of Discrimination against Women* requires the national parties to guarantee to men and women "the same rights and responsibilities during marriage and at its dissolution". The signatory Arab countries objected this article[1].

According to the Christian concept of marriage, it is [contracted by God and] indissoluble. Switzerland, as most Western countries of Christian culture, however now admit that the separation of the two spouses, in certain cases, can be preferable to their union. Shared between its two Catholic and Protestant communities, Switzerland opted for two institutions: the separation of body, only accepted by the Catholic Church, and divorce. But a Catholic that wants to divorce will be able to do it before Swiss courts, even though the Catholic Church does not recognize this divorce and refuses the religious blessing to a divorced person in case of a subsequent marriage.

What is the attitude of Switzerland while considering the three Muslim modes of marriage dissolution?

Muslim divorce is not a problem in Switzerland, whether obtained before Swiss or foreign courts. As for repudiation and ransom, they are forbidden in Switzerland because only the judges can pronounce a divorce[2]. But one must distinguish what happens in Switzerland from what happens abroad in this respect.

Some Muslims living in Switzerland repudiate or divorce amicably either before an imam or a consulate of a Muslim country in Switzerland. Such a procedure is not admitted in Switzerland and the spouses remain married in the eyes of Swiss authorities[3]. In one such case, passed before the mosque of

---

[1] The most important reservation is that done by Egypt (*Traités multilatéraux*, p. 174-175. See also the reservations of Iraq, Jordan, Libya and Tunisia, p. 175-181).

[2] Mercier: *Conflits de civilisations*, p. 78.

[3] Federal office of justice, legal opinion, unpublished, dated 15.6.1984.

Geneva before two Muslim witnesses, the wife did not hesitate to turn against the husband in order to claim part of his real estate property, acquired by this one whereas he thought that his marriage was dissolved definitely. In spite of agreement in writing adjusting financial questions between the two parties, the wife invoked the nullity of this divorce, as a Swiss court had not pronounced it.

The dissolution of the marriage as well as its conclusion before an imam in Switzerland, sometimes implying Swiss partners, in violation of the Swiss law, can be the result of ignorance of the law: imams and Muslims coming from countries that accept the religious marriage and repudiation could think that Switzerland has the same system as that of their countries of origin. But it can also be about a will to cheat the Swiss law. A Muslim foreigner that gets married civilly in Switzerland, getting a residence permit this way, risks being returned to his country if the marriage is dissolved by a Swiss court. He is tempted then to dissolve the marriage before an imam without endangering his stay in Switzerland.

It is also likely that some Muslims try to cheat and circumvent Islamic law. Outside of marriage, Islamic law and social customs forbid boys and girls to have sexual intercourse or even to frequent each other. The girl must arrive to marriage a virgin. To neutralize these norms in Switzerland, some resort to religious marriage before the imam with the authorization of the parents who may think that such a marriage is valid. Once he got from the girl what he wanted, the young man abandons her pregnant. There begins the drama. To find a solution, the Muslim family pushes the two spouses to proceed to repudiation before an imam to save face, and so one cannot blame the girl for the loss of her virginity. This same procedure can take place when a Muslim frequents a Muslim girl out of marriage and decides to end this relation. Before separating, he marries her before the imam; some time later he repudiates her, giving her thus a final favor.

If Swiss law assumes that each of the two spouses has the right to ask for divorce, the fact that a woman dares to ask for it can cost her dearly. One Tunisian has been condemned to fourteen years of reclusion for his wife's murder. According to the Criminal Court of Lausanne, the death of his Swiss wife constitutes "the convict's ultimate oppressive act to dominate a wife who escaped him". The day of the drama, the woman had gone to her husband to sign divorce papers. Wounded in his pride, the husband strangled her[1]. In certain cases, the Muslim husband manages to convince the woman to withdraw divorce action and immediately afterward he demands the divorce before a Court; a way not to lose face.

Some Muslim couples living in Switzerland go to their country of origin or hire a lawyer to dissolve their marriage before a Muslim court, believing that it is more in accord with their religion. Such a process, while done in good conscience, can have some tragic consequences for the woman, because the material consequences of such a divorce gotten abroad are unfavorable for her. Thus, returning to Switzerland, she attempts to benefit from Swiss law in this domain, but it is often too late since the Swiss courts officially recognize such a divorce. The woman falls thus in destitution or finishes in relying on public aid.

Some Muslim husbands living in Switzerland go to their country of origin or elect a parent in order to get repudiation, this then being communicated to the woman. Thinking that he freed himself thus of his wife, the husband hurries to contract another marriage abroad, and tries to take his new wife in Switzerland. He discovers that neither the repudiation nor the new marriage is recognized in this Western country. It is not without problems for foreign woman of good faith, unaware of any Swiss law. In a concrete case implying an Egyptian couple staying for years in Switzerland, the repudiated woman instituted an action against her husband before a Geneva Court. The husband was obliged to undertake the procedure of divorce according to Swiss legal norms, before a Swiss court[2].

---

[1] *24 Heures*, 18.2.1997.

[2] See on this affair: Decision of the Federal office of justice, unpublished, dated 7.2.1990; Decision of the Justice civil court dated 14.11.1991 (La semaine judiciaire, 114, n° 13, 31.3.1992, p. 209-224). For other cases of repudiation, see the decision of the Civil court of the district of Zurich dated 26.11.1963 (Schweizerische Juristen-Zeitung, 1964, p. 289 ss); Federal Court decision, unpublished, dated 29.1.1971; Legal opinion dated 7.12.1981 of the Federal office of justice (JAAC, 46 1982, p. 168-69); Federal Court decision 110 II 5 dated 15.3.1984; Federal Court decision dated 3.9.1996 (French translation in: *Revue de l'état civil*, n° 1/1997, p. 17-20).

Already in 1962[1], the Federal Court had decided, "repudiation, according to Egyptian law, of a Swiss wife by an Egyptian husband is not recognized in Switzerland nor registered, even though the wife agreed to divorce and required the enrollment". In this case, the marriage had been celebrated in Alexandria and the repudiation took place in Moscow, according to Egyptian law, at the Egyptian embassy[2].

However, in a particular case, there was recognition of repudiation. Born in Morocco, a Swiss citizen converted to Islam had married, in Morocco, a Moroccan woman (becoming thus a dual-national). He pronounced repudiation, in June of 1969, before a cadinotary. In January of 1971, the wife agreed to the dissolution of her marriage in writing. Invited by the Federal office of civil status to register the dissolution of the marriage in the family register of the origin municipality, the Authority of Surveillance in Aargau Canton answered favorably in its decision of May 4th, 1971. It claimed that the link between spouses in question and their country, where repudiation had taken place, was stronger than the link that bound them to Switzerland, even though the spouse, a dual-national, had kept the Swiss citizenship. The two spouses were domiciled in Morocco, they were Muslim and they had the citizenship of this country[3].

Today, by reason of the laxity of divorce procedure in Switzerland, which became as simple as the Muslim repudiation in case of mutual consent of the two spouses, the Swiss doctrine is shared facing the recognition of repudiation made abroad, notably when there is consent of both parties[4].

---

[1] Federal Court decision 88 I 48-52.

[2] See on this decision: Annuaire suisse de droit international, 1962, p. 218, note Lalive; L'ordre public dans le droit de la famille, in: Revue de l'état civil, 1969, p. 327; Vischer: Das Problem der Kodifikation des schweizerischen internationalen Privatrechtes, Rapports et communications de la Société suisse des juristes, fasc. n° 1, 1971, p. 86.

[3] *Schweizerische Juristen-Zeitung*, 1973, p. 25-26; *Revue de l'état civil* 1973, n° 2, p. 40. See the commentary of Lalive in: *Annuaire suisse de droit international*, 1972, p. 390.

[4] In favor: Bucher: *Droit international privé suisse*, tome II, p. 200;. opposed: Dutoit: *Commentaire de la loi fédérale*, p. 173.

7) Authority of the husband over his wife

A) Islamic norms

When a girl gets married, she passes from her father's control (or that of her male guardian) to her husband's authority. This one can impose her the Islamic norms concerning the modesty. He can also require of her to achieve her religious duties, and to forbid her voluntary fasting (by opposition to Ramadan fasting) so that she remains at his sexual disposition[1].

Although the Muslim woman occupies currently all social functions, the husband keeps the right to forbid her to work out of the house. Article 11 of the Egyptian Constitution brings an interesting precision, "The State shall guarantee coordination between woman's duties toward her family and her work in the society, considering her equal to man in the political, social, cultural and economic spheres without detriment to the rules of Islamic jurisprudence".

One Muslim asked the *Egyptian commission of fatwa* if he could prevent his wife from continuing to work. The Commission answered that the woman could not, without authorization of the husband, leave the conjugal house to work, whatever is her work and even though it is necessary for others as for example the work of physician or midwife. Therefore, the woman must obey her husband, abandon her work and remain home. The conjugal duties are bilateral: the woman must remain home but the husband must provide to her subsistence. The Commission mentions the verse 4:34, which institutes the husband's authority on his wife; this verse ends by the husband's right to hit her in case of disobedience[2].

An Egyptian professor of Al-Azhar still teaches his students that the husband has to care for his wife. She is thus not required to work. However, if the woman has no support (a husband, a father, a brother, a parent), she can work in the strict setting of Islamic morals[3].

---

[1] Al-Qaradawi: *Min huda al-islam*, p. 483-490.

[2] Al-fatawi al-islamiyyah min dar al-ifta, Cairo, vol. 9, 1983, p. 3076-77.

[3] Mahmud: *Huquq al-mar'ah*, p. 91.

B) Swiss norms

Hani Ramadan, Director of the *Islamic Center of Geneva*, writes, "Contrary to the idea commonly admitted in the West, according to which the Muslim woman is mistreated and despised, one can affirm that Islam has in fact given to the woman, so much on the spiritual level than on the communal level, a value never equaled by any other human society until our days"[1]. Evidently, the author of these lines could not pretend the opposite without denying his faith, which considers the Islamic norms (of divine origin), more perfected than the modern laws (of human origin). Still there are differences between Islamic norms and international or Swiss norms.

Besides the aforementioned norms which forbid discrimination, and establish an equality between man and woman in marriage, the *Convention on the Elimination of all Forms of Discrimination against Women* requests the national parties "to modify the social and cultural patterns of conduct of men and women, with a view to achieving the elimination of prejudices and customary and all other practices which are based on the idea of the inferiority or the superiority of either of the sexes or on stereotyped roles for men and women" (article 5).

The new Swiss Constitution guarantees the equality between men and women (article 8) as well as the freedom of religion (article 15 par. 3 and 4). With regard to work, article 167 CCS stipulates, "in the choice of a profession or occupation and in the exercise of these activities, every spouse has consideration to the person of the other spouse and to the interests of the marital union". The findings of the Swiss Federal Council add, "in case of lack of understanding, it is necessary to make prevail the individual freedom"[2].

The LPIL submits marital rights and duties to the law of the spouses' domicile. If they are not domiciled in the same country, is applicable the law of the country of the domicile that has the closest link with the case (article 48 par. 1 and 2).

These norms lead to the application of the Swiss law for Swiss citizens as well as for foreigners living in Switzerland, whatever

---

[1] Ramadan: *La femme en islam*, p. 9.
[2] *Feuille fédérale* 1979 II 1245.

their religion. The Muslim husband cannot invoke Islamic law that recognizes him an authority on his wife. So he will not be able to forbid her to work, nor to impose her the religious duties. To oblige his wife to accomplish her religious duties would be considered an objective reason of dissension and divorce[1].

The practice, however, can differ from the principles, whatever is the national or religious adherence of the spouses. Article 167 CCS is besides one of the rare articles on which there are no court decisions, and the legislator did not foresee any direct sanction[2]. Women cannot always address themselves to judicial authorities or the police to claim rights. Those that make it may expose themselves to reprisals on behalf of their husband and incur the threat of a divorce. This last measure can represent an efficient means to dissuade women, especially foreign, to face their husband's caprices. These women must often choose between the bad and the worse. It has been related the case of a Muslim husband who shut in his wife in the cellar during two days for the least mistake.

8) Relations between parents and children

A) Islamic norms

Islamic law distinguishes between guardianship (*hadanah*) and paternal authority (*wilayah*). Muslim State norms look alike on the essential points. We limit us to the Moroccan norms, which underwent a liberal modification in 1993.

So long as the marriage lasts, a child generally lives with his parents. The mother has the child's guardianship; it means that she must look after his elementary needs[3]. Article 99 of the Moroccan Family Law, amended in 1993, brought a nuance while specifying, "a child's guardianship is the responsibility of both father and mother, as long as they stay united by marriage".

---

[1] See Federal Court decision 74 II 1, JdT 1948 I 425, SJ 1949 335; RSJ 63/1967 380.

[2] Grosse: *Le statut patrimonial de base*, p. 18.

[3] Article 62 of the Algerian Family Code gives the following definition of the guardianship: "The right of guardianship consists of the maintenance, the scolarisation and the education of the child according to the religion of his father and the safeguarding of his physical and moral health".

The father is always invested with paternal authority. So article 109 of the Moroccan Family Law gives him the "right to look on what concerns education or school attendance". Article 148 adds, "The legal representation (of the incapable) is assured in the following order by: 1) father; 2) major mother, in case of father's death or loss of capacity. However, the mother cannot alienate the minor's possessions without the judge's authorization". The father acts as matrimonial guardian: he must give his agreement for marriage of his minor son as well of his daughter whatever her age (articles 9-12). He can even force his daughter into marriage. This last point changed in Moroccan Family Law only in 1993.

In case of marriage dissolution, the father preserves his rights over his children, as during marriage. The mother only receives their guardianship. In default of a mother, article 99 of the Moroccan Family Law assigns the guardianship to the father. In default of a father, the priority is granted to the mother's female lineage. This guardianship, according to article 102, continues for the boy until twelve years of age and for the girl until the age of fifteen. After this age, a child can choose to reside at the person of his choice: father, mother or any other relative mentioned in article 99. The guardianship extends to the following person if one who exercises it fails. It is notably the case when a child is Muslim and the guardian is non-Muslim. Article 108 stipulates:

> When the guardian has a religion different from the one of the child's father that has been confided her and that she is not his mother, she can exercise the guardianship during the first five years of the child's life.
>
> When the guardian is the child's mother, she fully exercises the guardianship, provided that she does not abuse of her right by raising the child in another religion than that of his father.

The doctrine stipulates:

> The non-Muslim mother cannot be attributed the guardianship in a permanent way. The child can be withdrawn if the mother attempts to influence him by teaching her own religion. Restrictions brought to the guardianship are dictated by the worry to preserve the faith of the minor of a deep influence exercised by the mother[1].

From the previous norms, one can conclude that the mother gets the child's guardianship during a limited period, and that period can either be reduced if the mother is not Muslim, or suppressed

---

[1] Charfi: *Code du statut personnel annoté*, p. 192.

if the mother apostatizes. The paternal authority remains between the father's hands. Children must be raised in the Muslim religion. Parents do not have another choice if one of them is Muslim, and the child cannot opt once major for another religion. In case of apostasy of the father, this one loses the paternal authority as well as guardianship.

One of the problems raised with Muslims is adoption, forbidden institution in the Muslim countries according to a Koranic verse (33:4-5). The only Muslim country that admits the adoption is Tunisia where, however, only one Muslim can adopt a Muslim child. In the other countries, parents can receive graciously a child, giving him affection and necessary material help, but the child cannot carry the name of the welcoming family nor have a share of inheritance, although he can benefit a bequest, and nothing prevents the welcoming person to marry the hosted girl.

When the Muslim couple cannot have any children, the husband often assigns the responsibility of it to his wife. As the artificial insemination is little developed, or even forbidden in the Muslim countries, and that the adoption is prohibited, the husband repudiates his wife or takes a second one.

B) Swiss norms

Besides the aforementioned norms which forbid discrimination, and establish an equality between man and woman in marriage, the *Convention on the Elimination of all Forms of Discrimination against Women* says that the State shall take all appropriate measures to eliminate discrimination against women, in all matters relating to marriage and family relations and in particular shall ensure, on a basis of equality of men and women, "the same rights and responsibilities with regard to guardianship, wardship, trusteeship and adoption of children, or similar institutions where these concepts exist in national legislation; in all cases the interests of the children shall be paramount" (article 16.f). In any case, parents cannot force their children to get married. The *Convention on Consent to Marriage, Minimum Age for Marriage and Registration of Marriages* says, "No marriage shall be legally entered into without the full and free consent of both parties, such consent to be expressed by them in person after due publicity and in the presence of the authority competent to solemnize the marriage and of witnesses, as prescribed by law" (art. 1 par. 1).

According to the Swiss Civil Code, "during a marriage the parents exercise parental care jointly" (article 297 par. 1). Article 159 par. 2 foresees that spouses "mutually bind themselves to cooperate with each other in safeguarding the interests of the union and in caring and providing for the child". Article 303 says, "the father and the mother shall provide for the religious training of the child" (par. 1); "a contract which restricts this power is void" (par. 2). It adds that a child who completed his sixteenth year has the right to choose faith (par. 3). If spouses diverge in opinion, in this domain, it is incumbent on them to look for understanding. In disagreements on an important question, they can, if a case arises, resort to an office of consultation or solicit judicial mediation (articles 171 and 172)[1]. Article 49 par. 3 aCst foresaw, "The holder of paternal or tutorial authority shall determine the religious education of children ... until they have completed their sixteenth year". This disposition has not been kept in the 1998 Constitution, since It is part of Swiss Civil Code.

Switzerland suppressed the possibility of minor marriage on the basis of the consent of the parents or guardian (article 94 CCS). The freely expressed consent is an imperative condition for the validity of the marriage. A marriage without consent is, in principle, sanctioned by the nullity (article 107 par. 3 CCS).

In case of divorce, the judge gives the parental care to one of the parents and fixes the relation between the parents and the children (article 133 CCS). The guardianship board may also transfer parental care to the father and the mother who request it, have agreed upon their personal share in the care and the distribution of the cost, if this is compatible with the well-being of the child (article 298a par. 1). The holder of the paternal authority arranges the child's religious education freely. He cannot be hindered in this respect in liberty, not more by the judgment of divorce than by a convention[2].

As one notes, the Swiss norms are not compliant to the Islamic norms. How is the conflict resolved between these two norms?

---

[1] Deschenaux and Steinauer: *Le nouveau droit matrimonial*, p. 34-35; *Feuille fédérale* 1979 II 1232.
[2] Federal Court decision 79 II 344.

According to article 82 par. 1 LPIL, "the relationship between parents and child is governed by the law at the child's habitual residence". Article 82 par. 2 adds, "If, however, neither parent is domiciled in the country of the child's habitual residence, but the parents and the child are citizens of the same country, the law of the country of their common citizenship applies".

Mixed marriages represent problems in this field. The Muslim husband generally requires that his children be educated in Islamic religion, requiring the non-Muslim spouse to accept, which she often agrees to easily. In the case where the two spouses do not agree, they generally decide to divorce. In one concrete case, the Muslim father wanted to mark his son religiously through circumcision, but the Christian mother was opposed. The two ended up divorcing and the child was assigned to the mother. In another case, the Muslim husband agreed that his children be educated in the Christian faith, but he had to cut all his links with his family and his country of origin.

In 1990, a tragic case involved a French-Swiss man who converted to Islam and married a Malaysian woman who also converted to Islam; they had two daughters. The family settled in France. The husband blamed his wife of being a bad Muslim. She run away to Geneva and found shelter in a women's center where her husband kidnapped the two little daughters in the night of September 16th, 1993, and disappeared for three years. He reappeared in Malaysia, where he asked the court for the annulment of his marriage and obtained guardianship of his two daughters[1]. His wife became Swiss, asked for a divorce that she obtained May 17th, 1994, with parental authority over her daughters. Returning two years later to Switzerland, without his daughters, the husband was stopped by the police and convicted, in 1997, with five years of prison by the Criminal Court of Geneva for abduction and sequestering. He refused to indicate where the children are, and nobody knows if they are even living. He declared in court:

> My main worry consists in preserving the education of my daughters.
> If I indicate to you where they are, I lose the control and the responsibility of this education. Whereas, at the end of my jail sentence, I will have the possibility of recovering them and exercising

---

[1] *Tribune de Genève*, 12.12.1996 and *24 Heures*, 12.12.1996; *LM*, 10.12.2000.

> my role as a Muslim father. My religion tells me that I should not indicate where they are[1].

As he keeps silent on the fate of his daughters, he is submitted to stern treatment. No holidays. No conditional freedom in view. His jail sentence may also be prolonged. He is accepting the eventuality of remaining in jail until the majority of his daughters, for ten years more[2]. Interrogated by the Swiss French Radio, Hafid Ouardiri, spokesman of the Mosque of Geneva, commented, "The respect of God's laws supercedes the mother's grief". Hani Ramadan, Director of the *Islamic Center of Geneva*, justified the father's behavior:

> There is... in this suit a dimension that it is necessary to take into consideration. The ex-wife broke the engagement to found a family according to the practices of Islam. Therefore, we can understand the motive that pushed the husband to act in this way[3].

Hani Ramadan does not explain what are the mother's torts. These declarations constitute incitements to transgress Swiss law.

One should ask whether the decision of a Muslim country to assign parental authority to the father because of his predominance in the education of children is not contrary to Swiss public order, either because the child's efficient interest is not taken in consideration, or because there is violation of the principle of sexual equality. In the event that a Muslim Egyptian would institute an action in divorce against his Swiss wife of Christian faith in Egypt, it is obvious that the Egyptian court would deprive the Swiss any guardianship over her children because of her religion. Switzerland would not execute this judgment without considering the interest of children. The only criteria of religion on which is based the Egyptian decision would be considered contrary to Swiss public order.

With regard to the father's authority on the marriage of his children, the Muslim parents living in Switzerland cannot force their children to get married, and they cannot oppose their marriage, for example with a non-Muslim. To solve this problem of conscience, some Muslim parents send their daughters back to their country of origin to impose on them a marriage arranged by the family. Article 45 LPIL recognizes as valid in Switzerland a

---

[1] Quoted by *Le Nouveau Quotidien*, 4.9.1997, p. 22.
[2] LM, 10.12.2000.
[3] Quoted by *Le Nouveau Quotidien*, 4.9.1997, p. 22.

marriage validly concluded abroad. But if one of the two spouses is Swiss or domiciled in Switzerland, such a marriage, done without the consent of the two spouses, will not be recognized. It would be contrary to the Swiss public order (article 27 par. 1). Such a marriage has a relative nullity, which means that it remains valid until it is attacked. We have to notice that the girl's refusal to obey orders of parents sometimes has dramatic consequences; she may be killed.

An important problem on which it is necessary to already get along before the marriage is the forename of children. Forenames in Arabic language can be with Muslim, Christian or neutral connotation. In Switzerland, the choice of forenames is incumbent upon the two parents if they are married; if not, the choice is incumbent upon the mother[1]. It is announced at the same time as the birth[2]. This question should be adjusted before the marriage or at the latest before the birth.

With regard to adoption, Swiss law permits it. Some Muslims may host a child because the adoption is forbidden in Islamic law. But hosting a child does not give the right to take him in Switzerland as if it had been adopted. Because of the problems relating to adoption, the booklet published by the Swiss institute of comparative law advises the mixed couples to submit to the premarital exams (barrenness, venereal illnesses, AIDS, etc.), which are also required by certain Muslim countries. If one of the two spouses is sterile, the project of marriage could meet some difficulties, even though the spouses accept the marriage without children. Indeed, the husband's family will very rarely accept a so serious breach to the social rule, even though the spouses live in Switzerland, far away from the husband's family.

Some information circulating in social service surroundings indicates the existence of groups in Switzerland who bring children from the Muslim countries. As a Christian cannot adopt a Muslim child according to the laws of these countries, these groups push Christian families to convert to Islam.

---

[1] Article 301 par. 4 CCS; article 69 par. 1 of the Ordonnance on the civil status.
[2] Article 69 par. 2 of the Ordonnance on the civil status.

One of the sharpest problems is the one of the child abduction. No Muslim country signed the *Hague Convention on the Civil Aspects of International Child Abduction*.

9) Matrimonial regime and economic relations

A) *Islamic norms*

In Islamic law, the legal regime is the one of the separation of goods. This means that every spouse keeps the property of his possessions acquired before or during the marriage. This system penalizes the woman if she remains at home, makes the household and takes care of children. This work not being remunerated, she comes out of the marriage with the only resources she had before the marriage. As for the husband, he keeps all what he had before the marriage and what he gained during the marriage by his lucrative activities. This inequality is particularly flagrant as the husband can forbid his wife to work. It is necessary to add here that a divorced wife has the right of maintenance for only a limited period, variable according to countries between a few months and up to two years.

To remedy the woman's precarious economic situation, Islamic law foresees the obligatory payment of a dower on behalf of the husband to his wife. A part of this dower is generally paid before marriage, and the remainder at the time of divorce. If the divorce is attributable the woman's torts, she loses the right to the remainder of this dowry. On the other hand, to get free from her husband, she may be obliged to give up the remainder of the dower and to repay him what she already received. The dower can be a symbolic amount, aiming not to overwhelm the husband. However, it may constitute an important amount to assure the economic future of a divorced wife. This dower is in principle the woman's exclusive property, but sometimes her parents take it[1].

B) *Swiss norms*

In Switzerland, if the spouses do not choose one of the regimes provided by the Civil Code, they are submitted to the legal regime of participation to the acquests. This means that in case of dissolution of the marriage by the divorce or by the death of a spouse, the assets acquired during the marriage will be shared in

---

[1] A Marriage contract between an Egyptian woman and an Algerian living in Canada mentions as dower 500'000.- DM!

equality. As for assets that each possessed before the marriage, they remain the property of the concerned spouse. On the other hand, divorce does not necessarily end the material reports of spouses since the law foresees maintenance obligations. These norms apply to all Swiss whatever is their religion.

If a spouse is foreign, the LPIL allows spouses to choose the law governing their marriage. They can "choose between the law of the country in which they both have their domicile, or will have their domicile after the marriage, and the law of one of their countries of citizenship" (article 52 par. 1 LPIL). The choice of law must be made in writing or be clearly evident from the marital property contract (article 53 par. 1 LPIL). It may be made or altered at any time. If it is made after the conclusion of the marriage, it is effective retroactively from the time of conclusion of the marriage, unless otherwise provided by the parties (article 53 par. 2 LPIL).

If the spouses have not made a choice of law, their marital property is governed by the law of the country in which both spouses are domiciled at the same time, or, if there is none, the law of the country in which both spouses were last domiciled at the same time. If the spouses were never domiciled at the same time in the same country nor have common citizenship, the provisions of the Swiss law on separation of property apply (article 54 LPIL). If the spouses move their domicile from one country to another, the law of the new domicile applies retroactively from the time of the marriage, unless the spouses excluded the retroactivity by an agreement in writing (article 55 LPIL). On the basis of these rules, the Islamic law will be applicable only to spouses having the same citizenship, but domiciled in two different countries.

The booklet published by the Swiss Institute of Comparative Law advises the mixed couples to submit their matrimonial regime to Swiss law. If the woman chooses to remain home, it is necessary that her work be taken into consideration in the sharing of possessions acquired by the husband. If the woman works, she must avoid that her possessions fall entirely in the household or in her husband's hands. She must require that the husband also participate in the expenses of the household. Indeed, some Muslims - and others - marry a Swiss woman to get a residence permit and the right to work in Switzerland. There are cases where husbands charged the wife of the household and sent back all their gains to their country of origin. When they think that they won enough in Switzerland, they divorce or repudiate their wives and leave to their country to marry other wives. If the spouses would like to settle abroad, it is important to regulate the economic rights depending on whether the woman wishes to work or to remain home. The wife should care not to find herself on the street, after a divorce or the death of her husband, with nothing in her hands. It may be useful that she requires of her husband the remittance of an amount of money, as important as possible, as dower. These are the rules of the game among Muslims. For this reason, the Swiss embassy in Cairo insists that the dower be sufficiently important to provide to the woman's needs in case of divorce. In spite of this insistence, some contracts of marriage between Swiss women and Egyptian Muslims indicate that the dower is one Egyptian pound (less than 50 Swiss cents, paid sometimes by the woman)!

10) Inheritance law

A) Islamic norms

Islamic law includes some discriminatory norms against women in inheritance matter. This discrimination is based on the Koran that bestows to sons double of what is given to girls (4:11) and to the husband double of what his wife inherits (4:12-13). This discrimination is explained by the fact that men had more duties than women [1]. These justifications are unacceptable, particularly when women provide for all needs of their families.

Islamic law also includes some discriminatory norms because of religious adherence. Thus, a Muslim that apostatizes can inherit from no one, and his succession is opened during his life, notably if he abandons his country to escape suits. Alone Muslim heirs can inherit from him. If he returns to Islam, he recovers his possessions [2]. On the other hand, the Muslim cannot inherit from a Christian and vice versa. Thus, if a non-Muslim wife marries a Muslim and get children (necessarily Muslim according to the Islamic law), she cannot inherit from her husband or her children. On the other hand, Muslim children cannot inherit their non-

---

[1] *Colloques sur le dogme musulman*, p. 201-202.
[2] This is indicated in the article 294 of the Kuwaiti Family Code.

Muslim mother. If a Christian becomes Muslim, only his children who convert to Islam can inherit. To get round this rule, one should constitute a bequest to competition of a third of the succession in favor of the heir deprived of the inheritance for reason of religious difference. The Islamic norms concerning succession incite non-Muslim wives married to Muslims to convert (for the show) in order not to lose their share in their husband's inheritance and so their children (in general Muslim) are not excluded of their own inheritance.

B) Swiss norms

International documents do not directly speak about succession. But article 17 of the UDHR says, "Everyone has the right to own property alone as well as in association with others. No one shall be arbitrarily deprived of his property".

The signatory Arab countries of the *Convention on the Elimination of all Forms of Discrimination against Women* gave out reservations concerning article 16 par. 1.c that prescribes the same rights and responsibilities of the man and the woman during marriage and at its dissolution, and article 16 par. 1.h that foresees "the same rights for both spouses in respect of the ownership, acquisition, management, administration, enjoyment and disposition of property, whether free of charge or for a valuable consideration". They considered these articles as contrary to Islamic law[1].

In Switzerland, article 8 nCst forbids discrimination based on sex or religion. It has its application in inheritance law, contravening to the Islamic norms. When the deceased has his last domicile in Switzerland, the Swiss authorities are competent (article 86 par. 1 LPIL) and apply Swiss law (article 90 par. 1 LPIL). If the deceased is Muslim, the Islamic norms are excluded by the conflict of laws rules.

The problem exists when the foreign deceased has chosen in his or her will the application of Islamic law, since Swiss law permits the choice of applicable law (article 90 par. 2 LPIL)[2]. In the same

---

[1] *Traités multilatéraux*, p. 175-181; http://untreaty.un.org/ENGLISH/ bible/englishinternetbible/partI/chapterIV/treaty9.asp

[2] Bucher: *Droit international privé suisse*, tome II, p. 396. A Swiss cannot subject his succession to the law of another country of citizenship

way, if the foreign deceased had his or her last domicile abroad, Swiss authorities have no jurisdiction over assets in Switzerland, unless the foreign authorities do not deal with them (article 88 par. 1). In this case, the estate is governed by the law determined by the conflict of laws rules of the country of domicile (article 91 par. 1 LPIL). Here also, Islamic law may be applicable. Finally, it is necessary to take account of the international conventions, notably of the convention between Switzerland and Iran of 1934, which foresees application of the national law of the deceased.

When Islamic law is applicable, it is likely, according to the doctrine, that rules excluding some people of the succession for motives based on the race, citizenship or religion are considered contrary to the Swiss public order, when there are meaningful links with Switzerland[1]. What about the assignment of an unequal share because of sex? This question was answered neither by the jurisprudence nor by the doctrine. We think that if heiresses agree to the application of Islamic norms that discriminate against them, the Swiss authorities called to share the succession and the Swiss banks solicited to transfer the succession to heirs must not point out the discriminatory character of Islamic norms. It is not necessary to be more royalist than the king. It should go otherwise if some heiresses ask the respect of the constitutional principle of sex equality. It is necessary to recall indeed that numerous voices in the Muslim countries ask the application of such equality in matters of inheritance[2].

Chapter V.
Food prohibitions

1) Religious norms

One finds food prohibitions everywhere in the world; they differ from a social group to the other, even though sometimes some of them may be the same. Rare are people who are

---

[1] *Ibid.*, p. 317.

[2] Aldeeb Abu-Sahlieh: *Unification des droits arabes*, p. 198-199. Similar opinion in: Al-Ashmawi: *Al-shari'ah al-islamiyyah*, p. 35-53, and Shahrur: *Al-Kitab wal-Qur'an*, p. 458-459 and 602-603.

omnivorous. What interest us here are the prohibitions that can be considered common to Muslims according to religious considerations and that create problems in Switzerland. To understand these prohibitions it is necessary to situate them summarily in relation to Jewish and Christian norms. For more detail, the reader can refer to two articles I published on Internet[1].

A) Jewish Norms

Permitted foods are called *kosher* nowadays, i.e. adequate, good for the consumption, but the Bible uses the term *tahor* (pure) by opposition to term *tame* (impure).

a) Prohibited Foods

Animal that has a split hoof divided in two and that chew their cud (Deuteronomy 14:6) are considered pure. All other mammals are impure. It is the case of the camel (which chews the cud but has no split hoof), and of the pig (which has split hoof but does not chews the cud) (Deuteronomy 14:7-8).

Birds are pure to the exception of 24 species considered impure (Leviticus 11:13-19; Deuteronomy 14:12-18) covering in particular wild birds and birds of prey. But it is not easy today to identify all these prohibited birds. Impure bird's eggs are impure.

The aquatic animals that have fins and scales at the same time are pure (Leviticus 11:9-12). All other fish, crustaceans, shellfish, seafood is impure.

The other species as rodents, reptiles, batrachians, bugs and invertebrates are impure, to the exception of locust, katydid, cricket or grasshopper (Leviticus 11:22)[2]. The bee is a prohibited animal, but its honey can be eaten.

The consumption of blood is prohibited "because the blood is the life, and you must not eat the life with the meat" (Deuteronomy 12:23; see also Genesis 9:4; Leviticus 17:12-14). For this reason, the animal must be slaughtered and emptied of its blood, and then its meat is salted two times and rinsed with water three times to suppress all trace of blood. One can also resort

---

[1] http://www.lpj.org/Nonviolence/Sami/articles/frn-articles/abattage.htm; http://www.lpj.org/Nonviolence/Sami/articles/frn-articles/Aliments. html.

[2] *Les lois alimentaires*, p. 3.

directly to the grating of meat on the flame; juice cannot then be recovered.

It is prohibited to eat the meat of an animal found already dead (Deuteronomy 14:21) or torn by wild beasts (Exodus 22:30). The ritual slaughter consists in cutting by means of a perfectly sharp knife, the most quickly possible and while causing the minimum of suffering to the animal, the trachea, the esophagus, the jugular vein and the carotid. The butcher must be Jewish. The Bible foresees to throw the meat of carrion to the dogs (Exodus 22:30), or to sell it to a foreigner (Deuteronomy 14:21). The butcher must remove all the fat from the animal (Leviticus 4:19) as well as the tendon attached to the socket of the hip (sciatic nerve) (Genesis 32:33). And as it is difficult to remove this nerve, it was decided to give up the consumption of the rear part of mammals and to sell it to non-Jews. The sciatic nerve of birds is not removed. Slaughtered animals must be in perfect health, neither sick, nor injured (Exodus 22:30; Leviticus 17:15), nor castrated. Rabbis reject the pre-slaughter stunning[1] although there is nothing in the Bible or the Talmud prohibiting it if the animal is not injured and remains alive before being slaughtered[2].

Hunt is not allowed because an animal cannot be consumed unless it is killed ritually[3].

It is prohibited to mix meat (fish is not a meat) and milk or their derivatives because of the verse, "Do not cook a young goat in its mother's milk" (Exodus 23:19 and 34:26; and Deuteronomy 14:21). For this reason, fervent Jews have utensils for the carnal food and other ones for the milky food. A third set of utensils so-called *parve* (neutral) are used for foods that are neither meat nor milk[4]. After having consumed milk or meat or their derivatives, it is necessary to wait between a half-hour and six hours before eating the other food[5]. Is prohibited the bread in which one adds animal or lactic fat or leaven from a wine alcohol if rules concerning these components are not respected[6].

---

[1] *Ibid.*, p. 4-5.
[2] Aldeeb Abu-Sahlieh: *Faux débat sur l'abattage rituel en Occident*.
[3] 24.4.2001: pyb@viejuive.com (Pierre-Yves Bauer).
[4] Bauer: *La nourriture cacher*, p. 10-12 and 20.
[5] *Les lois alimentaires*, p. 7-8.
[6] *Ibid.*, p. 6-7 and 9-11.

Products of the land are pure to the exception of fruits of a tree during the first three years (Leviticus 19:23) and of a portion (so-called *halah*) of bread or cake prepared with one of five kinds of cereals. The mistress of house takes a small piece of the bread and the cake and burns it[1].

All fruits and vegetables as well as their juices are comestible. The milk of a pure animal, as the milk of cow, is permitted, whereas the milk of an impure animal, as the milk of donkey, is prohibited. Wine and alcohols based on wine as brandy are considered pure products and can be consumed[2].

A food consumed at the time of the *Sabbath* must be cooked in the respect of the norms of *Sabbath*. That day, thirty-nine kinds of work, including to light fire, is prohibited (Exodus 35:3). Therefore, one lights fire one hour before the beginning of the *Sabbath* and lets it alight all *Sabbath* until the following day[3]. It is also prohibited to consume leaven during the eight days of Easter (Exodus 12:15, 19 and 20). For this reason, one uses particular utensils for Easter so that there is no trace of leaven[4].

In case of necessity, notably in case of deadly illness, which can be treated only by the absorption of prohibited foods or medicaments based on impure components, the food laws fade away completely. If the illness is not very serious and one has therapeutic choice, medicaments with permitted components should be chosen. On the other hand, non-oral consumption (as injections, suppositories, ointments and spray) is permitted[5].

b) *Justification of the prohibitions*

On Internet, a rabbi writes, "The definition of an impure animal emanates from the Creator's only will. It has nothing to do with hygienic criteria, nor nutritional qualities"[6]. This concept did not prevent some from presenting explanations, notably pseudo-medical, as numerous than little probable, to apologetic goal: God

---

[1] Bauer: *La nourriture cacher*, p. 10-14.
[2] *Les lois alimentaires*, p. 6.
[3] Bauer: *La nourriture cacher*, p. 18-20.
[4] *Ibid.*, p. 10-12 and 20.
[5] *Les lois alimentaires*, p. 6-8.
[6] *Ibid.*, p. 2.

knows what is good for us and the best proof of this goodness is that the prohibited foods are bad for health[1].

The justification advanced by the Bible concerning animals is as follows, "You must distinguish between the unclean and the clean, between living creatures that may be eaten and those that may not be eaten" (Leviticus 11:47)[2]. The Bible indicates further:

> You are to be my holy people. So do not eat the meat of an animal torn by wild beasts; throw it to the dogs (Exodus 22:30).
>
> Do not eat anything you find already dead. You may give it to an alien living in any of your towns, and he may eat it, or you may sell it to a foreigner. But you are a people holy to the Lord your God (Deuteronomy 14:21).

Several Jewish norms exclude non-Jews from pure food preparation. The use and consumption of drinks based on grape or alcohol of grape, and all products of the press not manufactured under the control of a competent rabbi, or if handled by a non-Jew, are likewise prohibited. This norm extends to vinegar, the oil of grape pips or the sugar of grapes. A Jew must kindle the oven. A devout Jew only consumes milk milked or prepared in presence of a Jew. The kitchen utensils and table service must be immersed in a ritual bath to purify them, when they have either been manufactured or sold by non-Jews[3].

Moshe Menuhin, father of the famous violinist Yehudi Menuhin, reports that his grandfather's house in the Jewish colony of Bokhara in Palestine was opened to Gentiles at the time of the Jewish Passover. He provided them a separate table. Menuhin adds:

> As soon as the foreign guests had left, grandfather went to the table of guests and, with a smile, took all bottles of wine that had been opened (there was a good number), carried them away and emptied them in the gutter. Some of bottles were nearly full and I did not understand such a wasting. I asked him, "What pain *goyim* did they

---

[1] Maïmonide: Le guide des égarés, p. 594-596. See also Philon: De specialibus legibus, 4:118; Bauer: La nourriture cacher, p. 29-36; Henninger: L'impureté des aliments et du sang chez les peuples sémitiques, p. 476-482; Henninger: Nouveaux débats sur l'interdiction du porc dans l'islam, p. 29-40; Vaux: *Les sacrifices de porcs en Palestine et dans l'ancien Orient*, p. 499-516.

[2] It would be too long to mention here all the racist texts of the Bible. See for example chapters 9 and 10 of the book of Esdras.

[3] *Le vin et les sous-produits de la vigne*, p. 6-8 and 11; Les lois alimentaires, p. 1-2.

make to wine?" Grandfather smiled and explained that, according to the Jewish law code, all wine opened by a *goy* became wine *nesek*, of the pagan and therefore undrinkable wine[1].

c) Respect of the prohibitions

It does not seem that Jews have always respected food prohibitions. These prohibitiond have even been attacked by the Pittsburgh Platform (November of 1885), adopted by American Reform Rabbis who declared, "We hold that all Mosaic and Rabbinical laws that regulate diet ... originated in ages and under the influence of ideas altogether foreign to our present mental and spiritual state. They fail to impress the modern Jew with a spirit of priestly holiness; their observance in our days is apt rather to obstruct than to further modern spiritual elevation"[2]. But the religious authorities always insisted on these prohibitions. Isaiah thunders forth against those that violate these prohibitions, "Those... eating the flesh of pigs, vermin, and rodents, shall come to an end together, says the Lord" (Isaiah 66:17)[3]. These authorities do not hesitate to resort to the coercive means to impose *kosher* food, using their privilege to deliver certificates of purity in all domains of the feeding, the restoration and the hotels. In some countries, these authorities have the monopoly, recognized by the State, of the certification of purity, on which they collect a tax.

B) Christian Norms

a) Abolition of the prohibitions

Christians mostly made Jewish food prohibitions obsolete. One finds a prelude of this abolition in Jesus' words, "There is nothing outside a person that by going in can defile, but the things that come out are what defile". And Mark commented, "Thus he declared all foods clean" (Mark 7:15, 19-22).

Since its beginnings, the Christian community broke away from Jewish food prohibitions. Christians of Jewish origin blamed Peter for having accepted the invitation of Cornelius, a Roman

---

[1] Menuhin, p. 34-35 (our translation from the French version).

[2] Dietary laws, col. 44; Declaration of Principles, 1885 Pittsburgh Conference, in: http://www.ucalgary.ca/~elsegal/363_Transp/ PittsburgPlatform.html.

[3] See also Ezekiel 4:14; Tobit 1:10-11; I Maccabees 1:62; II Maccabees chap. 6 and 7.

centurion, "Why did you go to uncircumcised men and eat with them"? (Acts 11:3). Peter knew such a prohibition, and recalled it to his host, "You yourselves know that it is unlawful for a Jew to associate with or to visit a Gentile; but God has shown me that I should not call anyone profane or unclean" (Acts 10:28). Peter justified his behavior by a vision in which a voice ordered him to eat everything that was presented him, "What God has made clean, you must not call profane" (Acts 10:15). Paul tells us that Peter, "until certain people came from James, he used to eat with the Gentiles. But after they came, he drew back and kept himself separate for fear of the circumcision faction" (Galatians 2:12).

If Christians, of Jewish origin, continued to observe biblical food prohibitions, the conversion of pagans to Christianity brought the Apostles to limit these prohibitions to the minimum. Thus, at the time of the *First Council* in Jerusalem, the Apostles asked the non-Jewish converts to abstain "from what has been sacrificed to idols and from blood and from what is strangled" (Acts 15:29). One notices here that this council abolished also the obligation of the circumcision. For Jews, uncircumcised persons were considered impure, and therefore could not even visit their homes. Henceforth, one can be Christian and be saved without being circumcised or observing the Jewish food prohibitions.

The question of these prohibitions was discussed in Paul's epistles. He establishes a large rule concerning food, "Eat whatever is sold in the meat market without raising any question on the ground of conscience, for the earth and its fullness are the Lord's". But he recommends avoiding scandalizing others (I Corinthians 10:25-30). He even permits Christians to eat meat offered to idols because "we know that no idol in the world really exists and that there is no God but one (I Corinthians 8:4). He thinks, "nothing is unclean in itself; but it is unclean for anyone who thinks it unclean ... The kingdom of God is not food and drink but righteousness and peace and joy in the Holy Spirit" (Romans 14:14 and 17).

The prohibition against consuming blood, now obsolete, was respected by Christians. Tertullian (d. ca 222) speaks about it in his writings [1]. As late as 692, the *Council in Trullo* (Constantinople) declared:

---

[1] Tertullian: *On the Resurrection of the Flesh*, chapter 6.

> The divine Scripture commands us to abstain from blood, from things strangled, and from fornication. Those therefore who on account of a dainty stomach prepare by any art for food the blood of any animal, and so eat it, we punish suitably. If anyone henceforth ventures to eat in any way the blood of an animal, if he be a clergyman, let him be deposed; if a layman, let him be cut off[1].

The *Council of Florence* took a liberal position on foods February 4th, 1442, even passing besides the decision of the Apostles. It is said, "[The church] condemns ... no kind of food that human society accepts and nobody at all, neither man nor woman, should make a distinction between animals, no matter how they died"[2].

If the Apostles abolished food prohibitions, allowing Christians to eat the food of pagans, some Councils reintroduced the prohibition concerning Jewish food[3].

b) Maintenance of the prohibitions by some groups

Some sectarian religious groups with Christian affiliations continue to observe some Jewish food prohibitions. Seventh-Day Adventists recommend an ovo-lacto-vegetarian diet, the respect of the biblical prohibition concerning animals and blood (but they do accept blood transfusions), the abstinence from smoking and consuming foods containing theine, caffeine and alcohol[4]. Jehovah's Witnesses do not observe the biblical prohibitions concerning the animals, they drink wine, but they prohibit blood consumption and transfusion, as well as tobacco (I Corinthians 7:1). Mormons do not observe the biblical prohibitions concerning animals, but recommend not consuming blood (pudding, etc.). On the other hand, they abstain from smoking and consuming foods containing theine, caffeine and alcohol[5]. However, these three groups do not require ritual slaughter as

---

[1] The Quinsext Council, (or the Council in Trullo), 692, canon 67.

[2] *Les conciles oecuméniques*, tome II.1, p. 1181-1182. http://www.ewtn.com/ library/COUNCILS/FLORENCE.HTM

[3] See Canon 12 of the Council of Vannes (465) (Hefele, vol. II.2, p. 905); Canon 40 of the Council of Agde (506) (Hefele, vol. II.2, p. 997); Canon 15 of the Council of Mâcon (583) (Hefele, vol. III.1, p. 204) and Canon 7 of the Council of Metz (888) (Hefele, vol. IV.2, p. 689).

[4] *Ce que croient les Adventistes*, p. 286 and 288-290.

[5] See *The word of wisdom*: http://wordofwisdom.ldsteach.com/

practiced by Jews, and do not follow biblical norm that prohibits mixing meat and milk.

Catholics are not supposed to eat meat on Fridays and during Lent, but this is no longer mandatory, whereas previously violation of this norm was punished severely. Today one notes a slip from religious prohibitions to dietary norms: one abstains from some foods out of tradition instead of saving one's soul[1]. There are also some religious orders such as the Carthusians who abstain from all meat as fundamental part of their rules[2].

Therefore, we may conclude that Christians, except for some small groups, do not observe religious food prohibitions. If today Western Christians do not eat rats or dogs, it is due much more to custom rather than because religious law prohibits the practice.

C) Islamic norms

The position of Muslims constitutes a nearly complete return to the Jewish prohibitions. We will explain here these prohibitions referring especially to the modern Sunnite Arab books, which we will supplement with the Shiite books when their norms differ from those of the Sunnites. It is necessary to note in this respect that the Muslim authors classify foods mainly in the following categories:

- *Halal* (licit): a food that one can consume.
- *Haram* (illicit): a food whose consumption is prohibited.
- *Mubah* (permitted): a food whose consumption is left to the choice of the person.
- *Makruh* (reprobated, repugnant): a food from which it is preferable to abstain although it is not prohibited.

One finds on the Internet lists classified according to *halal*, *haram* and *mashbuh* (suspect). The authors of these lists say that it is necessary to abstain from consuming suspect products.

a) The prohibitions in the Koran

According to Islamic law, everything that is not prohibited is permitted. God gave human beings mastery over all animals and fruits of the earth so that they can use them. But they must avoid wasting[3]. In the same way, it is prohibited to kill a licit animal for

---

[1] Branlard, p. 244-246.

[2] Chapter 7 of the *Statutes of the Carthusian Order* (French text in: http://chartreux.org/textes/-fr/st-fr-1.htm).

[3] See Koran 2:60, 168 and 172; 6:142; 7:160; 20:81.

any reason save to eat it[1]. Classic Muslim jurists condemned hunting for pleasure and not for food[2].

The Koran insists on the fact that man does not have the right to declare a food as illicit. Only God can do this (5:87; 16:116). What God declares illicit is unclean, and what he declares licit is good (7:157), but God remains free in his decision and he need not give reasons to anyone (5:1; 21:23).

The Koran speaks of some food prohibitions among the Arabs before Islam, prohibitions that it abrogates because it considers them as inspired by the devil[3]. It does not say anything of food prohibitions among Christians, but lingers on Jewish food prohibitions. It states that before the revelation of the Torah, all foods were licit, but Israel (Jacob?) prohibited some of these foods for himself (3:93) and God prohibited Jews some foods to punish them (4:160-161; 6:146). Elsewhere the Koran indicates that God had prohibited to Jews what he prohibited to Muslims. If Jews added to these prohibitions other foods, it is by their own decision (16:118). Therefore Muslims must not follow Jewish prohibitions, but those that God indicates them. These prohibitions are fixed in four verses:

- He only prohibits for you the eating of dead animals, blood, the meat of pigs, and animals dedicated to other than God. If one is forced to eat these, without being malicious or deliberate, he incurs no sin (2:173).
- Prohibited for you are dead animals, blood, the meat of pigs, and animals dedicated to other than God. Dead animals include those strangled, struck with an object, fallen from a height, gored, attacked by a wild animal-unless you save your animal before it dies - and animals sacrificed on altars (5:3).
- I do not find in the revelations given to me any food that is prohibited for any eater except: dead animals, running blood, the meat of pigs, for it is contaminated, and the meat of animals blasphemously dedicated to other than God. If one is forced to eat these, without being deliberate or malicious, then your Lord is Forgiver, Most Merciful (6:145).
- He only prohibits for you the eating of dead animals, blood, the meat of pigs, and animals dedicated to other than God. If one is forced to eat these, without being malicious or deliberate, then God is Forgiver, Most Merciful (16:115).

---

[1] Abd-al-Hadi: Ahkam al-at'imah, p. 184; Al-Fawzan: Al-at'imah, p. 138.
[2] Aldeeb Abu-Sahlieh: *Limites du sport*, p. 366.
[3] See 2:168-169; 5:103; 6:138-139 and 143-144.

The Koran prohibits eating: carrion (called by the Koran *mayyitah*, dead animal), blood, pork and what has been offered to deities other than God. Recall that in the *First Council* held in Jerusalem, the Apostles asked the non-Jewish converts to abstain "from what has been sacrificed to idols and from blood and from what is strangled" (Acts 15:29). The Koran uses the same formulation and adds pork, either with the goal of winning Jews to his side, or because some Arab Christians from Jewish origin observed such a prohibition[1]. Classic jurists think that any part of a pig is prohibited: its meat, its fat, its bones, its skin, and its hair. But Ibn-Hazm wrote that the Koran only prohibits pig meat[2]. Malikites considers the pig hair as pure, provided it is not pulled, but it is necessary to wash it. Hanbalites permit making a sifter of them provided it is used to sift dry products[3].

The Koran prohibits eating food offered to any deity other than the God, in verses 2:173, 6:145, 16:115 and 5:3. This last verse adds to this prohibition the "animals sacrificed on altars".

Concerning blood, verse 6:145 specifies "running blood". It means that the flowing blood of an animal either living or dead is prohibited, but not the blood remaining in the meat of a slaughtered animal. The animal must be emptied of its blood as much as possible but, contrary to Jews, one must not rinse and salt meat or grill it to eliminate the remainder of blood. Besides, Muhammad permitted Muslims to eat the liver and the spleen, contrary to the Jewish practice[4].

The Koran prohibits eating carrion (dead animals) and adds in verse 5:3, "Dead animals include those strangled, struck with an object, fallen from a height, gored, attacked by a wild animal- unless you save your animal before it dies". Carrion is an animal that died without human interference, or by a means judged illicit as for example by beating it. Game animals are licit even though not formally slaughtered, except if there was possibility to slaughter them, but not done. There is no need to slaughter aquatic animals according to a narrative of Muhammad that says,

---

[1] See Aldeeb Abu-Sahlieh: *Circoncision masculine*, p. 106-109.
[2] Ibn-Hazm: *Al-muhalla*, vol. 7, p. 391-392. See Musa: *Ahkam al-at'imah*, p. 58-62
[3] *Al-mawsu'ah al-fiqhiyyah*: Khanzir, vol. 20, p. 35.
[4] Musa: *Ahkam al-at'imah*, p. 139-142.

"God slaughtered all what is in the sea for Adam's sons". But some classic jurists require slaughtering those that live also out of water and have blood, such as crocodiles. Grasshoppers can be eaten if one finds them dead[1]. Animal slaughter is regulated in Islamic law:

- It is necessary to pronounce God's name on the living animal when one passes the knife on its neck (6:121; 22:36) and for the hunt, when one sends dogs behind the animal (5:4). The reason for which one pronounces God's name on the animal is to make its meat better and to expel the devil from the animal and the butcher[2]. We have to notice that the Koran prohibits killing game during the period of pilgrimage or eating the eggs of game birds (5:2 and 95-96).
- The butcher must be adult, capable of discernment, either a Muslim, or one of the *People of the Book* (Christian, Jew, Samaritan or Sabian). The dominant opinion at the Shiites is that the slaughter must be one of their community; they do not accept a slaughter from the *People of the Book*[3].
- Slaughter can be either by cutting (*dhabh*) the throat of animals with short neck as it the case with cow, sheep and bird, or by carrying the knife to the collarbone in the bottom of the neck of the animal (*nahr*) when this last has a long neck, as with the camel, or by wounding a game animal (*aqr*) that one cannot grasp or an agitated cattle. To slaughter an animal consists of cutting the trachea (respiratory tube), the esophagus (digestive tube) and the interior and the exterior jugular veins (blood vessels).
- The tool can be a knife, a sword or a blade. For game and unseizable animals, it can be a wounding tool as a spear or a projectile. In these two cases blood must sink. If one strangles an animal, or kills it by a shock or by beating it, its meat is illicit; it becomes a carrion. If an animal is killed by a stroke of rifle and that the projectile transfixes the animal, its meat is licit. Such an animal does not need to be slaughtered. But if it dies because of the shock of a stone or a projectile or by the sound of this last, its meat is illicit unless one can reach the animal still alive to slaughter it. So it is necessary that the slaughterer intervene on a living animal[4].
- During the slaughtering, the butcher and the animal should face Mecca[5]. The goal is to do the opposite of what polytheists did by facing their idols[6].

---

[1] Abd-al-Hadi: *Ahkam al-at'imah*, p. 289-292.
[2] *Ibid.*, p. 165.
[3] Al-Tabatba'i: *Riyad al-masa'il*, vol. 8, p. 166-174.
[4] Musa: *Ahkam al-at'imah*, p. 87-128.
[5] Al-Fawzan: *Al-at'imah*, p. 137.
[6] Musa: *Ahkam al-at'imah*, p. 131.

b) *Widening of the prohibitions by jurists*

If we refer to the Koran, we can say that only four foods are prohibited: pork, blood, carrion and foods offered to idols. The Koran considers licit everything that is not prohibited, as aforementioned. Therefore, nothing else should be prohibited. But the classic jurists attempted to widen the list of the prohibitions through an extensive interpretation of certain Koranic verses and contradictory narratives of Muhammad, probably to accommodate some local customs.

Thus, referring to the verses 6:143, 16:5 and 36:71-73, they consider as licit the animals entering in the category of *an'am*, herd animals, i.e. ovine, bovine, and camels. As for equines (horses, mules and donkeys), the Koran says that God created them "to ride, and for luxury" (16:8). Contrary to the verse on herd animals, the Koran does not indicate equines serve for food. It is also reported that Muhammad prohibited eating them. But the dominant opinion considers the meat of the horse and the wild donkey as licit because Muhammad and his Companions ate it[1]. Thus, the domestic donkey and the mule are prohibited, except by Malikites who consider them either licit, or repugnant[2].

According to the dominant opinion, the meat of all animals using their canines to attack other animals, such as the lion, the tiger or the wolf, is illicit. Certain narratives of Muhammad prohibited them. Some Malikites permit them because the Koran does not mention them among the prohibited foods, but Malik's opinion is that their meat is repugnant[3]. There are divergences among the classic jurists about some animals with canines as hyenas, foxes, bears, domestic and wild cats, elephants and monkeys. Some jurists say that it is permitted to eat their meat, others are opposed, yet others permit it reluctantly[4].

Concerning rodents, rats are prohibited but the dominant opinion permits eating hedgehogs, porcupines[5] and rabbits[6]. Some

---

[1] Abd-al-Hadi: *Ahkam al-at'imah*, p. 16-23.
[2] *Ibid.*, p. 23-30.
[3] *Ibid.*, p. 32-35.
[4] *Ibid.*, p. 35-44.
[5] *Ibid.*, p. 45-50.
[6] See Al-Bukhari, narratives 2384, 5066 and 5109, and Ahmad, narrative 12949.

Companions of Muhammad consider repugnant to eat rabbit because Muhammad said that it menstruates and therefore he did not eat it, but without prohibiting it to others[1]. The classic jurists permit Muslims to eat grasshoppers as well as fruit worms[2].

Birds are licit in principle. The dominant opinion prohibits eating birds of prey having claws, but some jurists permit eating them because the Koran does not mention them among the prohibited foods. The dominant opinion permit eating bats, flying mammals, but some jurists consider them repugnant[3].

The Koran permits eating animals living in water (5:96; 16:14; 35:12), but the dominant opinion among Shiites, citing narratives of Muhammad, follows the biblical classification, only allowing animals which have scales[4]. They do not speak of fins as in the Bible, probably because any fish with scales has fins. As for the classic Sunnite jurists, they are less categorical. One can summarize their position as follows:

- All classic jurists agree that fish dead for an obvious reason (killed while fighting, by strong wave, or a blow from a stick, or been thrown by water on the beach) is licit. If it died for unobvious reason, the majority of jurists consider it licit, except Hanafites.
- If the aquatic animal is not a fish or does not look like a fish, Hanafites consider it illicit and others as licit except if expressly prohibited (e.g., frogs), or excluded because of its venomous nature (e.g., eels), its aggressiveness (e.g., crocodiles), or its filth (e.g., sea turtles). Amphibian animals must be slaughtered to become licit.
- Some classic jurists think that an aquatic animal looking like a prohibited terrestrial animal is also prohibited. It is the case of the dolphin (called the pig of the sea), of the shark (called the dog of the sea), and of the eel (called the snake of the sea). Some think that the dolphin is prohibited for people who call it the pig of the sea, and permitted for those who call it by another name[5].

If a licit animal feeds upon rubbish, the dominant opinion says that one cannot eat it before quarantine, a period during which

---

[1] See Ibn-Majah, narrative 3236, Al-Tirmidhi, narrative 1711, Abu-Da'ud, narrative 3298. See also Abd-al-Hadi: *Ahkam al-at'imah*, p. 14-16.
[2] Abd-al-Hadi: *Ahkam al-at'imah*, p. 52-54.
[3] *Ibid.*, p. 59-63.
[4] Al-Amili: *Wasa'il al-shi'ah*, vol. 16, p. 397-399. Al-Tabatba'i, *Riyad al-masa'il*, vol. 8, p. 217-225. See list in: *Dalil al-muslim*, p. 93-108.
[5] Abd-al-Hadi: *Ahkam al-at'imah*, p. 76-89 and Musa: *Ahkam al-at'imah*, p. 47-54.

they are fed with clean food, so that its meat is not contaminated anymore by what they eat. This period varies between three and forty days[1].

Muhammad ordered some animals to be killed, such as snakes, ravens, rats, aggressive dogs and *dabs* (a kind of lizard), and he prohibited killing some other animals, such as frogs, ants, bees, crests, magpies, partridges and bats. These two categories cannot be eaten. But some jurists say that whatever can be killed should be edible.

Concerning animal products other than meat, classic jurists say that the bone and the skin of pure animals are pure if they have been slaughtered according to the religious rules. If the pure animal is carrion, tanning its skin makes it pure. As for the skin of impure animals, the classic jurists have varied opinions. Thus, Hanafites permit the use of the tanned hide of lions, wolves or dogs, but they exclude the skins of rats and pigs. We mentioned earlier that some jurists permit the utilization of the hair of pig. It is prohibited to eat fat taken from a living animal even if they are pure (as the fat from the hump of a camel or the tail of certain species of sheep); such fat is considered as coming from carrion[2]. Eggs and milk of pure animals are licit. So it is not permitted to eat turtle or eagle eggs, nor drinking donkey milk. In the same way one should not consume milk or eggs of an animal that fed upon rubbish before quarantine. If one finds eggs of an unidentified animals, classic jurists think one can eat them from the moment their two tips are different (this rule is also in the *Talmud*), or their cockle is rough (for fish eggs)[3]. Some parts of the animal are prohibited, such as genitalia, bladder, urine and stool. But Muhammad recommended camel urine as a medicine, so it is licit to consume.

All fruits of the earth and of trees are licit (16:69; 36:33-35). Products that damage health are prohibited (2:195; 7:157). So it is prohibited to eat a venomous fruit or to consume alcohol (5:90); the prohibition can be extended to drugs and tobacco[4].

---

[1] Abd-al-Hadi: *Ahkam al-at'imah*, p. 72-75.

[2] Al-Tirmidhi, narrative 1400 and Abu-Da'ud, narrative 2475. Musa: *Ahkam al-at'imah*, p. 143-147.

[3] Al-Tabatba'i: *Riyad al-masa'il*, vol. 8, p. 228-229 and 251.

[4] Abd-al-Hadi: *Ahkam al-at'imah*, p. 131-140.

All prohibited foods become licit when necessary to protect health or life (2:173; 5:3; 6:145). But a Muslim may consume no more than necessary, and not to satiate. May one steal a licit food instead of consuming a prohibited food? The answer is no. Can one eat human flesh? The answer is yes, if the person is dead, but no, if he is alive, even if he has been condemned to death as an apostate or a polytheist[1]. According to the dominant doctrine, it is prohibited to consume wine in case of thirst, because wine does not quench thirst and can even increase it. Wine may be used as medicine, if there is no other means to save life, provided a Muslim physician worthy of confidence prescribed the medicine[2].

A licit food can become an illicit food, and vice versa. So the juice of fruits, once fermented, becomes illicit. Wine in time turns into vinegar, which is a licit food; some think that this transformation must be made without manipulation[3]. Carrion is impure, but when it decomposes, it becomes pure ash. Water, licit food, becomes urine, which is a prohibited food. In the same way milk is licit although it is formed, according to the Koran, from two illicit foods, blood and food decomposed in the stomach (16:66). We also saw that an animal fed upon rubbish becomes pure after quarantine. To judge a food as licit or illicit, some classic jurists refer to the name of the food in question. Wine, illicit, once it became vinegar changes in name. As vinegar is not mentioned in the list of prohibited foods, it is considered licit. In the same way the dog, an impure animal, becomes pure salt when it falls in a salty swamp and decomposes. Excrement, impure matter, is put in a garden and becomes with time earth, a pure matter used for ablution in the absence of water[4].

If someone had a sexual relationship with an animal, this animal becomes prohibited for consumption and must be killed and burnt; according to Muhammad's narratives the person in question must also be killed[5]. This norm has its equivalent in the Bible (Leviticus 20:15-16). If the licit meat enters in contact with

---

[1] *Al-fatawi al-islamiyyah*, vol 10, n° 1300, p. 3558-3562.
[2] *Ibid.*, vol. 10, n° 1307, p. 3581-3582.
[3] See *fatwa* on Internet: www.gueteli.fr/home/mohmedpat/food2.html.
[4] Musa: *Ahkam al-at'imah*, p. 241-251.
[5] Abu-Da'ud, narrative 3871, Al-Tirmidhi, narratives 1374 and 1376; Ibn-Majah, narrative 2554; Ahmad, narratives 2294 and 2597.

pork, it becomes contaminated and therefore inedible. In the same way, if one slaughters a lamb with a knife that had been used to slaughter a pig, the meat of a lamb becomes illicit. If a rat falls in a vase of oil, the oil becomes impure. But if it falls on hard butter, only the part touched must be removed. All products that contain a prohibited ingredient become entirely prohibited. This norm applies to foods, food additives and pharmaceutical products as vitamins. One finds on the Internet lists of products classified into *halal* (licit), *haram* (illicit) and *mashbuh* (suspect, and therefore prohibited)[1]. Such lists are not very reliable because producers constantly change the ingredients of their products.

Finally, Muslims fast during the month of Ramadan. They must abstain from all food, from sunrise, to sunset. Besides this obligatory fast, there are some optional fasts, sometimes one day a week. On the other hand, the dominant opinion, based on narratives of Muhammad, prohibits eating or drinking from gold or silver utensils. The goal of this prohibition is to not imitate the pride of unbelievers. Notice also that it is prohibited for Muslim men (but not women) to wear gold rings or jewels[2].

c) Justification of the prohibitions

One finds explanations aiming to justify these prohibitions among both classic and modern authors. Certainly, the first reason is that God proscribed them, either through the Koran, or through Muhammad's narratives. As God is omniscient, and Muhammad, infallible, the believer must submit to these prohibitions. As God and Muhammad dictate norms only for the man's good, a Muslim cannot doubt that these norms are beneficial for health and social behaviors. To be qualified as good on a culinary level, or even on only a physiological level, a food must be religiously licit. A food both good and illicit constitutes a contradiction[3]. So one reads in *Wasa'il al-shi'ah* that eating carrion weakens the body, procures barrenness and provokes death by heart attack. As for blood, it accumulates yellow water in the stomach, causes bad odor, and develops cruelty to the point

---

[1] www.uh.edu/campus/msa/articles/*halal*.html;
www.soundvision.com/*halal*healthy/ingri-dient.shtml
[2] Abd-al-Hadi: *Ahkam al-at'imah*, p. 140-143.
[3] Benkheira, p. 46.

that one who eats it may kill his son and parents. Wine provokes tremors, weakens strength and provokes adultery and murder[1].

Some also advance arguments connected with Koranic beliefs that God transformed certain humans into animals to punish them. The fact that God chose these animals indicates that the latter are impure and, therefore, cannot be consumed. To consume such animals means to minimize his sanctions. This possibility of transforming humans is mentioned in verse 36:67. Three verses indicate that God changed some human beings into monkeys and pigs (2:65; 5:60; 7:166). Narratives of Muhammad offer other examples for such metamorphoses[2]. According to one narrative, God transformed seven hundred human groups who had disobeyed prophets; four hundred of these groups took the shape of terrestrial animals, and three hundred, the shape of aquatic animals. To sustain this belief, Muhammad recited verse 34:19 that says, "We made them bywords and we broke them into pieces. In that, verily, are signs for every steadfast and grateful person"[3]. The metamorphose argument is not mentioned in modern books on food, probably due to their irrational and shocking character, sounding more like Hinduism or Buddhism.

We saw that Muhammad ordered to kill some animals, such as snakes, ravens, rats, aggressive dogs and lizards[4]. The order to kill them is probably motivated by the fact that they are harmful. These animals cannot be eaten. Muhammad also prohibited the killing of some animals that, moreover, cannot be eaten. Among these animals the Sunnites mention ants, bees, crests, magpies and frogs[5]. The reason for this prohibition is religious. So the prohibition on killing ants, bees and crests is motivated by the fact that the Koran mentions them in positive way. A Shiite

---

[1] Al-Amili: *Wasa'il al-shi'ah*, vol. 16, p. 377, 378.
[2] See for example Muslim, narratives 3609, 4814 and 5316; Al-Tirmidhi, narrative 2987; Ahmad, narratives 3560, 3580, 3797 and 11171. See also Al-Kasani: *Kitab bada'i al-sana'i*, vol. 5, p. 37.
[3] Al-Amili: *Wasa'il al-shi'ah*, vol. 16, p. 379-387. See also Al-Shaykh Al-Saduq: *Ilal al-shara'i*, p. 483-489.
[4] See for example Al-Bukhari, narratives 1697 and 3067; Muslim, narratives 2071 and 2075; Al-Tirmidhi, narrative 767.
[5] Abu-Da'ud, narrative 4583; Ibn-Majah, narratives 324 and 3215; Ahmad, narratives 2907 and 3073; Ibn-Majah, narrative 3214. Abd-al-Hadi: *Ahkam al-at'imah*, p. 63-71.

narrative says that on the wing of every crest it is written in Syriac, "The family of Muhammad is the best of creation"[1]. The magpie was the first being to observe the fast. Muhammad considers the voice of the frog like a prayer, but maybe its consumption was prohibited because its flesh could contain venom[2]. The bat tried to extinguish the fire in the Temple of Solomon at the time of its destruction[3]. The partridge gives thanks to God and ends its prayer saying, "God curses those that hate the family of Muhammad"[4].

As among Jews, food prohibitions are also connected to contact with non-Muslims. The Koran stipulates:

> Today, all good food is made lawful for you. The food of the people of the scripture is lawful for you. Also, you may marry the chaste women among the believers, as well as the chaste women among the followers of previous scripture (5:5).
> You shall eat from that upon which God's name has been pronounced (6:118).

The first verse explicitly associates eating and inter-marriage. The matrimonial exchange is permitted with those whose foods are permitted.

The dominant opinion among the Shiites is that a person from the *People of the Book* cannot slaughter an animal, on the basis of narratives of their imams. Some think indeed that verse 5:5 concerns other foods than meat[5]. The Shiites are also more reticent than the Sunnites about marriage between a Muslim man and a non-Muslim woman from the *People of the Book*.

The Sunnites permit eating meat of an animal slaughtered by a non-Muslim, provided that he is monotheist (Christian, Jew, Samaritan or Sabian). He should not however pronounce over the animal another name than that of God. If he pronounces the name of Jesus or Abraham instead of God's name, the meat becomes inedible[6]. It is prohibited to eat the meat of an animal slaughtered

---

[1] Al-Amili: *Wasa'il al-shi'ah*, vol. 16, p. 301.
[2] Al-Aqfahsi: *Kitab li-ma yahil wa-yuharram min al-hayawan*, p. 131; Al-Bayhaqi: *Al-sunan al-kubra*, vol. 9, p. 534, narrative 19382.
[3] Al-Bayhaqi: *Al-sunan al-kubra*, vol. 9, p. 534, narrative 19381.
[4] Al-Amili: *Wasa'il al-shi'ah*, vol. 16, p. 302.
[5] Al-Tabatba'i: *Riyad al-masa'il*, vol. 8, p. 166-174.
[6] Musa: *Ahkam al-at'imah*, p. 88-90.

by an apostate[1], or even by a Muslim who is not circumcised, according to Ibn-Abbas. However, classic jurists thought that if one is permitted to eat the meat of an animal slaughtered by a Christian, there is even more reason to permit eating the meat of an animal slaughtered by an uncircumcised Muslim[2].

In any case, the animal must be slaughtered alive and must be drained of its blood. To insure that these two norms are respected, an Egyptian author proposes creation of Muslim slaughterhouses in countries that export meat to Muslim countries; the butchers should be Muslim because they are preferable to non-Muslims even though it is permitted to eat the meat of animal slaughtered by them[3]. A *fatwa* on the Internet indicates that the non-Muslim butcher must believe in God. It adds, "One who considers himself Christian or Jewish, but does not believe in God, nor in a holy book, nor truly believes in the religion that he pretends to follow, is actually an atheist, and the animal that he slaughters will be therefore not permitted to Muslims"[4].

In addition to restrictions concerning meat, it is prohibited for a Muslim to sit down at table with anyone who drinks wine. The Shiites prohibit even eating food prepared by a non-Muslim, if he touches it and transmits to it the humidity of his body[5].

Some Muslim religious scholars think that meat of uncertain source must be considered as licit according to verse 5:5, "The food of the people of the scripture is lawful for you". Muhammad once ate the meat of a goat that a Jew had offered him without asking how the goat had been slaughtered. Muslims are not obliged to ask how each animal has been slaughtered, but should ask if the butcher is a Muslim, or member of the *People of the Book*, because Muhammad ate the meat of the goat while knowing that it came on behalf of a Jew. One also notes a narrative about Aishah, according to which someone brought some meat to Muslims, without knowing if God's name was pronounced on this meat or not. When questioned, Muhammad

---

[1] Al-Fawzan, p. 149.
[2] Ibn-Qudamah, vol. 11, p. 138. See Aldeeb Abu-Sahlieh: *Circoncision masculine*, p. 177.
[3] Abd-al-Hadi: *Ahkam al-at'imah*, p. 224.
[4] www.guetali.fr/home/mohmdpat/food2.html.
[5] *Dalil al-muslim*, p. 69-70.

answered, "Pronounce God's name over the meat yourselves and eat"[1]. A Shiite book addressed to Muslims living abroad says:

> Many foods sold by unbelievers contain prohibited components as wine, meat of carrion, pork, and fishes without scales. For this reason, Muslims must be careful that their food does not contain any such prohibited foods.
>
> Muslims ought not ask about the content of food, unless it is meat. He cannot eat meat if it has not been slaughtered according to Islamic norms... He can eat any other food available without asking questions, even though such a food has been cooked with lard or wine. But it is preferable to try to avoid these foods for the sake of health, even when the appearance makes one think that it contains licit foods.
>
> If a Muslim learns that meat has not been slaughtered according to Islamic norms, he must consider it impure and illicit, and everything that is cooked with this meat becomes illicit, even if the meat is separated. In case of doubt concerning meat, one may separate it and eat the remainder of the food[2].

d) Respect of the prohibitions

Food prohibitions are not always treated with the same rigor. Although the prohibition on alcohol seems clear, Aishah reports that Muhammad drank the *nabith* (slightly fermented wine) from dates, barley or other grains macerated in water until fermentation[3]. Caliph Umar allowed Muslims to add water to the wine and to drink it[4]. Some classic jurists, including Abu-Hanifah, said that wine coming from fruits other than grapes and dates, such as the barley and corn, is only prohibited if alcohol is present to an intoxicating degree. According to Abou-Yousof, one should not punish a Muslim if he is not taken in the act. Some Muslims in the first century of the Islamic era believed that wine was allowed for those that did good deeds according to the Koranic verse 5:93 that stipulates, "Those who believe and lead a righteous life bear no guilt by eating any food, so long as they observe the commandments, believe and lead a righteous life, then maintain their piety and faith, and continue to observe piety and righteousness". This position remained a minority one[5] and those who consumed wine were punishable (but not necessarily

---

[1] Abd-al-Hadi: *Ahkam al-at'imah*, p. 206-235.

[2] Dalil al-muslim, p. 70-71.

[3] Abu-Da'ud, narrative 3511 and Ibn-Majah, narrative 3398. See also Ahmad, narrative 3315.

[4] Al-Nisa'i, narrative 5609.

[5] Abd-al-Hadi: *Ahkam al-at'imah*, p. 112-130.

punished). Today some Muslim countries do not foresee a sanction against the violation of such prohibition. In these countries, the manufacturing and the sale of wine are reserved to Christians, but Muslims drink most of the wine. Although some Muslim groups intervene to castigate those that consume wine and even attack stores and hotels that sell it, the drinking of wine in the Muslim community continues.

If a Muslim consumes pig, dog or donkey meat, he transgresses a religious law, but classic jurists cite no penal sanction against the transgressor[1]. Although the prohibition on eating pork is not punished in the Penal Code, unlike wine, one can say that Muslims do avoid pork more than wine. The pig is in fact considered impure and repugnant animal. One pointed out to me however that, in Cairo, Muslims breed pigs and sell them to Christians. Finally, the Qarmatians (9th–11th centuries), a Muslim dissident group now extinct, permitted butchers to expose the meat of any animal, including pigs and dogs, provided that they displayed the head of the animal so that people might eat what they liked, freely and knowingly, each according to his own conscience[2].

e) Comparison of Jewish and Muslim prohibitions

Jews and Muslims have similar food prohibitions, as in the case of pork, carrion, blood and sacrificial foods offered to idols. The Koran does not make the Jewish distinction between animals that have a cloven hoof and chew a cud, considered pure, and other animals considered impure[3]. Some foods are prohibited for Jews,

---

[1] Notice here that the resolution no 146, dated 30 August 1998 says:

1) There shall be deemed of selling meats of dogs or donkeys or other meats not prepared or not fit (good) for human consumption as a crime of the crimes relating with health and general principles of the Constitution.

2) The perpetrator of the crime stipulated in item (firstly) of this resolution shall be punished with imprisonment for a period not less than seven years and not exceeding ten years.

3) Committing the crime stipulated in this resolution in the circumstances of the war shall be considered as aggravating circumstance (*Iraqi Official Gazette* no 44, 4 November 1998, p. 2).

[2] Zakkar, vol. 1, p. 334-335.

[3] The Koran says: "For those who are Jewish we prohibited animals with undivided hoofs; and of the cattle and sheep we prohibited the

while being permitted for Muslims (e.g., the rabbit and the camel). The opposite is also true, e.g., for wine, permitted to Jews and prohibited to Muslims. On the other hand, Muslims do not have the prohibition to mix meat with milk. Finally, Jews do not allow the eating of meat slaughtered by a non-Jew, whereas the Muslim Sunnites allow eating meat slaughtered by a non-Muslim, provided he belongs to a *People of the Book*.

These divergences between Jews and Muslims probably aim at not offending some Arab culinary customs. One cannot indeed imagine the Koran prohibiting the meat of the camel. The desire to differentiate Muslims from the Jews after Muhammad's failure to convert them may also have played a role. Note the prohibition for Muslims to look or act like non-Muslims (6:153; 59:19). Muhammad would also have affirmed, as already noted, "One who looks like a group becomes part of it". Some classic jurists foresee even the death penalty for those that look like unbelievers and refuse to retract[1]. The system of Koranic food prohibitions presents Jews as bad believers, contrary to Muslims that are considered as connected to the authentic religion[2].

2) Swiss norms

The difference between the norms of all three communities creates for Jews and Muslims the same problems concerning the ritual slaughter, the respect of food prohibitions in the collective restoration in schools, the army, hospitals and jails, and the availability of these products. There are also the same social sanctions.

A) Ritual slaughter

The food prohibitions are especially noticeable for meat. A Jew or a Muslim often asks if the meat served is pork, rarely if bread is compliant to the religious norms. After the identification of the animal, they may ask, but more rarely, if the animal has been slaughtered in conformity with the religious norms. We will study in the following points the Swiss norms concerning

---

fat, except that which is carried on their backs, or in the viscera, or mixed with bones. That was a retribution for their transgressions, and we are truthful" (6:146).

[1] See Al-Luwayhiq, p. 126-127.
[2] Benkheira, p. 51.

slaughter and grievances formulated by Jews and Muslims in opposition to these norms.

a) Swiss norms on ritual slaughter

Jews and Muslims slaughter animals without prior stunning. [This method is generally called *ritual slaughter*.] Moreover, the butcher must be Jewish for the Jews, and Muslim for the Shiites. Muslim Sunnites require the butcher to be either a Muslim or one of the *People of the Book*.

The butcher's religious adherence violates the principle of non-discrimination affirmed in national and international law. But what raises problem is the prohibition in Switzerland of the ritual slaughter, prohibition integrated in 1893 in article 25bis aCst which stipulates:

> It is expressly prohibited to bleed animals being slaughtered without stunning them beforehand; this provision applies to all methods of slaughtering and all types of livestock.

This article was introduced in the Constitution by a popular initiative proposed by associations for protecting animals, following abolition of cantonal laws that imposed pre-slaughter stunning, at the request of the Jews. Against the opinion of the Swiss Federal Council and the Parliament, the people accepted this initiative August 20th, 1893 by 191,527 votes against 127,101. It has been approved by ten cantons and three half-cantons, while nine cantons and three half-cantons rejected it.

As formulated, at least in the German and French versions, article 25bis did not apply to poultry. The Federal Court decreed October 24th, 1907, that as the law hindered the freedom of worship, the prohibition had to be interpreted restrictively and, therefore, does not concern poultry[1] On the other hand, it was not prohibited to import meat of animals ritually slaughtered[2].

Switzerland was the first Western country to prohibit ritual slaughter, but does not have a monopoly on this prohibition. Sweden (in 1929), Norway (in 1937) and some German and Austrian Länder have similar prohibition[3].

---

[1] Federal Court decision 33.I.723, dated 24.10.1907.
[2] *Feuille fédérale* 1898.III.165.
[3] Steiner: *Einige notwentige Betrachtungen*, p. 12-13.

Article 25bis was replaced, December 2nd, 1973, by a new text that gives the Confederation the prerogative to legislate the protection of animals. The prohibition of the ritual slaughter was maintained, by article 12 of transitory norms of the Constitution. The decree of the Swiss Federal Council of 1972 concerning the modification of article 25bis explains divergences that appeared at the time of proceedings concerning this question:

> Organizations to protect animals, besides large surroundings of the population, call for the prohibition of bleeding animals of all species without prior stunning. One wants to save animals, whose slaughter is necessary to feed the population, from useless sufferings. Yet, prescriptions of the Jewish religion (besides those of Islam) prohibit stunning before slaughter, which is practiced by incision of the soft parts of the animal's neck. In surroundings that protect animals, this manner of slaughter has always been considered particularly cruel[1].

This decree added that the Jewish population considered article 25bis aCst discriminatory and a violation of the freedom of worship guaranteed by articles 49 and 50 of the Constitution. Therefore, the Swiss Jewish Federation community opposed inclusion of article 12 in the transitory norms of the Constitution, fearing that the question of ritual slaughter would be prejudged when forming legislation on the protection of animals. In opposition, the Swiss Association for the Protection of Animals and the Alliance of Independents wanted to extend the prohibition for poultry slaughter[2]. Both propositions have been rejected.

The debate on the ritual slaughter without stunning emerged during preparation of the law on the protection of animals of March 9th, 1978. The Swiss Federal Message of 1977 concerning this law recalls, without indicating any source, that the prohibition against ritual slaughter contravenes Jewish and Islamic norms, but simultaneously, Organizations for the Protection of Animals and, extensive population support, think that ritual slaughter is especially cruel. Considering the debates that took place in Federal chambers and the clear result of popular vote concerning the new article 25bis aCst (Article on the Protection of Animals), the Federal Council maintained a strict prohibition of animal slaughter without prior stunning. Answering to religious freedom arguments:

---

[1] *Feuille fédérale* 1972 II 1479.
[2] *Feuille fédérale* 1972 II 1482.

> We agree that this prohibition restricts the freedom of belief, opinion and worship of a religious minority. However, any freedom is submitted to limits imposed by the Constitution and the law; the same applies for the freedom of belief, opinion and worship... The debates in Parliament and the result of the popular voting concerning the constitutional article on the protection of animals do not leave any doubt about the fact that the methods used for ritual slaughters until now constitute, at least to eyes of large surroundings of the population, a violation of the principles governing the protection of animals. Therefore, they must be prohibited[1].

The decree notes that a delegation of an expert commission examined a device developed by the *American Federation for the Protection of Animals* with collaboration of rabbis. This device permits bleeding standing animals, suppressing so the reversing or projection of an animal. But use of this device does not solve in a satisfactory way the problem of animal protection. For this reason, the prohibition to bleed animals before stunning was maintained and applied to animals of the equine, bovine, ovine, caprine, porcine and rabbit (that Jews do not eat) species. Concerning poultry, this decree states that electronarcosis is considered inadequate. This means that poultry will be slaughtered without stunning until other methods are developed[2].

The Law of animal protection of 1978 affirms in article 2 par. 3, "Nobody may, in unjustified ways, cause pain, suffering or damage to animals nor put them in a state of anxiety". Article 20 adds:

> The slaughter of mammals without prior stunning is prohibited.
> The Swiss Federal Council can also prescribe, for extensive exploitations, the stunning of poultry before their slaughter.

Article 22 prohibits practices that make the animal needlessly suffer, and article 27 foresees in the case of rough handling of animals fines up to 40,000.- Sfr, and/or imprisonment up to three years. If the contravening is acting for financial reasons, the judge may pronounce heavier sanctions. Article 28 foresees in case of violation of the norms concerning the slaughter the prison or a maximum fine of 20,000.- Sfr, unless article 27 of the present law is applicable. The prohibition of ritual slaughter is confirmed in the Decree of May 27th, 1981, modified May 14th, 1997. Stunning methods are specified by article 64f. Article 64g

---

[1] *Feuille fédérale* 1977 I 1108-1109.
[2] *Feuille fédérale* 1977 I 1109-1110.

par. 3 makes an exception for poultry. It specifies, "Poultry must be stunned before being bled, except in case of decapitation and ritual slaughter".

Note here that the *European Convention for the Protection of Animals for Slaughter* of 1979, approved by Switzerland May 4th, 1994, worries also about animal suffering. It could not prohibit ritual slaughter in all signatory countries but tried to reduce the suffering of the slaughtered animals. Article 17 stipulates in this respect:

1) Each Contracting Party may authorize derogations from the provisions concerning prior stunning in the following cases:
- slaughtering in accordance with religious rituals;
- emergency slaughtering when stunning is not possible;
- slaughter of poultry and rabbits by authorized methods cause instantaneous death;
- killing of animals for health control where special reasons make this necessary.
2) Each Contracting Party availing itself of provisions of par. 1 of this article shall, however, ensure that at the time of such slaughter or killing animals are spared any avoidable pain or suffering.

The Swiss Federal Decree of 1992 concerning this convention says that it does not abolish the prohibition of ritual slaughter foreseen by the Swiss law[1].

Ritual slaughter always causes a debate on the federal level. Thus, a parliamentarian put September 25th, 1996, to the Swiss Federal Council a question concerning the fear to see the ritual slaughter of poultry prohibited in Switzerland. The petitioner thought that such a prohibition would hit directly the Jewish community, that will not be able to practice this form of slaughter anymore, and would constitute a reach to the freedom of belief. In answer dated November 20th, 1996, the Swiss Federal Council said that the prohibition of the ritual slaughter of animals restricts the freedom of belief and worship of a religious minority. However, any freedom is submitted to limits imposed by the Constitution and the law; the same applies for the freedom of belief and worship[2]. Therefore, the ritual slaughter of animals remains prohibited, exception made of poultry. The goal of this exception is "to provide both Jewish and Muslim religious communities of our country with indigenous poultry and, hence,

---

[1] Feuille fédérale 1992 V 959.
[2] *Feuille fédérale* 1977 I 1108-1109.

to reduce the dependence concerning the importations". The Message adds, "Because of the particular importance of the ritual slaughter for certain religious communities, the Swiss Federal Council does not have the intention today, as before, to prohibit the ritual slaughter of poultry"[1].

In his answer of the same day to a similar question dated September 6th, 1996, the Swiss Federal Council reiterated, "At the present time, the Swiss Federal Council does not have the intention to prohibit the ritual slaughter of poultry", adding:

> The respect of minority rights, whether they are linguistic, ethnic, religious or of another nature, is one of the fundamental maxims of our federal State. While adhering to the *Convention on the Elimination of all Forms of Racial Discrimination*, Switzerland committed itself on the international level to eliminate them. ... The constitutional aspects of the prohibition of the ritual slaughter have been discussed in detailed manner during the parliamentary debates concerning the law and the constitutional article on the protection of animals. The result of these debates was the maintenance of the prohibition of the ritual slaughter except for certain religious communities and the possibility for the Federal Council to introduce, for the extensive exploitations, the obligatory prior stunning of poultry[2].

According to the content of the two questions, it is obvious that the two petitioners wanted to reopen, by mean of ritual slaughter of poultry, the debate on the ritual slaughter for all animals. But the Swiss Federal Council did not accept this demand. Furthermore, it kept the right to impose the prior stunning of poultry, but only in extensive exploitations to avoid hurting the freedom of belief of Jews and Muslims.

December 8th, 1996, a parliamentarian submitted to the Swiss Federal Council and Parliament a petition going farther in the prohibition of the ritual slaughter of animals, asking to prohibit the importation in Switzerland of products coming from tortured animals (that is: animals slaughtered ritually). This petition followed a similar petition of 1995 by the Association against factories of animals (95.2024, BO 1995 NS 2163) that aimed also to prohibit the importation in Switzerland of ritually slaughtered animals. This demand was however rejected by the *Commission on Science, Education and Culture* that presented the following arguments:

---

[1] http://www.parlament.ch/afs/data/f/gesch/1996/f_gesch_19963429.htm
[2] http://www.parlament.ch/afs/data/f/gesch/1996/f_gesch_19961083.htm

> - Parliament rejected such a prohibition in 1977 during the debates of the federal law on the protection of animals. It had considered at that time that Jewish and Muslim communities would with difficulty have accepted such a disposition which could be taxed as a violation of the religious freedom or even anti-Semitic act.
> - The Agreements of the GATT do not allow national parties to prohibit the importation of food commodity unless it is proved that this commodity constitutes a danger for the health of people and animals - a condition that, concerning the ritually slaughtered meat, cannot evidently be fulfilled. Such a prohibition would be interpreted therefore as a protectionist measure incompatible with the objectives of the liberalization of agricultural market pursued by the GATT[1].

Such is therefore the legislative situation in Switzerland concerning ritual slaughter. This solution reflects the opinion of the majority of the Swiss population. But the Swiss Federal Council submitted to the consultation September 21st, 2001 a draft law on the protection of animals whose article 19 puts back in question the prohibition of the ritual slaughter. This article stipulates:

1) The slaughter of mammals without prior stunning is prohibited.

2) The Federal Council can prescribe the stunning for other animal slaughter.

3) The Federal Council designates the permitted methods of stunning.

4) The slaughter of mammals without prior stunning can be done with authorization of the concerned authority and in authorized slaughterhouses, titular of the prescribed authorization in article 16 of the federal law of October 9th, 1992 on food commodities and usual objects. This slaughter is allowed to answer to religious community needs whose coercive rules prescribe slaughter without prior stunning or prohibit the consumption of meat of animals stunned prior to slaughter.

5) It can fix the requirements to which must satisfy the formation of the slaughterhouse personnel.

This draft law risks provoked a large debate in Switzerland. The Swiss Animal Protection Society already announced the launch of a constitutional popular initiative to reintroduce in the Swiss Federal Constitution the obligation of pre-slaughter stunning of livestock; this initiative even prohibits Swiss importations of ritually slaughtered animals. If the draft law is adopted, a referendum will be launched[2].

---

[1] http://www.parlament.ch/Poly/Suchen_amtl_Bulletin/cn97/ete/1236.HTM

[2] *Courrier des bêtes*, n° 383, October 2001, p. 1.

Those who want to abolish the prohibition of ritual slaughter invoke religious freedom and accuse their adversaries of anti-Semitism and anti-Islamism. Those opposed to ritual slaughter invoke the suffering of animals and think that ritual slaughter constitutes a cruel treatment. Therefore, it is necessary to develop three basic questions.

b) Ritual slaughter and religious freedom

Jewish and Muslim religious surroundings think that the prohibition of ritual slaughter violates the religious freedom. Fawzia Al-Ashmawi writes about Muslims:

> The question of the access to *halal* meat remains a major problem, since Swiss law prohibits the slaughter of animals according to Islamic ritual and foresees that animals be stunned before being slaughtered. For this reason, Muslims continue to import *halal* meat from France or Belgium[1].

Echoing this reproach, the Message of the Swiss Federal Council of 1972 says that the "prescriptions of Jewish religion (besides those of Islamic religion) prohibit stunning before slaughter"[2]. In its decree of 1977, the Swiss Federal Council states, "We agree that this prohibition restricts the freedom of belief and worship of a religious minority. However, any freedom is submitted to limits imposed by the Constitution and the law; the same applies for the freedom of belief and worship"[3]. Article 50 par. 1 aCst indicates in this respect, "The freedom of worship is guaranteed within the limits set by public order and morality". If the new Constitution of 1998 affirms in article 15 par. 1, "the freedom of religion and conscience is guaranteed", it does not mean that this freedom is absolute. Haller and Schraner note in this respect that Jewish and Islamic religions permit polygamy, but Swiss law prohibits it. Therefore, one cannot invoke religious freedom for maintenance of ritual slaughter[4].

The answer of the Swiss Federal Council does not satisfy the religious surroundings, or law professors. Professor Antoine Favre comments on article 25bis aCst as follows:

> According to article 25bis aCst, it is expressly prohibited to bleed animals (livestock, not poultry!) without stunning them beforehand.

---

[1] Al-Ashmawi: *La condition des musulmans en Suisse*, p. 33.
[2] *Feuille fédérale* 1972 II 1479.
[3] *Feuille fédérale* 1977 I 1108-1109.
[4] Haller and Schraner, p. 22.

> This disposition restricts the freedom of worship. It is sufficient that the slaughter of livestock does not constitute a mistreatment toward animals (article 264 of the Penal Code). The article 25bis aCst must be abrogated[1].

Annotating the prohibition of ritual slaughter without prior stunning, professor Fleiner writes, "According to Jewish and Islamic religions, animals must not be stunned before being bled"[2]. He adds:

> The legislator cannot... restrict the freedom of conscience and belief while prohibiting the ritual slaughter unless such restriction is necessary for the public interest and provided that the principle of proportionality is respected. Therefore, the prohibition of the ritual slaughter is incompatible with the freedom of conscience and belief if it is not justified by motives of police or by the protective motives of animals...
>
> In our opinion, the necessity of an absolute restriction of a fundamental right does not exist. Indeed, there is no reasonable report between the aimed goal (reasonable protection of animals!) and the used means (total prohibition of the ritual slaughter). ... For these motives, the general prohibition of ritual slaughter should in our opinion be replaced by a different norm, preserving the constitutional Jewish and Muslim religious minority rights[3].

This point of view of the doctrine seems to be shared currently by the Swiss Federal Council that, as we saw before, submitted to the consultation September 21st, 2001 a draft law on the protection of animals allowing ritual slaughter. In the *Explanatory Report*, it is specified that the prohibition of ritual slaughter "is considered by some as a disproportionate limitation of the freedom of religion and conscience guaranteed by article 15 of the Constitution. The Swiss Federal Council shares this point of view. It thinks that public interest to protect livestock from pain and suffering is not sufficient to maintain the prohibition in force in Switzerland since 1893"[4]. Annotating the aforementioned article 19, Swiss Federal Council adds:

> Article 15 nCst guarantees the freedom of religion and conscience. A law can certainly restrict this freedom, but a legal basis is not sufficient to limit it. Any limitation of a fundamental right must also be justified by the public interest and proportioned to the pursued goals (article 36 nCst). The protection of animals is a public interest

---

[1] Favre: *Droit constitutionnel suisse*, p. 284.

[2] Fleiner-Gerster: Article 25bis, par. 16.

[3] *Ibid.*, par. 19 and 21.

[4] Révision de la loi sur la protection des animaux: rapport explicatif de l'avant projet, 21.9.2001, p. 7.

recognized by the Constitution that could justify the restriction. However the Federal Council thinks that the condition of proportionality is not fulfilled in the case of the prohibition of the ritual slaughter. Slaughter without prior stunning is an important ritual act for Jews and Muslims.

It is foreseen not to allow the ritual slaughter than to answer to religious communities' needs whose coercive religious rules prescribe this type of slaughter. It could not be practiced than on cantonal authorization and solely in the authorized slaughterhouses according to the law on food commodities.

The authorization of ritual slaughter methods makes void the present derogation that allows importing *kosher* meat and *halal* meat[1].

The argument that the prohibition of animal slaughter without prior stunning restricts the religious freedom lacks consistence. Jewish and Muslim holy texts recommend limiting the suffering of animals as much as possible. On the other hand, these texts do not treat the question of stunning, and nowhere pre-slaughter stunning is prohibited[2]. All that they prohibit is eating carrion (for Jews and Muslims) or injured animal (for Jews) and to consume blood.

Stunning an animal does not necessarily kill or injure it. New Zealand[3] and Australia[4] resort to electronarcosis, which is accepted by Muslims. The *Egyptian Fatwa Commission* already decided in 1978 that it is licit to eat the meat of an animal that has been stunned prior to slaughter, provided the animal does not die before being slaughtered. It considers pre-slaughter stunning conforms with the injunction of Muhammad, "God prescribed kindness in all thing. If you kill, do it with kindness, and if you bleed an animal, do it with kindness"[5]. An Egyptian author

---

[1] *Ibid.*, p. 16-17.

[2] Steiner: *Einige notwentige Betrachtungen*, p. 14; Haller and Schraner, p. 22.

[3] Discussion paper on the animal welfare standards, p. 13, par. 7.2.

[4] Grandin and Regenstein: *Religious slaughter and animal welfare*, p. 115-123.

[5] *Al-fatawi al-islamiyyah*, vol. 10, *fatwa* n° 1295, p. 3548-3549. See also Jad-al-Haq: *Buhuth wa-fatawi islamiyyah*, vol. 4, p. 227-254 and the *fatwa* of Ibn-Baz in: *Ahkam al-dhabh wal-luhum al-mustawradah*, p. 59-61. The reader can find two other *fatwas* in Hartinger: *Das betäubungslose Schächten der Tiere im 20. Jahrhundert*. For more details, see my article: Aldeeb Abu-Sahlieh: *Faux débat sur l'abattage rituel*.

invokes even the Koran in favor of the pre-slaughter stunning, "When the Lord appeared in Mountain, It put it in crumbs and Moses fell thunderstruck" (7:143). He notices that Moses fell vanished under the shock, but he remained alive[1].

Concerning the prohibition of blood consumption, the stunning of animals does not impede blood flow. Foundation Brigitte Bardot says, "meat of an animal emptied of its blood and stunned previously contains as much blood as the meat of an animal slaughtered without prior stunning"[2]. Dr. Samuel Debrot has a similar opinion:

> Blood (of a ritually slaughtered animal) comes out red, well-oxygenated, because the animal breathes after the stroke of knife; but disorganized movements often close the wound again; it is surprising to note how much the slaughtered animal without prior stunning bleeds ... I challenge the proponents of ritual slaughter to obtain more blood from an animal ritually slaughtered according to their method. Besides, it is impossible to bleed an animal and drain the whole of its blood. If Moses prohibited all consumption of blood, give us then meat that does not contain any trace of blood! It is impossible... Then why not to use meat coming from an animal appropriately stunned rather than the meat of an animal brutalized, agonized with suffering, a meat which, in any case must be washed with water to eliminate all trace of blood[3].

Therefore, we can say that we face a false problem and a faulty interpretation of a religious text. The real reason behind the claims of Jews is economic. One author points out that the Consistorial Jewish Association of Paris has a yearly budget of 150 million French francs. Half of this budget is collected through taxes on so-called "right of the knife"[4]. One multiplies rules to multiply control and fees. Maybe it is necessary to add the inability of some persons to put themselves in question. Therefore, we may conclude that it is false to say that the pre-slaughter stunning of the animal is contrary to both Jewish and Muslim religious rules. In any case, freedom of religion and worship does not mean the absolute acceptance of everything that

---

[1] Abd-al-Hadi: *Ahkam al-at'imah*, p. 216-217.

[2] http://www.fondationbrigittebardot.fr/fr/journal/10_98/10_3.html

[3] Debrot: L'opinion d'un directeur d'abattoir, p. 20-21.

[4] See on the economic aspect Bauer: *La nourriture cacher*, p. 50-68. See also Décision de la Cour européenne des droits de l'homme, June 27th, 2000, *Sha'are Shalom ve Tsedek vs. France* (request n° 27417/95).

others profess. We may add here that even among traditionalists, religious laws and practices have changed because of reconsideration and evolving social environments. This is for example the case for offences such as adultery (Leviticus 20:10; Deuteronomy 22:21), homosexual acts (Leviticus 20:13), blasphemy (Exodus 21:17) and stubbornly disobeying one's parents (Deuteronomy 21:18-21). The Bible decrees the death penalty for these acts. In addition, according to Torah law, only a man can divorce his spouse (Deuteronomy 24:1) and inheritance is restricted to sons (Deuteronomy 21:15-17). However, all these rules have been abandoned. We should, then, be able to change the rules on animal slaughter, if such rules really exist, as the pre-slaughter stunning reduces suffering of the animal, an eminent consideration in Jewish and Islamic law, as we will see further.

c) *Religious freedom for the Jews and other's freedom*

Law professors and the Swiss Federal Council invoke respect for the religious freedom of the Jewish and Muslim minorities in favor of the abolition of the pre-slaughter stunning in spite of the absence of coercive religious rules that forbid this procedure. There is however another aspect, which should also be taken into consideration: respect for the convictions of those opposed to slaughter without prior stunning.

It is worth noting that Jews slaughter more animals than they consume as meat. This for two reasons: on one hand, the slaughtered animals may be declared as non-*kosher* after being bled; however, Jews do not eat the hind legs of the animal because of the command not to eat the sciatic nerve (Genesis 32:33) which is difficult and expensive to remove entirely[1]. Meat [slaughtered in a manner following kosher rules, but] classified as inedible for Jews, is sold on the market, generally without indication. The Swiss Federal veterinary office states in its *Basic Information on Ritual Slaughter* of September 20th, 2001:

> The incision that kills an animal is not the only condition that must be fulfilled. For this reason, only about 10% of veal slaughtered ritually are sold as *kosher* meat; for the thick livestock this rate rises to about 30%. Besides, only the first part of the animal admitted as *kosher* meat is consumed; the remainder is sold on the market of normal meat[2].

---

[1] Discussion paper on the animal welfare standards, p. 13, par. 7.1.

[2] Office vétérinaire fédéral: *Informations de base sur l'abattage rituel*, 20.9.2001, par. 5.

This important element is passed under silence by law professors and by the *Explanatory Report* of the Swiss Federal Council joined to the draft law on the protection of animals submitted to the September 21st, 2001 consultation. Besides, the draft law does not require labeling the package whether or not meat comes from slaughter without prior stunning.

However, if law professors and the Swiss Federal Council worry about the religious freedom of Jewish or Muslim minorities (in spite of the absence of coercive religious norms!), it is also important to respect convictions of those opposed to slaughter without prior stunning who ask that packing indicate the manner of slaughtering the animal. It would be necessary besides to mention that it is meat rejected by Jews[1]. Evidently, such a mention would have repercussions on the price of *kosher* meat, if the public refuses to consume meat rejected by Jews. This is why Jews are opposed that the European Parliament imposes such a mention on packing[2]. Such a repercussion in price is not sufficient reason to defy moral convictions of those opposed to slaughter without prior stunning.

d) Ritual slaughter and accusation of racism

We saw that the Swiss Federal Council refuses to prohibit ritual slaughter of poultry and importation of meat of ritually slaughtered animals, for fear of being accused of anti-Semitism[3].

The idea that the prohibition of ritual slaughter is inspired by anti-Semitism is hawked by professor Jean-François Aubert who says, "The revision of 1893 was no more than a small eruption of anti-Semitism, an imitation of what was proposed at that time in certain parts of Germany"[4]. A recent doctoral thesis in law presented by a Jewish Swiss to the University of Zurich is constructed entirely on the hypothesis that the prohibition of ritual slaughter in Switzerland is motivated by racism of the

---

[1] Gellatley: Going for the kill; See also Hartinger: *Das betäubungslose Schächten der Tiere in unserer Zeit*.

[2] Decision by European Parliament could raise cost of kosher food, *The Midwest Jewish Week*, 17.7.1992, p. 4, in: http://www.ukar.org/ronen02.shtml

[3] http://www.parlament.ch/Poly/Suchen_amtl_Bulletin/cn97/ete/1236.HTM

[4] Aubert: *Traité de droit constitutionnel suisse*, vol. 2, par. 2067.

Swiss people and xenophobia against Jews and Muslims[1]. The author affirms, "Again today, anti-Semitic components dominate the movement opposed to ritual slaughter"[2]. Claude Nordmann, President of the Jewish Community in the canton of Fribourg, uses the same argument[3]. Without negating the existence of an anti-Semitic trend, it seems to us that such accusation errs by too much generalization. One can be opposed to corrida or wale hunting without necessarily being anti-Spanish or anti-Japanese.

To accuse opponents to the ritual slaughter of being anti-Semitic aims to intimidate and avoid discussion[4]. Evidently, these opponents reject this accusation of anti-Semitism and point out that some Jews are also members of the Association for the Protection of Animals[5]. December 3rd, 1978, most Swiss have accepted the law for protection of animals prohibiting ritual slaughter, and it is pretentious to say that the majority of Swiss people are anti-Semitic.

If some Jewish and Muslim groups consider, wrongly, the prohibition of ritual slaughter as a discriminatory measure and do not miss an opportunity to denounce this discrimination, we must also remember that both Jewish and Islamic norms are discriminatory and violate the law against racism. This discrimination is rarely denounced by organizations that fight against racism and discrimination. The Swiss norm denunciation and the silence concerning Jewish and Islamic norms do not constitute an auspicious attitude to solve community problems. On the other hand, there are Jews and Muslims who reject ritual slaughter and consider it as cruel[6]. Let us set aside economic interests and political incentives, and consider the suffering of animal, which is the most important element in this debate.

---

[1] Krauthammer: *Das Schächtverbot in der Schweiz* 1854-2000.

[2] *Ibid.*, p. 274.

[3] See the letter to the Editor of Claude Nordmann: À propos d'abattage rituel, in: *La Liberté*, 24.10.2001, p. 2.

[4] See the answer of ACUSA to the letter of Claude Nordmann, in: http://www.acusa.ch/news-of-the-day/011025.htm

[5] Steiner: *Einige notwentige Betrachtungen*, p. 7-9.

[6] Steiner: *Einige notwentige Betrachtungen*, p. 7-9 and 13.

e) *Ritual slaughter and suffering of animals*

We saw that the Association for the Protection of Animals decided in favor of the prohibition of ritual slaughter. Commenting on this prohibition, Jean-François Aubert writes:

> It is difficult for men to say if the incision of an artery is more painful for victims than a stroke of a mallet on the forehead. Some people however were clearly convinced, and they knew how to communicate their feeling to the majority of the electoral body. Actually, the supplying of meats will never go without cruelty, however one operates. It is not at all established that the Jewish method is worse. The revision of 1893 was no more than a small eruption of anti-Semitism; an imitation of what was proposed at that time in certain parts of Germany [1].

This famous Swiss constitutionalist thus leaves the argument of animal suffering and prefers to see behind the prohibition of ritual slaughter a demonstration of anti-Semitism. But he contradicts himself since he recognizes, "some people however were clearly convinced, and they knew how to communicate their feeling to the majority of the electoral body".

Whereas, in 1893, the Swiss Federal Council was opposed to constitutional article 25bis, it rallied to majority opinion in its Message concerning the law on the protection of animals, in force since 1981, and whose goal is to reduce their suffering to the minimum. The Message notes that a delegation of the expert commission examined a device developed by the *American Federation for the Protection of Animals* with the collaboration of rabbis. This device permits bleeding of a standing animal, thus suppressing reversing or the projection of the animal. But the use of this device does not sufficiently solve the problem of animal protection [2]. The law even spread the prohibition of ritual slaughter to rabbits, which Jews do not eat.

To invoke the argument of animal suffering raises a fundamental question of religious surroundings. According to such surroundings, their religious norms concerning animal slaughter are of divine origin. These surroundings cannot recognize that their "divine norms" are less respectful of animals than "human norms". Such recognition means questioning their faith in a perfect God. Thereby, these religious surroundings try

---

[1] Aubert: *Traité de droit constitutionnel suisse*, vol. 2, par. 2067.
[2] *Feuille fédérale* 1977 I 1109-1110.

to prove that their method is more merciful than that proposed by opponents to ritual slaughter.

One rabbi wrote on the Internet that slaughter, as practiced by Jews, "provoke immediate bleeding, an instantaneous cerebral death. It is probably the least painful slaughter method". He adds that a scanner demonstrates, "the brain of the animal slaughtered by rabbis were in a perfect state, whereas that of animals previously stunned were strongly damaged... A brief look at literature, or a countryside walk will recall conditions of slaughter, not to say execution, of rabbits, pigs and even pets, and, if not, stages of a hunt: our conditions of slaughter infinitely faster and less traumatic than those used by other nations"[1].

This Jewish point of view is not shared by various Associations for the Protection of Animals[2], the Swiss Veterinarian Society[3], the Swiss Union of Master-Butchers[4], the Swiss Federal Council, the Federal Veterinary Office or the Western Legislators, who all require pre-slaughter stunning to reduce animal suffering. The Federal Veterinary Office indicates that, July 24th, 2001, it visited the slaughterhouse of Besançon, where animals are ritually slaughtered for the Swiss market. After this visit, "the delegation cannot confirm that ritual slaughter does not cause any pains to animals. Many animals correctly slaughtered according to ritual presented, after the incision, strong reactions of defense; the corneal reflex, that serves criteria for loss of conscience, was sometimes again distinctly observable up to 30 seconds after the incision provoking bleeding"[5].

We may mention in this respect among objectors to the ritual slaughter the Foundation Brigitte Bardot that wages a campaign

---

[1] *Les lois alimentaires*, www.alliancefr.com/users/kacher/Kcacher1-genr.htm, mis à jour November 2000, p. 4.

[2] See the letter of Bernard Lavrie and the answer of ACUSA, in *Acusa*, 1998, 1: www.acusa.ch/an1998-1/01-lutte.html. See also Massacres sans anesthésie, in: http://www.ragecoeur.itgo.com/rituel3.html; Abattages rituels autorisés, in: http://www.svpa.ch/evenements.html

[3] La Société des Vétérinaires Suisses ne veut pas d'une autorisation de l'abattage rituel, in: http://www.gstsvs.ch/cug/gst_vet/index.nsf?Open

[4] Union suisse des maîtres-bouchers, 28.9.2001, in: http://www. qualiteduboucher.ch/pages/francais/polit.htm#p151

[5] Office vétérinaire fédéral: *Informations de base sur l'abattage rituel*, 20.9.2001, par. 5.

against Jewish and Muslim ritual slaughter. In a text distributed on the Internet, this Foundation explains, "millions of cattle, sheep and poultry are slaughtered each day in a cruel way, to observe religious rituals. Either for *halal* meat, or *kosher* meat, sufferings endured at the time of slaughter are unacceptable at the end of the 20th century". This Foundation desires adoption of legislation imposing animal stunning prior to any slaughter. It notes, "neither the Torah nor Talmudic texts on animal consumption specify that it is obligatory to slaughter the animals, nor that any animal killed by another method is unfit for consumption, and it is nowhere mentioned that the animal should not be stunned before death.... On the contrary, it is specified in these two books that man must respect all animals". The Foundation explains, with photographs, how cattle and sheep are slaughtered, and their atrocious sufferings[1].

Answering Mr. Claude Schwab who wished, in a televised broadcast, in the name of leading Switzerland toward Europe, to suppress the prohibition of ritual slaughter, prohibition that he qualifies as a blemish, Samuel Debrot, president of the *Society for the Protection of Animals* of the canton of Vaud, said that killing mammals without prior stunning is considered cruel death by Swiss law. He adds:

> When one attends a normal slaughter, then a ritual slaughter, one is easily persuaded that ritual slaughter is a cruelty and infringes upon the most elementary principles of animal protection. There is no longer any doubt about that. Breeders, butchers, consumers want to slaughter livestock without suffering and not an intolerable jugulation, dating back 4000 years, whether according to Jewish or Islamic ritual. Mr. R. Bloch, president of the Federation of the Jewish Communities of Switzerland declared to us that the Jews of Switzerland would not ask for the reintroduction in Switzerland of ritual slaughter; strictly practicing Jews are content with ritual slaughter of poultry, that was legalized in 1981[2].

One viewer answered Pastor Schwab:

> Everyone knows that most religions, institutions based on ritual acts created by men for men, never worry about animal conditions, and *a fortiori* of suffering of these lower "beings". But a man who calls himself a representative of God and fighting to reintroduce torture toward creatures of this same God appears somewhat paradoxical! ... No, Mr. Pastor, ... animals have not been conceived by your own Creator to serve as an outlet

---

[1] http://www.fondationbrigittebardot.fr/fr/journal/10_98/10_3.html
[2] *Courrier des bêtes*, February 2001, n° 379, p. 5.

> for human silliness... The love of humans starts with the respect of all Creation[1].

The idea that pre-slaughter stunning of an animal reduces its suffering is now admitted by Muslim religious authorities, who think stunning conforms with the injunction of Muhammad, "God prescribed kindness in all thing. If you kill, do it with kindness, and if you bleed an animal, do it with kindness". Therefore, these authorities do not oppose pre-slaughter stunning provided it does not cause death of the animal before being bled[2].

f) Economic considerations

The project of the Swiss Federal Council to abolish the prohibition of animal slaughter without prior stunning not only follows moral considerations (the respect of religious freedom of Jews and Muslims), but also follows economic considerations.

The Federal veterinary office says in its *Basic Information on Ritual Slaughter* of September 20th, 2001, "To assure the provision of religious communities that consume meat of animals slaughtered ritually, the competent authorities allow importation of this meat". This means that if the prohibition of animal slaughter without prior stunning is abolished, Switzerland will no longer be obliged to import *kosher* or *halal* meat, and will even be able to export such meat, notably to Muslim countries[3].

The economic argument is based on the assumption that Jewish and Islamic norms require that animals be slaughtered without prior stunning. However, we saw that this assumption is false, at least with regard to Muslims. New Zealand and Australia, two big exporters of *halal* meat for neighboring Muslim countries, practice pre-slaughter stunning by electronarcosis. Switzerland could therefore, without any problem, maintain the prohibition of slaughter without prior stunning and export *halal* meat to Muslim countries.

B) Collective restoration

In the name of religious neutrality, the State must avoid discriminating against people for religion, especially in the

---

[1] *Ibid.*, p. 5.

[2] *Al-fatawi al-islamiyyah*, vol. 10, *fatwa* n° 1295, p. 3548-3549.

[3] Office vétérinaire fédéral: *Informations de base sur l'abattage rituel*, 20.9.2001, par. 4.

setting of public services. Food prohibitions constitute an element of religious freedom. Therefore, it must look after their respect as much as possible in the collective restoration in schools, army, hospital or jail. Such an obligation should also be observed by enterprises that provide collective services to their employees. But such prohibitions raise problems of organization and feasibility, because this restoration is not *à la carte*. As this question has never been studied in Switzerland, we will propose here some avenues for reflection.

a) Public schools and universities

Because of religious diversity and irreconcilable food requirements, an academic restaurant cannot satisfy all demands, as it cannot prepare dishes that answer all allergy concerns.

At the academic site of Lausanne where we are, there is no collective restoration that assures food compliance to aforementioned Jewish or Islamic norms. Besides a normal restaurant, customers at the university's dining hall have different choices to follow various religious dietary requirements: a self-made salad, a main dish, a vegetarian dish and a complete meal with a pre-established menu. The personnel indicate if pork is served. The customer can ask then for another meat in the context of the complete meal. On the other hand, the chaplainry allows students to meet Monday and prepare convivial meals called *à la fortune du pot* (pot-luck). Cooks are two or several voluntary students who prepare the meal for the entire group of about forty persons. Some avoid using pork. Having frequented this chaplainry for about ten years, I noticed that few Muslim students come. As for Jewish students, they meet another day of the week and prepare their own *kosher* meal. Nothing prevents Muslim students to do the same, but there was no demand on their part.

In fault of information concerning the situation of schools in Switzerland, we indicate here the report of the *High Council for integration* in neighboring France:

> The collective restoration raises the question of the respect of food ritual in collectivity. As a rule, the prohibition of pork consumption is respected in the canteen, when requested by parents, including in external classes and linguistic stays. In most establishments, a surrogate rich in proteins replaces the meat for "meals without pork".
>
> No general position has been taken. The testimony of the person in charge of the school of Bobigny is especially illuminating, "Demands arrive by the delegates of the parents. These are prompt demands that

> provoke debate. Not all demands are satisfied. We serve some substitute meals when there is pork. Demands to exclude pork represent about 30% of the meals, and in some districts such demands represent more than 50%. In some schools, some ask for *kosher* meat or vegetarian meals. We do not have a systematic position. Three schools decided that they would stop proposing substitution meals. They provoke problems in a secular school that regroup the Muslim children around one isolated table, for reasons of convenience. In these schools, children do not eat the main dish but compensate by vegetables. Parents protested".

> One observes that, besides the prohibition of pork, there is more frequently request for *halal* meat. This demand, formulated by an increasing number of parents at the time of the enrollment to the canteen and defended by their associations, did not even receive an answer on behalf of the school institution[1].

Concerning this matter, this Council recommends "the setting up, on request, in canteens of meals without pork that guarantee a surrogate rich in proteins". On the other hand, it thinks unacceptable "the introduction of *halal* meals in the collective context, more by principle than by reason of difficulties of canteen management that it would create"[2].

b) Army

The Swiss army does not prepare a particular meal for either Jews or Muslims. But paragraph 182 of the Regulation concerning the Organization of the courses of the Swiss Army stipulates[3]:

> On demand, and as far as the progress of service is not considerably disturbed, soldiers can be allowed by troop commanders to take their meals, for religious motives, separately or out of the military locals. As compensation for missed meals and with the commander's assent, soldiers beneficiary of such a measure receive a part or the totality of their subsistence indemnity in pension paid cash.

A rabbi in Lausanne informed me that his community could provide *kosher* meals to interested parties. Some Jewish soldiers receive *kosher* food from their families.

In France, the Commissariat of the Ground Troops produces, individual fight rations in the context of operational feeding; seven of the fourteen proposed menus do not include any pork product. Army restoration organizations must propose specific

---

[1] Haut Conseil de l'intégration, 3.3.1, p. 38.
[2] *Ibid.*, 4.4.2-3, p. 59 and 60.
[3] Regulation 51.23f, in force since 1.1.1999.

meals to soldiers wishing to conform themselves to prescriptions of their religion: *kosher* food for Jews, fast meals on occasion of Catholic religious feasts, *halal* meal without alcohol nor pork for Muslims[1].

c) Hospital

Fawzia Al-Ashmawi writes that Muslim organizations took the initiative to officially ask Swiss authorities to provide *halal* food in public institutions, in particular in jails and hospitals; some establishments respected these demands and applied them[2].

In France, Branlard indicates that in hospitals, especially private ones, it is not easy to organize meals compliant to all religious norms. A Jew of strict obedience, or a Muslim, who cannot have a food regime conforming to his convictions in a French hospital, looks for suitable care abroad. The patient may try to receive recompense for the foreign treatment from the French government. A decision of the Court of Colmar refused such a payment for a Jew. The social security objected that because of the multiplicity of religions with ritual food, it would lose control of a considerable number of expenses, and that a religious motive is a personal one and does not constitute a medical reason[3].

d) Jail

All penitentiary establishments offer meals of choice when the main meal includes pork. However, some more advanced demands can appear, as was the case, summer 1999, in Champ-Dollon (Geneva), where Muslim convicts asked for *halal* meals, but their request has not been granted by the administration, as ritual slaughter is prohibited in Switzerland. At the same time they requested cable TV in the cells, to receive Islamic broadcasts[4].

C) Availability and control of foods

To respect prohibited food, it would be necessary to get a stock on the compliant food market to the religious norms and to insure

---

[1] Branlard, p. 233.

[2] Al-Ashmawi: *La condition des musulmans en Suisse*, p. 33.

[3] Branlard, p. 233-234, quoting 6.4.1967, Cahn, JCP 1968, II, 15508, obs. P.L.

[4] Arbez: *Détenus musulmans dans les prisons suisses*, p. 6.

that these norms are respected. Article 19 of the *European Convention for the Protection of Animals for Slaughter* of 1979, approved by Switzerland May 4th, 1994, stipulates:

> Each Contracting Party permitting slaughter in accordance with religious ritual shall ensure, when it does not itself issue the necessary authorizations, that animal sacrificers are duly authorized by the religious bodies concerned.

Switzerland, as noted already, does not allow the ritual slaughter of animals, excepted for poultry. For other meats, Jews and Muslims obtain them in France. In France, the *Intra-Community Rabbinical Commission on Ritual Slaughter* has the responsibility of *kosher* meat. It chooses the butchers, supervises them and controls the meat from slaughter to sale to individuals. A court rejected the authorization delivered by the Chief Rabbi of Tunisia since it does not have any authority in France[1]. The European Court of Human Rights decided that the monopole over ritual slaughter reserved, in France, to only sacrificers approved by the main Jewish organization, was compatible with religious freedom[2]. With regard to *halal* meat, it is submitted to the Paris mosque's control and that of other mosques approved by the State. These mosques are competent to authorize butchers to practice ritual slaughter. Jewish and Muslim religious authorities collect taxes on *kosher* and *halal* meat to support their cash-boxes. In cities where *halal* meat is not available, Muslims of Switzerland often frequent Jewish butcher shops that sell *kosher* meat. Swiss Jews informed me that the price of *kosher* meat is nearly twice that of non-*kosher* meat. The rabbi of Lausanne assured me that he does not collect a tax on this meat and that the high price is due to importation from France.

Because of the small Jewish community and lack of organization of the Muslim community, Switzerland does not know a system of *kosher* or *halal* food labeling in supermarkets, as is the case in the United States. In this country, about 23,000 products carry *kosher* labels, and about 300 Jewish agencies certify the kosher quality of these products. There are also Muslim organizations of certification in this country. These

---

[1] Trib. Correct. Seine 6.1.1964, Abraham et Isaac Y., Gaz. Pal. 1964, 1, 447.

[2] See decision of the European court dated 27.6.2000: Cha'are Shalom ve Tsedek c/France, in: http://hudoc.echr.coe.int/hudoc/ViewRoot.asp

organizations not only work to win their paradise! The Jewish community of Lausanne arranges a list of *kosher* products on the Internet: http://home.urbanet.ch/urba9410/. But this community ordered a survey on the economic feasibility of the *kosher* market.

One can however not underestimate difficulties of enterprise. Certification of a *kosher* or *halal* food requires a lot of technical means in order to discover ingredients of food commodity and a permanent control of these ingredients that constantly change. Besides the technical difficulties, some certificators deliver certificates of conformity from afar, without ever examining products. Even though a product comes from Muslim countries or Israel, this is not a guarantee that the product respects religious norms. Sellers of *halal* meat buy a part of their meat from a *halal* butcher, and get the remainder from a stock market. Then they mix the two meats and sell them as *halal* while showing the invoice delivered by the *halal* butcher. This procedure opens the way for all kind of abuse. Therefore, we wonder if the State can, in these conditions, guarantee the respect of different religious communities whose requirements are varied and often irreconcilable.

D) Social sanction

The law is not supposed to regulate all human reports, and judges cannot intervene on every social problem. Some human reports obey to cultural dictates and are punished by social mechanisms. For example, no one can ask a judge to condemn a neighbor because he does not say "hello". But the refusal to say hello will be judged by society as anti-social and will have implications that will affect life in community, or even provoke ostracism and xenophobia. The religious food prohibitions may have such effects in some circumstances. I will start with my own experience.

Every foreigner that asks for Swiss citizenship must get the agreement of the Confederation, a canton and a municipality. Every stage is accompanied by an exam that can vary from region to region. For the lowest stage, I presented my demand to the municipality of Vuissens, of about 150 inhabitants, in the canton of Fribourg. I needed a positive vote from the population and an acceptance by the Municipal Council composed mainly of farmers. The meeting with the Municipal Council was satisfactory and my request was accepted. After the meeting, the members of the Council invited me to the village restaurant to drink a "glass of friendship", an excellent white wine of the region They told me, laughing, that it is a condition, "If you do not drink wine, we cannot welcome you among us". But not being accustomed to wine and being on an empty stomach, I had difficulty finishing the glass. They poured me one glass after another. Exiting the restaurant was a relief for me; I needed to lean on the parapet to avoid falling down the staircases. Such a meeting could be a failure if I were a Muslim not drinking wine. As the law does not oblige any municipality to bestow its citizenship, the Municipal Council could have refused me, without any possibility of recourse. To drink wine is part of the social culture of this municipality.

One Swiss diplomat confessed to me that he does not oppose the naturalization of Muslims in Zurich, but he hardly appreciates such new citizens in his small countryside municipality. In his municipality, at the time of public and social demonstrations, one generally serves a small glass of wine and cakes containing, among their ingredients, both pork and alcohol. A Muslim of strict observance will not feel at ease in such a municipality, and municipality inhabitants will feel constrained facing such a newcomer. This diplomat explained to me that every time he invites Muslims, he does not know how to avoid offending their religious sensitivities concerning food. When invited by these Muslims, he informs his hosts that he does not eat sheep, meat often served to guests. Muslims are then very surprised and constrained, not knowing what meat to offer him either.

Food prohibitions can have implications when looking for a job, notably in branches linked to food services. A Muslim *au pair* girl coming from ex-Yugoslavia finds work in a Swiss family. This girl refuses to prepare food with pork or to put the dishes used for pork or wine in the dishwasher. The Christian family, little accustomed to these customs, dismissed her immediately. The *au pair* girl will not be able to resort to any court to require that the Christian family respect her Islamic norms. Similarly, this girl and her Muslim family will probably interpret her dismissal as a discriminatory measure against Muslims. The same can happen with a cleaning woman, a cook or a butcher. Fawzia Al-Ashmawi reports the case of two Muslim women who refused to work as waitresses, because they wanted to avoid touching or serving alcohol[1].

The Guide for the Muslim in Foreign Countries lingers on these problems. It thinks that a Muslim can pick the grape even when he knows that it could serve to make wine, but he does not have the right to work in that sector of wine production. The Muslim can work in the supermarket where one sells both wine and pork, provided he himself is not required to handle or sell these foods[2]. He can eat in restaurants where one serves wine, provided he does not sit at a table where others drink wine, and that he does not encourage such illicit activities in that restaurant[3].

The problem is even sharper in mixed marriages. The law cannot intervene to say what one may eat at home. [It remains in the private domain, not touched by the issue of the separation of Church and State.] Certainly, a Christian woman cannot force her Muslim husband to eat pork or drink wine. But can he force his wife not to bring pork or wine into his house or to either drink wine or eat pork, either in or out of the house? Is it necessary for him to make separate tables? And what of their children? Some Muslim husbands forbid their Christian wives from eating pork or drinking wine during pregnancy and in the period of nursing, so they do not transmit these substances to their children. What about a Muslim husband who observes the Ramadan fast? Can he require his Christian wife and children to fast with him? In the booklet on the mixed marriages published by the Swiss Institute of comparative law, it is recommended that the two spouses discuss these problems before marriage and agree to terms in a notarized contract.

The problem can also have repercussions outside the family. Muslims who come to Switzerland are accustomed to a society that prohibits the daytime public consumption of food or drink during the month of Ramadan. Certainly Switzerland will not be able to prohibit such consumption in respect of Muslims' fasting, but there is a risk of Muslims trying to impose such abstinence for their coreligionists, as they are known to do in Muslim countries. In a symposium held in Turku (Finland) in 1996, one

---

[1] Al-Ashmawi: *La condition des musulmans en Suisse*, p. 112.
[2] *Dalil al-muslim*, p. 78.
[3] *Ibid.*, p. 73.

participant noted that fundamentalist Muslim refugees in that country led some punitive operations against Muslims who frequented Turku bars during the month of Ramadan. Finns told me their indignation, "These Muslims come to make the police at home!" In the French report of the *High Council for integration*, it is said:

> In the college Edgar Quinet, in the center-city of Marseille, pupils, who are all Muslim, follow in their almost-totality the Ramadan. If a child eats in his corner, there is always a friend who makes the sign of slaughter. Such behaviors reveal the risk that develops between over zealous pupils concerning religious observance[1].

Certainly this behavior of intimidation is reprehensible, but it is difficult to monitor it in practice. This is not a simple matter for the child in question who risks more problems with his friends. If one wishes to end such behavior, it is necessary to develop mutual respect through education of individual freedom; a slow developing process that eventually requires serious questioning of preconceived religious norms and practices.

Chapter VI.
Religious Cemeteries

Islamic law prescribes burial of the dead where he dies. One must accept the destiny that God reserves to him. According to Muhammad, every person, at the time of creation, is mixed with earth that is predestined for his tomb[2]. However, classic jurists permitted, with reticence, the transfer of the dead to the holy cities - Mecca, Medina, and Jerusalem - to benefit their blessing[3].

It is estimated that between 90 and 95% of deceased Muslims are repatriated to their countries of origin, and this repatriation can cost up to 15,000.- Sfr[4]. Why such a repatriation? Muslims answer that Switzerland does not grant them the right to be buried according to their religious norms. It is what we will see

---

[1] Haut Conseil de l'intégration, 3.3.5, p. 42.

[2] Al-Qurtubi: *Al-tadhkirah*, p. 88-89.

[3] Al-Nawawi: *Al-majmu*, vol. 5, p. 303. See Al-Zuhayli: *Al-fiqh al-islami*, vol. 2, p. 509-510.

[4] *Tages-Anzeiger*: Toleranz gegenüber Muslimen, 22.8.96, p. 19; *Der Bund*, 11.8.98: Bundesstadt öffnet Friedhöfe für Andersgläubige.

summarily here, referring the reader back to our book dedicated to the Islamic cemetery question in Switzerland[1].

1) Separation of tombs

A) Islamic norms

Islamic law prescribes between dead persons the division that exists between living persons. Muslims must be buried in their own cemetery, and it is prohibited to bury an unbeliever among them. According to Muhammad, the dead undergoes punishment or enjoys the happiness already in the tomb. For this reason, it is necessary to avoid putting a believer close to an unbeliever so that he does not endure the condition of his neighborhood. Muhammad said, "I am discharged of any Muslim who is found with a polytheist"[2]. If a Christian woman dies pregnant from a Muslim, she must be buried in a separate place, neither in the Muslim cemetery (so these last are not prejudiced because of her presence), nor in the one of Christians (so the child, supposedly already Muslim, does not undergo a prejudice by their presence)[3].

The apostate is thrown into a pit "as one throws a dog". If he has a Muslim parent, it would be preferable to let him wash him as one washes an impure dress and roll him up in a worn-out dress[4]. Concerning someone who commits suicide or one who was convicted to death for a reason other than apostasy, they are buried in the Muslim cemetery, but the imam should not pray for them, as a sign of disapproval of their offences[5].

The unbeliever is buried in the cemetery of unbelievers. A Muslim will not take care of his unbelieving father unless the latter has nobody else. He will not pray for him. The Koran orders, "You shall not observe the funeral prayer for any of them

---

[1] Aldeeb Abu-Sahlieh: *Cimetière musulman*.

[2] See Ibn-Qayyim Al-Jawziyyah: *Ahkam ahl al-dhimmah*, vol. 2, p. 725-727; Al-Qurtubi: *Al-tadhkirah*, p. 100-101; Ibn-Rushd: *Al-bayan wal-tahsil*, vol. 2, p. 255-256; Khalid: *Al-islam wa-ru'yatuh fima ba'd al-hayat*, p. 123-124.

[3] Ibn-Hazm: *Al-muhalla*, vol. 5, p. 142-143; Ibn-Qudamah: *Al-mughni*, vol. 2, p. 423; Al-Nawawi: *Al-majmu*, vol. 5, p. 285; Al-Nawawi: *Rawdat al-talibin*, vol. 2, p. 134, 143.

[4] Ibn-Abidin: *Rad al-muhtar*, vol. 2, p. 230-231.

[5] See article Intihar, in: *Al-mawsu'ah al-fiqhiyyah*, vol. 6, p. 281-295; *Fatawi al-lajnah al-da'imah*, vol. 8, p. 394, 395.

when he dies, nor shall you stand at his grave. They have disbelieved in God and His messenger, and died in a state of wickedness" (9:84)[1]

It is prohibited to bury an unbeliever in Arabia. If one is buried there, he must be exhumed and repatriated because, according to Mawerdi, "burial is equivalent to a stay for ever". He quotes Muhammad who, on his deathbed, called Umar (d. 644), the future 2nd caliph, and told him, "Two religions must not coexist in the Arabian Peninsula"[2]. A Saudi *fatwa* says that if one cannot give back the unbeliever's body to the rightful parties, or if an amputed part of the body cannot be returned to its owner and it is not possible to take it out of the country, bury it in an anonymous ground belonging to nobody[3].

As we said in the first part of this book, Islamic law does not allow that a Muslim stay in the Land of Disbelief, except in necessity. Some consider such a Muslim an apostate and refuse him burial in a Muslim cemetery[4]. As it is not possible to prevent Muslims from entering the Land of Disbelief, it was necessary at least to prevent their burial in a cemetery of unbelievers. *The Guide for the Muslim in Foreign Countries* indicates:

> It is not permitted to bury a Muslim in a cemetery of unbelievers unless there is no cemetery for Muslims and that it is not possible to transfer the dead to a nearby Muslim country. If thereafter it becomes possible to exhume the Muslim to transfer him to a Muslim cemetery, this transfer becomes an obligation[5].

After long debate, the *Academy of Islamic Law* that depends on the *Organization of Islamic Conference* decided that burial in a cemetery of unbelievers is possible only in necessity[6]. The *Saudi Fatwa Commission* permits burial of a Muslim in an Islamic cemetery in the Land of Disbelief, but recalls that a Muslim must in principle leave the Land of Disbelief for the Land of Islam.

---

[1] Al-Nawawi: *Rawdat al-talibin*, vol. 2, p. 118; 134 and 143; Al-Nawawi: *Al-majmu*, vol. 5, p. 285; Al-Bahuti: *Kashshaf al-qina*, vol. 2, p. 124-125; Ibn-Rushd: *Al-bayan wal-tahsil*, vol. 2, p. 277 and 284; Al-Qalyubi and Umayra: *Hashiyah*, vol. 1, p. 337.

[2] Mawerdi: *Les statuts gouvernementaux*, p. 357.

[3] Fatawi al-lajnah al-da'imah, vol. 9, p. 8-9.

[4] Al-Jaza'iri: *Tabdil*, p. 25-27.

[5] *Dalil al-muslim*, p. 89.

[6] *Majallat majma al-fiqh al-islami*, n° 3, part 2, 1987, p. 1339-1341.

Only the Muslim who knows the norms of Islam, feels secure in his religion and works to propagate Islam may remain there[1]. Concerning one case in France, the Commission says that if there is no Islamic cemetery and no possibility of transferring the dead, it is necessary to look for a place in the desert (*sic*) to bury him; his tomb will be leveled so the dead is not exhumed[2].

B) Swiss norms

The *Swiss Islamic Cemetery Foundation*, created in 1987 by Swiss converts, sent in 1993 about 900 letters to French-speaking municipalities in view of obtaining a cemetery for Muslims[3]. These letters remained without result. A memorandum, indicating that Muslim tombs must occupy a specific locale in the cemetery, apart from tombs of other religions, accompanied them. The circular by the *Islamic Cultural Foundation of Geneva* states:

> Islamic Tradition recommends that the dead be buried close to the place of death, "Bury the dead where their souls left them" (*Narrative of Muhammad*). The transfer for no valid reason is not recommended (except for example if the Muslim died in a city where it does not exist an Islamic cemetery)...
>
> The best place is a cemetery to benefit from the prayers of visitors. It is strictly prohibited to bury a non-Muslim with a Muslim, as the opposite. All Islamic schools agree on this point. This religious obligation requires the exclusive right as much as possible. It is not segregation as some pretend. In Islam, there are other religious obligations where it is possible to a non-Muslim to either participate or benefit (for example during the festivities) as well as in some recommended religious practices as charity (*sadaqah*)[4].

Instead of giving the real reason for which Muslims must not be buried close to an unbeliever, the *Islamic Cultural Foundation of Geneva* advances the argument of the prayer so that one does not interpret Muslims' attitude as "segregation".

Muslims accuse Switzerland of discrimination against them by refusing a decent funeral and obliging transfer of their dead

---

[1] Fatawi al-lajnah al-da'imah, vol. 8, p. 451-452.

[2] *Ibid.*, vol. 8, p. 454-455.

[3] *La Suisse*, 13.10.1993: À quand un cimetière musulman?

[4] See also the interview of Hafid Ouardiri, representative of the Islamic Cultural Foundation, March of 1999 by the Youth and Social Commission, in: *Mémorial des séances du conseil municipal de la ville de Genève*, 12.10.1999, p. 1440.

abroad at great expense[1]. In fact, anyone who dies in Switzerland has the right to be decently buried there, even if just traveling through. The problem is Muslims refuse to be buried randomly, in public cemeteries, next to an unbeliever. They require their own cemetery or a separate plot in a public cemetery, exclusively reserved for their use. By this request, they oblige cantons to retreat and give up a secular advancesd dearly acquired in the debate over cemeteries.

Indeed, before 1874 the cantons had Catholic, Protestant and Jewish cemeteries, each community refusing to be buried with others. Catholics, especially, refused to bury in their cemeteries the unbaptized, the apostates, those who committed suicide, the excommunicated, etc. These discriminatory norms are prescribed in the Canon Law Code of 1917[2] and 1983[3]. Jews also refused, and still refuse - with exceptions – to be buried with others. If a non-Jew is buried close to Jews, they forbid him any non-Jewish sign or ceremony[4]. They also refuse to bury a non-circumcised Jew unless he is circumcised after his death[5].

To put end to the conflict between Catholics and Protestants, article 53 par. 2 aCst stipulates, "The disposal of burial grounds is a concern of the civil authorities. They shall make sure that every deceased person may get a decent burial".

According to this article, any deceased, including a suicide and a non-baptized, has the right to be buried decently, independently of his religion. The Swiss Federal Council was charged to look after the respect of this decency by the cantons. It has been called to decide many litigious cases between Catholics and Protestants, notably concerning non-baptized, suicide and… tooting of bells at the time of funeral ceremony. In its decisions, it did not exclude the presence of private religious cemeteries, cemeteries

---

[1] Al-Ashmawi: *La condition des musulmans en Suisse*, p. 46; Burkhalter: *La question du cimetière*, p. 93-94.

[2] See the canons 1212, 1239 and 1240.

[3] See the canons 1183-1185 and 1240-1241.

[4] Burial of non-Jewish wives in Jewish cemeteries, 1916, in: http://www.ccarnet.org/cgi-bin/respdisp.pl?file=98&year=arr; *Non-Jewish burial in a Jewish cemetery*, in: http-://www.ccarnet.org/cgi-bin/respdisp.pl?file=99&year=arr

[5] See on this question Aldeeb Abu-Sahlieh: *Circoncision masculine*, p. 52-53.

that the cantons could accept or refuse to create. However, its final aim was the unification of cemeteries, without religious barriers, finding "that a common cemetery, without distinction of confession, was certainly the most compliant system to the equality of citizens and the better of any to moderate the religious contrasts in life"[1]. This desire to unify cemeteries was already present in a draft-law prepared in 1880. But the Swiss Federal Council renounced to adopt it to avoid crumpling the population, preferring punctual interventions, counting on the factor time[2]. Today, neither Catholics nor Protestants have their own cemeteries. The only group that have separate cemetery are Jews, some arranged after 1874. To our knowledge, no Jewish cemetery has become a common cemetery. The non-Jew can never be buried there, while a Jew can be buried in cemeteries that were previously reserved for Catholics or Protestants.

Invoking the exception made to Jews in some municipalities, Muslims require today their own cemeteries according to the religious freedom and the right to a decent funeral, but they carefully dissimulate the deep, discriminatory reasons, which motivate such a demand. Four cantons have already been confronted to this problem: Geneva, Bern, Basel-city and Zurich.

Geneva

In Geneva, there was in the 19th century cemeteries for the Protestants and for Catholics and a cemetery for Jews in Carouge. In 1876, Geneva adopted a law that considers that cemeteries are all "municipal properties" (article 1 par. 1) and foresees, "burials must take place in pits established one following the other, in a regular and pre-determined order, without any distinction based on religion or other" (article 8 par. 1). With regard to the Jewish cemetery, the High Council decided that once it is saturated, Jews should follow the law as everybody else. And as the authorities refused to enlarge this cemetery, the Jewish community decided to construct a cemetery in the French territory, at Veyrier-Étremblières, whose entrance is on the Swiss territory, with tombs on French territory.

---

[1] *Feuille fédérale* 1895 I 61-63; see also 1886 I 811 and 1886 II 395.
[2] See *Feuille fédérale* 1875 III 283 and 541; 1881 II 230, 541-542 and 817.

Giving up to "political pressures"[1], the city of Geneva created in 1979, in violation of the law of 1876, a separate Muslim square in the cemetery of Petit-Saconnex[2]. News having spread quickly, this square immediately turned into a cantonal Islamic cemetery. In the beginning of 1992, Michel Rossetti, Administrative Counselor in charge of the Social Affairs Department, decided to forbid the burial of any Muslim not domiciled in the territory of Geneva[3], and that, when the square would be full, "the law of 1876 would apply indistinctly to all communities, including Muslims"[4].

This wrong step of Geneva, that consisted in creating a separate square in violation of the law and then in trying to close it, continues to provoke an acrid debate between proponents and opponents to confessional cemetery in the cantonal and municipal level in Geneva[5], as well as in other cantons. Now, not only Muslims ask for their own cemeteries, but also liberal Jews, Armenians and Anglicans. To attempt to put end to these claims, June 19, 1997, paragraph 3 has been added to article 4 of the Law of 1876. This new paragraph stipulates, "Sites are assigned without distinction of origin or religion". It reinforces the aforementioned article 8 par. 1. This modification does not have as much calmed minds, especially with the arrival of Manuel Tornare, favorable to the confessional cemeteries, in replacement of Michel Rossetti.

Bern

The municipality of Bern adopted in September 1997 a new Regulation on cemeteries permitting to create separate areas for

---

[1] Answer of Michel Rossetti 15.10.1996: *Mémorial des séances du conseil municipal de la ville de Genève*, séance du 15.10.1996, p. 1705-1705.

[2] Letter of Guy-Olivier Segond, Administrative councillor of the city of Geneva to Mr. Henri Schmitt dated 22.8.1979.

[3] Letter to the author from the State councillor Gérard Ramseyer dated 10.6.1996.

[4] Answer of Michel Rossetti, 15.10.1996: *Mémorial des séances du conseil municipal de la ville de Genève*, séance du 15.10.1996, p. 1705-1706.

[5] See *Mémorial des séances du conseil municipal de la ville de Genève*, 15.9.1993, p. 977-990, and 12.1.1999, p. 2943-2958. See also 12.10.1999, p. 1432-1457.

religious or ethnic minorities (article 3)[1]. In application of this new disposition, the local parliament of the city of Bern accepted in August 1998 the principle of the creation of a separate zone for Muslims of any confession they are, provided to be domiciled in the city of Bern or Ostermundigen or that they died in a hospital of the city of Bern[2].

November 9th, 1999, it has been decided to assign a credit of 45,000.- Sfr for the creation of a separate Islamic square for 250 tombs in the cemetery of Bremgarten[3]. Muslims accepted that tombs be reused (by Muslims), without evacuating bones (so the rest of the dead is assured), at the end of twenty years, similarly to the other tombs of the cemetery. On the other hand, the municipality guaranteed that there would not be any ashes (of cremation) or urns for ashes in this land. The Islamic square of Bern was inaugurated in big pump in January of 2000, in the presence of cantonal and local persons responsible for Bern as well as ambassadors from Muslim countries and representatives from Muslim socio-cultural organizations[4].

Basel-city

In 1996, Basel-city also modified its law of 1931 concerning cemeteries to permit the creation of a free place for a community (article 7 par. 1 litt. c). Thus, a separate square was granted to Muslims, and provisions were made to grant them another subsequently. As in Bern, tombs can be reused (only by Muslims) after the legal period, without removing their bones.

I contacted Emanuel Trueb, responsible for cemeteries in this canton, and asked him why he gave up concerning discriminatory Muslim requirements. He answered that as a Christian he is merciful and thinks that it is necessary to allow time for Muslims to adjust to the Swiss reality. Progressively, he believes, they will be integrated and there will be no separation in cemeteries between Muslims and non-Muslims. It is necessary to have great faith to believe in such miracles, without a push from the State.

---

[1] *Der Bund*, 19.9.1997.
[2] *Der Bund*, 14.8.1998.
[3] *Der Bund*, 12.11.1999.
[4] Al-Ashmawi: *La condition des musulmans en Suisse*, p. 34-35.

Zurich

In the city of Zurich two solutions were presented. Muslims could buy a land for a private cemetery, but this project failed in 1997 because of its high price. The other solution was to get a separate square of 8000m^2 in the public cemetery existing in Eichbuehl-Altstätten. This last solution however was in opposition with article thirty-five of the cantonal decree of 1963 that forbids the creation of separate squares in the public cemeteries. Therefore, it was necessary to change this decree. The majority of municipalities of the canton rejected the idea of a separation inside cemeteries on the basis of the religion, but some municipalities kept the door open for a clause of exception in particular cases or a delegation of the decision to a municipality that would be free to decide on the subject.

This change intervened on June 27th, 2001, notably thanks to the support of the Catholic and Reformed Churches, opens the way for the concession of a separate square exclusively reserved for Muslims. Pastor Leonhard Suter wrote, in October of 1997, a report[1] for his Reformed Church, based notably on an article by Federal Judge Niccolò Raselli[2]. Catholic authorities solicited a legal opinion from professor Walter Kälin[3]. All three were in favor of a confessional cemetery. Referring to a minimal Islamic documentation, they just repeated the arguments of Swiss fundamentalist Muslims without questioning the real reason behind their request.

May 27th, 2001, I asked the head of the Islamic Center in Zurich for what reason he claimed a cemetery or a separate square exclusively reserved for Muslims. His answer was, "I do not want to be buried close to an unbeliever's tomb carrying a cross". Ismail Amin, president of the *Union of Muslim Organizations* in Zurich, affirms that one of the objectives of his organization is "the establishment of a cemetery where Muslims could be buried according to Islamic tradition". Yet, he specifies

---

[1] Suter: *Muslimische Gräber.*
[2] Raselli: *Schickliche Beerdigung für Andersgläubige.*
[3] Kälin; Rieder: *Bestattung von Muslimen auf öffentlichen Friedhöfen im Kanton Zürich.*

that he will never accept that a member of the non-conformist Ahmadite group be buried in this Muslim cemetery[1].

2) Direction of the tomb

A) Islamic norms

In the beginning, Muhammad turned in his prayer toward Jerusalem as Jews do. But sixteen months after his arrival to Madina, he decided to replace the direction of Jerusalem for that of the *Kaaba* in Mecca, to differentiate himself from the Jews[2] who had rejected his revelations. [Even though there is no evidence that Abraham was ever in Mecca,] Muslims believe Abraham constructed the *Kaaba* as a sanctuary for God's worship. It constitutes the most sacred object for Muslims after the Koran, and different norms are related to it: the Muslim must turn seven times around it in pilgrimage, to head toward it during prayer, and to avoid having the back or face oriented to it while performing bodily functions [3]. This spatially bound anthropomorphic concept of divinity, inherited from polytheistic Arabs, goes against the Koranic concept that God is omnipresent (2:115) and that religiosity does not depend on direction but on faith and good deeds (2:177).

Classic Muslim jurists thought that the deceased should be buried on his side facing the *Kaaba*, i.e. the axis of his tomb must be perpendicular to the *Kaaba*. This rule is based on a statement by Muhammad. He reportedly said that the *Kaaba* is the direction of all Muslims, both alive and dead[4]. But the classic jurists are divided about to know if it is necessary to put the dying toward the *Kaaba* and to do the same way while one washes him after death, or if this norm applies only in the tomb. Invoking verse 2:115, Ibn-Hazm requires orientation toward the *Kaaba* only in the tomb[5]. Note here that Jews bury the dead with feet turned toward Jerusalem so that they can stand up the day of the

---

[1] Interview given to Fawzia Al-Ashmawi (Al-Ashmawi: *La condition des musulmans*, p. 116).

[2] Koran 2:144-145 and 150. See on the changing of the direction, Ibn-Qayyim Al-Jawziyyah: *Zad al-ma'ad*, p. 391-392.

[3] Al-Bukhari, narratives 141 and 380.

[4] Abu-Da'ud, narrative 2490.

[5] Ibn-Hazm: *Al-muhalla*, vol. 5, p. 173-174.

resurrection and walk directly to Jerusalem[1]. Some rabbis suggested that if one does not manage to align tombs toward Jerusalem, a wall surrounds the cemetery with a door toward Jerusalem, the feet being directed toward the door[2].

B) Swiss norms

In the memorandum of the *Swiss Islamic Cemetery Foundation*, it is noted that tombs must be oriented according to an axis of 40° to 220°, and that the body must be laid down on his right side so that the face is oriented to 130° (direction of the Mecca). A circular of the *Islamic Cultural Foundation of Geneva* indicates, "It is necessary to direct the dead toward the *Kibla* (*Kaaba*) (obligatory!). The Prophet said: It is your *kibla*, alive and dead".

In the interview with a Geneva commission in March of 1999, Hafid Ouardiri, spokesman of the *Islamic Cultural Foundation of Geneva*, specifies, "For the Muslim, the main element is that the burial be in a tomb directed toward the Mecca, because it is from there that the resurrection will occur"[3]. No classic Muslim jurist, to my knowledge, mentions this reference to the resurrection in relation with the direction of the tomb. Probably Hafid Ouardiri borrows it from the Jews.

When pits are dug one after the other, according to a pre-established order, Islamic norm raises problem because of the order inside the cemetery. The cantons and municipalities have the right, or even the duty, to prescribe such an order. It pertains to decency of the burial. On the other hand, as the deceased are buried without distinction of religion, to modify the orientation of the tomb of a Muslim in a line, besides the disharmony generated in the cemetery, constitutes a distinction between the dead on the basis of the religion. In this respect, Muslims are required to form harmonious rows in their prayers.

The determination of the direction of the *Kaaba* is not easy. The Muslim architects of the Mosque of Geneva did a mistake with the niche indicating the direction of the *Kaaba*; the mistake was discovered several years later. On the other hand, the

---

[1] E-mail from David Lilienthal ravdav@ljg.nl du 14.5.2001.

[2] *Direction of graves in a cemetery*, 1980, in: http://www.ccarnet.org/cgi-bin/resp-disp.pl?file=104&year=arr

[3] Mémorial des séances du conseil municipal de la ville de Genève, 12.10.1999, p. 1440.

B) Swiss norms

The memorandum of the *Swiss Islamic Cemetery Foundation* indicates, "The funeral should take place the day of the death, or the following day at the latest". A pamphlet of the *Islamic Cultural Foundation of Geneva* says, "It is recommended to activate the preparations of the funeral, except valid reasons (for example autopsy)".

Besides the fact that the requirement of Muslims in Switzerland does not take account of the above quoted classic Muslim jurist suppleness, it contravenes to the cantonal norms. Thus, in answer to the *Islamic Cultural Foundation of Geneva*, the city of Fribourg writes in its letter of October 6th, 1993, "The fact that burial must take place the same day of death, or at latest the following day, requires an excessive availability (including weekends) of the personnel affected in the service of burials".

There is the question of personnel availability, but also the respect of the procedure and a minimal delay before burying the dead. This delay aims to assure the family in particular and all the population in general that none will be buried unless effectively dead. This delay is also dictated by the worry to avoid useless exhumations. Indeed one can suppose reasonably that in case of contentions about the reason or the circumstances of the death, a delay of 48 hours is sufficient so that arguments are presented to the judicial authorities and that an investigation can determine what really happened[1]. The spirit of these cantonal norms is in perfect concordance with the Islamic norm. Therefore, nothing justifies a special treatment for Muslims, contrary to what could suggest the aforementioned documents.

5) Permanence of tombs

Dead must not clutter the living. To solve the problem of the space, one proceeds to the periodic disaffection of cemeteries and the exhumation of human remainders to incinerate them or to put them down in ossuaries. A third system consists in immediately reducing bodies in ashes after the death, ashes which are preserved in small urns or dispersed in the nature. So one passed from the eternal pyramids of Pharaohs to the temporary tombs,

---

[1] La Harpe; Fryc: *La mort et la loi*, p. 3.

and from the temporary tombs to ashes that waters or winds transport. But this passage is not accepted without resistance.

A) Islamic norms

The Koran does not say anything concerning the permanence and disaffection of tombs. It is reported that Muhammad had disaffected tombs of polytheists to construct his own mosque in Medina. Some narratives of Muhammad incite the respect of tombs. So he forbad walking with shoes of leather among tombs[1]. He also said, "To break bones of a dead is as to break bones of one who is alive"[2]; "A person who sits on a tomb is similar to a person sitting on a brazier"[3]. These prescriptions are bound to the respect that humans owe to the dead, but also to the belief that the dead feel the steps of those who walk close to their tomb.

From these narratives, the classic jurists wondered if it was possible to exhume the dead, to reuse the tomb to bury another person therein, and to construct or to plant on a land containing a tomb after exhumation or without exhumation of bones. Ibn-Abidin writes that it is preferable to bury each in a unique tomb, except in case of necessity. One does not open a tomb to reuse it unless the first buried became again earth and no bones remain. But if bones are found there, they should be put aside and separated from the new dead by earth. He rejects the rigorist position that forbids reuse of the tomb, because it is not possible to prepare an exclusive tomb for every person in populated regions without that tombs invade the fertile plains and fallow regions. He indicates that some classic jurists permitted to construct on tombs and to use the ground of cemeteries for agriculture if bodies perished[4].

With the expansion of the urbanization, the Muslim countries wondered if it was possible to disaffect tombs. Several *fatwas* have been issued on this topic. Some of them were in the beginning opposed to the disaffection of cemeteries although they

---

[1] Abu-Da'ud, narrative 2811; Al-Nisa'i, narrative 2021.

[2] Abu-Da'ud, narrative 2792; Ibn-Majah, narrative 1605.

[3] Al-Nisa'i, narrative 2017; Muslim, narrative 1612; Abu-Da'ud, narrative 2809.

[4] Ibn-Abidin: *Rad al-muhtar*, vol. 2, p. 234. See also Al-Nawawi: *Al-majmu*, vol. 5, p. 284-285 and 298-300; Al-Nawawi: *Rawdat al-talibin*, vol. 2, p. 14.

permitted to bury the dead with others. But they ended up accepting the reuse of tombs as well as the total disaffection of cemeteries to make an agricultural land or to construct buildings and roads[1].

B) Swiss norms

One circular by the *Islamic Cultural Foundation of Geneva* indicates, "It is strictly prohibited to unearth a dead person without an imperious reason, as for example if the cleansing of the body has not been performed or he does not have a burial shroud". A memorandum of the *Swiss Islamic Cemetery Foundation* stipulates, "Exhumation is forbidden; therefore it is necessary to acquire perpetual concession".

Invoking the constitutional articles concerning the religious freedom and the right to a decent burial as well as international documents, in 1995, the President of the *Swiss Islamic Cemetery Foundation*, Abd-Allah Lucien Meyers, a convert, asked his municipality to guarantee a perpetual tomb and the regrouping of all Islamic tombs in one place of the public cemetery. The municipality accepted to grant him a concession of 50 years with possibility of renewal for 20 years, but refused to regroup Islamic tombs. He resorted to the State Council of Zurich, but without success. He then appealed to the Federal Court, which rejected his demand, on June 5th, 1999, finding, "such an obligation would put in question the planning and the exploitation of the public cemetery and would constitute a lasting private use of the public domain. Even religious freedom does not impose itself on collectivity as such a requirement would limit in an unacceptable manner its maneuver in front of subsequent developments. Besides, according to the principle of equality, perpetual tombs should be offered to all citizens, and that would drag important problems"[2].

Conscious probably of the problem, Hafid Ouardiri, spokesman of the *Islamic Cultural Foundation of Geneva*, accepted to put water in his wine while permitting to bury a dead over another

---

[1] *Al-Fatawi al-islamiyyah*, vol. 4, p. 1169-1170, n° 573; *Ibid.*, vol. 4, p. 1173-1174, n° 575. See also Al-Qaradawi: *Min huda al-islam*, vol. 1, p. 729-733; Bukhal, p. 58.

[2] Federal Court decision 125 I 300. French translation in: *Revue de droit administratif et de droit fiscal*, vol. 56.6.2000, p. 636.

after body decomposition. He affirmed to a Geneva commission in March 1999, "For Muslims, it is not necessary that the tomb be eternal. One can bury a deceased over another after the decomposition of the body.... They are opened to discuss how long should be the lapse of time before burying a new deceased in the same tomb, because they are well conscious of the question of the space"[1].

Muslims accepted giving up on the condition of the perpetual concession in Bern and Basel-city. The Muslim tombs, like all tombs in line, can be reused after twenty years, without evacuation of bones. But this reuse is limited to Muslims since tombs are in a separate square exclusively reserved for Muslims. Muslims do not accept that a Muslim be put on an "unbeliever ", nor an "unbeliever" on a Muslim.

6) Cremation

Rejected through the centuries by Jewish, Christian and Muslim communities alike, cremation is now rehabilitated in the West among Christians in particular for practical, philosophical, economic, ecological, hygienic, and legal reasons (respect of the will of the deceased). Condemned by Pope Leo XIII in 1886, and the Canon Law Code of 1917, it was finally admitted by the Catholic Church in 1963[2]. Acceptance of cremation differs from country to country. So the rate of cremation in 1998 is 4.09% in Italy, 14.90% in France, 67.9% in Switzerland, 71.42% in England and 98.42% in Japan[3]. Liberal Jews and Muslims resort to cremation, but nobody knows the percentage, probably minute.

A) Islamic norms

The Koran mentions the first funeral. After the murder of Abel by Cain, God sent a raven to scratch the soil, to teach him how to bury his brother's corpse (5:31). Elsewhere it is said, "From it we created you, into it we return you, and from it we bring you out once more" (20:55).

---

[1] Mémorial des séances du conseil municipal de la ville de Genève, 12.10.1999, p. 1440.

[2] Louveau: *L'incinération*, p. 1-2.

[3] http://members.aol.com/CremSoc/LegalEtc/Stats/Interntl/1998/StatsIF.html.

One finds narratives where Muhammad forbad putting someone to death by fire. Thus, after Ali had burnt alive some apostates, Ibn-Abbas objected saying that he would not have burnt them, but executed them according to the word of Muhammad, "One who changes his religion, kill him". He invokes against the use of fire a word of Muhammad that says, "Do not punish with God's sanction"[1]. In another narrative, Muhammad ordered to Hamzah Al-Aslami, "If you take that person, burn him", then he called him and said, "If you take that person, kill him and do not burn him because no one can castigate by the fire other than the master of fire"[2]. Muhammad forbad also destroying an anthill by fire[3]. The prohibition to use cremation in these narratives relates to the cremation as sanction of a person alive.

According to another narrative of Muhammad, a man gathered his children around him on his deathbed and asked them what they thought about him. His children answered that he was the best of fathers. He then told them, by humility, that he did not accomplish any good, and that if God could seize him, he will punish him as no one has been punished before. He ordered his children to swear that they would burn him after his death until he becomes coal, to reduce him to ashes and to disperse his ashes on a windy day, half on earth and half on sea, thinking thus to escape God. After death, his sons executed their father's will. God then gave the order to the earth and the sea to give back the parts of the deceased and the man stood in presence of God. God asked him, "What pushed you to give such an order?", and the deceased answered, "My fear of you, Lord". God filled him then with mercy[4]. This narrative aims to demonstrate that God is

---

[1] Al-Bukhari, narrative 2794. See also Al-Bukhari, narratives 1378 and 6411; Ahmad, narratives 1775, 1802, 2420 and 2421; Al-Tirmidhi, narrative 1378; Al-Nisa'i, narrative 3992; Abu-Da'ud, narrative 3787. Muhammad ordered to burn a village called Abna (Ibn-Majah, narrative 2833; Ahmad, narrative 20786).

[2] Abu-Da'ud, narrative 2299. Classical jurists allow the recourse to the fire as punishment in application of the law of retaliation (Koran 16:126, 2:174) or against homosexual (see article Ihraq, in: *Al-mawsu'ah al-fiqhiyyah*, vol. 2, p. 120 and 124-125).

[3] Abu-Da'ud, narrative 2300; Ahmad, narrative 3814.

[4] See different forms of this narrative in: Al-Bukhari narratives 3219, 6000 and 6954; Muslim, narratives 4950 and 4952; Al-Nisa'i,

capable to revive the human being even though he is incinerated and his ashes dispersed by the wind. It does not include any disapproval of the cremation since God can save the incinerated person.

In some Arab countries, there are crematories for those whose religious norms permit the cremation. It is the case in Egypt[1]. Books in Arabic do not consider cremation since it is not permitted. July 29th, 1953, the *Egyptian Fatwa Commission* says:

> All Muslims agree that the human being has immunity and dignity as much alive as dead, according to God's word, "We have honored the children of Adam" (17:70). According to true narratives of the Prophet, elaborated by his Companions, their successors and all Muslims until now, burial in a niche or a pit is part of the dignity of a human being after his death. Therefore, it is not permitted to incinerate a Muslim's corpse. And if the deceased had asked for it by will, his will is void and non-executable. The cremation of corpses has been known only in the traditions of Zoroastrians, and we have been ordered to behave differently and in accordance with our noble law[2].

One finds other *fatwas* on the Internet, solicited by Muslims living in the West[3]. In answer to my demand of May 10th, 2001, the service of *fatwa* of Islam-online wrote:

> Islam strictly forbids castigating a living person by fire. For this reason, when the Prophet saw that his Companions had burnt an anthill, he told them, "Cannot castigate by fire other than the master of fire". Furthermore, it is prohibited to burn the dead because of the narrative of Muhammad, "What provokes suffering for a living person provokes also suffering for the dead". Islam insists that water used to wash the dead must be heated to a tolerable middle degree to not provoke suffering. We must imagine as if the dead were alive and take into consideration what may provoke suffering and what may be useful for him. So water will not be heated to boiling point so that his skin is not peeled. To stronger reason, it is prohibited to burn the dead.
>
> Cremation of dead Muslims does not exist in the Arab countries because this ritual is connected to non-celestial religions and religious groups. Such a practice does not exist among Muslims, or Jews, or Christians. And I do not know any Muslim in a Western country who

---

narrative 2052; Ibn-Majah, narrative 4245; Ahmad, narratives 7327, 10674, 10704, 11237, 11312 and 19184.

[1] Law 5/1966 (article 6) and execution decree 418/1970 (article 19).

[2] *Al-Fatawi al-islamiyyah*, vol. 7, p. 2517, n° 1074.

[3] See www.sunnah.org/msaec/articles/cremation.htm; www.isna.net /iq/cremtn.htm; www.understanding-islam.com/ri/mi-072.htm; www.islam-online.net/completesearch/english/*fatwa*Display.asp? h*Fatwa*ID=233.65.10.05.2001

> asked to be incinerated, unless he followed before his death non-Islamic teaching or changed his religion. In this case we cannot count him among Muslims nor can we take account of him in our *fatwa*[1].

This *fatwa* refers to Muhammad's narrative, "What provokes suffering for a living person provokes also suffering for the dead". However if one wants to follow this narrative, one should not put the dead under ground, nor throw him in the sea if he dies on a boat since these two measures, if applied to a living person, provoke suffering. Certainly, cremation among Muslims remains unaccepted. But the Koran permits a change in this domain since it forbids wasting money uselessly (17:26) and harming nature (2:60). Besides, some Muslims already resort to cremation in the West, notably among those married to non-Muslim women[2]. If today Jewish, Christian or Muslim religious authorities remain hostile to cremation, it is mainly because burial is more profitable for them on the financial and power levels.

B) Swiss norms

The memorandum of the *Swiss Islamic Cemetery Foundation* indicates, "cremation is absolutely forbidden". An *Islamic Cultural Foundation of Geneva* flier develops this prohibition:

> All Koranic schools are unanimous that the earth is the final place for every corpse. The Koran says, "Did we not make the earth an abode? For the living and the dead?" (77:25). It also says, "From a tiny drop, He creates him and designs him. Then He points out the path for him. Then He puts him to death, and into the grave" (80:19-21). We deduce therefore that cremation is absolutely forbidden.

Switzerland has had the same debate over cremation as other Western countries. When the Constitution of 1874 was written, the question of cremation had not yet begun. Therefore, article 53 par. 2 aCst only speaks of the right to "get a decent burial". In 1884, a lawyer from Chaux-de-Fonds presented a petition to the Swiss Federal Council asking that cremation be considered "a decent burial, therefore authorizing it through the Swiss Federal Constitution, for all cantons and municipalities that want to introduce it". Swiss Federal Council decided it was not necessary to legislate the subject, and left the decision to cantons. It added:

> It did not appear necessary to proponents of cremation in Zurich and to the authorities of Zurich to consult the legislative or executive federal

---

[1] WebmasterE@islam.online.net, answer to request dated 10.5.2001.

[2] See the case of a Tunisian living in Canada, in: Chaïb: *L'émigré et la mort*, p. 140 and 147.

authority on the question to know whether this method of burial is decent; one can only approve them. They thought, rightfully, that the cremation, recommended by scientists, declared compatible with the Christian religion by clergymen, and sung even by poets in antique and modern times, could not be booed by you or us as something of indecent! A similar objection, indeed, was never presented, up to our knowledge, by any authority having had to deal with it[1].

There are fifty-nine crematories in Switzerland and, according to the yearly report of the Swiss Union of Cremation 1997/1998, 67.97% of the dead in Switzerland were incinerated in 1998, which puts Switzerland in the lead of Western countries, following England. All cantonal laws allow cremation even though some cantons do not always arrange facilities of cremation for religious considerations. It is the case notably of the Catholic canton of Fribourg that, yet, allows the cremation (Decree of December 5th, 2000, article 4 par. 4). Those who like to be incinerated in that canton must pass through another canton.

No canton imposes cremation. Article 1 of the Jura Decree, December 6th 1978, stipulates, "This kind of burial cannot be made obligatory". This does not exclude the imposition of cremation in case of epidemic[2]. On the other hand, some cantons incinerate bones after disaffection of tombs[3].

Cremation is often practiced on request of the deceased or his close relatives. In the canton of Jura, article 1 of the Decree related to cremation, dated December 6th, 1978, allows it:

When the deceased demonstrated, in writing, his desire to be incinerated, or when his relatives ask for his cremation, as long as no opposition is raised among them, or when the people caring for his burial ask for the cremation, unless there is a contrary will.

This decree does not define the term *relatives*. There is no problem if the relatives are from the same degree. But what if there are several relatives from different degrees? One can presume in this case that the opinion of the nearest parent prevails. The Federal Court confirmed that people who have narrow relations with the deceased and were the more affected by his disappearance have the right to take care of the corpse[4].

---

[1] *Feuille fédérale* 1884 IV 225-231.
[2] Spöndlin, p. 91.
[3] Article 51 of the decree of the canton of Vaud dated 5.12.1986.
[4] Federal Court decision 111 Ia 234.

The decease's religious community has no right to intervene and forbid cremation. Can it refuse depositing the urn in the confessional cemetery? This question received a negative answer by Basel authorities in a case concerning the Jewish community. Wyler, who thinks civil authorities cannot grant a religious community a private cemetery and at the same time force this community to act against its convictions, criticized this decision[1]. But this stance is unfounded, because the Jewish community cannot consider cremation indecent. If this community refuses the incinerated person the right to be buried in a Jewish cemetery, this means a return to a practice like the Catholic Church that put the suicide out of the cemetery; the Swiss Federal Council condemned this practice. Far more serious is the concession made by the city of Bern that, while bestowing to the Muslim community a separate plot in the public cemetery, promised that there would not be any ashes (of cremation) or urns for ashes in this plot[2]. This means that the cremation is considered indecent burial and that the municipality gives Muslims the possibility to refuse burial in the Muslim plot to those who chose cremation. This attitude of the canton of Bern constitutes a breach of religious freedom as guaranteed by the Constitution.

The problem of Muslim cremation arose in Lausanne, in March of 2001[3]. Ben Younes Dhif, a Muslim Moroccan married to a Christian woman from Vaud Canton, expressed the wish to be incinerated, and his wife wanted to respect his wishes. Two of Ben Younes' nephews, came from France, to oppose and alert the press, Moroccan Embassy, mosques and Islamic centers. A petition was even launched. Hani Ramadan, Director of the *Islamic Center of Geneva*, threw himself in the battle, declaring:

> It is the first time that such a case is raised. In Switzerland, there are more and more Muslim-Christian mixed couples, but until now, to my knowledge, religious convictions of the deceased have always been respected. Cremation is simply illicit in Islam. Prophet Muhammad said, "To break bones of a dead is as to break bones of an alive". The

---

[1] Wyler: *Die staatsrechtliche Stellung*, p. 143.
[2] Session du 9.11.1999, GRB o 2052.
[3] A similar case happened in Geneva. A Tunisian working at the UN, married to a Christian, asked for his cremation, but his Muslim parents were opposed in spite of the favorable position of his wife. He was then buried in the Muslim cemetery of Geneva.

> corpse must be respected. It is even required to proceed very quickly in burial to preserve intimacy and avoid decay.

Hafid Ouardiri, spokesman of the *Islamic Cultural Foundation of Geneva*, declared, "This situation is astonishing. I do not understand why the widow of this Moroccan and her family opposed a Muslim ritual. Maybe it is necessary to explain to the widow better why the cremation is forbidden in the Koran". He concludes, "In any case, it is imperative to respect the husband's faith!" To prevent cremation, the nephews of Ben Younes hired a lawyer, Mr. Jean-Pierre Moser, who immediately intervened at the District Court of Lausanne. Having faced pressure, the widow gave up in court, renouncing that the justice decides on this case. She did not want to fight over her husband's corpse:

> I try to understand their incentives. But what they did is odious. They do not simply respect my husband's last will. When we called them to tell them his health is very serious, three months before death, they promised to come. It is only after death that they appeared[1].

Islamic centers could have benefited from this case to educate their coreligionists instead of maintaining them in ignorance and pushing them to contravene the last will of the deceased. This case left a bitter taste among several Christians who have been confirmed in their idea that Muslims are incapable of or refuse to integrate. But we think Muslims living in Switzerland will not be able to escape this debate and will finish by adopting the cremation as the majority of Swiss population.

To conclude the question of cemeteries, only the first argument (refusal to be buried close to an unbeliever) could justify concession of a separate zone exclusively reserved for Muslim burials. This argument is distriminatory and thus creates problems. The State should not make itself guarantor of this discrimination. If I refuse to sit down next to a Jew or Muslim, I would be called racist. Why would what is forbidden during life be permitted after death? Thus, we advocate suppressing all existing religious cemeteries in Switzerland, including Jewish ones. Any contrary demand falls under the law against racism.

---

[1] *Le Matin*, 7 and 10.3.2001, articles by Jean-A. Luque.

CONCLUSION

---

1) Shared responsibility

In their writings in Arabic or in various Western languages, Muslims often present themselves as victims of the West. In the West, one notes three currents. There are those that think Muslims constitute a danger for Western society. Others, on the contrary, share worries of Muslims and wish to give them help on all levels. Others think that Westerners and Muslims carry joint responsibility for the present situation and that an effort must be undertaken on all sides. We side with this group.

We blame the unbalanced, immoral political position of the West. While being proud to defend human rights, the West contributes to the violation of these rights. As a Palestinian, I can mention as example the Western attitude toward my own people. The injustice committed against Palestinian people provokes anger not only on behalf of Muslims, but also on behalf of eastern Christians. It is not necessary that the West, in the name of a guilty feeling toward Jews, accept and contribute to a group that has become executioners of others and behave as capricious children who believe themselves above laws and morals (concerning Palestine, see appendix 3 at the end of this book).

We blame the West for having transformed the UN into a mafia-like organization, without democratic representation, at the service of superpowers and Zionism to the detriment of justice for all. Charged initially with respecting human rights and peace keeping, the UN has become an instrument of Western crimes against the Arab and Muslim populations. This organization is notably responsible for the Palestinian tragedy and the maintenance of sixty-one concentration camps in the Middle East, where hundreds of thousands of Palestinian refugees are heaped up for the sole crime of not being Jewish.

We blame the West for sustaining corrupt Arab dictators, often maintaining their own power thanks to this support. For material reasons, the West sacrifices moral principles. The boomerang effect is unavoidable in this domain. When the West pretends to punish dictators, it makes a mistake in target, as in the case of Iraq, provoking the death of hundreds of thousands of innocent Iraqi children. Now we see the same thing happening in Afghanistan. What Muslim nation will be next? On the other hand, the West sows its military bases in Arab and Muslim countries, accentuating the impression in those populations that it has a new phase of colonization and domination.

We blame the West for its lack of support to the free thinkers and movements who defend human rights. Their support should interest the West. We live in a system of communicating vessels. What happens in Muslim countries will end up arriving in the West, one way or the other. If you let your neighbor's house burn the fire will end up by destroying your own house.

We blame the West for its attitude of dismissal in considering foreigners, in particular Muslims. I mention for example: Algerians who chose France (the *Harkis*) and live today in a tragic situation there; victims of massage lounges and other repressive activities in sexual exploitation; employees of diplomatic mission houses, treated as slaves on Western soil; foreigners that are brought to work in the West for distinctly lower wages than those of the citizens of their host countries.

We blame the West for its lack of firmness toward those that breach the laws. I think about the development of drug mafias, of money laundering and of terrorist groups, some of them coming from Muslim countries. No less serious is the lack of firmness facing violations of human rights, notably as regards to family law. Western countries endure a demographic deficiency that requires them to open borders to the migratory fluxes in order to remedy population decrease. To avoid entrance of people whose culture risks problems, Switzerland had recourse to the politics of the three circles in foreign candidate selection to immigration. The *Federal Commission Against Racism* wrongly condemns this politics. Every person merits respect, but it is necessary to realize that the acceptance of others includes risks that it is necessary to size up: risks for the person in question having difficulties adjusting in Switzerland, and risks for Swiss citizens and those that live there. Switzerland possesses a legal system decided by population majority. One can in this respect, find material profit and enterprises interest for underpaid salaried employee, to allow entry without considering long-term effects of these persons' presence on the Swiss legal system. To accept the other, yes: but not at any price. If certain control must be exercised on the entrance of either temporary or long-term workers, such a control must be much more consequential for those that naturalize or ask political asylum in Switzerland.

One can make reproaches in this respect to the system of exams that precedes naturalization, system caricatured by the movie "Swiss makers", but the principle in itself remains valid even though its modes must be improved. Thus, naturalization must be refused to someone that refuses to submit to the Swiss law. This one must be tested by a set of questions and social behaviors. Certainly, one should not require a Muslim to eat pork or drink wine to obtain naturalization. However, is it not right to ask him to respect fundamental principles such as freedom of religion and norms that ensue? For example, a Muslim that refuses that his son has freedom to change religion at the age of sixteen, or refuses that his daughter marry a Christian should not be naturalize. An imam who would marry the couple before the civil marriage must not only excluded from naturalized, but also forbidden to live in Swiss territory. It would be necessary to determine the foreigners' norms, which enter into conflict with Swiss norms, and see which the foreigners must ultimately respect.

This rigor must be observed also with regard to claimants of political asylum. Article 2 of the *Convention relating to the Status of Refugees* states, "Every refugee has duties to the country in which he finds himself, which require in particular that he conform to its laws and regulations as well as to measures taken for the maintenance of public order". Some Western countries wish to even require immigrants not to practice the excision of their girls.

The mixed marriage being a most sensitive domain, it seems to us necessary to take the adequate measures to prevent abuses. One sometimes hears that Muslims look currently to marry Western women to accelerate the Islamization of the West. Some of these Muslims require besides that their wives convert to Islam, and that their children be Muslim. When their daughter wants to marry a Christian, they require that he convert to Islam. However, it is contrary to fundamental principles of human rights. There is a duty of information and precaution on behalf of the civil authorities. Today one gets married as easily as one buys a box of chocolate. The civil status officer proceeds to marriages without realizing motives and stakes of this marriage. The Italian bishops began to refuse to grant religious dispensation to any Italian who marries a Muslim. They think indeed that these marriages often end up a failure. Certainly, the Italian can still get married before the civil status officer. But the position of the bishops can bring this Italian to a hold of conscience and a bigger prudence. They ask that the Italian State insure that values of the Constitution, notably concerning family law, are respected before signing an agreement with the Muslim community[1].

Our booklet on marriages between Swiss and Muslim partners (published by the Swiss Institute of Comparative Law) suggests that couples sign a contract of marriage dealing with all questions up to the grave. The reader can find in the 4th appendix of this book a *Model of contract for mixed marriage between Muslims and non-Muslims*. This contract must be signed before a notary so it has legal effect and psychological impact on the spouses. Different religious communities also have their own booklets, and organize sessions whose goal is to illuminate the couple and resolve difficulties. But we think it necessary to follow an efficient procedure of information. No State allows someone to drive a car without first passing an exam. However, marriage is much more difficult to accomplish than driving a car. We thus think that marriage, especially mixed marriage, must be preceded by an exam. Some nations require a medical exam of the two parties, but it seems to us insufficient. This exam must concern the most important questions. Meanwhile, it is prudent to require the two parties sign a detailed marriage contract, and not merely to be satisfied with general norms. On this level, the adage should not be "No one is supposed to ignore the law", but "No one is supposed to know the law". To make exams supposes to also undergo consequences of failure. If for example a Muslim insists that his children are raised Muslim and that his daughter only

---

[1] *Le Matin*, 7 and 10.3.2001, articles of Jean-A. Luque.

marries a Muslim, we think that the civil status officer must refuse to celebrate this marriage for the same reason it refuses to celebrate a marriage that is obviously a marriage of convenience, whose goal is only to get a residence permit. We do not deny that every marriage can potentially fail, even between native Swiss citizens, but the failure of a mixed marriage has more serious implications because it creates generalizations and sows faction and xenophobia between communities. Thus, it is necessary to take all precautions so such a marriage succeeds.

It is not sufficient however that Swiss authorities inform the foreign Muslims of rights and duties, it would be necessary again that religious persons responsible for the Muslim community not follow the contrary sense of one extolled by the Swiss authorities. A Muslim that would come in Switzerland and hope to get married before an imam of a mosque, not passing before civil authorities, will not be able to do so if no imam agrees to collaborate with him. But if the imam is ignorant of Swiss norms, or if he takes a shrewd pleasure to violate them while considering them as unbelievers' norms, Swiss authorities must be especially heedful facing this imam, to inform him and guard against Swiss norm violation, to send him back to his country or put him in jail.

The West must seriously consider the growth of the Muslim community within its borders and prepare well for integration, not to be confronted with a situation of implosion one day, as in USSR or Yugoslavia. This is particularly important with the current migratory fluxes.

2) Muslim migratory fluxes

Today, in Western countries, one observes migratory fluxes without precedent. This phenomenon follows the communicating vessels principle: the poor head toward the rich Western countries, ready to work for even minimal wages. On the other hand, Western countries endure an important demographic deficit and a lack of workers for their factories. These factors create alarming consequences for old age pensions. So, these countries open their doors to foreigners [who provide low cost manual labor.] This situation will have terrifying consequences on the Western legal systems and risks to create insurmountable tensions inside the Western countries, not only by reason of the economic competition, but also by reason of the difference of the legal concepts: some believe in a democratic system freely settled, and the others in a revealed and indisputable legal system.

It is little likely that the West can contain the migratory fluxes without a lucid and just political vision. The earth is one and more global than ever. One cannot say in this respect, "Every man for himself and God for all". A man who does not come to his neighbor's help whose house burns, risk sooner or later to see the fire spreading to his own house. Therefore, it would be necessary to review in depth the relations between the rich countries and the poor countries on the basis of justice and solidarity.

Certainly, one can say that the West cannot complain about immigrants if one knows that Southern countries receive the great majority of the 100 million migrants in the world (83%). Three quarters of these immigrants are in Africa, in Asia and in the Middle-East; they represent primarily migrations in its simplest most existential form: those caused by hunger, or for the sake of survival in the face of natural catastrophes. Thus, migratory flows are chiefly within the Third World. But seen the aforesaid problems, the West cannot open doors nor can close them completely[1]. What to make then? A French author of Algerian origin made the following proposition:

> The fact that France cannot receive immigrants in a lasting manner could be transformed in an *asset*. Why not substitute the policy of the locked door for that of co-operation? ... The countries of the South are lacking professionals trained in new technologies, health care, hygiene and education. Why, instead of fixating dogmatically on either integration or expulsion, not think of a situation more fluid where for example engagements are taken to employ and train workers here and who would be paid for a defined proportion of their salary in currency automatically invested in their country of origin, and who would not be allowed to stay in France after a certain contractual period? This would be real co-operation: it brings currency to countries that need it, it raises the technical level of these countries and, by receiving these *coopérants* only for a limited time, it favors the return, and it dedramatizes the uprooting of the immigrants[2].

This problem of immigration itself deserves more research. We hope that our modest contribution will be useful for further progress.

---

[1] Naïr: *Lettre à Charles Pasqua*, p. 87.
[2] *Ibid.*, p. 97.

3) Role of philosophers

Measures described above must be accompanied by a renewal of the philosophical thought and a profound debate in Western and Muslim countries.

The confrontation between religious norms and the secular norms occurs because the religious norms of divine origin refuse neither to compromise nor to allow any recourse to reason, two indispensable conditions in any dialogue and pacific co-existence.

Some Arab philosophers do not hesitate to overtly extol the abandonment of revelation and the de-sacralization of the holy books. So Egyptian philosopher Zaki Najib Mahmud (d. 1993), adept of scientific positivism, believes that one should take from the Arab past or the Western present only what is useful to the Arab society[1]. To judge what is useful and what is not, one only needs to consider reason, whatever the examined source: revelation or non-revelation[2]. This attitude supposes the dismissal of all holiness from the past[3]. Things must be appreciated in practice, without falsifying historic data or falling into generalizations[4]. "The key to truth today", he writes, "is to digest the idea that we are well in transformation, therefore in mutation; so, the past cannot govern the future"[5]. He adds that to be able to construct a modern society, Arab countries must eradicate from their mind the idea according to which "Heaven ordered and the Earth must obey; the Creator drew and planned, and the creature must be satisfied with its destiny and its fate"[6].

Husayn Fawzi (d. 1988), Egyptian freethinker, adopts a similar speech. In the Egyptian intellectual meeting with Kadhafi, April 6th, 1972, he said that modern societies could not be directed by religion. "That personal conviction intervenes in the domain of human relations, it does not create a problem. But we should not

---

[1] Mahmud: *Tajdid al-fikr al-arabi*, p. 18-20; Mahmud: *Al-ma'qul wal-la ma'qul*, p. 34.

[2] Mahmud: *Tajdid al-fikr al-arabi*, p. 21; Mahmud: *Thaqafatuna fi muwajahat al-asr*, p. 96.

[3] *Ibid.*, p. 51-53.

[4] *Ibid.*, p. 65, 79 and 80.

[5] *Ibid.*, p. 228.

[6] *Ibid.*, p. 294-295. For more details on the position of this philosopher, see Aldeeb Abu-Sahlieh: *L'impact de la religion*, p. 132-134.

consider that any religion directs modern society. Each keeps for himself his relation with his own God and His Apostles. But it cannot mean that any people that progresses toward civilization is obliged by principles or norms of conduct established in one time or another. I cannot admit what my reason rejects, whatever pressures the government exercises against me. My reason is the leader and the master"[1]. In fact, this philosopher rejects all revelation. At the time of my meeting with him, September 8th, 1977, he told me that God had created the world in six days and that he had taken a rest the seventh day, and continuously henceforth he is still resting. Therefore, God could not send all prophets who came after the sixth day.

The philosopher and physician, Mohammad Ibn Zakariyya Al-Razi (in Latin: Rhazes; d. 935) already expressed distrust of revelation, "God has provided what we need to know, not in the arbitrary and divisive gift of special revelation, which only foments bloodshed and contention, but in reason, which belongs equally to all. Prophets are impostors, at best misled by the demonic shades of restless and envious spirits. But ordinary men are fully capable of thinking for themselves and need no guidance from another". Asked if a philosopher can follow a prophetically revealed religion, Al-Razi openly retorts, "How can anyone think philosophically while committed to those old wives' tales, founded on contradiction, obdurate ignorance and dogmatism[2]?"

Muslims, wherever they live, must make a real effort to separate completely the religious law and give to the reason the pre-eminence on faith. However, the West must also make an effort in this regard. The West - that pretends to have freedom of thought - must begin to teach in its theology schools that revelation as definitive and forever enclosed text is a false and dangerous concept for humanity, that every human has a mission to fill on this earth, and that the Spirit never stops to blow. The Prophet Joel said in this respect:

> I will pour out my Spirit on all flesh. Your sons and your daughters shall prophesy, your old men shall dream dreams, and your young men shall see visions. Even on the male and female slaves, in those days, I will pour out my Spirit (Joel 3:1-2).

---

[1]*Al-Ahram*, 7.4.1972, p. 6.
[2]*The Encyclopaedia of Islam*, CD, Brill, Leiden, vol. 8, 1999, p. 474a.

This idea is confirmed by Paul who writes to the Corinthians, "You can all prophesy one by one, so that all may learn and all be encouraged" (I Corinthians 14:31). To consult the Bible, the Gospel and the Koran means to have a look in the inheritance of humanity. But this must serve to watch better ahead, in our time. It is not possible to live the present exclusively with norms of the past. This attitude would condemn humans to immobility, and therefore stagnation. Imam Mahmud Shaltut (d. 1964) wrote:

> One who immobilizes himself on opinions of predecessors and is satisfied of their knowledge, and their system of research and investigation, commits a crime against the human nature and deprives the man of the grant of the reason, which characterizes him[1].

If this idea is taught in the West, it can make its path progressively thereafter among Muslims and Jews alike. Without it, the 21st century will be ravaged by religious wars, stirred by hallucinated and radical Jews, Christians or Muslims, all pretending to obey God's orders, given long ago; orders whose veracity is impossible to prove since God remains, at present, unattainable by our means of communication.

To finish, I must guard against inter-faith dialogue if it is not founded on frankness and the respect of human rights. Christian Churches do a dis-service to their followers and Muslims while adopting flattering speech and sustaining Muslim demands, not accounting for ulterior motives and consequences. Very often this dialogue only serves to travel and eat well. It is sufficient to note that decades of inter-faith dialogues between Church leaders and Muslims have not even successfully put an end to abuses of Muslims who get married with non-Muslim women, but forbid the marriage of a non-Muslim man with a Muslim woman.

---

[1] Shaltut: *Min tawjihat al-islam*, p. 126.

APPENDICES

We produce here six texts. Two relate to the tragedy of September 11th, 2001. The third, written before that tragedy, concerns the Palestinian question that is a principal point of political tension between the West and Muslims. The fourth is a *Model of contract for mixed marriage between Muslims and non-Muslims.* [The final two are reproductions of historic documents by the Founding Fathers of the United States. They are presented here by the editor as a resourcc for understranding the principle of the separation of Church and State.]

Appendix 1. Barbarism is the Fruit of Injustice

(Letter to the Editor published by many Swiss newspapers before the American intervention in Afghanistan).

The tragedy in the United States stirs passions. Words miss to describe it. After all, when the knell bell sounds, nobody has the right to ask for whom it tolls. All innocent victims, wherever they are, deserve our sympathy.

In love as in hate, it is necessary to keep cool and to remember some principles that may help us understanding and acting correctly.

The preamble of the Universal Declaration of Human Rights says, "Disregard and contempt of human rights have resulted in barbarous acts which have outraged the conscience of mankind"; "it is essential, if man is not to be compelled to have recourse, as a last resort, to rebellion against tyranny and oppression, that human rights should be protected by the rule of law".

The Prophet Isaiah, 2700 years ago, said, "Peace will be the fruit of justice" (32:17). It is obvious that Washington and New York, as well as the Middle East, wherefrom probably come the perpetrators of the present tragedy, are not in peace. Therefore, there is somewhere an injustice.

U.S. President Bush and other politicians, who let the situation in the Middle East fester, shout their horror and swear vengeance. This is not the first time that such acts against American interests have taken place. Americans took the path of vengeance each time. Probably they will take it again this time; but with what result? Attacks may only intensify. Everybody fears that what happened in New York and Washington may repeat itself elsewhere. One is therefore faced with an infernal cycle of violence. One easily forgets Jesus' words, "All who take the sword will perish by the sword" (Matthew 26:52). Not one of these leaders remembers the words of Isaiah, "Peace will be the fruit of justice".

Instead of driving the world in the spiral of violence and unforeseeable mutual destructions, instead of pushing people to despair and suicide, politicians have the duty to come back to justice and to solve the problem of the Middle-East according to justice. Today, more than ever, the world is called to choose between barbarism on behalf of all, and justice for all. What we say about the Middle East applies to any other situation based on injustice. "One who swallows bones, cannot sleep", says an Arab proverb. One who sows injustice harvests barbarism.

Appendix 2. United States Must put Justice on their Side

(Interview by Etienne Dubuis, published in *Le Temps*, Geneva, October 10th, 2001).

Le Temps: That do you think you about the American riposte to the attacks of September 11th, 2001?

Sami Aldeeb: I think that the United States missed a good opportunity to do a conscience examination. They avoided carefully asking why they are today hated in the Muslim world and what they could do to avoid such hate. They preferred to answer to the attacks with strength. However, the true name of Ben Laden, is "Misery and Injustice". And the United States must fight against these two factors. If you caught malaria, it does not serve any good to run after the mosquito which pricked you; you should rather know where does it come from, why there are swamps and how one can purify them.

Le Temps: About what injustice do you think?

Sami Aldeeb: About the injustice that reigns in Middle East, since the presumed guilty comes from there. Oussama Ben Laden himself makes reference to facts that deserve discussion. I think about the American military presence in many countries of the region, which is a form of colonialism, about the support of the United States, since long time, to various dictatorships, and about the drama the Palestinians live.

Le Temps: Is Oussama Ben Laden not a fanatic before being a justiciary?

Sami Aldeeb: He is certainly a fanatic. The Kamikazes themselves were certainly victims of brainwashing. But the first duty of the United States is to maintain justice on their side. This may not be sufficient, but it is absolutely necessary. As long as they do not accomplish it, they are responsible in the drama that touches them. You know it well: people are suitable to be much more easily manipulated in situations without an exit and when they feel desperate.

Le Temps: After what happened, the United States are in the right to ask for justice.

Sami Aldeeb: In the case that occupies us, there are two possible ways to do justice. The first consists of dragging the guilty before courts as done by the Allied Powers following World War II. The problem is that it is a biased justice: it judges others by its own standards; losers only are recognized as guilty, whereas winners are always right. It ensues uneasiness, a confusion of values that can only be harmful. The second manner to proceed consists in creating reconciliation commissions, as in South Africa. Crimes of apartheid were very serious. When Nelson Mandela obtained power, he had good reason to want to judge persons responsible before the whole world. And yet, he did not, he attacked the evil at its roots and henceforth he is even appreciated by Whites. The United States should have done the same, to name wise men, to encourage freedom of speech. Instead, they are condemning all objectors to silence, including journalists that dare criticize their politics. Their attitude is not going to serve morals, or society.

Appendix 3. No justice, no peace: for a Canaanite Republic

(Text written before the events of September 11th, 2001 for the *Panoramiques Magazine*).

"The worst of miseries is one which causes laughter", says an Arab proverb. I will add that the worst of miseries is not to know how to laughter in misery. Allow me therefore some overflow of language to relieve my deep sadness while thinking about my homeland of origin. To arrive at wisdom, a man often needs to reach the limits of lunacy. I start with place. Where am I from? What is my homeland called? Today, my adopted homeland is called Switzerland. As for my homeland of origin, it is located somewhere between the Mediterranean and the Jordan River. I hesitate to pronounce its name and I want so much to rename it:

- "Israel"? Recognized by the United Nations, it is not recognized by (all) countries that surround it. The name itself causes hate and contempt among Arabs and Muslims. I will not go into the motivations.

"Palestine"? It is the only country recognized by the countries that surround Israel, but not by the United Nations or Israel, and it provokes hatred and contempt among fundamentalist Jews and Christians. Every time I write a letter to the editor (signed Christian of Palestinian origin) in the Swiss newspapers, I receive one or several letters from these fundamentalists telling me that Palestine is a myth that has no existence in history and that Palestinians came from an island somewhere in the Mediterranean. Here too I will not delve into the motivations.

Yet, we have to name for this plot of land, even if it seems to be the size of a handkerchief. I've decided therefore, to avoid annoying anyone, by using the name Canaan. It is the name that God, according to the Bible, used to designate this land when He spoke to Abraham (mythic or real, carnal or spiritual father of all Jews, Christians and Muslims):

> I will give to you, and to your offspring after you, the land where you are now an alien, all the land of Canaan, for a perpetual holding (Genesis 17:8).

By using the name Canaan, I wish also to do justice to the ancient inhabitants of this land, whose descendants still existed at the time of Jesus. The Gospel according to Matthew reports that a Canaanite woman came to Jesus asking him humbly to heal her daughter who was "tormented by a demon". Jesus granted her prayer and praised her faith, "Woman, great is your faith! Let it be done for you as you wish!" Matthew adds, "And her daughter was healed instantly" (Matthew 15:21-28). Sometimes, I start dreaming with those Jews who believe in the arrival of the Messiah, just to ask him for a miracle, one alone: to heal all inhabitants of the land of Canaan who are tormented by the demon of violence these days.

Someday, inhabitants of this plot of ground should meet again to speak, to eat, to drink and to rebuild this ravaged country. They should then settle on a name that does not remind them anymore of their past silliness and does not wake up the demon of the past. I propose here and now to call their country "Canaan", a neutral name, without spite and without bad memories. They will be called then among nations "the Canaanites".

But how will we ever arrive at this utopian day while the Jews, Christians and Muslims who populate Canaan are tearing one another to pieces, threatening each other with atomic and chemical bombs, delighting in the death of the others and glorifying their martyrs who sacrifice their life to kill and wound the greatest number of the other clan?

In the days of the apartheid regime of South African, not a long time ago, some twisted minds proposed a solution of the problems between Blacks and Whites: to paint the Blacks white, or the Whites black; some cans of paint and that would be it! One could propose today a similar solution for Jews, Christians and Muslims in Canaan: two of these groups should convert to the religion of the third. No matter which; all are the same.

The paint can solution has not been adopted in South Africa. They preferred the ballot box solution, the way of democracy. Instead of creating courts to judge criminals of war as Whites did after the Second World War, ex-Yugoslavia war and Rwanda war, the South Africans preferred commissions of conciliation. Blacks, the majority, chose recourse to their ancestral wisdom, i.e. the discussion of their problems under the palaver tree. Mali knows a similar wise system to solve problems: people meet in a hut with a very low roof. They must remain sitting to discuss. If one of them sets up to use his hands against another, he hits his head against the roof. Blacks and Whites discuss in South Africa. All is not rosy, but good will is there. The Whites are still white, and Blacks are still black, but they decided to work shoulder to shoulder, to construct their future together. Instead of changing the color of their skin with paint, they decided to change their hearts. In spite of years of jail and persecution, President Mandela knew how to inspire fellow citizens with a sense of justice. And today a great many White South-Africans pay homage to him.

Justice, changing the heart, working together elbow to elbow shoulder to shoulder instead of destroying each other, these may be the passwords to solve problems between the inhabitants of Canaan: Jews, Muslims and Christians. We are in this respect against the idea of partitioning the country of Canaan. Just as we are against apartheid that reigns over the inhabitants of this country today, unity brings strength. Division provokes hatred and frustration.

About fifteen years ago, I took a tourist bus in Rome to get a general view of it. At one stop, I saw this sentence in Latin engraved in the stone on the portal of a Church: *Fructus justitiae pax* (Peace will be the fruit of justice). Coming from a country torn by war, this sentence unsettled me. I wanted to know the origin. After some research, I discovered that it is a word from the Prophet-poet Isaiah (32:17) who lived in the country of Canaan 2700 years ago. I wish to quote here the entire passage that is exceptionally beautiful:

> Justice will dwell in the wilderness,
> and righteousness abide in the fruitful field.
> Peace will be the fruit of justice,
> and the result of justice, quietness and trust forever (Isaiah 32:16-17).

Think about it for a moment: a sentence from Isaiah who states, "Peace is the fruit of justice" engraved on a Church portal in Rome, capital of the Romans whose strategists said: *Si vis pacem, para bellum* (If you want peace, prepare for war). What a contrast! I was filled with emotion, and today again when I think about it I have the same thrill. Immediately after that, together with friends I founded in Switzerland an association called *Association for the Reconstruction of Emmaus*, and the association's letterhead includes the phrase: "Peace will be the fruit of justice" (Isaiah 32:17). My friends and I wanted to make this village a symbol of justice and peace in a country of Canaan.

Emmaus is that famous village on the road to which the resurrected Christ met two of his disciples. They invited him to spend the night with them, and they only recognized him after having shared bread with him (Luke 24:13-35). The breaking of bread, gesture of solidarity between humans! ... not the breaking up of a country, a gesture of hate and silliness. Jews occupied this village in 1967, destroyed it completely with bulldozers and expelled its inhabitants. On the site of this village they established a picnic area called Park Canada. Trees replaced humans. My friends and I wanted to help inhabitants of this village to return, as a gesture of justice and solidarity. But Jews still turn a deaf ear to the request of its inhabitants[1]. As with this village, Jews destroyed 384 other villages since the creation of

---

[1] See photos of the destruction of this village taken by an Israeli soldier in: http://www.lpj.org/Nonviolence/Sami/Album.html.

Israel, according to Jewish maps[1]. Inhabitants of these destroyed villages became refugees of which a good part live in 61 concentration camps: 13 in Lebanon, 10 in Syria, 10 in Jordan, 20 in West-Bank and 8 in Gaza Strip, therefore a few kilometers from their lands and their destroyed houses. Jews refuse their return whereas they welcome their coreligionists from the United States, Russia, West Europe, Ethiopia, India and other countries and install them on the lands and houses of these refugees whose only crime is not being Jews!

Let us return to the paint cans. Over the centuries, thousands of people converted to Judaism. You cannot tell me that these blue-eyed blonds are the sons and daughters of the Semitic Abraham unless he assiduously frequented whorehouses of Eastern Europe. Today again, one finds conversion to Judaism. One must also add non-Jewish partners in mixed marriages and children of these marriages. All of these people may claim, according to Israeli law, the "right to return" in the country of Canaan. Once there, they benefit from all social, economic and political advantages of Israeli laws. These advantages are only partially provided for non-Jews who are born in the land of Canaan and have an Israeli passport. Their only crime is that they are not Jewish, precisely as South African Blacks' crime was not being White. The non-Jews who live in the territories occupied by the Jews in 1967 and the Palestinian refugees living in concentration camps under Jewish occupation or in adjacent countries do not have the right to advantages recognized to the "Jewish" Russian, American, Swiss, Polish, Italian, English, Dutch, Ethiopian, French, German, Austrian, Australian, Canadian, etc. The only crime of these Palestinians is that they are not Jews, precisely as South African Blacks' crime was not being White. We are therefore confronted with a real racist regime of apartheid, whatever one says. Those who do not consider this regime as racist are either blind or dishonest.

What to do with this racist regime of apartheid based not on skin color, but on religious faith? There is still the paint cans solution, mentioned above. It would only take a well-intentioned reformed rabbi to deliver a certificate of Judaism to Christian and Muslim Palestinians. Immediately thereafter, they will join the

---

[1] See Uehlinger: *Localités palestiniennes détruites après 1948.*

"Chosen People" and have the right to consume the "milk and honey" of the country of Canaan with other Jews. Another solution would be to convert all inhabitants of the country to just one faith – Judaism, Christianity or Islam – and to make a law that gives them all the same rights.

The conversion solution, the paint cans, does not seem feasible on a large scale, at present at least, even though some hope may be there. On the Internet one finds a site of Jews converted to Islam called "Jews for Allah"[1]. One also finds "Jews for Jesus"[2]; as well as former Christian Russians converted to Judaism, in order to escape Russia. One may recognize them by their uncircumcised penis. Some even get circumcised, exchanging their foreskin for an Israeli passport. Should we pity them?

In the meantime, we need another solution. Non-Jewish Palestinians of Canaan, with their Arab brothers or pseudo-brothers turned to the United Nations, to Western and other countries to convince the Jews to recognize their rights. They also tried traditional war. Currently, they resort to primitive weapons: stones, without counting invectives. Nothing makes Jews move even one millimeter… whose projects are unknown and staggering. Ben Gourion said the borders of Israel spread over all lands where an Israeli soldier puts his foot. Some fundamentalist Jews (as well as fundamentalist Christians in the United States and Europe) think the borders of the *Promised Land* should spread from the Euphrates to the Nile. This would explain the fact that the Israeli embassy in Egypt is located on the other side of the Nile: one cannot put an embassy to a foreign country on ones' own territory! Jews in the country of Canaan can count on their indefectible American and European allies as well as on their atomic weapons to dissuade Arab and Muslim countries and prevent them from winning the war. Continual American and British bombing against Iraq is probably intended as a signal to any Arab country that would consider a war against Jews. In a panic, Arab countries content themselves with sending some money to Palestinians. In the meantime, they provide Jews and their allies the necessary Arab oil to make and run their tanks and

---

[1] http://jews-for-allah.org/.
[2] http://www.jewsforjesus.org/.

planes that destroy and sow desolation among non-Jewish inhabitants of Canaan.

But one does not know how long Palestinians will accept to be abused by Jews. The Arab poet Al-Mutanabbi (d. 965) said, "It is necessary to never underestimate a weak one in a quarrel: a mosquito is capable of covering the lion's eye with blood". The Internet edition of the *Jerusalem Post* of August 14th, 2001 presents information that sounds an alarm in the deteriorating Middle East situation. The information is based on an article written by the director of a Palestinian Center in Gaza published by the Palestinian weekly *Al-Manar* issued in Lebanon. According to this information, Palestinians think seriously about the biologic weapons to counter Jewish military strength. About a hundred experts would be capable of handling and using them. A few bombs lobbed at water resources, beaches, markets and residential centers would do the job, and they would be difficult to detect according to the information in the *Jerusalem Post*[1]. We are faced with an apocalyptic script with unpredictable consequences. It will be then Hitler's posthumous victory: the extermination of Jews and non-Jews in the Middle East.

Jörg Shimon Schuldhess, an anti-Zionist Jewish Swiss artist, writes that one found hair, bones and shoes of the Jews who died in concentration camps. But their passports, where are they now? He speculates that some Nazi soldiers used these passports to go to Israel under the identity of their Jewish victims, in order to continue Hitler's policy in that region. This would explain, according to him, the presence of an important German community in Israel[2]. Whatever be the fate of the Jewish passports, human foolishness does not limit itself in time or space: one can be a Hitler without being an Aryan, and a Nazi while being Semitic or Pseudo-Semitic. Do you want proofs?

The Bible tells the story of Samson. His enemies, the Philistines, seized him and gouged out his eyes. They brought him down to Gaza, today's famous city manhandled by the Jews, and bound him with bronze shackles; he ground at the mill in the prison. One day, his enemies made a feast in honor of their

---

[1] www.jpost.com/Editions/2001/08/14/LatestNews/LatestNews.32587.ht ml.

[2] Jörg Shimon Schuldhess, *Flugblatt*, October 16, 1986.

divinity. They called Samson out of the prison to entertain them. Samson said to the attendant who held him by the hand, "Let me feel the pillars on which the house rests, so that I may lean against them". The house was full of men and women who looked on while Samson performed. Samson grasped the two middle pillars on which the house rested, and he leaned his weight against them. He strained with all his might; and the house fell on all the people who were in it (Judges 16:21-30).

Does this remind you of something? History repeats itself! Is this the prelude to what awaits all the region of the Middle East, if Jews and their allies persist with the present politics? No one in the Middle East is strong enough to insure victory and crush his enemies completely, nor weak enough to be reduced to perpetual slavery. We advance inexorably toward ultimate war and destruction of the entire Middle East. No one will be left unscathed in this next war, all programmed as a delay-action bomb. After the first madman pushes a button, it will be too late to stop him. The country of Canaan, or even the neighboring countries, will become an uninhabitable desert for many centuries. Even lizards will not be able to reside there. Hate on all sides is so strong that dry and green, innocent and guilty, young and old man alike, will end up in smoke and ashes.

The solution of despair toward which Jews and their allies are pushing Palestinians will bring peace for noone. We need to come quickly out of the gears of war and abandon the Roman strategist principle, "If you want peace, prepare for war", to come back to the principle of the Prophet Isaiah, "Peace will be the fruit of justice" (32:17). Peace requires that one returns most quickly to the table of negotiations and open all cases, notably the most delicate, the ones concerning refugees and the 385 Palestinian villages destroyed by the Jews. Without a solution to this case, the region will never, never, know peace. It is necessary that Jews stop claiming for themselves the title "Chosen People" and accept others as equal human beings, just as Whites of South Africa finally accepted Blacks as human beings. It is necessary to end the present politics of religious apartheid, politics unfortunately sustained by the West, for the same reason as racial apartheid had to end in South Africa. Jews must accept the creation of a new State, regrouping Jews, Christians and Muslims; a State we could call "The Canaan Republic". They must, like

Switzerland, suppress religious borders between the three communities. In the same time, the three communities must change the legal system concerning family law and create only one law and only one court for all: for Jews, Christians and Muslims, with laws permitting mixed marriages (to mix the bloods) and suppress discrimination against women. Thus one may have a free society. No society can live on two or three levels of law. Again two measures are needed:

- To create mixed schools where Jews, Christians and Muslims study together, the same matters and the two languages: Arabic and Hebrew.

- To suppress religious cemeteries and bury people together, whatever their faith, so that they remember that they are united before life as before death.

In a speech pronounced May 5th, 1991 before the Knesset, the violinist and humanist Yehudi Menuhin said:

Those who live by the sword shall die by the sword and terror and fear provoke terror and fear. Hatred and contempt are fatally infectious ... One fact is surely abundantly clear, namely this wasteful governing by fear, by contempt for the basic dignities of life, this steady asphyxiation of a dependent people should be the very last means to be adopted by those who themselves know too well the awful significance, the unforgettable suffering of such an existence ... It is unworthy of my great people, the Jews[1].

In an interview, Father Elias Chacour, originally of Biram, a village destroyed by the Jews, said:

We are citizens of second zone, yes, if there are zones. I believe in fact there is now only one zone in Israel, the Jewish citizenship zone. There are non-zones, the margin, where non-Jews are tolerated, but not accepted, because Jews do not have a solution to rid themselves of it. Fortunately, there are very few Jews - but they exist - that protest against this segregation. I fear that in a very short time, if Israel does not fundamentally change politics, does not convert to a new political direction, I believe that we will only have the military option to survive here. It cannot make any roots here, because Palestine, since before Abraham, since Melchizedeck, did not accept a conqueror who does not try to make roots. They are not making roots. They

---

[1] *Washington Report on Middle East Affairs*, July of 1991: Address given by violinist Sir Yehudi Menuhin to the Knesset upon receiving Israel's highest honor for his accomplishments as a musician, May 5, 1991, in: http://www.washington-report.org/ backissues/0791/ 9107039a.htm.

> are planting hate in the heart of Palestinians. It is necessary to change, if they want to survive with any quality of life in the Middle East[1].

The authors of the Universal Declaration of Human Rights affirm in the preamble:

> It is essential, if man is not to be compelled to have recourse, as a last resort, to rebellion against tyranny and oppression, that human rights should be protected by the rule of law.

This affirmation rejoins the word of the Prophet Isaiah, "Peace will be the fruit of justice" (32:17). The day when Christians, Muslims and Jews will be considered by Jews as equal human beings and agree to treat them on equal footing, that day will be the first day of peace in the Middle East. The Middle East has today to choose between justice for all and the extermination of all. Many speak these days of a Palestinian State. Let's be straightforward. Instead of solving problems, such a State would only create new ones.

Certainly, this nation state would be recognized by all countries but will have a divided people, with thousands of refugees living as livestock in sixty-one concentration camps in Palestine/Israel and the adjacent countries. These refugees coming from 385 Palestinian villages destroyed by the Israeli-American weapons and bulldozers wait since more than one half-century to return home. With the creation of a Palestinian State, they should put end to their dream and accept the misfortune that hit them, keeping their eyes watching their lands some kilometres far from their camps, lands occupied and exploited by Jews coming from Russia, Poland and elsewhere.

These refugees will never forgive their leaders or their usurpers. They will intensify the violence in the manner of Samson that made the temple collapse on his head and the head of his enemies. The region will live even darker hours where all strokes will be permitted. Fire will swallow the dry and the green, and mutual extermination will await Israelis and Palestinians. It will be Hitler's posthumous victory.

How to come out of this situation? The solution is very simple. Instead of creating a new State that dedicates the injustice, I propose to Israel to annex the occupied territories in 1967, to

---

[1] Interview given to the Agence de presse internationale catholique, May 1988.

allow the Palestinian refugees to return home and to rebuild their villages, to abolish the discriminatory laws against non-Jews, to promulgate a constitution that guarantees equality for all its inhabitants, to organize general elections and to allow the participation of the non-Jews in the political, legislative, economic and military life. In short, to make a modern State with secularised laws without discrimination because of religion or sex. A State called the Canaanite Republic. It is the name that God, according to the Bible, used while addressing himself to Abraham: "I will give to you, and to your offspring after you, the land where you are now an alien, all the land of Canaan, for a perpetual holding" (Genesis 17:8). God did not mention to Abraham either Israel or Palestine, but Canaan. What we look for by this solution is a State based on justice and not on division or discrimination. Only justice can bring Middle-East peace.

To conclude, if Jews are truly looking for peace in the Middle East, they must conform themselves to the principles of justice instead of persisting in their current policy contrary to human rights. In this regard, they should allow Palestinian refugees to return home and treat non-Jewish Palestinians on an equal footing, irrespective of their religion. Why the fact of being Christian or Muslim makes a Palestinian a candidate for refugee camps, jails, torture, deportation or death? Why?

Appendix 4. Model of Contract for Mixed Marriage

(This model of contract for mixed marriage between Muslims and non-Muslims is taken, with light modifications, from our booklet, Sami Aldeeb: *Mariages entre partenaires suisses et musulmans: connaître et prévenir les conflits*, Swiss Institute of Comparative Law, Lausanne, 3rd edition, reprint May 2000, p. 35-37)

This model of contract should be filled separately by the two future spouses that proceed to the comparison of answers. The agreed final text should be signed before a notary that keeps a copy of it. Cancel or modify passages that do not fit.

After due consideration, the undersigned

Mr............... Born on ....

Nationality............... Religion...............

Civil status (single, divorced, widow)

and

Mrs................ Born on ....

Nationality............... Religion...............

Civil status (single, divorced, widow)

agreed what follows:

The marriage takes place

in.... (name of the country)   before the civil status of...............

abroad (name of the country)......   before...............

The civil marriage is followed by a religious ceremony (specify the ceremony)...............

or

The civil marriage is not followed by a religious ceremony.

Their common domicile will be (name the country)...............

The woman keeps her nationality.

She keeps her family name, (or) she adopts the family name of her husband (specify the form).

Religious freedom of spouses

Each partner keeps his religion and commits to respect the freedom of religion and worship of the other, including the right to change religion.

The spouses commit to not impose one to the other their respective food norms.

Fidelity and monogamy

The husband and the wife promise mutual help and fidelity. They attest that they are not married at the time of the marriage. Each one commits not to marry another person so much that the present marriage is held. In case of false attestation or violation of the mentioned engagement, each one acquires the right to ask for divorce for this reason.

Children

The husband and the wife affirm they submitted themselves to the premarital exams and informed each other of the results of these exams.

Children's religion will be................

They will be educated in this religion. They will benefit the religious freedom when they complete their sixteenth year, including the right to change religion, without any constraint on behalf of parents or their respective families.

Children will carry European, Christian, Muslim, Arabic, neutral forenames. The choice of the forename will be made by mutual understanding between the two parents (indicate eventual forenames of boys and girls).

Children will be baptized at the age of...............

They will choose freely to be circumcised or excised when they complete their 18 years if they want to.

Children will be schooled in public, Muslim, Christian, Jewish schools (specify).

Children will be registered exclusively on their mother's passport.

The Muslim partner will not oppose the marriage of his daughters with a non-Muslim.

Economic relations

The two spouses contribute on a basis of equality, according to their respective means, to the expenses of the household and the education of children. They jointly decide the affairs of the couple.

The matrimonial regime is submitted to the law of ..... (mention a Western country). The spouses opt for the regime (name the regime)...............

Sartorial norms, work and travel

The husband and the woman commit to not impose one another, nor to their children, the Islamic sartorial norms or the Islamic norms concerning social life, school education and sport.

The wife decides herself of her work. She does not need the husband's authorization for her leisure, her travels and the obtaining of travel titles and identity documents for herself and for her children.

Dissolution of the marriage

The husband and the wife commit to resolve their conflicts amicably. In the event that one spouse wants to put end to the marriage, he/she commits to make it before the judge and not to resort to the repudiation.

If the husband or the two spouses are domiciled in a country that allows the husband to repudiate his wife, the husband recognizes to his wife the right to repudiate him in the same conditions.

In case of divorce, the assignment of children will be decided according to the law and on decision of the judge of..... (mention a Western country). If children are assigned to the mother, the father commits to respect this decision and not to withdraw them, whatever is their place of residence. In case of death of a spouse, children will be assigned to the surviving spouse.

The sharing of the assets and the maintenance between spouses will be adjusted according to the law of.... (mention a Western country), even though the husband or the two spouses reside in a Muslim country.

In any case, assets acquired during the marriage by one or the other spouse are considered as common property of the two and will be shared in equality, except if the two spouses opt for the regime of separation.

Succession

The husband and the wife submit their successions to the law of…. (mention a Western country). They reject all restriction to the right to inherit based on religion or sex. In the event that the succession is opened abroad, partially or completely, and that the foreign judge refuses to apply the law chosen by the spouses, each of them recognizes in advance to the surviving spouse the right to the third of his inheritance after liquidation of the matrimonial regime.

Death and funeral ceremony

In case of death of the husband, his body will be buried in the nearest secular cemetery, in a religious cemetery, incinerated, repatriated in the country of origin (specify the choice).

In case of death of the wife, her body will be buried in the nearest secular cemetery, in a religious cemetery, incinerated, repatriated in the country of origin (specify the choice).

In case of death of a descendant, his body will be buried in the nearest secular cemetery, in a religious cemetery, incinerated, repatriated in the country of origin of the foreign spouse (specify the choice).

If the transfer of the body of the spouse or the descendant in a country of origin is chosen, the spouse that makes this choice commits to contract an insurance that covers expenses of the transfer.

Modification of the present contract

The husband and the wife commit to respect the terms of this contract in good faith. The present contract cannot be modified than with the free consent of the two spouses, before a notary.

Name of the husband

His signature   place and date.................

Name of the wife

Her signature   place and date.................

Name and address of the 1st witness

Signature   place and date.................

Name and address of the 2nd witness
Signature   place and date.................
Name and address of the notary
Signature   place and date.................

P.S.: In the event that spouses decide to proceed to a Muslim religious ceremony after the civil marriage or to conclude an abroad religious or consular marriage, it is indispensable to mention expressly in the document established following the ceremony or the marriage

-       that the contract of marriage signed before notary by the two spouses is an integral part, and

-       that in case of contradiction between the two, the present contract has the priority on the document established by the religious or consular authority.

Appendix 5. James Madison's Memorial and Remonstrance

To the Honorable the General Assembly of the Commonwealth of Virginia

Memorial and Remonstrance

We the subscribers, citizens of the said Commonwealth, having taken into serious consideration, a Bill printed by order of the last Session of General Assembly, entitled "A Bill establishing a provision for Teachers of the Christian Religion," and conceiving that the same if finally armed with the sanctions of a law, will be a dangerous abuse of power, are bound as faithful members of a free State to remonstrate against it, and to declare the reasons by which we are determined. We remonstrate against the said Bill,

1. Because we hold it for a fundamental and undeniable truth, "that religion or the duty which we owe to our Creator and the manner of discharging it, can be directed only by reason and conviction, not by force or violence." The Religion then of every man must be left to the conviction and conscience of every man; and it is the right of every man to exercise it as these may dictate.

This right is in its nature an unalienable right. It is unalienable, because the opinions of men, depending only on the evidence contemplated by their own minds cannot follow the dictates of other men: It is unalienable also, because what is here a right towards men, is a duty towards the Creator.

It is the duty of every man to render to the Creator such homage and such only as he believes to be acceptable to him. This duty is precedent, both in order of time and in degree of obligation, to the claims of Civil Society. Before any man can be considered as a member of Civil Society, he must be considered as a subject of the Governor of the Universe: And if a member of Civil Society, do it with a saving of his allegiance to the Universal Sovereign.

We maintain therefore that in matters of Religion, no man's right is abridged by the institution of Civil Society and that Religion is wholly exempt from its cognizance. True it is, that no other rule exists, by which any question which may divide a Society, can be ultimately determined, but the will of the majority; but it is also true that the majority may trespass on the rights of the minority.

2. Because Religion be exempt from the authority of the Society at large, still less can it be subject to that of the Legislative Body. The latter are but the creatures and vicegerents of the former. Their jurisdiction is both derivative and limited: it is limited with regard to the co-ordinate departments, more necessarily is it limited with regard to the constituents.

The preservation of a free Government requires not merely, that the metes and bounds, which separate each department of power be invariably maintained; but more especially that neither of them be suffered to overleap the great Barrier which defends the rights of the people. The Rulers who are guilty of such an encroachment, exceed the commission from which they derive their authority, and are Tyrants. The People who submit to it are governed by laws made neither by themselves nor b y an authority derived from them, and are slaves.

3. Because it is proper to take alarm at the first experiment on our liberties. We hold this prudent jealousy to be the first duty of Citizens, and one of the noblest characteristics of the late Revolution. The free men of America did not wait till usurped power had strengthened itself by exercise, and entagled the question in precedents. They saw all the consequences in the principle, and they avoided the consequences by denying the principle. We revere this lesson too much soon to forget it. Who does not see that the same authority, which can establish Christianity, in exclusion of all other Religions, may establish with the same ease any particular sect of Christians, in exclusion of all other Sects? that the same authority which can force a citizen to contribute three pence only of his property for the support of any one establishment, may force him to conform to any other establishment in all cases whatsoever?

4. Because the Bill violates the equality which ought to be the basis of every law, and which is more indispensable, in proportion as the validity or expediency of any law is more liable to be impeached. If "all men are by nature equally free and independent," all men are to be considered as entering into Society on equal conditions; as relinquishing no more, and therefore retaining no less, one than another, of their natural rights.

Above all are they to be considered as retaining an "equal title to the free exercise of Religion according to the dictates of Conscience." Whilst we assert for ourselves a freedom to embrace, to profess and to observe the Religion, which we believe to be of divine origin, we cannot deny an equal freedom to those whose minds have not yet yielded to the evidence, which has convinced us.

If this freedom be abused, it is an offence against God, not against man: To God, therefore, not to man, must an account of it be rendered. As the Bill violates equality by subjecting some to peculiar burdens, so it violates the same principle, by granting to others peculiar exemptions.

Are the Quakers and Menonists the only sects who think a compulsive support of their Religions unnecessary and unwarrantable? can their piety alone be entrusted with the care of public worship? Ought their Religions to be endowed above all others with extraordinary privileges by which proselytes may be enticed from all others?
We think too favorably of the justice and good sense of these denominations to believe that they either covet pre-eminences over their fellow citizens or that they will be seduced by them from the common opposition to the measure.
5. Because the Bill implies either that the Civil Magistrate is a competent Judge of Religious Truth; or that he may employ Religion as an engine of Civil policy. The first is an arrogant pretension falsified by the contradictory opinions of Rulers in all ages, and throughout the world: the second an unhallowed perversion of the means of salvation.
6. Because the establishment proposed by the Bill is not requisite for the support of the Christian Religion. To say that it is, is a contradiction to the Christian Religion itself, for every page of it disavows a dependence on the powers of this world: it is a contradiction to fact; for it is known that this Religion both existed and flourished, not only without the support of human laws , but in spite of every opposition from them, and not only during the period of miraculous aid, but long after it had been left to its own evidence and the ordinary care of Providence.
Nay, it is a contradiction in terms; for a Religion not invented by human policy, must have pre-existed and been supported, before it was established by human policy. It is moreover to weaken in those who profess this Religion a pious confidence in its innate excellence and the patronage of its Author; and to foster in those who still reject it, a suspicion that its friends are too conscious of its fallacies to trust it to its own merits.
7. Because experience witnesseth that ecclesiastical establishments, instead of maintaining the purity and efficacy of Religion, have had a contrary operation.
During almost fifteen centuries has the legal establishment of Christianity been on trial. What have been its fruits? More or less in all places, pride and indolence in the Clergy, ignorance and servility in the laity, in both, superstition, bigotry and persecution. Enquire of the Teachers of Christianity for the ages in which it appeared in its greatest luster; those of every sect, point to the ages prior to its incorporation with Civil policy.
Propose a restoration of this primitive State in which its Teachers depended on the voluntary rewards of their flocks, many of them predict its downfall. On which Side ought their testimony to have greatest weight, when for or when against their interest?
8. Because the establishment in question is not necessary for the support of Civil Government. If it be urged as necessary for the support of Civil

Government only as it is a means of supporting Religion, and it be not
necessary for the latter purpose, it cannot be necessary for the former. If
Religion be not within the cognizance of Civil Government how can its
legal establishment be necessary to Civil Government? What influence
in fact have ecclesiastical establishments had on Civil Society?
In some instances they have been seen to erect a spiritual tyranny on the
ruins of the Civil authority; in many instances they have been seen
upholding the thrones of political tyranny: in no instance have they been
seen the guardians of the liberties of the people. Rulers who wished to
subvert the public liberty, may have found an established Clergy
convenient auxiliaries.
A just Government instituted to secure & perpetuate it needs them not.
Such a Government will be best supported by protecting every Citizen
in the enjoyment of his Religion with the same equal hand which
protects his person and his property; by neither invading the equal rights
of any Sect, nor suffering any Sect to invade those of another.
9. Because the proposed establishment is a departure from the generous
policy, which, offering an Asylum to the persecuted and oppressed of
every Nation and Religion, promised a luster to our country, and an
accession to the number of its citizens. What a melancholy mark is the
Bill of sudden degeneracy? Instead of holding forth an Asylum to the
persecuted, it is itself a signal of persecution.
It degrades from the equal rank of Citizens all those who see opinions in
Religion do not bend to those of the Legislative authority. Distant as it
may be in its present form from the Inquisition, it differs from it only in
degree. The one is the first step, the other the last in the career of
intolerance. The magnanimous sufferer under this cruel scourge in
foreign Regions, must view the Bill as a Beacon on our Coast, warning
him to seek some other haven, where liberty and philanthrophy in their
due extent, may offer a more certain respose from his Troubles.
10. Because it will have a like tendency to banish our Citizens. The
allurements presented by other situations are every day thinning their
number. To superadd a fresh motive to emigration by revoking the
liberty which they now enjoy, would be the same species of folly which
has dishonored and depopulated flourishing kingdoms.
11. Because it will destroy that moderation and harmony which the
forbearance of our laws to intermeddle with Religion has produced
among its several sects. Torrents of blood have been split in the old
world, by vain attempts of the secular arm, to extinguish Religious
disscord, by proscribing all difference in Religious opinion. Time has at
length revealed the true remedy. Every relaxation of narrow and
rigorous policy, wherever it has been tried, has been found to assuage
the disease.
The American Theater has exhibited proofs that equal and complete
liberty, if it does not wholly eradicate it, sufficiently destroys its

malignant influence on the health and prosperity of the State. If with the salutary effects of this system under our own eyes, we begin to contract the bounds of Religious freedom, we know no name that will too severely reproach our folly. At least let warning be taken at the first fruits of the threatened innovation.

The very appearance of the Bill has transformed "that Christian forbearance, love and charity," which of late mutually prevailed, into animosities and jealousies, which may not soon be appeased. What mischiefs may not be dreaded, should this enemy to the public quiet be armed with the force of a law?

12. Because the policy of the Bill is adverse to the diffusion of the light of Christianity. The first wish of those who enjoy this precious gift ought to be that it may be imparted to the whole race of mankind. Compare the number of those who have as yet received it with the number still remaining under the dominion of false Religion s; and how small is the former! Does the policy of the Bill tend to lessen the disproportion?

No; it at once discourages those who are strangers to the light of revelation from coming into the Region of it; and countenances by example the nations who continue in darkness, in shutting out those who might convey it to them. Instead of Leveling as far as possible, every obstacle to the victorious progress of Truth, the Bill with an ignoble and unchristian timidity would circumscribe it with a w all of defense against the encroachments of error.

13. Because attempts to enforce by legal sanctions, acts obnoxious to go great a proportion of Citizens, tend to enervate the laws in general, and to slacken the bands of Society. I f it be difficult to execute any law which is not generally deemed necessary or salutary, what must be the case, where it is deemed invalid and dangerous? And what may be the effect of so striking an example of impotency in the Government, on its general authority?

14. Because a measure of such singular magnitude and delicacy ought not to be imposed, without the clearest evidence that it is called for by a majority of citizens, and no satisfactory method is yet proposed by which the voice of the majority in this case may be determined, or its influence secured.

The people of the respective counties are indeed requested to signify their opinion respecting the adoption of the Bill to the next Session of Assembly." But the representatives or of the Counties will be that of the people. Our hope is that neither of the former will, after due consideration, espouse the dangerous principle of the Bill. Should the event disappoint us, it will still leave us in full confidence, that a fair appeal to the latter will reverse the sentence against our liberties.

15. Because finally, "the equal right of every citizen to the free exercise of his Religion according to the dictates of conscience" is held by the same tenure with all our other rights.

If we recur to its origin, it is equally the gift of nature; if we weigh its importance, it cannot be less dear to us; if we consult the "Declaration of those rights which pertain to the good people of Virginia, as the basis and foundation of Government," it is enumerated with equal solemnity, or rather studied emphasis.

Either then, we must say, that the Will of the Legislature is the only measure of their authority; and that in the plenitude of this authority, they may sweep away all our fundamental rights; or, that they are bound to leave this particular right untouched and sacred:

Either we must say, that they may control the freedom of the press, may abolish the Trial by Jury, may swallow up the Executive and Judiciary Powers of the State; nay that they may despoil us of our very right of suffrage, and erect themselves into an independent and hereditary Assembly or, we must say, that they have no authority to enact into the law the Bill under consideration.

Conclusion:

We the Subscribers say, that the General Assembly of this Commonwealth have no such authority: And that no effort may be omitted on our part against so dangerous an usurpation, we oppose to it, this remonstrance; earnestly praying, as we are in duty bound, that the Supreme Lawgiver of the Universe, by illuminating those to whom it is addressed, may on the one hand, turn their Councils from every act which would affront his holy prerogative, or violate the trust committed to them: and on the other, guide them into every measure which may be worthy of his [blessing, may re]bound to their own praise, and may establish more firmly the liberties, the prosperity and the happiness of the Commonweath.

This and other writings of James Madison found at:

http://members.tripod.com/~candst/tnppage/memorial.htm
http://www.matisse.net/files/madison.html

James Madison - a Mainstream Revolutionary

Appendix 6. Jefferson's Bill for Religious Freedom

JEFFERSON'S DRAFT (1779)

A Bill for Establishing Religious Freedom

SECTION I. Well aware that the opinions and belief of men depend not on their own will, but follow involuntarily the evidence proposed to their minds; that Almighty God hath created the mind free, and manifested his supreme will that free it shall remain by making it altogether insusceptible of restraint; that all attempts to influence it by temporal punishments, or burthens, or by civil incapacitations, tend only to beget habits of hypocrisy and meanness, and are a departure from the plan of the holy author of our religion, who being lord both of body and mind, yet chose not to propagate it by coercions on either, as was in his Almighty power to do, but to extend it by its influence on reason alone; that the impious presumption of legislators and rulers, civil as well as ecclesiastical, who, being themselves but fallible and uninspired men, have assumed dominion over the faith of others, setting up their own opinions and modes of thinking as the only true and infallible, and as such endeavoring to impose them on others, hath established and maintained false religions over the greatest part of the world and through all time: That to compel a man to furnish contributions of money for the propagation of opinions which he disbelieves and abhors, is sinful and tyrannical; that even the forcing him to support this or that teacher of his own religious persuasion, is depriving him of the comfortable liberty of giving his contributions to the particular pastor whose morals he would make his pattern, and whose powers he feels most persuasive to righteousness; and is withdrawing from the ministry those temporary rewards, which proceeding from an approbation of their personal conduct, are an additional incitement to earnest and unremitting labours for the instruction of mankind; that our civil rights have no dependance on our religious opinions, any more than our opinions in physics or geometry; that therefore the proscribing any citizen as unworthy the public confidence by laying upon him an incapacity of being called to offices of trust and emolument, unless he profess or renounce this or that religious opinion, is depriving him injuriously of those privileges and advantages to which, in common with his fellow citizens, he has a natural right; that it tends also to corrupt the principles of that very religion it is meant to encourage, by bribing, with a monopoly of worldly honours and emoluments, those who will externally profess and conform to it; that though indeed these are criminal who do not withstand such temptation, yet neither are those innocent who lay the bait in their way; that the opinions of men are not the object of civil government, nor under its jurisdiction; that to suffer the civil magistrate to intrude his powers into the field of opinion and to restrain the profession or propagation of principles on supposition of their ill tendency is a dangerous falacy, which at once destroys all religious liberty, because he being of course judge of that tendency will make his opinions the rule of judgment, and approve or condemn the sentiments of others only as they shall square with or differ from his own; that it is time enough for the rightful purposes of civil government for its officers to interfere when principles break out into overt acts against peace and good order; and finally, that truth is great and will prevail if left to herself; that she is the proper and sufficient antagonist to error, and has nothing to fear from the conflict unless by human interposition disarmed of her natural weapons, free argument and debate; errors ceasing to be dangerous when it is permitted freely to contradict them.

SECT. II. WE the General Assembly of Virginia do enact that no man shall be compelled to frequent or support any religious worship, place, or ministry whatsoever, nor shall be enforced, restrained, molested, or burthened in his body or goods, nor shall otherwise suffer, on account of his religious opinions or belief; but that all men shall be free to profess, and by argument to maintain, their opinions in matters of religion, and that the same shall in no wise diminish, enlarge, or affect their civil capacities.

SECT. III. AND though we well know that this Assembly, elected by the people for the ordinary purposes of legislation only, have no power to restrain the acts of succeeding Assemblies, constituted with powers equal to our own, and that therefore to declare this act irrevocable would be of no effect in law; yet we are free to declare, and do declare, that the rights hereby asserted are of the natural rights of mankind, and that if any act shall be hereafter passed to repeal the present or to narrow its operation, such act will be an infringement of natural right.

This and other writings of Thomas Jefferson found at:
http://etext.virginia.edu/jefferson/quotations/
http://members.tripod.com/~candst/tnppage/qjeffson.htm

Bibliography

- Abd-al-Hadi, Abu-Sari Muhammad: *Ahkam al-at'imah wal-dhaba'ih fi al-fiqh al-islami,* Dar al-jil, Beirut; Maktabat al-turath al-islami, Cairo, 2nd edition, 1986.
- Abd-al-Qadir Al-Jaza'iri, Muhammad: *Tuhfat al-za'irin fi tarikh Al-Jaza'ir wal-Amir Abd-al-Qadir,* Dar al-yaqdhah al-arabiyyah, Beirut, 1964.
- Abou-Yousof Ya'koub (d. 798): *Le livre de l'impôt foncier,* Paul Geuthner, Paris, 1921.
- Abu-Da'ud: *Sunan Abu-Da'ud,* CD Al-Alamiyyah, Beirut, 1991-1996.
- Abu-Zahrah, Muhammad (d. 1974): *Al-ahwal al-shakhsiyyah,* qism al-zawag, Cairo, 2nd edition, 1950.
- Abu-Zahrah, Muhammad (d. 1974): *Al-ilaqat al-duwaliyyah fil-islam,* Dar al-fikr al-arabi, Cairo, (1984?).
- *Ahkam al-dhabh wal-luhum al-mustawradah min al-kharij, majmu'at min al-fatawi,* Dar al-thaqafah, Riyad, 1979.
- Ahmad: *Musnad Ahmad,* CD Al-Alamiyyah, Beirut, 1991-1996.
- Al-Amili, Muhammad (d. 1692): *Wasa'il al-shi'ah ila tahsil masa'il al-shari'ah,* Al-maktabah al-islamiyyah, Teheran, 1982.
- Al-Ansari, Zakariyya (d. 1520*): Sharh al-manhaj, in margin of: Hashiyat Al-Jamal,* Al-Maktabah al-tijariyyah al-kubra, Cairo, s.d.
- Al-Aqfahsi, Ahmad: *Kitab li-ma yahil wa-yuharram min al-hayawan,* Dar al-Kutub al-ilmiyyah, Beirut, 1996.
- Al-Ashmawi, Fawzia: *Kalimah, in: Al-islam wal-muslimun bi-Uropa, symposium, March 20-21, 1997,* Wazarat al-awqaf, Casablanca, vol. 2, p. 311-318.
- Al-Ashmawi, Fawzia: *La condition des musulmans en Suisse,* CERA Éditions, Geneva, 2001.
- Al-Ashmawi, Muhammad Sa'id: *Al-shari'ah al-islamiyyah wal-qanun al-masri, dirasah muqaranah,* Maktabat Madbuli, Cairo, 1986.
- Al-Bahuti, Mansur (d. 1641): *Kashshaf al-qina an matn al-iqna,* Alam al-kutub, Beirut, 1983.
- Al-Bayhaqi, Abu-Bakr (d. 1066): *Al-sunan al-kubra, Dar al-kutub al-ilmiyyah,* Beirut, 1994.
- Al-Bukhari: *Sahih Al-Bukhari,* CD Al-Alamiyyah, Beirut, 1991-1996.
- Aldeeb Abu-Sahlieh, Sami A.: *Cimetière musulman en Occident: normes juives, chrétiennes et musulmanes, le cas suisse,* L'Harmattan, Paris, 2002.
- Aldeeb Abu-Sahlieh, Sami A.: *Circoncision masculine - circoncision féminine: débat religieux, médical, social et juridique,* L'Harmattan, Paris, 2001
- Aldeeb Abu-Sahlieh, Sami A.: L'enseignement religieux en Égypte: Statut juridique et pratique, in: *Praxis juridique et religion,* 6.1.1989, p. 10-41.

- Aldeeb Abu-Sahlieh, Sami A.: *Les musulmans face aux droits de l'homme: religion, droit et politique, étude et documents*, Winkler, Bochum, 1994.
- Aldeeb Abu-Sahlieh, Sami A.: Les ONG de défense des droits de l'homme en quête de légitimité en droit arabe, in: *Associations transnationales*, 1/1998, p. 12-27.
- Aldeeb Abu-Sahlieh, Sami A.: Limites du sport en droit musulman et arabe, in: *Droit et sport, Staempfli*, Bern, 1997, p. 349-371.
- Aldeeb Abu-Sahlieh, Sami A.: *L'impact de la religion sur l'ordre juridique, cas de l'Égypte, Non-musulmans en pays d'islam*, Éditions universitaircs, Fribourg, 1979.
- Aldeeb Abu-Sahlieh, Sami A.: Unification des droits arabes et ses contraintes, in: *Conflits et harmonisation: mélanges en l'honneur d'Alfred E. von Overbeck*, Éditions universitaires, Fribourg, 1990, p. 177-204.
- Aldeeb Abu-Sahlieh, Sami A: Droit familial des pays arabes, statut personnel et fondamentalisme musulman, in: *Praxis juridique et religion*, 5.1.1988, p. 3-42.
- Aldeeb Abu-Sahlieh, Sami A.: Faux débat sur l'abattage rituel en Occident: Ignorance des normes juives et musulmanes, cas de la Suisse, in: http://www.lpj.org/Nonviolence/Sami/articles/frn-articles/abattage.htm
- Aldeeb Abu-Sahlieh, Sami A. et Bonomi, Andrea (ed.): *Le droit musulman de la famille et des successions à l'épreuve des ordres juridiques occidentaux*, Schulthess, Zürich, 1999.
- Aldeeb, Sami: *Mariages entre partenaires suisses et musulmans: connaître et prévenir les conflits, Institut suisse de droit comparé*, Lausanne, 3rd edition, reprint 2000.
- *Al-fatawi al-islamiyyah min dar al-ifta al-masriyyah*, Wazarat al-awqaf, Cairo.
- Al-Fawzan, Salih: *Al-at'imah wa-ahkam al-sayd wal-dhaba'ih*, Maktabat al-ma'arif, Riyad, 1988.
- Al-Ghazali, Muhammad (1996): *Qadaya al-mar'ah bayn al-taqalid al-rakidah wal-wafidah*, Cairo and Beirut, 4th edition, 1992.
- Al-Hasan, Muhammad Ali: *Al-ilaqat al-duwaliyyah fil-Qur'an wal-Sunnah, Maktabat al-nahdah al-islamiyyah*, Amman, 2nd edition, 1982.
- Al-Jaza'iri, Abu-Bakr Jabir: *I'lam al-anam bi-hukm al-hijrah fil-islam, Rasa'il Al-Jaza'iri*, Maktabat Linah, Damanhur, 3rd edition, 1995, p. 711-729.
- Al-Jaza'iri, Muhammad Ibn Abd-al-Karim: *Tabdil al-jinsiyyah riddah wa-khiyanah*, s.l. and without publisher, 2nd edition, 1993.
- Al-Jaza'iri, Muhammad Ibn Abd-al-Karim: *Zawag al-muslim bi-ghayr al-muslimah wa zawag al-muslimah bi-ghayr al-muslim fi mizan al-islam*, [Cairo], 2nd edition, 1993.
- Al-Jurjani, Ali Ibn-Muhammad (d. 1413): *Al-ta'rifat*, Dar al-kitab al-masri, Cairo and Dar al-kitab al-lubnani, Beirut, 1990.

- Al-Kasani (d. 1191): *Kitab bada'i al-sana'i fi tartib al-shara'i*, Dar al-kitab al-arabi, Beirut, (1982?).
- Allègre, Claude: *Dieu face à la science*, Fayard, Paris, 1997.
- Al-Luwayhiq, Jamil Habib: *Al-tashabbuh al-munha anh fi al-fiqh al-islami*, Dar al-Andalus, Jeddah, 1999.
- Al-Mahdawi, Mustafa Kamal: *Al-bayan bil-Qur'an*, Al-dar al-jamahiriyyah lil-tawzi wal-i'lan, Casablanca, 1990.
- *Al-mawsu'ah al-fiqhiyyah, Wazarat al-awqaf wal-shu'un al-islamiyyah*, Dhat al-salasil, Kuwait.
- Al-Nawawi, Abu-Zakariyya (d. 1277): *Al-majmu sharh al-muhadhdhab*, Dar al-fikr, Beirut, 1990.
- Al-Nawawi, Abu-Zakariyya (d. 1277): *Rawdat al-talibin wa-imdat al-muftin*, Al-maktab al-islami, Beirut, 3rd edition, 1991.
- Al-Nisa'i: *Sunan Al-Nisa'i*, CD Al-Alamiyyah, Beirut, 1991-1996.
- Al-Qalqili, Abd-Allah: *Al-fatawi al-urduniyyah, qism al-ta'amul ma al-aduw wa ahkam al-jihad*, Al-maktab al-islami, Beirut, 1967.
- Al-Qalyubi and Umayra: *Hashiyah*, Dar ihya al-kutub al-arabiyyah, Cairo, s.d.
- Al-Qaradawi, Yusuf: *Min huda al-islam, fatawi mu'asirah*, Dar al-qalam, Kuwait, 3rd edition, 1987.
- Al Qurtubi, Muhammad Ahmad (d. 1273*)*: *Al-tadhkirah fi ahwal al-mawta wa-umur al-akhirah*, Dar al-manar, Cairo, (s.d.).
- Al-Sanhouri, Muhammad Ahmad Faraj: *Al-usrah fil-tashri al-islami*, Wazarat al-tarbiyah wal-ta'lim, Cairo, 1987.
- Al-Shafi'i (d. 820): *Kitab al-um*, Dar al-fikr, Beirut, 1980.
- Al-Sha'rawi, Muhammad Mitwalli (d. 1998): *Qadaya islamiyyah*, Dar al-shuruq, Beirut and Cairo, 1977
- Al-Shawkani, Muhammad (d. 1834): *Nayl al-awtar min ahadith sayyid al-akhyar, sharh muntaqa al-akhbar*, Dar al-jil, Beirut, s.d.
- Al-Shaykh Al-Saduq, Abu-Ja'far (d. 991): *Ilal al-shara'i*, Dar al-balaghah, Beirut, s.d.
- Al-Sukkari, Abd-al-Salam Abd-al-Rahim: *Khitan al-dhakar wa-khifad al-untha min manzur islami*, Dar al-manar, Heliopolis, 1988.
- Al-Tabatba'i, Al-Sayyid Ali: *Riyad al-masa'il fi bayan al-ahkam bil-dala'il*, Dar al-huda, Beirut, 1992.
- Al-Tirmidhi: *Jami Al-Tirmidhi*, CD Al-Alamiyyah, Beirut, 1991-1996.
- Al-Wansharisi (d. 1508): *Al-mi'yar al-mu'rib wal-jami al-mujrib an fatawi ahl Afriqya wal-Andalus wal-Maghrib*, Wazarat al-awqaf, Rabat, 1981.
- Al-Wazani, Muhammad Al-Mahdi: *Al-nawazil al-sughra al-musammat al-minah al-samiyah fil-nawazil al-fiqhiyyah*, Wazarat al-awqaf, Rabat, 1992.
- Al-Zuhayli, Wahbah: *Al-fiqh al-islami wa-adillatuh*, Dar al-fikr, Damascus, 1991.
- Al-Zuhayli, Wahbah: *Athar al-harb fil-fiqh al-islami*, Dar al-fikr, Damascus, 1983.

- Arbez, Alain René: *Détenus musulmans dans les prisons suisses, réflexions d'un aumônier catholique*, April 2000 (under press).
- Aubert, Jean-François: L'islam et l'école publique, in: *Der Verfassungsstaat vor neuen Herausforderungen, Festschrift für Yvo Hangartner*, Dike Verlag, St. Gall, 1998, p. 479-495.
- Aubert, Jean-François: *Traité de droit constitutionnel suisse, Éditions idées et calendes, Neuchâtel*, vol. 1 and 2, 1967, and supplement 1967-1982, 1982.
- Azeroual, Yves: *Foi et République*, Dalil Boubakeur, Jacques Delaporte, Guy Le Neouannic, Joseph Sitruk, Jacques Stewart, Éditions Patrick Banon, Paris, 1995.
- Badran, Badran Abu-al-Aynayn: *Al-ilaqat al-ijtima'iyyah bayn al-muslimin wa-ghayr al-muslimin*, Beirut, 1980.
- Barreau, Jean-Claude: *De l'immigration en général et de la nation française en particulier*, Le Pré aux Clercs, Belfond, 1992.
- Basset, Jean-Claude: Aux sources de l'anti-islamisme en Suisse, in: *Tangram*, 7, October 1999, p. 20-23.
- Bauer, Julien: *La nourriture cacher*, Que sais-je n° 3098, PUF, Paris, 1996.
- Belguendouz, Abdelkrim: Les jeunes maghrébins en Europe: deuxième génération, deuxième chance pour le développement au Maghreb? in: *Revue juridique*, politique et économique du Maroc, n° 21, 1988, p. 69-102.
- Benkheira, Muhammad Hocine: *Islam et interdits alimentaires, juguler l'animalité*, PUF, Paris, 2000.
- Branlard, Jean-Paul: *Droit et gastronomie aspect juridique de l'alimentation et des produits gourmands*, LGDJ and Gualion, Paris, 1999.
- Bucher, A.: *Droit international privé suisse, Personnes, Famille, Successions*, vol. 2, Helbing and Lichtenhahn, Basel and Francfort-sur-le-Main, 1992.
- Cardaillac, Louis: *Morisques et chrétiens, un affrontement polémique 1492-1640*, série historique 6, Librairie Klincksieck, Paris, 1977.
- *Ce que croient les adventistes, 27 vérités bibliques fondamentales*, Éditions Vie et Santé, Dammarie les Lys, 1990.
- Chaïb, Yassine: *L'émigré et la mort, la mort musulmane en France*, Edisud, Aix-en-Provence, 2000.
- Charfi, Mohamed: *Code du statut personnel annoté*, Walili, Marrakech, 1996.
- *Chrétiens, musulmans et juifs dans l'Espagne médiévale: de la convergence à l'expulsion*, under the direction of Ron Barkaï, Cerf, Paris, 1994.
- *Dalil al-muslim fi bilad al-ghurbah*, Dar al-ta'aruf lil-matbu'at, Beirut, 1990.
- Debrot, Samuel: L'opinion d'un directeur d'abattoir, in: *Das sogenannte Schächtverbot, Schriftenreihe des Schweizerischen Tierschutzverbandes*, n° 6, Basel, 1971, p. 17-21.

- Deschenaux, H.; Tercier, P.; Werro, F.: *Le mariage et le divorce*, Staempfli, Bern, 4th edition, 1995.
- Deschenaux, Henri et Steinauer, Paul-Henri: *Le nouveau droit matrimonial, effets généraux, régime matrimonial, succession*, Staempfli, Bern, 1987.
- *Deuxième et troisième rapports périodiques présentés par la Suisse au Comité de l'ONU pour l'élimination de la discrimination raciale conformément à l'article 9 de la Convention internationale de 1965 sur l'élimination de toutes les formes de discrimination raciale*, Bern, May 2000
- Dietary Laws, in: *Encyclopaedia judaica*, vol. 6, 1978, col. 26-46.
- *Discussion paper on the animal welfare standards to apply when animals are commercially slaughtered in accordance with the religious requirements*, Wellington, April 2001, in: http://www.maf.govt.nz/biosecurity/animal-welfare/nawac/papers/religious-requirements.pdf
- Dutoit, Bernard, *Commentaire de la loi fédérale du 18 décembre 1987*, Helbing and Lichtenhahn, Basel, Francfort-sur-le-Main, 2nd edition, 1997.
- *Egypt demographic and health survey, 1995*, National population council, Cairo, September 1996.
- Ennaceur, Mohamed: L'immigration maghrébine en Europe et l'avenir des relations Maghreb-Europe, in: *Revue tunisienne de droit social*, 1992, n° 6, p. 111-136.
- *Être français aujourd'hui et demain, rapport remis au Premier Ministre par Marceau Long, président de la Commission de la nationalité*, 2 tomes, La documentation française, Paris, 1988.
- *Fatawi al-lajnah al-da'imah lil-buhuth al-ilmiyyah wal-ifta*, Dar al-asimah, Riyad, 1996.
- Favre, Antoine: *Droit constitutionnel suisse*, Éditions universitaires, Fribourg, 2nd edition, 1970.
- Fleiner, Thomas: Article 25bis, in: *Commentaire de la Constitution fédérale de la Confédération suisse du 29 mai 1874*, Helbing and Liechtenhahn, Basel, date: 1989.
- Gellatley, Juliet: *Going for the kill: A Viva! report on religious (ritual) slaughter: Do supermarket chains sell religiously slaughtered meat?* in: http://www.viva.org.uk/Viva!%20Campaigns/Slaughter/goingforthekill3.htm#Stunning%20Abroad.
- Gozlan, Martine: *L'islam et la République: des musulmans de France contre l'intégrisme*, Belfond, Paris, 1994.
- Grandin, Temple and Regenstein, Joe M.: *Religious slaughter and animal welfare: a discussion for meat scientists*, Meat Focus International, Published by: CAB International, March 1994, p. 115-123. in: http://www.grandin.com/ritual/kosher. slaugh.html
- Grosse, Jacques-Michel: Le statut patrimonial de base, les effets généraux du mariage, in: *Le nouveau droit du mariage*, Cedidac, Lausanne, 1986.
- Haeri, Shahla: *Law of desire, temporary marriage in Iran*, Tauris, London, 1989.

- Haller, Hans-Joachim; Schraner, A.: Die Schächtfrage aus religiöser Sicht: Der Standpunkt der Theologen, in *Das sogenannte Schächtverbot, Schriftenreihe des Schweizerischen Tierschutzverbundes*, n° 6, Basel, 1971, p. 22-24.
- Hamidullah, Muhammad: *Documents sur la diplomatie musulmane à l'époque du prophète et des khalifes orthodoxes*, Maisonneuve, Paris, 1935.
- Hamidullah, Muhammad: *Majmu'at al-watha'iq al-siyasiyyah lil-ahd al-nabawi wal-khilafah al-rashidah*, Dar al-nafa'is, Beirut, 5th edition, 1985.
- Hammad, Suhaylah Zayn-al-Abidin: *Masirat al-mar'ah al-su'udiyyah ila ayn*, Al-dar al-su'udiyyah, Jeddah, 3rd edition, 1984.
- Hartinger, Werner: *Das betäubungslose Schächten der Tiere im 20. Jahrhundert*, eine Dokumentation, Die grüne Reihe, Fachverlag für Tierschutzliteratur Fred Wipfler, Munich, (s.d.).
- Hartinger, Werner: *Das betäubungslose Schächten der Tiere in unserer Zeit*, Conference September 8, 2000, Berlin, in: http://www.vgt.ch/news/000926.htm
- Haut Conseil de l'intégration: *L'islam dans la République*, November 2000.
- Hefele, Karl Joseph von: *Histoire des conciles d'après les documents originaux*, Letouzey and Ané, Paris, 1907-1952.
- Henninger, J.: L'impureté des aliments et du sang chez les peuples sémitiques, in: *Supplément au Dictionnaire de la Bible*, Paris, 1975, IX, p. 476-482.
- Henninger, J.: Nouveaux débats sur l'interdiction du porc dans l'islam, in: *Le cuisinier et le philosophe, Hommage à Maxime Rodinson*, Paris, 1982, p. 29-40.
- Hunter, W. W.: *The Indian Musalmans, are they bound in conscience to rebel against the Queen?* reprinted from the 1871 edition, Premier Book House, Lahore, 1974.
- Ibn-Abidin, Muhammad Amin (d. 1836): *Rad al-muhtar ala al-dur al-mukhtar*, Dar al-fikr, Damascus, 1979.
- Ibn-Arabi (d. 1240): Al-wasaya, Dar al-jil, Beirut, 1988.
- Ibn-al-Arabi (d. 1148): Ahkam al-Qur'an, Dar al-fikr, Beirut, 1972.
- Ibn-Hazm, Ali (d. 1064): *Al-muhalla*, Dar al-afaq al-jadidah, Beirut, s.d.
- Ibn-Hazm, Ali (d. 1064): *Ma'rifat al-nasikh wal-mansukh, en marge de Tafsir al-Qur'an al-azim lil-imamayn al-jalilayn*, Matba'at Al-Halabi, Cairo, 1923.
- Ibn-Khaldun (d. 1406): *Muqaddimat Ibn-Khaldun*, Matba'at Ibn-Shaqrun, Cairo, (s. d.)
- Ibn-Majah: *Sunan Ibn-Majah*, CD Al-Alamiyyah, Beirut, 1991-1996.
- Ibn-Qayyim Al-Jawziyyah, Shams-al-Din (d. 1351): *Ahkam ahl al-dhimmah*, Dar al-ilm lil-malayin, Beirut, 2nd edition, 1981.
- Ibn-Qayyim Al-Jawziyyah, Shams-al-Din (d. 1351): *Zad al-ma'ad fi huda khayr al-ibad*, Dar Ibn-Hazm, Beirut, 1999.
- Ibn-Qudamah, Abu-Muhammad Abd-Allah (d. 1223): *Al-mughni*, Dar al-kitab al-arabi, Beirut, 1983.

- Ibn-Rushd (Averroès), Muhammad Ibn-Ahmad (d. 1198): *Bidayat al-mujtahid wa-nihayat al-muqtasid*, Dar al-kutub al-ilmiyyah, Beirut, 1996.
- Ibn-Rushd, Muhammad Ibn-Ahmad (d. 1126): *Al-bayan wal-tahsil wal-sharh wal-tawjih wal-ta'lil fi masa'il al-mustakhrajah*, Dar al-gharb al-islami, Beirut, 1984.
- Ibn-Rushd, Muhammad Ibn-Ahmad (d. 1126): *Kitab al-muqaddimat al-mumahhidat*, Dar Sadir, Beirut (s.d.).
- Ibn-Salamah, Hibat-Allah (d. 1019): *Al-nasikh wal-mansukh*, Mustafa Al-Halabi, Cairo, 2nd edition, 1967.
- *Immigration et nationalité, quelles réponses?* Under the direction of Jacques Trémolet de Villers, Dominique Martin Morin, Paris, 1990.
- Jad-al-Haq, Ali Jad-al-Haq: *Buhuth wa-fatawi islamiyyah fi qadaya mu'asirah*, Al-Azhar, Cairo, 1995.
- Jelen, Christian: *Ils feront de bons français, enquête sur l'assimilation des Maghrébins*, Laffont, Paris, 1991.
- Kabbashi, Al-Mukashifi Taha: *Tatbiq al-shari'ah al-islamiyyah fil-Sudan bayn al-haqiqah wal-itharah*, Al-Zahra lil-i'lam, Cairo, 1986.
- Kälin, Walter; Rieder, Andreas: *Bestattung von Muslimen auf öffentlichen Friedhöfen im Kanton Zürich*, Gutachten im Auftrag des Kirchenratspräsidenten Pfarren R. Reich, des Generalvikars von Zürich und Glarus, Weihbischof P. Henrici, und des Präsidenten der römisch-katholischen Zentralkommission des Kantons Zürich, Dr R. Zihlmann, September 1st, 2000.
- Karrer, Pierre A.; Arnold, Karl W. and Patocchi Paolo Michele (trans): *Switzerland private international law*, Kluwer, Boston; Schulthess, Zurich, 2001.
- Khadduri, Majid: *War and peace in the law of Islam*, The Johns Hopkins Press, Baltimore and London, 1979.
- Khalid, Hasan: *Al-islam wa-ru'yatuh fima ba'd al-hayat*, Dar al-nahdah al-arabiyyah, Beirut, 1986.
- Khelil, Mohand: *L'intégration des Maghrébins en France*, PUF, Paris, 1991.
- Krauthammer, Pascal: *Das Schächtverbot in der Schweiz 1854-2000, Die Schächtfrage zwischen Tierschutz, Politik und Fremdenfeindlichkeit*, Schulthess, Zurich, 2000.
- *La Bible de Jérusalem*, Cerf, Paris, 1984.
- La Harpe, R.; Fryc, O.: La mort et la loi, in: *La mort devant la loi*, Société d'études thanatologiques de Suisse romande, 8th symposium, Genève, November 9, 1989.
- Lathion, Stéphane: *De Cordoue à Vaulx-en-Velin, les musulmans en Europe et les défis de la coexistence*, Georg, Geneva, 1999.
- Le Pen, Jean-Marie: *Pour la France*, Albatros, Paris, 1985.
- *Les conciles œcuméniques*, Cerf, Paris, 1994.
- *Les lois alimentaires*, www.alliancefr.com/users/kacher/Kcacher1-genr.htm, updated November 2000.

- Levrat, Jacques: *Une expérience de dialogue, les centres d'étude chrétiens en monde musulman*, Christlich-Islamisches Schrifttum, Altenberg, 1987.
- Lewis, Bernard: La situation des populations musulmanes dans un régime non-musulman. Réflexions juridiques et historiques, in: Lewis Bernard & Schnapper, Dominique: *Musulmans en Europe, Actes Sud*, Poitiers, 1992, p. 11-34.
- *L'impôt d'Église*, Commission intercantonale d'information fiscale, Bern, 1999.
- Louveau, Philippe: *L'incinération: qu'en penser?* updated December 5, 1999, in: www.portstnicolas.org/soc/soc82.htm.
- Mahmud, Zaki Najib (d. 1993): *Al-ma'qul wal-la ma'qul*, Dar al-shuruq, Beirut and Cairo, 1976.
- Mahmud, Zaki Najib (d. 1993): *Tajdid al-fikr al-arabi*, Dar al-shuruq, Beirut and Cairo, 1974.
- Mahmud, Zaki Najib (d. 1993): *Thaqafatuna fi muwajahat al-asr*, Dar al-shuruq, Beirut and Cairo, 1976.
- Mahnig, Hans: L'intégration institutionnelle des musulmans en Suisse, in: *Tangram*, n° 8, March 2000, p. 102-109.
- Maïmonide, Moïse (d. 1204): *Le guide des égarés*, Verdier, Lagrasse, 1979.
- Maimonides, Moses (d. 1204): *The book of knowledge*, transl. Russell and Weinberg, Royal College of Physicians, Edinburgh, 1981.
- Malik: *Muwatta Malik*, CD Al-Alamiyyah, Beirut, 1991-1996.
- Manaf, Abdelouahed: *Problèmes du couple mixte face au droit et à la société* (cas franco-marocain), Imprimerie Najah el-jedida, Casablanca, 1990.
- Masud, Muhammad Khalid: The obligation to migrate: the doctine of hijra in Islamic law, in: Dale F. Eickelman and James Piscatori (ed.): *Muslim travellers: pilgrimage, migration, and the religious imagination*, Routledge, London, 1990, p. 29-49.
- Mawerdi (d. 1058): *Les statuts gouvernementaux*, Le Sycomore, Paris, reproduction, 1982.
- Mawlawi, Faysal: *Al-usus al-shar'iyyah lil-ilaqat bayn al-muslimin wa-ghayr al-muslimin, Dar al-irshad al-islamiyyah*, Beirut, 1988.
- Menuhin, Moshe: *La saga des Menuhin, autobiographie de Moshe Menuhin*, Payot, Paris, 1986.
- Mercier, Pierre: *Conflits de civilisations et droit international privé: Polygamie et répudiation*, Dros, Geneva, 1972.
- *Message relatif à une nouvelle constitution fédérale*, November 20, 1996.
- Muhammad: (d. 632): Koran, translated by Rashad Khalifa. It can be found at http://www.moslem.org/English.html.
- Mursi, Muhammad Abd-al-Alim: *Hijrat al-ulama min al-alam al-islami*, Dar alam al-kutub, Riyad, 1991
- Musa, Kamil: *Ahkam al-at'imah fi al-islam*, Dar al-basha'ir al-islamiyyah, Beirut, 1996.
- Muslim: *Sahih Muslim*, CD Al-Alamiyyah, Beirut, 1991-1996.

- Naïr, Sami: *Lettre à Charles Pasqua de la part de ceux qui ne sont pas bien nés*, Seuil, Paris, 1994.
- Neirynck, Jacques and Ramadan, Tariq: *Peut-on vivre avec l'islam? Le choc de la religion musulmane et des sociétés laïques et chrétiennes*, Favre, Lausanne, 1999.
- Oualalou, Fathallah: L'immigration maghrébine en Europe un choix économique et culturel (un dossier UMA-CEE), in: *Économie et culture, actes*, Wallada, 1992, p. 41-49.
- Pahud de Mortanges, René: Fragen zur Integration der nichtchristlichen Religionsgemeinschaften, in: *Annuaire suisse de droit ecclésiastique*, 1998, p. 89-108.
- Peters, Rudolph: Dar al-harb, Dar al-islam und der Kolonialismus, in: *Zeitschrift der Deutschen Morgenländischen Gesellschaft*, supplement III, 1, 1977, p. 579-587.
- Philon d'Alexandrie (d. 54): *De specialibus legibus*, Cerf, Paris, 1975.
- Quesada, Miguel-Angel Ladero: La population mudéjare, état de la question et documentation chrétienne en Castille, in: *Minorités religieuses dans l'Espagne médiévale, Revue du Monde musulman et de la Méditerranée*, n° 63-64, 1992/1-2, p. 131-142.
- Qutb, Sayyid (d. 1966): *Fi dhilal al-Qur'an*, Dar al-shuruq, Beirut, 10th edition, 1981.
- Ramadan, Hani: *Articles sur l'islam et la barbarie*, Centre islamique de Genève, Genève, 2001.
- Ramadan, Hani: *La femme en islam*, Éditions Maison d'Ennour, Paris, 1996.
- Ramadan, Tariq: *To be a European Muslim: a study of Islamic sources in the European context*, The Islamic foundation, Leicester, 1999.
- Ramadan, Tariq: *Les musulmans dans la laïcité, responsabilités et droits des musulmans dans les sociétés occidentales*, Tawhid, Lyon, 1994.
- *Rapport sur la protection de l'État*, Bern, 1998.
- Raselli, Niccolò: Schickliche Beerdigung für Andersgläubige, in: *AJP* 9/1996, p. 1103-1110.
- Riad, Fouad: Pour un code européen de droit musulman, in: *Le statut personnel des musulmans, droit comparé et droit international privé*, under the direction of Jean-Yves Carler and Michel Verwilghen, Bruxelles, 1992, p. 379-382.
- Sabbagh, Leila: La religion des Moriscos entre deux *fatwas*, in: *Les Morisques et leur temps*, CNRS, Paris, 1983, p. 43-56.
- Salamah, Ahmad Abd-al-Karim: *Mabadi al-qanun al-duwali al-islami al-muqaran*, Dar al-nahdah al-arabiyyah, Cairo, 1989.
- *Sectes ou mouvements endoctrinants en Suisse, la nécessité de l'action de l'État ou vers une politique fédérale en matière de sectes: rapport de la Commission de gestion du Conseil national*, 1er juillet 1999.
- Shahrur, Muhammad: *Al-Kitab wal-Qur'an, qira'ah mu'asirah*, Sharikat al-matbu'at, Beirut, 1992.
- Shaltut, Mahmud (1964): *Min tawjihat al-islam*, Dar al-shuruq, Beirut and Cairo, 7th edition, 1983.

- Siegenthaler, Toni: Fascination des mers du sud et mariage, problèmes de la bigamie et de tenue des registres, in: *Revue de l'état civil*, 1985, p. 295-298.
- Spöndlin, Wilhelm: *Rechtsverhältnisse an Friedhöfen unter besonderer Berücksichtigung des zürcherischen Rechtes*, Schulthess, Zurich, 1910.
- Steiner, Richard: Einige notwendige Betrachtungen zu BV Art. 2bis, in: *Das sogenannte Schächtverbot, Schriftenreihe des Schweizerischen Tierschutzverbandes*, n° 6, Basel, 1971, p. 3-14.
- Suter, Leonhard: *Muslimische Gräber auf kommunalen Friedhöfen, Wissenschaft Spiritualität Gesellschaft*, Zurich, October 1997.
- Tertullian (d. vers 220): *On the resurrection of the flesh*, trad. Holmes, in: http://www.ccel.org/fathers2/ANF-03/anf03-41.htm#P9676_2650295.
- The Galileo case, holy Father's address, in: *L'Osservatore Romano*, 44 (1264), 4.11.1992, English translation in: www.its.caltech.edu/~newman/sci-cp/sci-9211.html.
- *The Swiss Civil Code*, translated by Robert P. Sick, Hyperion, Westport, 1980 and vol. II completely reset by Wyler, Siegfried and Wyler, Barbara, Remak Verlags, St. Gallen, 1987, with supplementary in 2000.
- *The Gospel of Barnabas*, trad. Lonsdale and Laura Ragg, Clarendon Press, Oxford, 1907; reprint: Al-Kitab, Lahore, 1981; Ministry of Awqaf and Islamic Affairs, Doha, 1996.
- *The Quinsext Council, (or the Council in Trullo)*, in: http://www.fordham.edu/halsall/basis/trullo.html.
- *Traités multilatéraux déposés auprès du secrétaire général*, état au 31 décembre 1991, Nations Unies, New York, 1992.
- Tupuliak, Sulayman Muhammad: *Al-ahkam al-siyasiyyah lil-aqalliyyat al-muslimah fi al-fiqh al-islami*, Dar al-nafa'is, Amman and Dar al-bayariq, Beirut, 1997.
- Turki, Abdel-Magid: Consultation juridique d'Al-Imam Al-Mazari sur le cas des musulmans vivant en Sicile sous l'autorité des Normands, in: *Mélanges de l'Université St-Joseph*, I, Beirut, 1980, p. 691-704.
- Uehlinger, Christoph: *Localités palestiniennes détruites après 1948*, Association pour reconstruire Emmaüs, CH-1025 St-Sulpice, 1989.
- Vaux, R. de: Les sacrifices de porcs en Palestine et dans l'ancien Orient, in: *Bible et Orient*, Paris, 1967, p. 499-516.
- Wyler, Fritz: *Die staatsrechtliche Stellung der israelitischen Religionsgenossen-schaften in der Schweiz*, Buchdruckerei Glarner Nachrichten, Glarus, 1929.
- Zakkar, Suhayl: *Al-jami fi akhbar al-qaramitah*, Dar Hassam, Damascus, 1987.
- Zukaghi, Ahmad: *Ahkam al-qanun al-duwali al-khas fil-tashri al-maghribi, al-jinsiyyah*, vol. I, Dar Tobgal, Casablanca, 1992.

KEY WORD INDEX

GENERAL INDEX

Detailed table of contents

SAMI A. ALDEEB ABU-SAHLIEH

MUSLIMS IN THE WEST

Redefining the Separation of Church & State

This work is dedicated to problems brought about by the presence of Muslims. Even though the precise data for these problems differs slightly in other countries, these problems are everywhere practically identical in Western countries where currently between fifteen and twenty million Muslims live.

After a description of the Muslim view of minorities, this work presents Muslim demands to see to what extend these demands can be taken in account: the recognition, freedom of religion and worship, school, family law, forbidden foods and cemeteries.

If the Muslim community continues at its present growth rate without adapting a more tolerant system of values, this community will represent a serious risk to the future of the democratic and legal system of Western countries, and will be able to endanger their territorial sovereignty, as in former Yugoslavia.

This work is written on a critical topic in this period of extreme global tensions. It is exceedingly beneficial for the Muslim community as well as the West. Both paradigms must learn to co-exist if we are to survive. To analyze problems is the first step in their solution.

The Author

Sami A. Aldeeb Abu-Sahlieh, born in 1949, is a Christian Arab of Palestinian origin and Swiss citizenship, holds a doctorate in law from the University of Fribourg. He graduated in political sciences from the Graduate Institute of International Studies of Geneva. For the past several decades Dr. Aldeeb has been Director of Arab and Islamic Law in the Swiss Institute of Comparative Law in Lausanne. He has written many books and articles on Arab and Islamic law and the Middle East political situation, and has lectured extensively across the world on these topics (http://go.to/samipage).